Love and Good Reasons

FRITZ OEHLSCHLAEGER

Love and Good Reasons

POSTLIBERAL APPROACHES

TO CHRISTIAN ETHICS AND

LITERATURE

Duke University Press   Durham and London   2003

© 2003 Duke University Press

Printed in the United States of

America on acid-free paper ∞

Designed by C. H. Westmoreland

Typeset in Weiss with Din Mittelschrift

display by Keystone Typesetting, Inc.

Library of Congress Cataloging-in-

Publication Data appear on the last

printed page of this book.

"Love has nothing to do with good reasons."

—Isabel Archer to Lord Warburton, in Henry James,

The Portrait of a Lady

Charity is not a figurative precept.

It is a horrible thing to say that Christ, who came to replace

figures by the truth, came only to set up the figure of charity

in place of the reality that was there before.

"If the light be darkness, what will the darkness be?"

—Blaise Pascal, *Pensees*, 849,

trans. A. J. Krailsheimer

contents

acknowledgments

I am convinced that our reasons for acting morally are rooted deep in our loves. Most people do not ask, Why be moral? They simply act from something like Aquinas's assumption that the good must be loved and made real. Simone Weil argued that one of the illusions created by "imaginative literature" was that evil is "romantic and varied," whereas good is boring. She thought just the opposite to be true in life and great art: real evil "is gloomy, monotonous, barren, boring." "Real good," on the other hand, is "always new, marvelous, intoxicating."

My experience confirms Weil's judgment. I have been the recipient of many real and extraordinary goods, and I have always found them varied, engaging, and inexhaustible. They have often come, of course, in the form of people, some of whom I can try to thank here.

My intellectual debt to Stanley Hauerwas and Alasdair MacIntyre is enormous. George Hendrick has provided me with a model of scholarship and friendship for nearly thirty years. James F. Childress kindly included me in a National Endowment for the Humanities seminar where I first encountered the work of Hauerwas, MacIntyre, Nussbaum, and others integral to this study. J. D. Stahl introduced me to the work of John Howard Yoder; Rob Patzig, to that of Emmanuel Levinas. Tom Gardner and Robert Benne read sections of the manuscript and provided important suggestions and encouragement. Katherine Soniat kept me apprised of articles chronicling literary study's decline from where it ought to be, at the center of humanistic education. Peter Graham has been a wonderful conversation partner in all things literary and ethical for many years. My understanding of religious ethics has benefited greatly from discussions with Ned Wisnefske and Paul Hinlicky.

My readers at Duke University Press provided me with extraordinarily detailed and helpful reviews of an earlier version of this book. Editors Reynolds Smith and Sharon Torian insisted I write a better book than I would have without their care and attention. I have received so much daily good from my coworkers in the English Department at Virginia Tech that I cannot begin to thank them adequately.

I first glimpsed love in the process of making the good real in my parents and other members of my family. I have been very lucky in them. Finally, to adapt a phrase from Jane Austen, the "best blessings" of my existence are my wife, Deb, and my children, Amy and Matthew. This book is for them.

Love and Good Reasons

introduction

The central effort of liberal ways of doing ethics has been, as Alasdair MacIntyre argues, "to specify universally binding principles or rules whose universality has the scope of humanity itself."[1] Both Kantianism and utilitarianism identify ethical action with what can be justified from the standpoint of anyone. Another way to put this is that liberal ethics has tried to do without a sustaining narrative or story. As Christian ethicist Stanley Hauerwas likes to say, the liberal story is that there is no story.[2] Rather, the primary task of liberal ethics has been to give an account of obligation sufficient to enable diverse groups of strangers to live together without violence. And this has been no mean task. What the dominance of liberal ethics has done, however, is to render the specific convictions of particular communities irrelevant to moral deliberation. No longer is there any intimate connection between right action and the kind of people we understand ourselves to be.

I subscribe to George Grant's sense that insofar as "'liberalism' is used to describe the belief that political liberty is a central human good, it is difficult . . . to consider as sane those who would deny that they are liberals."[3] Nevertheless, there is now a substantial body of opinion in the universities, if not yet in the general populace, that we have moved to a postliberal period. The Enlightenment metanarrative of tradition-free reason has lost its credibility for many elites and largely been replaced by frank commitment to Nietzschean will to power, "that power over ourselves and everything else which is itself the very enhancement of life."[4] No doubt this movement from liberalism to postliberalism is part of the logic of technology itself, as that blending of *techne* and *logos*, making and knowing, fashions the subjects it requires. Following Heidegger, Grant has been particularly prescient about the way technology puts into question liberal reason. "The chief fact," Grant writes, is that "technology organises a system which requires a massive apparatus of artisans concerned with the control of human beings . . . The machinery reaches out to control more and more lives through this apparatus, and its alliance with the private and public corporations necessary to technological efficiency."[5] Perhaps the irony of liberalism is to prepare for the regime of technology that undermines it. Or, to put this another way, perhaps liberalism served technology by providing an account of reason that enabled the relentlessly manipulative quality of human relations to be screened from view.

In any case, postliberal or postmodern teachers of literature and other "humanistic" disciplines increasingly argue that manipulation or transformation of the students is their primary goal. The dominant model of the classroom is often quite different from that of liberal education as classically understood. On the one hand, the conversionist pedagogue's explicit confession of ideological aim seems refreshing. Surely all teaching in the humanities involves, in some way, moving students toward implicit or explicit goods. But there is an important difference between teaching that aims at goals shared by student and teacher within a common account of authority and the kind of elitist pedagogy that assumes "the teacher must recognize that he or she must influence (perhaps manipulate is the more accurate word) students' values through charisma or power." "Otherwise," as one "emancipationist" pedagogue puts it, "one must depend on the assumption that those values are latent in students, and the teacher's job is merely to help the student bring them to the surface. It must be recognized, then, that emancipation is not a transcendental vision, but is a value, which, like all values, is contingent, and that if the teacher wishes to instill such a vision in students, he or she must accept the role as manipulator."[6] The elitist and Gnostic assumptions of such pedagogy are too obvious to need remarking. What the writer misses is the possibility that students and teachers might work together in a mutually enriching way from within a shared tradition of value. The passage resonates with anxiety over loss of cultural authority, the one shared ground between defenders of "liberal" education on both the right and the left. What needs to be asked of the transformationists, in my view, is the following question: Absent a tradition devoted to defending and upholding the unique unsubstitutable identity of every person, what prevents those to be transformed from becoming what Heidegger called "standing reserve," material "to be done with," resources to be transformed into power?[7]

It is little wonder, then, that students seem increasingly uninterested in the humanities, literature especially. Students are generally quite willing to regard their lives as projects to be fashioned, but they see little reason to let others do the fashioning. Like Thoreau when he "knew for a certainty that a man was coming" to his house "with the conscious design of doing [him] good," they run for their lives.[8] Such reading as continues becomes purely a private pleasure, a subversive activity that escapes the corporate realm dominated by the powers that claim our lives. How completely English departments have become part of the technocracy is illustrated rather drearily by the stream of articles assessing the state of the profession through such measures as wages, benefits, ratio of doctorates to "dignified" professional positions, and "market share" of resources relative to other disciplines.[9]

If literary study is not to become an exclusively private pursuit, it must be brought into more explicit relationship to the substantive ethical convictions of various traditions. We must learn to read very specifically in relation to the varying accounts of the good that remain in this culture. To what degree this involves reorganizing learning communities is a matter that university departments might fruitfully discuss. MacIntyre's idea of the "university of constrained disagreement" offers a model for reconfiguring communities that would enable more specifically traditioned literary and ethical studies. I make some proposals drawing on MacIntyre's ideas in the last part of my first chapter. At the same time, I recognize the seriousness of theologian John Milbank's explicitly Christian reservations about MacIntyre's paradigm of the virtues.[10]

This study seeks to articulate a particular moral vision, a Christian one, and discover what it entails for reading texts. To be thus explicit and particular about my position seems to me the only honest way to recognize the truth of Stanley Fish's contention that the ethical can never be free from political and ideological construction, for anyone seeking to construct the category is always already embedded in a "local network of beliefs, assumptions, purposes [and] obligations."[11] Hauerwas has argued that "ethics always requires an adjective or qualifier—such as Jewish, Christian, Hindu, existentialist, pragmatic, utilitarian, humanist, medieval, modern."[12] A Christian ethics will be that marked by the specific convictions of a body of people formed by the history of Israel, Jesus, and the Church. The narrative of Scripture that forms Christians does move from a local and particular history to universal claims. But that history is ongoing, not yet complete. The Kingdom has appeared in Jesus, who invites us into His life, but it awaits its definitive fulfillment in God's own time. Any Christian reflection about the universal, then, should occur from within Jesus and the community formed by his life, death, and resurrection: the church.

The approach to Christian ethics I explore in the following chapters is greatly indebted to the work of Hauerwas, the main proponent of a Christian ethics whose central terms are narrative, vision, character, the virtues, community, and church. For Hauerwas, doing ethics is *not* primarily a matter of developing principles by which quandaries or dilemmas might be resolved by impersonal choosers. Rather, Christian ethics is a practical activity—closely allied to the practical activity of theology, or, I might add, literary criticism—whose "first task is to help us rightly envision the world."[13] Doing Christian ethics, then, involves giving people the linguistic skills to understand "what is going on," in H. R. Niebuhr's phrase, in relation to the narratives and traditions that form the Church.[14] Even what we define as moral decisions depends on the kinds of people we have learned to be and thus on the descriptive skills we have learned from the communities that form us—communities that are themselves sustained by narratives. The questions that arise for a community and its members are a function of the practices and commitments of the community: "Only in view of baptism," for instance, does the question of military service become a question for the Christian at all. Similarly, "people consider questions of sexual immorality only if they first presume that those in their community are pledged to live lives of fidelity."[15] Christian ethics, in this view, is not about what we can justify doing in our freedom, or justify doing to others; rather, it is part of the ongoing effort of a community to get its descriptions right as it lives out a substantive understanding of the good.

This book is devoted, then, to articulating a way of doing Christian ethics and literary criticism in conjunction with one another. The studies that follow represent attempts to get the descriptions right from a Christian point of view. I am concerned throughout with the kinds of questions Hauerwas teaches us to ask: How will readers formed by Scripture, by the narrative of Israel, Jesus, and the Church, go about reflecting on this text? What kinds of questions will they ask? How will they construe the complex, manifold realities confronted by the figures in this fictional world? This is not to simply invite Christian interpreters to pour into the text whatever content they wish. They will be prevented from doing so precisely by Christian themes: hospitality to the stranger, love of the neighbor, a fidelity to the other rooted in the "discipline of repentance."[16] Nevertheless, there will be some consistent features of Christian insight into literary texts, and thus readers will find me turning repeatedly to several concerns: the insufficiency of liberal ideas of autonomy, the consequences of creatureliness, the cruciality of forgiveness to life conceived as a narrative unity. These are matters involving the closest kind of relationship among the narratives of the books we read and love, the narratives we live, and the great narrative that seeks to incorporate Christians within it: that of Israel, Jesus, and the Church.

To some extent, I share Edward Said's concern about the "disappearance of literature itself" from the curriculum and its replacement by "fragmented, jargonized subjects."[17] An Arnoldian return to a high culture version of literature, the kind implicitly advocated by the genre of literary jeremiads, seems to me, however, neither possible nor desirable in today's university. Such a return is prevented, on one hand, by the increasingly multicultural character of the university and, on the other, by the presentist provincialism of suburban students. In short, I think the only way to revive literary study in the university is to bring literature back into connection with what Martha Nussbaum calls "our deepest practical searching," our basic ethical questions about how we should live.[18] To do so will be a difficult matter, however, for liberal culture has itself encouraged the increasing privatization of those very questions: "how one should live" is, for most people, not a public, civic, communal, or religious question but a purely private one—at least as long as one refrains from overt harm to others. Moreover, this privatization of ethical questions is a perfectly understandable response to the increasing manipulation and domination of life by corporate and state powers in modern mass society. Sensing the impotence of individuals in the public sphere and also perhaps the "aridity" of a realm where all relations are purely contractual, individuals retreat to the private.[19] In a recent lament called "The Decline and Fall of Literature," Andrew Delbanco comments on "the mysterious and irreducibly private experience" of literature without recognizing how his very description undercuts the reason for studying literature in a classroom or within a discipline or tradition.[20] If literature is primarily about "irreducibly private experience," why talk about it? Moreover, why pay the extraordinary fees charged by contemporary universities to hear a professor talk about it, particularly if one knows in advance that the sum of the teaching is likely to be the confirmation of an ideology already clearly understood without reference to the literature?[21]

Today's literary Jeremiahs infrequently confront the issue of the authority to teach. Delbanco is a case in point. He cites approvingly a journal passage of Emerson's from the period in which Emerson was moving from being a preacher to a lecturer: "The whole secret of the teacher's force lies in the conviction that men are convertible. And they are. They want awakening." Delbanco believes that we have forgotten this, but I suspect just the opposite is the case. The students have been awakened, specifically to the broadly relativist understanding, itself indebted to Emerson, that authorized ways of reading are the more or less arbitrary behaviors of disciplinary communities—and that part of their function is to determine who counts and who does not. The problem is not that we have forgotten Emerson, but that everyone has become Emersonian. Students generally accept the Emersonian notion that all history is merely biography, and they sensibly concentrate on the biography that concerns them most: their own. Many unthinkingly accept, with American naïveté, that genius amounts to believing that what is true for them in their "private heart is true for all men." The result is solipsism and a lack of interest in what would take them out of themselves. Elsewhere, Delbanco quotes Emerson saying that "the use of literature is to afford us a platform whence we may command a view of our present life, a purchase by which we may move it."[22] Surely there is today no shortage of students seeking to use knowledge of one sort or another as a tool to move the present, but students so motivated wisely choose the technological subjects rather than literary study. In short, a definition of literature that positions it as a kind of technology is unlikely to compete well against more powerful and rewarding technological disciplines.

My own approach is to confront the issue of authority directly by locating it within a specific tradition, the Christian one. No doubt my literary-ethical descriptions will be of most interest to Christians, but I offer them, too, as hopeful enrichments of a conversation that has not often welcomed explicitly religious interpretations. If they serve no other purpose for non-Christian readers, perhaps they can at least provide interpretations for criticism in a process of "teaching the conflicts" along the lines advocated by Gerald Graff.[23] The challenge for all nonscientific disciplines in the university, and for our democracy as a whole, is to devise forms in which people can contribute to the ongoing conversation without ceasing to be the people they are formed to be by their particular commitments. I hope in this book to suggest how Christians can contribute to the conversation about ethics and literature without bracketing the convictions that define who they are.

One final word here about my title. Doing Christian ethics and literary criticism in conjunction with one another seems inevitably to involve working out concrete, particular correlations between love and good reasons. Each of the studies that follow this introduction will, I hope, make some contribution to our thinking about these terms, even though I do not take them up in the abstract way more appropriate to a systematic work. I do want to focus attention, however, on how Christian accounts of action—the good reasons we are rightly compelled to offer—are related to love. To be sure, the God who loves in freedom needs no good reason to love us, and we need no good reason to love one another except that God commands it, appears in the very form of love, and teaches that to fail to love is to remain in death.[24] But, to the Christian, these will appear the very best reasons of all, and thus all our good reasons for acting, our ethics, will be rooted, in some way, in the love that moves the universe and comes to us in the rabbi Jesus from Nazareth.

chapter 1

LITERARY CRITICISM AND CHRISTIAN ETHICS

IN SERVICE TO ONE ANOTHER

The recent critique of liberal ethics, whether Kantian or utilitarian, has come from a variety of voices and viewpoints. After suggesting the chaotic and fragmented quality of contemporary moral language, Alasdair MacIntyre has argued that there can be no tradition-free account of practical rationality. Judgments about what is just or rational must take place within traditions dependent on narratives about the good life for human beings.[1] Stanley Fish has claimed that references to "the realm of the ethical in general" are merely efforts to "pass off" some particular and "contestable set of values." "The ethicists are not *the* ethicists," according to Fish, if that word is used to denominate a group of experts operating in a value-free way to solve, as if by special technical competence, dilemmas that are beyond the rest of us. Rather, they are the "purveyors of a *particular* moral vision" that must make its way against competing moral visions.[2]

Bernard Williams has emphasized the way demands for objectivity in moral deliberation cause agents to adopt a "mid-air stance" that alienates them from their projects and commitments. Divorced from what they care about, agents have difficulty answering the question Why be moral?—for to do so seems to depend on our having particular cares and commitments.[3] Stanley Hauerwas has pointed out the problems inherent in picturing the moral life primarily as a matter of confronting quandaries or hard choices as if from the standpoint of anyone. Such an account of ethics severs our moral choices from our character, diminishes the importance of the virtues, and overlooks the way vision determines the kinds of quandaries we confront.

Several works of the past decade on ethics and literature, or the virtues in academic life, attempt to redress the separation of morality from the rest of life promoted by liberal ethics. At the forefront of this work are

Martha Nussbaum's interdisciplinary studies of literature and philosophy, with their foregrounding of the Aristotelian "starting point," "How should one live?" Wayne Booth has similarly turned to Aristotle, specifically to the virtue of friendship, to work out an ethics of fiction. Historian Mark Schwehn has advocated the importance of the virtues for academic work, suggesting that the character of scholarship is, or ought to be, related to the character of the scholar. J. Hillis Miller has taken a somewhat different tack in proposing an ethics of reading that insists literature includes within it an "ethical moment" resistant to technique. Miller's work stands in ambiguous relationship to the liberalism of Kant, whose notion of respect Miller seems to want to preserve while simultaneously undermining the value of Kant's narrative exemplifications of the law.

The works of Schwehn, Booth, Miller, and Nussbaum offer important insights to one seeking ways to think about literature and ethics in relation to one another. I turn momentarily to examining the proposals of each, suggesting both their strengths and the ways a Christian ethics of literature will differ. Following my engagement with these theorists, I offer an exposition of Hauerwas's understanding of Christian ethics, showing how it specifically informs the larger arguments of this study. The penultimate section of the chapter suggests how the specific literary-ethical studies of the following chapters contribute to the overall conception. In the final section, I suggest the way literary study might flourish within MacIntyre's "university of constrained disagreement," and, at the same time, I acknowledge the reservations of theologian John Milbank about MacIntyre's paradigm of the virtues.

I

Mark Schwehn makes the case for virtue in academia in *Exiles from Eden: Religion and the Academic Vocation in America*. Schwehn traces the academic calling, as understood in American research universities, to Max Weber. For Weber, the academic life required Puritan asceticism and renunciation even though the academic pursued his calling in a rationalized, secular world. Pursuing his "impersonal and solitary undertaking," the Weberian scholar "wait[ed] alone, in disciplined attention, for the chance infusion of mundane grace that would lead him to a temporary salvation through his making a correct conjecture in his manuscript."[4] Noting the turn to interpretive communities and the communal epistemologies of antifoundationalism, Schwehn calls for a changed conception of the academic vocation, one that would emphasize the virtues—specifically humility, charity, faith, and gratitude—and simultaneously move teaching to the center of the academic calling. There is much to commend in Schwehn's argument. An infusion of these virtues into contemporary academics would likely promote a more communal, less competitive approach to disciplinary knowledge. Placing teaching at the center of the academic's life would diminish the isolation of the scholar, giving him or her an increased sense of the life and values of communities larger than the university. That kind of change ought, in turn, to change the nature of research, making it less specialized, more available to wider publics.

Schwehn writes as a Christian but wants to make his case for humility, charity, faith, and gratitude without reference to theological warrants. He acknowledges that there is a "historical connection between religious beliefs and these virtues," and he insists on "an epistemological connection between the exercise of these virtues and the communal quest for knowledge and truth." He vigorously insists, however, on "nowhere argu[ing] that there is some sort of absolute and necessary connection between religious belief and the virtues of humility, faith, self-sacrifice, and charity" (53). Obviously, Schwehn does not want to be in the position of arguing that only professing theists can be humble, self-sacrificial, or charitable. He repeatedly uses the work of the "pious and genuinely virtuous secularist" Jeffrey Stout to illustrate the virtues he commends in those without theistic convictions. Schwehn's use of Stout, however, is a bit curious, as he quotes Stout to the effect that his secular piety is "analogous to and even . . . indebted to a central theme from the Reformed tradition."[5] Moreover, Schwehn invokes an argument that is a favorite of cultural conservatives: that liberal secular culture lives off a moral inheritance from the past that it simultaneously undermines. He worries that "our present-day academies as well as many academicians like Jeffrey Stout might be living off a kind of borrowed fund of moral capital," a fund they may not be able either to "replenish" or "transmit" to the next generation (53).

Schwehn seems a bit condescending in his need to argue that professed nontheists can be "genuinely virtuous." Of course there are humble, sacrificing, charitable nontheists. A more productive line of inquiry might work out the ways theists and nontheists understand these virtues. One might also ask whether these virtues are indeed vital to scholarship in academic communities of discourse and whether some accounts of truth are more likely than others to foster them. To further discussion along these lines, let me take up the conversation with Schwehn on two virtues in particular: humility and charity.

Schwehn's fullest account of humility does not avoid invoking theological warrants. He argues that what frequently passes for lack of motivation among today's students "really involves a lack of humility, stemming in part from a lack of piety or respect for that aspect of God's ongoing creation that manifests itself in works of genius" (48). He cites an example of his students' unwillingness to do the cognitive work to understand Augustine's discussion of friendship and loss, confesses that no doubt part of the failing is his own, but insists that the problem stems also from a lack of student humility, the kind of humility that would lead to "the *presumption* of wisdom and authority *in the author*"—any author, Kant, Aristotle, and Tolstoy as well as Augustine (48). Schwehn has nicely posed the problem of student dismissiveness here, but it cannot be addressed by simply urging the "practice of humility" (49). We must notice the way Schwehn's theological understanding of Creation underwrites the "presumption" of authority in his classic writers. God's creation is "ongoing" and "manifest[ing] itself" in the works of these geniuses, each of whom discovers some aspect of a truth available to all.

Now, for contrast, consider Richard Rorty's urging students "to see moral progress as a history of making rather than finding, of poetic achievement by 'radically situated' individuals and communities, rather than as the gradual unveiling, through the use of 'reason,' of 'principles' or 'rights' or 'values.'"[6] If moral progress or truth is understood to be a social construction, the product of relatively local acts of making by radically situated individuals, then why should the student bother to work through the nuances of Augustine's discussion of friendship and loss? Rorty's description undercuts any sense that Augustine and the student are engaged in a continuous process of discovery about the most important matters. Moreover, it seems to me that Rorty's pragmatic understanding of truth is much less likely to foster humility than one that insists the truth to be "something other and something more than warranted assertibility."[7] Individuals constructing reality, making moral progress, and articulating truth seem less likely to develop humility than those who think of themselves as seeking, discovering, and learning to love the truth. As Josef Pieper says of Thomas Aquinas's sense of humility, "The ground of humility is man's estimation of himself according to truth. And that is almost all there is to it."[8] The way to overcome the Christian student's dismissiveness of Augustine is to reaffirm the community between the student and the saint. The source of the presumed authority Schwehn wants the student to grant Augustine lies in their sharing commitment to the same central Truth and the Church's acknowledgment and validation of Augustine's teaching. I suggest a shift in the nature of the question implicitly raised, though not directly addressed, by Schwehn. Rather than pondering how to encourage students and academics to practice the virtues, we ought to think about changing the nature of learning communities in ways that will foster the virtues. One thing this means is bringing Christian students and instructors together more intentionally as seekers after a proper "estimation" of themselves "according to truth."

What's at stake for literary interpretation in the cultivation of the virtues and reformation of communities might be seen by contrasting my account of the way a Christian student would read Augustine with a comment of Annette Kolodny's on reading the classics: "The only 'perennial feature' to which our ability to read and reread texts written in previous centuries testifies is our inventiveness—in the sense that all of literary history is a fiction which we daily re-create as we reread it."[9] It is not my purpose to lament the diminishing cultural status of the classics. Attempts to restore teaching of the classics without the reformation of learning communities seem to me largely wrongheaded. Neither do I think that any such teaching will suddenly result in the quotient of civic virtue needed by a society of ordered liberty. But I do insist that there is a "perennial feature," for Christians, to Augustine's treatment of friendship and loss. Readers of Book 4 of the *Confessions* will remember how the mourning Augustine feels that the loss of his friend leaves him "with only half a soul" and how he comes to dread death himself because his own death would mean the abandonment of his friend to utter extinction: "I felt that our two souls had been as one, living in two bodies, and life to me was fearful because I did not want to live with only half a soul. Perhaps this, too, is why I shrank from death, for fear that one whom I had loved so well might then be wholly dead."[10] Eventually, Augustine comes to see this grief itself as a type of prideful unfaith, and he moves toward the recognition that he must love the lost friend, and other friends, in God. Now, I did not "invent" this interpretation of Augustine: I *recognize* the pattern in Book 4, in part because it is like the movement of Augustine's thought in many places and, in part, because I recognize in his experience something that describes my own. Augustine's recognitions and mine derive from our shared faith in the Trinitarian God, Whose revelation in the history of Israel, Jesus, and the Church has given us the very language, the descriptive skills, with which we understand ourselves and make sense of our experience.

Kolodny's and my sense of what we are doing when we read differs because of the kinds of communities in which we find ourselves. Kolodny's understanding of interpretation is that of the autonomous self inventing itself from moment to moment by inventing different versions of a past that point toward a culmination in the present. The Christian, on the other hand, understands himself or herself as a creature formed and sustained by God and as a participant in a living historical community, whose linguistic resources give him or her the ability to understand what it means to be a "self." The Christian looks toward the culmination of history in God's definitive future while at the same time knowing that an anticipation of that future has already been given in Jesus' life, death, and resurrection. History does not point to the individual Christian but to the Kingdom, a foretaste of which is manifest in Jesus. For Kolodny, when we read, "we appropriate meaning from a text according to what we need (or desire), or in other words, according to the critical assumptions or predispositions (conscious or not) that we bring to it" (280). I'm not sure that "critical assumptions or predispositions," presumably the learned behaviors of a disciplinary community, are quite the same as "what we need (or desire)." But Christians—and Kantians as well—will be troubled by the suggestion that we "appropriate meaning" according to our wishes and desires. To Kantians this will suggest violating the categorical imperative, using the author as a means rather than an end in himself or herself. Constructing a literary history to account for oneself will seem, to the Christian, like an attempt at self-justification, the process from which one has been freed by God's justification in Christ. Christians will be moved to "appropriate" meanings from literary or historical texts in accord with their "needs or desires," but their training in the dispossession of self and respect for the other ought to act as checks on this interpretive sinfulness. When Christian interpreters are tempted to construe a text in a self-justifying way, they should be restrained from doing so by fundamental notions, and disciplined habits, of fidelity, justice, and charity. In short, any account of an interpretive community should also include an account of the virtues it fosters—for the virtues it fosters are surely relevant to the interpretations it will produce.

Schwehn wants especially to foster charity in interpreters, but his account does not sufficiently distinguish charity from justice or offer convincing reasons for academics to be charitable. A historian, Schwehn notes the way virtue language "easily insinuates itself" into the criticism he has received from other scholars or directed at himself: " 'You have really not done [William] James full justice in your discussion of his religious views.' Or again, 'You really need to be more charitable to James in your analysis of his courtship and marriage' " (50). Notice how interchangeable the language of justice and charity seems; it's not clear why the second comment could not just as easily call for greater fairness or justice to James. Moreover, Schwehn does not confront the inevitable challenge to his call for charity. Why should a historian be charitable to James rather than simply just? Schwehn offers the argument that it will make him a better historian: "If I have grown to treat my colleagues and my students with justice and charity, am I more or less likely to treat historical subjects such as William James in the same manner? I am surely more likely to do so. And would such treatment increase or decrease the quality of my historical *thinking* ? Again, I think that the exercise of charity toward my historical subjects is bound to make me a better historian: more cautious in appraisal, more sympathetic with human failings, less prone to stereo-type and caricature" (50–51). What Schwehn fails to acknowledge are the value judgments embedded in his assumptions about what it means to be a good historian. How far, one might ask, is he willing to extend his sympathy? Should the good historian give a charitable or sympathetic treatment to the totalitarian dictators of our century? Would not such a treatment risk being inadequately condemnatory, opening the historian to an argument analogous to that Kantians sometimes make against for-giveness: that it insufficiently values appropriate resentment or what Jeffrie Murphy calls "moral hatred"?[11] Being a good historian is not a value-free description. Both what counts as history and the requisite virtues of the academic are at stake in differences among interpretive communities. Kolodny's community of feminist literary historians can be held together in their work of reenvisioning and reinventing the past by shared commitment to greater justice for women. A presumably loose community of Rortean pragmatists could measure the worth of their conceptual redescriptions of one another's work by the pragmatic differ-ences they make. Such a community would produce those devoted to strong misreading rather than cautious faithfulness—as long as such mis-reading leads to the extension of North Atlantic bourgeois democracy, whose institutions Rorty now sees as "prior" to philosophy.

Perhaps we should extend to communities Hauerwas's insistence that ethics always requires the "qualifier." Communities formed by particular narratives will give differing accounts of the virtues and even of what is going on in academic work. Perhaps we should also say with Fish that whenever one refers to oneself as a "communitarian," some specific understanding of community is being "passed off" under a deceptive generality. Schwehn's account is more dependent on Christian warrants than he acknowledges. He repeatedly insists on his brave modernity, saying that his "reconception of the academic vocation" should not be seen as "an atavistic undertaking," for he has "no patience for nostalgic returns to medieval syntheses of one sort or another" (22). After quoting Cardinal Newman on the differences between a university and a college, Schwehn states, "To think that we could reintroduce distinctions like these into the present United States is at best to be afflicted with a severe case of terminal wistfulness" (80). The last phrase echoes Rorty, who speaks of the "terminal wistfulness" with which the books of communitarian critics of liberalism typically end.[12] Among the wistful is MacIntyre, whose *After Virtue* closes by depicting us, among the ruins of contemporary moral culture, "waiting not for a Godot, but for another—doubtless very different—St. Benedict."[13] MacIntyre stresses the way accounts of rationality and the virtues are narrative and community-dependent. On his model, the attempt to revitalize specific virtues would depend on the simultaneous revivifying of the communal practices, traditions, and beliefs that gave those virtues meaning. Such an approach seems considerably less wistful than Schwehn's desire to reconceive the vocation of contemporary academics in secularized research institutions in terms of virtues whose primary warrants have historically been religious ones.

Wayne Booth, in *The Company We Keep*, seeks to move one of the Aristotelian virtues, friendship, to the center of "an ethics of fiction." In the Aristotelian tradition, Booth writes, "the quality of our lives was said to be in large part identical with the quality of the company we keep."[14] "Without friends no one would choose to live, though he had all other goods," Aristotle remarks in *The Nicomachean Ethics*. Booth works briefly through Aristotle's tripartite typology of friendships, focusing mostly on the "fullest" kind, which "arises whenever two people offer each other not only pleasures or utilities but shared aspirations and loves of a kind that make life together worth having as an end in itself. These full friends love to be with each other because of the quality of the life they live during their time together. As Aristotle says, a true friendship is a relation of virtue with virtue, or as we might translate—remembering again that 'virtue' was for him a much broader, less moralistic term than it is for us—a relation of strength with strength and aspiration with aspiration" (174). Booth uses friendship as his model for the relationship between a reader and the implied author of a text. The best kind of literary company we keep offers the "quality" of relationship Aristotle finds in the highest type of friendship. Booth speaks of giving a "loving response" to a text (34) and of asking the following types of questions as we read: "Should I believe this narrator, and thus join him? Am I willing to be the kind of person that this story-teller is asking me to be? Will I accept this author among the small circle of my true friends?" (39). Perhaps Booth's greatest ethical achievement lies in his modeling a rich friendly responsiveness to a variety of texts and authors.

Booth finds puzzling the "modern neglect of friendship as a serious subject of inquiry" (170), a neglect perhaps explainable by the ways of doing ethics that have dominated modernity. If ethics is devoted primarily to working out universal principles by which impersonal choosers resolve prearticulated dilemmas, then ethics will have little to do with friendship or the virtues more generally. But Booth himself remains committed to the idea of liberal autonomy that has undermined the serious consideration and teaching of the virtues. Commenting on a program of " 'bibliotherapy' that claims to use books, especially fiction and poetry, to cure," Booth indicates his agreement with the program's assumption but "doubt[s] that the good people" who "run [it] can have worked out any very subtle way of providing precisely the right book for a given patient at a given time." From the "problems one can foresee in any such program," Booth argues a conclusion that sounds like the relativism of today's students: "Every reader must be his or her own ethical critic" (236–237). Similarly, while reviewing the many myths that claim the attention of moderns, Booth argues that "most of us in our time are so thoroughly entangled in rival myths that only a rigorously pluralistic ethical criticism can serve our turn" (350). What he means by "entanglement" becomes clearer later in the argument: "Whenever I engage seriously with any metaphors, petty or grand, whenever I join in any narrative, religious or secular, and whenever I then choose to discuss my venture, after the fact, with those who have traveled the same way, I become part of a venture in self-education that is both supremely practical and at the same time the very end of life itself" (369). Clearly, Booth thinks here of a "self" that stands apart from the narratives it "engages" or "joins." Friendship no longer stands as the supreme good of life; rather, that place is taken by "self-education"—precisely the commitment to liberal autonomy that, over time, diminishes the seriousness of interest in the virtues, friendship included, as "matters of character," ethics. Booth will also have difficulty persuading others who really are "formed" by those narratives that he has engaged them seriously. The Christian will find a contradiction between the claim to serious engagement with the Christian narrative and the continuing claim that "self-education" is the "very end of life itself." Participation in the Kingdom of God, not self-education, is the end of life for the Christian.

At other points in *Company*, Booth critiques the idea of autonomy, arguing that we are ineluctably social selves. Citing a range of social disciplines, he concludes: "All these and many others have tried to teach us once again what ancient philosophy, classical rhetoric, and traditional religion took for granted: the isolated individual self simply does not, cannot exist. Not to be a *social* self is to lose one's humanity. As Aristotle insisted, we are 'political animals' precisely in the sense that we become human only in a polis" (238). Booth thus argues for a model of the self based on character, role, and Bakhtinian heteroglossia. Each of us "is constituted in a kind of counterpoint of inherited 'languages,'" often in tension or even irreconcilable with one another. We become our character by doing our "best to enact the various roles 'assigned'" to us (238–239). Literature offers a rich source of roles for us to try on, adopt, and then drop or make part of our repertoire. Booth admits that this process seems akin to hypocrisy but argues that moderns have overvalued sincerity and makes the case for productive hypocrisy: the practice of role playing in such a way that it leads to the development of a character's qualities, even the virtues. Booth's point about the overvaluation of sincerity seems well taken, but serious objection can be raised to the way he describes the movement from role playing to the practice of a virtue. (And we should notice from the first how the very notion of role playing still implies a centered self that stands back from, and chooses among, various possible roles.) Booth argues that one is more likely to become a better tennis player by telling oneself, "I'm getting better all the time" than by saying, "I'm a poor tennis player." He then asks, "Why should the same not be true of all the virtues? If I do not practice courage frequently enough to make it habitual, how can I ever become *courageous*?" (253).

Courage, as Aristotle understands it, does require practice, but it also requires more than a set of habits or skills achieved through practice. Aristotelian courage involves not just willingness to face danger, but doing so in particular ways: "The man who faces and fears (or similarly feels confident about) the right things for the right reason and in the right way and at the right time is courageous (for the courageous man feels and acts duly, and as principle directs); and the end of every activity is that which accords with the disposition corresponding to that activity. This is true of the courageous man."[15] Aristotelian courage requires a settled disposition, a willingness "to face things that are terrible to a human being, and that he can see are such, because it is a fine act to face them" and to do so "in virtue of the formed state of character" (*NE* 133–134). One might improve one's tennis skills by persuading oneself that one is improving, although I suspect this would be untrue if the description were counterfactual, that is, if one were being beaten continually by opponents. But, absent the settled disposition to courage, the willingness to face things terrible to a human being seems unlikely to grow simply because one decides to practice it. The practice Booth advocates is a necessary but not sufficient condition for the virtues as Aristotle understands them. The serious question for Booth is whether conceiving of life as a matter of trying on roles undermines the ability to develop the settled dispositions necessary for Aristotelian virtue. For Aristotle, courage involves not simply choosing a role (perhaps later to be discarded) from a variety that present themselves. Rather, it involves seeing that there is something real and fine about facing danger in this way and not some other—and that norm is always before the courageous person in the form of the virtuous figure who does the right thing at the right time in the right way and for the right reason.

Given Booth's pluralism, it would seem unlikely for him to offer any normative account of the good life. He does, however, offer at least a strong negative prohibition: what "we moderns" must guard against is the "temptation to allow some one voice" from the polyphony we inherit "to triumph, either within our souls or in the political order." Indeed, "our ills can be traced to our attempts to 'perfect' some one language at the expense of all the others" (239). A tolerant liberal pluralism thus serves as something close to a norm, and Booth is at his best when he demonstrates his ability to give voice to conflicting responses to ethically contested texts by Rabelais, Austen, Lawrence, and Mark Twain. He provides a powerful moral argument against *Huckleberry Finn*, a text he is personally committed to defending, and, in the process, proves himself the good listener, the good friend both to books and people that he seeks to be. No doubt Booth has learned much about understanding the requirements of particular roles and rehearsing different points of view from one of his most intimate literary friends, Jane Austen. These abilities are essential to the process of moral education in Austen's works, particularly in *Emma,* as I show in Chapter 3. There I stress the way imagining oneself into different roles—the way a novel allows one to do—might well be more constructive for moral education than insisting that learning to be moral involves assuming a moral point of view abstracted from particularity.

Fish has attacked Booth's general language about what literature offers—"a richer and fuller life than I could manage on my own"—by pointing out that there is no correlation between moral behavior and the reading of the most profound texts. Booth's language of fullness, richness, depth, and profundity begs all the difficult questions about the particularity of his moral vision. As Fish rightly sees, such language leaves Booth with little to say in defense of a particular canon of books. But Fish is unfair to Booth when he sets out the assumptions he claims must lie behind an attempt to define an ethical canon: "It would seem that in order to answer these questions one must *already* be in the state of ethical perfection to which the canon is supposed to bring one, which suggests the superfluousness or at least causal irrelevance of the canon to the very values it is said to produce" (41). Booth claims neither to be in a state of ethical perfection nor that the canon is able to produce such a state. He presents himself as an inquirer, a friend among friends engaged in conversation, trying on different roles and voices and doing his best to see things from other points of view. The works he engages are mostly classics of English literature, but he nowhere displays any rigidity about canonicity. He simply finds himself among the friends whom trusted others have commended to his attention. It is part of his friendliness, and humble assumption of imperfection, to be always making new friends.

More specifically theoretical than Booth is J. Hillis Miller's *The Ethics of Reading.* Miller contends that "there is a necessary ethical moment" in the "act of reading as such, a moment neither cognitive, nor political, nor social, nor interpersonal, but properly and independently ethical."[16] He situates his argument under the aegis of Kant's *Foundations of the Metaphysics of Morals* while also providing a deconstructive reading of Kant that stresses Kant's own need to provide narratives to flesh out his conception of the moral law and the gap that always exists between the law as such and any narrative claiming to exemplify it. Focusing on Kant's example of the inconsistency in willing a lying promise, Miller argues that the promise is a particular form of performative language whose fulfillment is never assured. Thus, the reader of Kant's little narrative "cannot decide whether the morality of promising is grounded in the law as such or whether it is an example of an ungrounded act which would define morality as a linguistic performative to be judged only by an internal temporal consistency which the example shows, as by a slip of the tongue, can never be attained" (38). Readers of literary narratives, then, are condemned to a kind of "betrayal" as they experience the "perpetually deferred fulfillment" of whatever particular promise "was the whole reason for being of the story" (33).

Despite the deconstruction of Kant, the primary "constructive" concept in Miller's ethics seems to be "respect," freely given by the reader to the text in an act that recognizes the text's claim on him or her. Miller suggests that the ethical moment in reading "faces in two directions": "On the one hand it is a response to something, responsible to it, responsive to it, respectful of it. In any ethical moment there is an imperative, some 'I must' or *Ich kann nicht anders*. I *must* do this. I cannot do otherwise. If the response is not one of necessity, grounded in some 'must,' if it is a freedom to do what one likes, for example to make a literary text mean what one likes, then it is not ethical, as when we say, 'That isn't ethical.' On the other hand, the ethical moment in reading leads to an act. It enters into the social, institutional, political realms, for example in what the teacher says to the class or in what the critic writes" (4). The analogous moment in the *Foundations* is Kant's footnote differentiating respect from both fear and inclination and associating respect for the law as such with rational autonomy. Respect, for Kant, is the "self-wrought" rational feeling by which we freely and autonomously impose on ourselves the law that we recognize to be necessary.[17] Miller's ethics would thus seem to ground a clear negative prohibition about what one must not do—one must not, as cited above, "make a literary text mean what one likes"—but its positive import is less clear. How one reads any particular text in the "social, institutional, and political realms" in which interpretation occurs is left unspecified. Miller does claim that his general position can be exemplified only through specific acts of reading, which he carries out in later chapters of *Ethics* and in *Versions of Pygmalion*. I show some ways in which a Christian ethics of interpretation must differ from him in both Chapter 2 and Chapter 4 of this book. Let it suffice here to say that Miller's attempt seems to be to save a universalizing language of the ethical—to do ethics without the qualifier—but he does so by severing nearly every connection between his overall position, based on respect for the text as such, and his specific examples or readings. What seems curious is Miller's situating himself under Kant, if, as the deconstructive moves argue, this results in our concluding that no promises can ever be believed, that reading literary narratives is only to repeatedly experience their unreadability, that the "ground" of any ethical act may be no more than an unwarranted "self-affection," and that we are left in a realm of universal lying where the only reasonable stance to adopt is a thoroughgoing suspicion.[18]

The influence of Kant is evident in Miller's marking out a specific sphere of life denominated the ethical, much as Kant marks off the moral sphere. Miller argues that "the political and the ethical are always intimately intertwined, but an ethical act that is fully determined by political considerations or responsibilities is no longer ethical." The ethical moment "must be sui generis, something individual and particular, itself a source of political or cognitive acts, not subordinated to them" (4–5). Miller's purpose—one surely shared by a Christian ethics—is to defend the integrity of the text as "something individual and particular" against methodologies that claim to exhaustively explain it by reference to forces outside it. At stake, for Miller, is the continued study of literature. Current critical models assume that a work of literature "is entirely to be accounted for and is accountable to forces, powers, surveillances from outside itself." Literature "expresses, in spite of itself, an ideology"; "no corner" remains "anywhere for deviation, idiosyncrasy, freedom, or performative power." Such assumptions make literary study a "dreary business" and one ultimately without legitimation, for all the inquirer discovers is what he or she already knows and "what can more clearly be known and seen elsewhere, for example by the study of history and society as such." The ethical "I must," however, "cannot . . . be accounted for by the social and historical forces that impinge upon it"; in fact, the ethical moment "contests these forces or is subversive of them." It is "genuinely productive and inaugural in its effects on history." This ethical "I must" operates not only "on the author writing the work," but also "on the narrator telling the story within the fiction of the novel, on the characters within the story at decisive moments of their lives, and on the reader, teacher, or critic responding to the work." Miller suggests that there are "analogies among all four of these ethical moments"—those claiming author, narrator, character, reader—but "the basis of these analogies, what *logos* controls them, remains to be interrogated" (8–9).

The Christian interpreter will join Miller in insisting that a literary work cannot be exhaustively explained by adducing a series of causes from outside the work: social, historical, political, economic, or psychological. Some margin of the unexplainable or mysterious will always elude the interpreter. The work is not a thing to be grasped, to be tackled or mastered by technique. Literary education that becomes the acquisition of rival techniques, like that in today's prestigious graduate departments, is not only "somewhat dreary" but deceiving, on Christian grounds, for its assumption that the work of ultimately mysterious persons can be totally accounted for by one or another explanatory model. A work can never be fully accounted for precisely because of its creation by one who has himself or herself been created by the infinite God. Where Christian interpreters will differ from Miller is in their sense of the way a community carries a tradition or life in time. Miller argues that literature's ethical moments are "radically inaugural," a phrase related to his resistance to totalizing explanations. "Radically inaugural moments" would be resistant to exhaustion by technique, but they presumably would be unrelated to moments preceding or following and thus uninterpretable. Some measure of coherence and continuity of phenomena—guaranteed for Christians by God's action as creator, sustainer, and redeemer—is necessary for all interpretation. To assert that "ethical moments" are "radically inaugural," tantamount to new beginnings of the world, is to defeat the impulse to totalization by making interpretation itself impossible.

An Aristotelian alternative to Miller's approach to ethics and literature is offered by Martha Nussbaum, whose work has been enormously important to those involved in the cross-disciplinary conversation of literary study and moral philosophy. Resisting any strong separation of experience into moral and nonmoral spheres, Nussbaum takes as her "starting point" the ancient question, "How should one live?"[19] Her "aim is to establish that certain literary texts . . . are indispensable to a philosophical inquiry without which the inquiry cannot be complete" (*LK* 23–24). A novel by Henry James embodies an ethical vision of life no less important to moral philosophy than a systematic work by a professional philosopher. What Nussbaum seeks methodologically is not just "to bring [novels] to some academic discipline which happens to ask ethical questions"; she wants to avoid using novels simply as material to approach with questions developed independently through traditional philosophical inquiry. Instead, Nussbaum seeks to bring novels "into connection with our deepest practical searching, for ourselves and others, the searching in connection with which the influential philosophical conceptions of the

ethical were originally developed, the searching we pursue as we compare these conceptions, both with one another and with our active sense
of life." Acknowledging that "no starting point is altogether neutral," that
no putting of the question is without "some hint as to where the answers
might lie" (LK 24), Nussbaum develops an "Aristotelian procedure" for
her comparative searching of major ethical conceptions:

> The inquiry proceeds by working through the major alternative posi-
> tions (including Aristotle's own, but others as well), holding them up
> against one another and also against the participants' beliefs and feelings,
> their active sense of life. Nothing is held unrevisable in this process,
> except the very basic logical idea that statement implies negation, that to
> assert something is to rule out something else. The participants look not
> for a view that is true by correspondence to some extra-human reality,
> but for the best overall fit between a view and what is deepest in human
> lives. They are asked to imagine, at each stage, what they can least live
> well without, what lies deepest in their lives; and, again, what seems
> more superficial, more dispensable. They seek for coherence and fit in
> the web of judgment, feeling, perception, and principle, taken as a
> whole. (LK 25–26)

Literary works—Nussbaum focuses on Greek tragedies in *The Fragility of
Goodness*, on novels in *Love's Knowledge*—are "not neutral instruments for the
investigation of all conceptions." The "very choice" to write a literary
work rather than a work of systematic philosophy "expresses already certain evaluative commitments" (LK 26). When Nussbaum tries to systema-
tize the evaluative commitments of literary works, she develops four
categories: literary works are committed to the "Noncommensurability of
the Valuable Things"; "The Priority of Perceptions (Priority of the Particular)"; the "Ethical Value of the Emotions"; and the "Ethical Relevance of
Uncontrolled Happenings" (LK 36–43). "Noncommensurability" seems
partly defined in distinction from utilitarianism's strategy of representing
all goods along a single scale or in terms of variable quantities of a single
quality, like pleasure or utility. "The organizing vision" of novels tends to
show "that one thing is not just a different quantity of another; that there
is not only no single metric along which the claims of different good
things can be meaningfully considered, there is not even a small plurality
of such measures." Novels are more likely to "show us the worth and
richness of plural qualitative thinking and engender in their readers a
richly qualitative kind of seeing" (LK 36). The emphasis on perception is

carried over to the second category, where she brings together Aristotle and Henry James. "The ability to discern, acutely and responsively, the salient features of one's particular situation" lies "at the core" of Aristotle's "practical wisdom," which Nussbaum regards not simply as a "tool" but as "an ethically valuable activity in its own right." She finds the same commitment to rich responsiveness in James and notes that such "commitment seems to be built into the very form of the novel as genre"—an observation no doubt true, at least, of the novel as James conceived it. Nussbaum wants to hold up perception and fine discernment over against "the ethical crudeness of moralities based exclusively on general rules." She grants that "rules and general categories still have enormous action-guiding significance in the morality of perception," but sometimes her rhetorical emphases belie a lower estimation of rules than this suggests— as in the reference to "ethical crudeness" quoted just above (*LK* 37).

Nussbaum regards the emotions not merely as "blind surges of affect" but as "discriminating responses closely connected with beliefs about how things are and what is important." Anger, for example, "seems to require and to rest upon a belief that one has been wronged or damaged in some significant way by the person toward whom the anger is directed" (*LK* 41). Literary works recognize and represent this cognitive dimension of the emotions, long suppressed in the dispassionate style of philosophical writing. While not wishing to suggest that the emotions are "self-certifying sources of ethical truth"—they can be just as wrong or unjustified as beliefs—Nussbaum does want to show "the richness of the connections between emotion and judgment" (*LK* 42). She is especially interested in the tensions between love, with its devotion to particular recipients, and the moral point of view as defined by philosophical ethics. "Moral luck," the influence on human flourishing of events that happen to persons "through no fault of their own," has also been a consistent emphasis of Nussbaum's, particularly in her arguments for the ethical value of the Greek tragedies in *The Fragility of Goodness*. Literary forms seem in their very conception to give a weight to uncontrolled and uncontrollable happenings that is quite unlike that of traditional moral philosophy. Nussbaum strongly objects to the Platonic project of isolating the good from harm. Human goods, she insists in *Fragility*, are vulnerable; indeed, their vulnerability is part of what makes them precious. Literary works can keep the vulnerability of particular persons before our eyes, filled perhaps with pity and fear, in ways that the detached style of philosophy cannot. Moreover, what a novel or tragic drama offers in such a case is not

simply an extended example of a philosopher's proposition; rather, the
novel or drama offers an extended experience in the qualitative discernment of particulars that makes it quite unlike the examples offered by
philosophers—tricked up, as they are so often, to serve conclusions arrived at in advance.

Doing justice to the rich and complex work of Martha Nussbaum
requires much longer treatment than I can give it here. She should be
thanked by those of us to whom literature matters for being bold enough
to assert again its ethical importance. She has pointed out persuasively
the failure of contemporary literary criticism to engage the great ethical
traditions, despite its intense interest in philosophical currents more generally. Nussbaum's foregrounding the problem of moral luck has been
immensely important to me, although I draw rather different conclusions
about it, and her focus on the tension between particular and universal
commitments has also been helpful. Above all, I see her as part of a group
of extraordinarily fine minds who have emphasized the centrality of
attention to morality, a group including Henry James, Simone Weil, and
Iris Murdoch, all of whom Nussbaum cites. Consider the moral import,
for instance, of James's famous advice to the novice writer: "Try to be one
of the people on whom nothing is lost!" Or James commenting more
specifically on the link between morality and fine disciplined seeing in
"The Art of Fiction": "The essence of moral energy is to survey the whole
field." James told H. G. Wells that literature *"makes* life, makes interest,
makes importance," and it does so by offering its readers extended experiences in the discernment of particulars, the kind of discernment necessary for good judgment.[20] Nussbaum has added immensely to this
Jamesian making of life, interest, and importance not only in her theoretical articulations but also in her readings of particular texts.

Troubling, however, is the logic of Nussbaum's treatment of moral luck.
She begins *The Fragility of Goodness* with a quotation from Pindar: "But
human excellence grows like a vine tree, fed by the green dew, raised up,
among wise men and just, to the liquid sky." The quotation serves to set "a
problem that lies at the heart of Greek thought about the good life for a
human being": the degree to which human flourishing is "dependent on
what is outside of us."[21] No one would deny that human lives are influenced by factors we might group under the large heading of luck or
fortune. The critical question, especially for the Christian, lies in whether
we would equate all of those things under luck's influence with human

worth. Nussbaum makes just such an equation: "What the external nour-
ishes, and even helps to constitute, is excellence or human worth itself"
(*FG* 1). She makes this comment partly as a gloss on Pindar, but it does
represent the tenor of her argument in *Fragility* and other texts. The move
from "excellence" to "human worth" must not go unchallenged. One must
ask whether a human life would be regarded as worthless if it failed to
realize excellence or lacked the fostering external circumstances helpful
to doing so. Christians must certainly insist on a strong separation between excellence and worth. They will want to encourage people to
realize excellence in a variety of practices; they will clearly recognize
that good fortune and fostering circumstances can be helpful to individuals in the development of excellences; and they will thus hope to exert at
least some control over fortune to assist people toward the excellences.
They will always realize, however, that the possession of excellences
is not to be equated with human worth, which derives from creation
by God.

Related to Nussbaum's equation of excellence and worth is a moral
vocabulary that frequently sounds oddly consumerist. She focuses her
discussion of Greek tragedy on situations of "practical conflict," described
as involving "a conflict of desires": "the agent wants (has reason to pursue)
x and he or she wants (has reason to pursue) y; but he cannot, because of
contingencies of circumstance, pursue both. We want ultimately to ask
whether among these cases there are some in which not just content-
ment, but ethical goodness itself, is affected" (*FG* 27). The easy equation
of "wanting" with "having reason" here seems more confusing than clar-
ifying; surely one can "want" all kinds of things that one would never
describe as objects of reason. Many of our everyday "practical conflicts"
involve tension between what we want and what we have reason to
pursue based on some end to which we aspire. From within Nussbaum's
conflation of want and reason, however, there appears a kind of universe
of desires, of things or "items," to use another of her recurrent terms. The
desiring self would have all of these things (and thus perhaps the greatest
possible worth), and it becomes a kind of tragedy when anything must be
"forgone," another characteristic phrase: "Sometimes what is, of necessity, forgone is a possession, reward, or some other item external to the
agent; sometimes it is an activity in which the agent wishes to (has reason
to) engage. Sometimes there will simply be an omission or a failure to
pursue one of the desired projects; sometimes the course chosen will

itself involve acting against the other project or commitment. Sometimes what is omitted is an 'extra' or luxury, peripheral to the agent's conception of value; sometimes it is more central—either a component part of his or her conception of living well or a necessary means to something that is a component" (FG 27–28).

Surely Greek tragedy deals with situations of "practical conflict": the chapter from which the above derives is devoted to the choice Agamemnon must make to sacrifice Iphigenia to have favorable winds for the voyage to Troy. My objection is to the contemporary consumerist language in which Nussbaum frames the conflicts of tragedy. Agamemnon's choice is tragic because he has been positioned by the pattern of fate in such a way that he must spill the innocent blood of his daughter to avenge his brother's honor. The tragedy lies not in Agamemnon's "forgoing an item," but in the killing of Iphigenia, killing that brings about more killing, as blood cries out to be answered by blood. One suspects that, for Nussbaum, there is tragedy involved whenever the desiring self cannot have everything it "wishes." Such a description of ethical conflict, or the ethical life, as primarily a matter of items or projects to be pursued or, tragically, forgone, seems quite alien to Aristotle, under whose authority Nussbaum situates her overall conception. Aristotle speaks in the *Nicomachean Ethics* of the need for his students to have received proper antecedent training of the dispositions: if the dispositions have not been trained in certain particular ways, then there is nothing he can do with those young men. Surely, training the dispositions means learning to have some desires and not others; it means learning to be directed toward some ends that one has good reasons to pursue—despite what other things one might wish to do. It means acquiring such habitual orientations toward certain actions that one has no sense of forgoing other projects. Aristotle associates virtue with the "fully formed state of character." This phrase suggests that when a person of virtue does *x*, we cannot imagine his doing *y*, because doing *x* is part of who he is: nothing has been omitted, nothing has been forgone, because these other possibilities simply do not exist for him.

I have developed some other reservations about Nussbaum's positions in Chapter 5 of this book, with reference especially to her reading of James. These have to do with the way she uses Kant in relation to James, with the adequacy of her "Aristotelian procedure," and with the question of translatability, that is, with whether she is really successful in casting the questions posed by one ethical language-in-use into the terms of another. I want to avoid overstating my differences with Nussbaum, however, for her insistence on perception and on the ethical contribution of literature has been extremely important to me.

II

Nussbaum's project can be understood as part of the broad questioning of ways of doing ethics that have focused on formulating principles by which actors stand back from the particularities that make them who they are in order to resolve dilemmas or "ethical issues." In this emphasis, her work has contributed to that of Stanley Hauerwas, who has repeatedly suggested the problems involved in thinking of the moral life as a matter of confronting quandaries or hard choices. In an essay written with David Burrell, Hauerwas explains the problems with this "standard account" of morality:

> [The standard account] simply ignores the fact that most of the convictions that charge us morally are like the air we breathe—we never notice them. We never notice them precisely because they form us not to describe the world in certain ways and not to make certain matters subject to decision. Thus we assume that it is wrong to kill children without good reason. Or even more strongly we assume that it is our duty to provide children (and others who cannot protect themselves) with care that we do not need to give to the stranger. These are not matters that we need to articulate or decide about; their force lies rather in their not being subject to decision. And morally we must have the kind of character that keeps us from subjecting them to decision.[22]

Hauerwas argues elsewhere that the emphasis on quandaries inadequately recognizes the way vision determines the kinds of ethical decisions we will be called on to make: "The kind of agent we are and the kinds of institutions and practices in which we are involved determine the kinds of cases we confront. Situations are correlative of the ways we have learned to see, and seeing depends on the language we use and the expectations we have encouraged through our character and roles" (*TT* 170). Defining ethics as impersonal decision-making theory has the effect of "alienating the moral agent from his or her projects," thus robbing the "moral life of those characteristics from which it derives its rationale—namely, the close identification of what we ought to do with

what we want to be as a concrete moral agent."[23] When we confront an
ethical quandary from within the "standard account" of morality, "the
only intentions or reasons for our behavior that are morally interesting
are those that anyone might have." If we, for example, confront the
dilemma of abortion, "questions like Why did the pregnancy occur?
What kind of community do you live in? What do you believe about the
place of children? may be psychologically interesting but cannot be
allowed to enter into the justification of the decision"—precisely because
these "vary from one agent to another" (*TT* 18). Such an account of ethics
can have little to say about moral growth, for it slices life up into a series
of unrelated decisions—while ruling irrelevant the "beliefs and dispositions" that cause the agent to identify certain situations as dilemmatic.
According to Hauerwas and Burrell, it is "character, inasmuch as it is
displayed by a narrative, that provides the context necessary to pose the
terms of a decision, or to determine whether a decision should be made at
all" (*TT* 20).

For Hauerwas, the central terms of Christian ethics are narrative, vision, character, the virtues, community, and church. He defines his approach in contrast to that of Christian ethicists who have sought to make
their arguments within the dominant terms of philosophical ethics. The
latter approach has, in Hauerwas's view, the effect of undermining the
seriousness of Christian claims: "If we know what we ought to do on
grounds separate from our religious beliefs, then what are we to make
morally of those theological convictions? Usually these ethicists relegate
such convictions to a 'higher morality' or to the 'motivational' aspects of
the moral life. Both alternatives entail a moral psychology which ar-
tificially severs agents and their actions; what we 'ought to do' is abstracted from the question of who we are" (*PK* 23). Hauerwas instead
emphasizes the agent's perspective and the distinctiveness of Christian
convictions. He typically asks first not "What should I do?" but "How
should we, as a Christian community, describe what is going on here
within the set of distinctive convictions that we hold?" When addressing
the issues of suicide and euthanasia, for example, he declares it his primary task "to help Christians get the meaning of suicide and euthanasia
right in terms of how those notions help them to understand the basic
story that defines the kind of community they are" (*TT* 104).

Among the skills of the Christian ethicist are the ability to give careful
attention to particulars and to describe what is going on in relation to the
narrative of Scripture. Doing ethics involves a particular kind of memory,

itself a moral discipline: "Ethics is the attempt to help us remember what kind of story sustains certain descriptions. It is, therefore, a discipline rather like history, in that we are forced to tell stories in order to capture our past, sustain our present, and give our future direction" (*TT* 104). To return to the examples of suicide and euthanasia, then, what the ethicist must first do is to recall the Christian themes that bear on the way we understand these matters. Hauerwas does this with special reference to the language of gift, to the centrality of trust in Christian existence, and to the need for communal solidarity. What emerges from his analysis, in this case and in many others, is the sharp illumination of an aspect of a moral "quandary" that the "standard account of morality," with its impersonal weighing of claims, simply could never discover. One of his chief concerns about euthanasia and suicide is the way they erode a sense of communal care and solidarity. Made aware of his own sinfulness by the Christian story—aware in a way that would be irrelevant to the moral chooser of the standard account—Hauerwas notes about euthanasia, "Humans never kill more readily than when we kill in the name of mercy. We must be careful that the mercy we dispense, especially when it takes the form of ending life, is not necessary because of our original uncare" (*TT* 112). Similarly, he asks whether suicide is not often "a sign of failure of community," a sign of significant abandonment in a society "where 'abandonment' is often called the pursuit of life, liberty and happiness, and hallowed by the ethics of individualism" (*TT* 113).

Part of the first of Hauerwas's "Ten Theses toward the Reform of Christian Social Ethics," then, is that "Christian social ethics too often takes the form of principles and policies that are not clearly based on or warranted by the central convictions of the faith." "The basis of any Christian social ethic," this first thesis continues, "should be the affirmation that God has decisively called and formed a people to serve him through Israel and the work of Christ."[24] Hauerwas assumes that accounts of practical reason are narrative-dependent; indeed, his second thesis begins, "*Every social ethic involves a narrative.*" The particular narrative that guides a Christian social ethic is the narrative of Scripture: of the history of Israel, the life, death, and resurrection of Jesus, and the creation of the Church. Liberal ethics has tried to do without a sustaining narrative or story, taking as its primary task instead the giving of an account of obligation sufficient to allow diverse groups of strangers to live together. Without question, this has been an important task. What it has done, however, is render specific Christian convictions irrelevant to moral deliberation,

sunder the virtues from accounts of obligation, and paradoxically leave
people increasingly under the dominion of "fate"—for insofar as one
accepts the story of autonomy as freedom from particular entanglements,
one will come to see anything (e.g., the family) that influences one as a
matter of "fate." Losing narrative as a "central category for social ethics"
has, according to Hauerwas's second thesis, "resulted in a failure to see
that the ways the issues of social ethics are identified—i.e., the relation of
personal and social ethics, the meaning and status of the individual in
relation to the community, freedom versus equality, the interrelation of
love and justice—are more a reflection of a political philosophy than they
are crucial categories for the analysis of a community's social ethic" (CC
9–10). What "counts" as social ethics is "a correlative of the content" of
the narrative that forms the community.

"The first task of Christian social ethics, therefore, is not to make the
'world' better or more just" (CC 10); neither is it to provide an ethos for
liberal social strategies, democracy, or the American nation-state. The
first task of the church is to be the church, and indeed it is only in being
the church that the church enables the world to know itself as "world." A
Christian social ethics must be concerned, at the very beginning, with
vision, with "help[ing] us rightly envision the world": "We can only act
within the world we can envision, and we can envision the world rightly
only as we are trained to see. We do not come to see merely by looking,
but must develop disciplined skills through initiation into that community that attempts to live faithful to the story of God" (PK 29–30). Doing
Christian ethics involves giving people the descriptive skills with which
to interpret "what is going on" in relation to the narratives and traditions
of the church.[25] In part, this means that Christians must learn to name the
powers, as Hauerwas emphasizes in the fourth thesis of his reformation:
"We live in a world of powers that are not our creation and we become
determined by them when we lack the ability to recognize and name
them" (CC 10). In addition, one cannot stress enough the need for transformation of the self if the world is to be seen truly. As sinners, "we do not
desire to see truthfully." This is not a self-evident proposition but something we come to understand as we allow the Christian narrative to
redescribe our lives, or, as Hauerwas puts it, as we "submit to [the] vigorous continuing discipleship" commanded by the Gospel (PK 30). The
lesson is "most disconcerting when the narrative asks us to understand
ourselves not only as friends of the crucified, but as the crucifiers": "Our
sin is so fundamental that we must be taught to recognize it; we cannot

perceive its radical nature so long as we remain formed by it. Sin is not some universal tendency of humankind to be inhumane or immoral, though sin may involve inhumanity and immorality. We are not sinful because we participate in some general human condition, but because we deceive ourselves about the nature of reality and so would crucify the very one who calls us to God's kingdom." "Learning to be a sinner" is part of what it means to "discover our true identity," which happens only insofar as we learn to "locat[e] the self in God's life as revealed to us through the life, death, and resurrection of Jesus Christ" (*PK* 30–31). Hauerwas's sense of "locating the self" here should not be taken to mean that we somehow "read ourselves into" Scripture or that "believers," as George Lindbeck puts it, "find their stories in the Bible." Hauerwas aligns himself firmly with the kind of postliberal approach to Scripture articulated by Lindbeck, whose "intratextual theology" "redescribes reality within the scriptural framework rather than translating Scripture into extrascriptural categories. It is the text, so to speak, which absorbs the world, rather than the world the text."[26]

Narrative is a crucial category precisely because the God Christians worship "has willed to be known through a very definite and concrete history" (*PK* 6). Christian ethics "begin[s]" not "by emphasizing rules or principles, but by calling our attention to a narrative that tells of God's dealing with creation" (*PK* 24–25). The narrative mode of Christian convictions is "neither incidental nor accidental." Rather, "the fact that we come to know God through the recounting of the story of Israel and the life of Jesus is decisive for our truthful understanding of the kind of God we worship as well as the world in which we exist" (*PK* 25). Doctrines about God are not the real meaning of the stories; the stories are not ways of saying things that can just as well be put in discursive or propositional language. Doctrines such as Creation should be understood as simply "shorthand ways of reminding us that we believe we are participants in a much more elaborate story, of which God is the author" (*PK* 26). "Knowledge" of God, world, and self are interdependent and in need of "concrete display" in narrative. Selfhood requires learning to tell a particular story or stories, which is why liberalism—the story that there is no story—leads to discontinuity in the self and to experience's seeming "just one damn thing after another." For Christians, the Socratic directive to "Know thyself" involves knowing the self as it is storied by Scripture: "Not only is knowledge of self tied to knowledge of God, but we know ourselves truthfully only when we know ourselves in relation to God. We know who we are only when we place our selves—locate our stories—within God's story" (*PK* 27).

Even knowing who one is requires the extended discipline of allowing the scriptural stories and categories to redescribe one's life. One turns and turns again to the Scripture as one learns increasingly what it means to be a creature and a sinner whose life is a gift and whose justification lies in the death and resurrection of the God whom one has crucified. Learning to be a creature means "learn[ing] to recognize that our existence and the existence of the universe itself is a gift. It is a gift that God wills to have our lives contribute to the eschatological purposes for creation." That God has so willed is part of what we mean by theological shorthand referring to grace. "Grace is not an eternal moment above history render-ing history irrelevant" but "God's choice to be a Lord whose kingdom is furthered by our concrete obedience through which we acquire a history befitting our nature as God's creatures" (*PK* 27). In summarizing the reasons for narrative's centrality to an "explication of Christian exis-tence," Hauerwas makes three general claims: first, that "narrative for-mally displays our existence and that of the world as creatures—as *con-tingent* beings"; second, that "narrative is the characteristic form of our awareness of ourselves as *historical* beings who must give an account of the purposive relation between temporally discrete realities"; and third, that a particular narrative, that of "the covenant with Israel, the life, death, and resurrection of Jesus, and the ongoing history of the church as the re-capitulation of that life," constitutes the *"form of God's salvation"* as we know it (*PK* 28–29).

The second claim provides the connection to Hauerwas's understand-ing of community. Communities are identified by the accounts they give "of the purposive relation between temporally discrete realities"—those, for instance, between goods and the practices, intentions, virtues di-rected toward those goods. A community "joins us with others to further the growth of a tradition whose manifold storylines are meant to help individuals identify and navigate the path to the good." The self can be said to be "subordinate" to the community, then, in the sense that "we discover the self through a community's narrated tradition" (*PK* 28). Communities teach us what kinds of intentions are appropriate; they give us the linguistic skills we need to understand our lives truthfully. This is why the church must, first of all, *"be itself"* (Thesis 5), by which Hauerwas means *"a people who have been formed by a story that provides them with the skills for negotiating the danger of this existence, trusting in God's promise of redemption"* (*CC*

10). Hence one of Hauerwas's objections to the concentration, in liberal ethics, on rules and obligations: "The concentration on obligations and rules as morally primary ignores the fact that action descriptions gain their intelligibility from the role they play in a community's history and therefore for individuals in that community. When 'acts' are abstracted from that history, the moral self cannot help but appear as an unconnected series of actions lacking continuity and unity" (*PK* 21).

Hauerwas's understanding of narrative and community has specific consequences for the subject matter of ethics, for the relationship between theology and ethics, and for a stance on the virtues. The insistence that ethics concerns the way character is formed in particular ways by communities with particular commitments has the effect of bringing a much wider range of subjects into the purview of ethics than is ordinarily the case under the standard account. Hauerwas has written not only about such quandaries as euthanasia, abortion, and suicide but also about the moral value of the family, the commitment of medicine to be a presence in suffering, "the tyranny of normality," and "the moral challenge of the handicapped."[27] He is fond of saying that the church should *be* rather than *have* a social ethic (Thesis 8): on this view, the church is not primarily a generator of position papers but the carrier of a story that enables its people to live truthfully and the context for a continual reflection on the kind of people Christians are called to be. Being a social ethic means, among other things, "*recaptur[ing] the social significance of common behavior, such as acts of kindness, friendship, and the formation of families*" (*CC* 11).

It also means, for Hauerwas, a commitment to nonviolence that derives from the conviction that God is the "lord of history" and it is not our responsibility to make history "come out right" (*PK* 87). Nonviolence plays a central role in Hauerwas's thinking, which closely links violence with falsehood. We come to see the world truthfully insofar as we are formed and transformed by the story of Scripture, with its disarming of the powers in Jesus' cross and resurrection. "Our violence," then, "is correlative to the falseness of the objects we worship, and the more false they are, the greater our stake in maintaining loyalty to them and protecting them through coercion. Only the one true God can take the risk of ruling by relying entirely on the power of humility and love" (*PK* 79). The cross is "not merely a general symbol of the moral significance of self-sacrifice"; it is the "ultimate dispossession through which God has conquered the powers of this world" (*PK* 87). The resurrection is "God's decisive eschatological act," through which we see that "peace has been made possible," even though the world continues to be at war (*PK* 88–89). Critical to Hauerwas's analysis is the decisiveness of Jesus' cross and resurrection. It is precisely "because we have confidence that God has raised this crucified man," Jesus the Jew from Nazareth and not some other, that we "believe that forgiveness and love are alternatives to the coercion the world thinks necessary for existence" (*PK* 87).

As Hauerwas's approach brings far more than the usual quandaries into the purview of the Christian ethicist, so, too, it diminishes the difference between ethics and theology. Ethics is not something one does after systematic theology. Rather, "because truth is unattainable without a cor-responding transformation of self, 'ethics,' as the investigation of that transformation," must be done *"at the beginning* of Christian theological reflection" (*PK* 16). We are always *"already* in the moral adventure," and the task of ethics is to give us "a disciplined set of analytic skills" by which to navigate (*PK* 18). Theological convictions are eminently practical; they represent not some "primitive metaphysics" but the means by which we learn to describe the world, ourselves, what happens to us, what we undertake and do. Like the theology to which it is so closely related, Christian ethics is a "form of reflection in service to a community." Less concerned with abstract "ideas" than with practical construal of self and world, Christian ethics depends for its intelligibility ultimately "on a community's wisdom about how certain actions are prohibited or en-joined for the development of a particular kind of people" (*PK* 54).

The virtues have a central place in a Christian ethics concerned with construing self and world in relation to the narratives and traditions that form the church. The kinds of moral decisions we face are functions of the kinds of people we have learned to be, of the descriptive skills we have learned from the communities that form us: "If it is true that I can act only in the world I see and that my seeing is a matter of my learning to say, it is equally the case that my 'saying' requires sustained habits that form my emotions and passions, teaching me to feel one way rather than another" (*PK* 117). The point here recalls Nussbaum's insistence on the cognitive significance of the emotions. Hauerwas's sense that the virtues involve the directed training of the emotions suggests the possibility of criteria by which trustworthy emotions might be distinguished from un-trustworthy ones: "Questions of feeling are central for determining what I ought to do since they are signals that help remind us what kind of people we are" (*PK* 117). On this view, it is possible to have feelings that are inappropriate, unworthy of us, and plainly wrong—and these can be judged so by being referred to our character. If we have been formed to feel in ways that are worthy of ourselves, and the God who has created us, our feelings can provide important leadings as to what we ought to do.

Hauerwas has written widely on patience, hope, courage, peaceableness, and honor as well as justice and love. His writing on the virtues turns on two general conceptual claims. The first insists that the self is best understood narratively, its unity "like the unity that is exhibited in a good novel—namely with many subplots and characters that we at times do not closely relate to the primary dramatic action of the novel" (CC 144). The virtues are thus vital to the narrative unity of the self. Becoming oneself depends on developing certain dispositions in a sustained and disciplined way into formed states of character (i.e., the virtues). A particular value of the Christian narrative is that it continually calls into question any attempt of ours to appropriate our character, treating it as solely our achievement rather than a gift from God shaped by His story and the people it brings into being. The narrative "must provide skills of discernment and distancing. For it is certainly a skill to be able to describe my behavior appropriately and to know how to 'step back' from myself so that I might better understand what I am doing. The ability to step back cannot come by trying to discover a moral perspective abstracted from all my endeavors, but rather comes through having a narrative that gives me critical purchase on my own projects" (CC 144–145).

Following from this sense of the self as narrative is a second claim regarding agency: narrative, not freedom, is "the fundamental category for ensuring agency." Agency lies in our ability to describe both what we do and what happens to us in an "ongoing narrative" that constitutes our character. Two immediate implications follow from this position: that one's agency depends on one's descriptive abilities and the truthfulness of the story within which one locates one's life, and that being an agent is partly a social skill, for it depends on the interpretive narratives one learns from a community and its tradition: "There is no contradiction between claims of agency and our sociality, since the extent and power of any agency depends exactly on the adequacy of the descriptions we learn from our communities. Our 'freedom,' therefore, is dependent on our being initiated into a truthful narrative, as in fact it is the resource from which we derive the power to 'have character' at all" (PK 43). Freedom, understood as "some real or ideal state in which we have absolute control of our lives," is clearly impossible. When we understand freedom in this way, we cannot help coming to see our lives as increasingly determined. Rather than freedom, Hauerwas speaks of "agency," the "capacity to claim our lives by learning to grow in a truthful narrative." Finally, the skills to make our lives our own "are not just 'intellectual' but also moral." They depend on the virtues, particularly courage and hope: "To face our lives truthfully requires trust and courage, for if we are to be free we must learn to see what we have done without illusion and deception. So the formation of courage is even greater than the power of choice, as we must be trained to face our destiny of death, not with denial, but with hope" (*PK* 43).

III

My approach to setting Christian ethics and literary study into conversation assumes that theology is a practical activity devoted to construing the world in accord with the narrative of Scripture that forms and guides the Church. It would be impossible for me to characterize here all of the ways in which Hauerwas's work informs the readings that follow in this book. Nevertheless, let me emphasize three general points that I have found extremely helpful. The first concerns the inseparability of the kind of people we are from what we identify as matters of moral reflection; the second involves the insistence that doctrines such as Creation should be understood as second-order language, as shorthand ways of reflecting on the great narrative of God's relation to the world; the third involves Hauerwas's account of agency, with its insistence that claiming our lives as our own involves learning to understand ourselves from within a truthful narrative rather than seeking to escape narrative altogether.

As literary narratives involve extended opportunities for reflection on the way the "kind of quandaries we confront depend on the kind of people we are" (*PK* 117), a Christian ethics of literature will place great emphasis on character, with careful attention to the virtues. Accounts of the virtues must themselves be historicized, with a recognition of the difference Christian faith makes to an understanding of the virtues. Christian ethical reflection on the virtues must resist being captured by the general cultural call for inculcation of the "virtues," which seems to assume either that there is consensus about what these are or that any virtue is better than none at all. Accounts of the virtues are relative to convictions about the good life for human beings; Benjamin Franklin omits virtues from his list that were crucial to Aquinas because they differ about the ends of life. One's understanding of a virtue differs in relation to the paradigm case that one establishes, and the choice of paradigm case depends on one's polis. Aristotle's account of courage, with its paradigm of armed civic virtue in the Greek city-state, varies from Aquinas's, based on martyrdom for the Christian faith.[28] This means there is need for careful study of particular virtues as they are worked out in particular texts and in relation to particular understandings of the good for human beings. Several of my chapters take up specific virtues in this way.

Also important is Hauerwas's double insistence on the narrative sense of Scripture and the derived, or second-order, status of doctrines such as Creation. A repeated concern of this book is Gnosticism, a subject I address in Chapters 3 and 5. Chapter 5 takes up the issue directly, as I suggest the way Henry James's *Portrait of a Lady* might be read as, in part, a response to the theology of his father, Henry James Sr. The elder James's theology is particularly revealing for its connection between Gnosticism and the loss of a narrative understanding of Scripture. For James Sr., Creation is no longer second-order language pointing to our contingency, to our existence's being a gift, to our participation in a story authored by God. Rather, it has become a philosophical abstraction, completely removed from temporal understanding or display. Human being is set over against God in a vast antithesis. As James Sr. tries to understand how human beings can be, at once, created and yet, in a state of nature, completely opposed to God, he formulates two ways of understanding Creation. One way suggests that the human being must be composed of a real, essential or created self that lies within a shadow self and must be liberated—a Gnostic formulation. The second is to argue that Creation names the process by which God turns self-loving human being toward the pure other-regarding quality of Divine love, manifested, for James, in society. This turns creatures into pure negativities as God goes about loving himself. Both of James Sr.'s ways of resolving the problem are profoundly anti-Trinitarian, and it is part of my argument that James Jr., in *Portrait*, reflects a perhaps more orthodox Trinitarian understanding of love precisely because he understands life in narrative terms. The point to be stressed here, however, is that James Sr.'s theology reflects the problems caused by treating Creation, nature, and grace as abstractions rather than as shorthand reminders of themes from the scriptural narrative.

Hauerwas's account of agency provides an alternative to the assumptions about autonomy and heteronomy implicit in the approaches of critics I engage in several chapters, particularly those on Austen, James,

and Crane. Those assumptions bear out what Hauerwas has argued about
the consequences for notions of freedom when the self and its agency are
no longer understood in narrative terms. When autonomy is claimed for
the unstoried self, then the self comes to seem increasingly determined,
its actions frequently heteronomous. In discussing Crane's "The Monster," for example, Michael Warner argues that Dr. Trescott's saving
Henry "fails" and that the story problematizes notions of "agency" and
moral action itself. Although "freedom obtains" for Trescott, "pure intent
does not," in Warner's view, and it is the latter "that we must assume in
order to understand our machinery of valuation."[29] The problem here lies
not in the story, but in Warner's assumption that moral action depends on
the ability of a "pure intent" to enact value. For where has such an intent—
free, apparently, even from the agent's history—ever existed? Warner's
argument illustrates the dead end for moral reflection to which we are
brought by notions of autonomy as freedom from any determining context. I agree with Warner that Crane problematizes Trescott's decision,
but he invites us to see the problem as one specifically of interpretation,
of "storying" a faceless man who returns from death. Interestingly, a "pure
intent," though of a slightly different kind, is what some feminist critics
find lacking in Mr. Knightley. His correction of Emma must thus be
disregarded because it is not disinterested. Such a view turns again on the
model of the unstoried autonomous self able to be persuaded only by
objective or impartial reason giving. Approaching *Emma* without the assumption that moral suasion must be "objective" frees us from the suspicious reading of Knightley as a sinister male forming Emma for himself.
We can thus see him as a Christian friend whose saying what he "must" to
Emma assists in destroying her illusion of perfection and helping her to a
real sense of conscious worth.

IV

As my approach to Christian ethics emphasizes discernment, the literary-
ethical chapters that follow represent extended attempts to get the descriptions right from a Christian point of view. Chapter 2 focuses on
Herman Melville's "Bartleby, the Scrivener," working out specific consequences for literary interpretation of central Christian doctrines, especially as they make for a difference from the ethics of reading as practiced
by Miller. The chapter demonstrates how reflection on the story can be

enriched by introducing the ways various traditions have thought about the issues of law and love posed by Melville. I emphasize the literary-ethical implications of Christological particularism and show how other Christological assumptions are implicit in critical arguments about the story. I also show how the story might focus a discussion of the sea change that has occurred in the conceptions of two virtues, prudence and charity, from their placement at the center of the good life by Aquinas to their curious appearance in "Bartleby." I argue further that Melville's story can help us to see some of the consequences of Kant's means-end distinction and identification of rationality with personhood. The chapter closes with a reflection on the consequences for teaching of the means-end distinction and an argument for our adopting a renewed, and richer, sense of prudence.

Chapter 3 focuses on a rich source for ethical reflection, Jane Austen's *Emma.* I begin by suggesting the difficulties faced by a liberal critic like Lionel Trilling when reading a writer, like Austen, who was not a liberal. Trilling's work on Austen suggests the liberal imagination's uneasiness with virtue as well as the Gnostic tendency to insist that freedom lies in transcendence of all circumstance. I also engage Wayne Booth's attempt—unsuccessful, in my view—to defend the novel against feminist arguments that it endorses a dangerous romantic ideology. The feminist critique of Mr. Knightley's schooling of Emma, however, is itself based on an identi-fication of rationality with impartiality that my study challenges. *Emma* reflects quite specifically on moral partiality, suggesting both why we ought not to will its disappearance and how it must be balanced by love and respect for others. Austen also reflects specifically on what it means to be good. Does it involve primarily learning appropriate behaviors in particular roles, or does it involve a more general quality of heart and mind—a good will directed, indiscriminately, toward all? What, too, does it mean to do another good or to be another's good? Surely influence, appropriate and inappropriate, is one of the central concerns of the novel, as Gilbert Ryle noted when he suggested that an alternative title might be *Influence and Interference.*[30]

What Bernard Williams and Martha Nussbaum have called "moral luck" is another of Austen's concerns.[31] "Handsome, clever, and rich," Emma Woodhouse seems ideally positioned to enjoy the fullest human flourish-ing, yet Austen suggests that there is a better blessing even than rich ethical luck.[32] That better blessing is a conscious sense of worth, which can be achieved by Emma only after her illusion of perfection is shattered and she begins a conscious course of learning to respect others as centers of value in themselves and not as players in her fantasies. With the breaking of her illusion, Emma enters the world of ethics, of conflict over limited goods—in this case, Mr. Knightley—where principles must be developed in order to choose among competing claims or claimants. Early in the novel, Mrs. Weston defends Emma by saying that she "will never lead any one really wrong" or make a "lasting blunder" (68), propositions that are seriously tested when Harriet emerges as Emma's rival. Austen does, I believe, uphold Mrs. Weston's predictions, but in a way that the young Emma, convinced of her own omniscience, could never have conceived.

Chapter 4 concentrates on the way the virtues of honor and constancy are displayed in two novels by Anthony Trollope, *The Warden* and *He Knew He Was Right*. Prompted by a remark of Hauerwas's that the problem with Karl Barth is "that he did not read enough Trollope,"[33] the chapter seeks to bring Barth and Trollope into conversation on the matter of honor, a virtue that seems increasingly obsolescent in modern egalitarian societies. My attention to constancy in the novels is prompted similarly by MacIntyre's concentration on that virtue in Austen, the "last great representative of the classical tradition of the virtues." Constancy occupies such a central place for Austen because it is involved in affirming the narrative unity of the self. Thus, without it, "all the other virtues to some degree lose their point."[34] Hauerwas himself has explored the relationship between constancy and forgiveness in Trollope's *The Vicar of Bullhampton*, using his analysis to argue that forgiveness is vital to constancy because it makes possible the maintenance of standards within particular communities—standards on which constancy depends.[35] Forgiveness is that virtue that makes possible the upholding of standards while at the same time allowing for the reintegration of those who sometimes fail them. What needs further working out is the relationship between constancy and change, an issue at the center of the two novels the chapter treats. In *The Warden*, Mr. Harding remains constant, faithful to the communities that define who he is, while undergoing a major life-changing reversal. In *He Knew He Was Right*, on the other hand, Lewis Trevelyan's rigidly constant adherence to his own view of himself leads to madness. The latter novel can be read, I believe, as a richly theological one that explores what it means to live "under wrath."

Chapter 5 moves from wrath to envy, the deadly sin of Gilbert Osmond, which I explore through Kant's treatment of the vice in his lectures and *The Doctrine of Virtue,* part 2 of *The Metaphysics of Morals.* My reading of *The Portrait of a Lady* argues that the loveless Osmond looks very much like the Gnostic God of Henry James Sr., one for whom creatures are not truly other but rather only material for his own self-realization. *Portrait* suggests that Henry James Jr. was, at least implicitly, more Trinitarian in his understanding of love than his father, perhaps because of his greater commitment to a narrative-dramatic understanding of life. James's fiction has played a central role in Nussbaum's articulation of an ethics whose most important term is perception, the fine discernment of particulars. In *Love's Knowledge,* she delineates the "Aristotelian procedure" of her ethical inquiry through a reading of *The Ambassadors,* grouping James together with Aristotle and posing both against an understanding of morality she identifies with Kant.[36] Chapter 5 offers a brief alternative reading of *The Ambassadors* as part of a more general critique of Nussbaum's use of James in her ethical "procedure." The chapter also treats such matters of philosophical and Jamesian interest as curiosity, regret, the possibility of disinterestedness, and the relationship between love and good reasons. My reading of the novel's problematic ending builds on feminist challenges to the ideology of literary realism yet argues that Isabel's notorious return to Rome represents the response of love to Pansy Osmond's prior and completely gratuitous extension of an unlimited fidelity.

The strategy of Chapter 6 is to read two stories by Stephen Crane, "The Monster" and "The Blue Hotel," in relation to the Gospel of John, to which Crane alludes very broadly, especially in "The Monster." Critics have noted Crane's interest in John before, but they have nearly always sought to weave every detail remotely traceable to the Gospel into allegorical readings of the stories. My approach is different. Crane's very broad allusions to John in "The Monster" seem to me to resist precise allegorization; rather, they seem invitations to read the whole of the text in relation to the story of Lazarus's being raised from the dead and the Johannine motifs of light, glory, and eternal life. The story is opened further by the phenomenological terms of Emmanuel Levinas, particularly those from *Totality and Infinity,* with its emphases on light, glory, infinity, and the paradoxical relationship between war and peace. The central motif of Crane's story is the most fundamental term of Levinas's phenomenology: the face, which, by resisting the subject's attempt to schematize it as part of its own projects, opens, for Levinas, the possibility of ethics. "The Blue Hotel," too, asks to be read in relation to the Johannine understanding of the lie and its relation to murder. The Johannine interpreter of that story will see the strong connection between the death of the Swede and the deceptions of the Blue Hotel, themselves rooted in the original lie, "Ye shall not surely die."

Conceived as an afterword, the final essay considers first the predicament of the Christian scholar in the postmodern multiversity and then what George Marsden has called "the outrageous idea of Christian scholarship."[37] Through an engagement primarily with Rorty and Stout, I argue that postmodern ethical differences do go considerably farther down than a liberal like Stout will allow. Christian scholars should begin, then, to discover the consequences of their faith convictions for the kinds of knowledge they produce. In doing so, they are following the lead of Rorty, who puts the community question first. In "The Priority of Democracy to Philosophy," Rorty argues that "we" must know who "we" are before we can begin to put the questions of philosophy. Rorty's is an important position for Christians to consider, in part because the Deweyan progressivism he endorses has been of such influence in the public schools and universities. People from all "solidarity groupings" need to think out the consequences for education of the abandonment of the Enlightenment project. My afterword seeks to articulate some Christian differences from Rorty and Stout, and then sets out some terms for conversation among Rorty, Stout, Hauerwas, and MacIntyre. The essay might be read, I hope, as an attempt to fulfill the task of the scholar required by MacIntyre's "university of constrained disagreement."

Some general matters remain to be addressed. Why these writers— Melville, Austen, Trollope, James, Crane—and not others? A partial answer to that question lies in my academic training, focused mostly on English and American writers of the nineteenth century. Several of my choices have been discussed by Booth, Miller, and Nussbaum, and thus they allow me to enter into conversation with these major voices in the discussion of literature and ethics. In each case, the texts raise important matters for Christian ethical reflection. Of the five writers, Austen, daughter of a clergyman and sister to two others, was the most orthodox Christian. Trollope was a member in good standing of the Church of England, but he "seems not to have thought very much about religion one way or the other," as Hauerwas puts it, reflecting the conventional judgment, one challenged by the chapter in this study.[38] Melville, influenced by the Calvinism of his family, has been treated as everything from a vigorous atheist to a negative theologian. No doubt the best-known judgment about his religious faith was that uttered by Hawthorne: "He can neither believe, nor be comfortable in his unbelief; and he is too honest and courageous not to try to do one or the other."[39] Henry James was the son of one significant American religious thinker and the brother of perhaps this country's most significant thinker about religion. James's life and work exhibit a continuing interest in religious matters, particularly as expressed in culture, and in spiritualism, but it would be very difficult to define his faith with any precision. Stephen Crane was the fourteenth child of a Methodist minister, the Reverend Jonathan Townley Crane, and a very devout mother, Mary Peck Crane. He is generally considered to have rejected this background and embraced late nineteenth-century naturalism. In much of his fiction, God seems either dead or irrelevant. Yet a persistent strain of critical opinion has held that Crane is a religious writer, though what is meant by that judgment is frequently left unclear.

Whatever their particular faith commitments, all five writers were formed by the culture of Christendom—another reason I have gravitated toward nineteenth-century texts. At this point, I should confess an inevitable ambiguity in these studies. At times, I emphasize the way Christian convictions affect analysis of, reflection on, or appropriation of a particular text. At other times, I seem less interested in providing readings that are compelling on Christian grounds than in drawing out continuing Christian presuppositions of texts. I know no way around this ambiguity, which seems implicit in the Christian interpreter's role as a critical voice from within culture.[40] My choice of nineteenth-century texts has been guided, too, by the sense that they offer rich, extended opportunities for loving attention and moral discernment, as Nussbaum has demonstrated so well. I believe, in fact, that the close study of literature should be defended precisely for its ability to train our capacity to attend. At the heart of a "Christian conception of studies is the realization that prayer consists of attention," Simone Weil writes, and thus a right ordering of "school studies" must be toward the development of the faculty of attention.[41] Rather than encouraging students of literature to flash in milliseconds through the information resources of the Internet, perhaps a literary education should direct them, time and again, to open themselves to the seemingly infinite nuances of a mind like Austen's or James's. If the students find this too difficult, too frustrating, the instructor should assure them, as Weil says of students struggling with geometry, that they "have nevertheless been making progress each minute . . . in another more mysterious dimension"—progress that will some day bear fruit where attention is needed. Perhaps the result will eventually "be felt in some department of the intelligence in no way connected with" literary criticism. Weil seems certain, for instance, that one day the fruits of studying geometry will be "discovered in prayer" (45). Who knows what students are learning as they attempt to stay with, and sort through, Isabel's complex reflections on her marriage to Osmond? If they are learning to give their attention, then that is more than enough. For "only he who is capable of attention," Weil writes, will be able to love the sufferer, the neighbor, by asking the question that he needs to hear: "What are you going through?" (51). What Weil writes of Latin translations and geometry problems could be said equally of James or Austen studies, provided they are done with the right kind of effort: "So it comes about that, paradoxical as it may seem, a Latin prose or a geometry problem, even though they are done wrong, may be of great service one day, provided we devote the right kind of effort to them. Should the occasion arise, they can one day make us better able to give someone in affliction exactly the help required to save him, at the supreme moment of his need" (52).

V

Doing Christian ethics as a traditioned inquiry and with frank acknowledgment of the qualifier would seem best suited to the university reorganized around the principle of "constrained disagreement" proposed by MacIntyre at the end of *Three Rival Versions of Moral Enquiry.* In MacIntyre's reconceived university, inquirers working from "rival standpoints" or alternative accounts of rationality would pursue work from within their own traditions while engaging in systematic encounters with representatives of other standpoints. Students and faculty would be involved in "reembody[ing]" a "particular tradition" not only by "reread[ing] the texts which constitute that tradition, but . . . do[ing] so in a way that ensures that the reader is put to the question by the texts as much as the texts by the reader."[42] Working in Christian ethics and literature would be inseparable from learning what it means to be good. At the same time, the sense of working from within a tradition would lead students and faculty to think beyond the university, and part of their work would necessarily be that of nurturing a public to receive it. Particularly compelling is MacIntyre's argument that the liberal university is, at present, almost completely unable to give an account to the public of what it is doing in such fields as philosophy or literary study.

MacIntyre's work has been important to Hauerwas, and it certainly lies behind much that I do here. Following MacIntyre, I assume that accounts of rationality are narrative-dependent; that the virtues are settled dispositions learned within communities committed to embodying particular narratives; that part of education in the virtues or character involves authoritative guidance; that the unity of the self depends on learning to read one's actions in relation to an interpretive narrative. Nevertheless, I do share John Milbank's sense that Christian interpreters must think out more fully the relationship between MacIntyre's account of virtue and the Christian virtues in particular. Milbank argues that the Aristotelian account of virtue is inherently linked to the agon and to a conception of the soul as self-contained in ways that one cannot carry over, without modification, to Christian thinking about the virtues. This means, on the one hand, that virtue "in the antique sense" is "ultimately related to victory in some sort of conflict," and, on the other, that "where virtue is conceived even in residually heroic terms (as by Aristotle) it will tend to reduce to a matter of self-control."[43] "The primacy of the mean," for example, "belongs with the idea of a soul that is ideally self-contained," for "'balance' can only be primary within fixed bounds" (361). Christian charity, however, is primarily "relational" and not a matter of balance; rather, the "very mode of being" of the person of charity is "a giving," a "constant outgoing" that does not diminish the person but "paradoxically recruits again her strength" (359–360). Thus it can be exercised by anyone, "even in negative situations of poverty and weakness," precisely because the charitable person "is first and foremost the *recipient* of charity from God." Charity is "inherently excessive": one cannot have "too much" of it (360).

Where this book is concerned with the virtues, I hope my analyses will assist thinking about the relationship between MacIntyre's account of virtue in general and the particular virtues in question. The chapter on *Emma* takes up the conversation with MacIntyre, primarily regarding the virtues of Miss Bates and the way the good for Emma relates to the social form of marriage in which she is to realize that good. My reading of Trollope's *The Warden* stresses the way Mr. Harding's constancy involves not simply willed self-consistency but the more relational virtue of fidelity: to his lost wife, to his friends at Hiram's hospital, to his sense of church carried primarily by its music. The fidelity to Pansy I ascribe to

Isabel Osmond seems excessive, and it is called forth by an extension of trust on Pansy's part that is infinite. Similarly, the hospitality and truthfulness called for by Stephen Crane's ironies are, in principle, unlimited. In each case, exercising the virtues in question seems less a matter of subduing an unruly self or finding a mean between extreme qualities than of establishing right relationships with others. In short, while I continue to think MacIntyre's paradigm of community, tradition, narrative, and character possesses great explanatory and pedagogical value, it must always be remembered that the Christian's character is enabled ultimately by the Trinitarian God, Whose perfection lies not in isolated self-containment or beautifully poised equilibrium but in the extravagant generosity that wills in Creation what is other than Himself and in the self-emptying on the Cross that the world regards as foolishness. Following that God may, as Milbank suggests, lead to such changes in the understanding of the virtues that they may cease to look like virtues in the antique sense at all.[44]

chapter 2

TOWARD A CHRISTIAN ETHICS OF

READING, OR, WHY WE CANNOT BE DONE

WITH BARTLEBY

I

In *Versions of Pygmalion,* J. Hillis Miller describes an experience familiar to many of us who have given our lives largely to reading. He suggests that the books lining the shelves of libraries "do not just passively sit there. They cry out to be read." Miller experiences this cry as a call directed to him, even as a demand, and argues further that an ethics of reading must begin with the reader's response to this demand: "The call is directed to me personally and with equal force by each text. I *must* read them all. There is no initial way or principle, other than arbitrary or contingent ones, by which I can decide an order of priority among all the books. I must get on with it and begin where I can. But in choosing to respond to the demand made by the book that has fallen by accident into my hands, I am betraying my responsibility to all the other books. This is a responsibility I can never fulfill. So I live in a perpetual condition of guilty arrears, which is my fate as soon as I have learned to read. I shall go to my grave still in debt and unable by the most heroic efforts to pay off my obligation."[1]

I have quoted at length because I wish to respond to Miller's assumptions carefully as a beginning toward a Christian ethics of reading, an ethics that would take seriously the idea that Christian convictions have specific consequences for the way people read. I have had something of the experience Miller describes, as I suspect many Christian readers have: the sense that one is related to all of the lives that books embody and articulate, the uneasy wish that one had more time to learn and remember the stories contained on those library shelves, sometimes the extraordinary frustration and irritation that other claims on one's time prevent one from doing more reading. But the Christian reader will no doubt take exception to the abstract universalism of Miller's position, to the assertion that all texts have an *equal* claim upon him, that he *must* read them *all*, and that any principle by which he chooses books to read must be merely arbitrary or contingent. It is difficult to see how one could follow such principles in the practice of reading, as Miller's assumptions would seem to dictate adopting some procedure for the random distribution of attention.

The Christian reader might further object that Miller's position reflects extraordinary hubris, a determined rejection of creatureliness. Only God is able to know and remember the stories of all people; to set that as the task of human readers is to confuse the distinction between creature and Creator. Miller's enterprise further strips the reader of all particular history; it seems an attempt to place the reader in something like the literary equivalent of a Rawlsian original position.[2] I am led to the books I read because I am a particular, situated, historical being, the product of a specific family, tradition, and culture. To understand oneself in those terms is part of what a Christian means by calling himself or herself a creature. Becoming the history-less liberal subject, or reader, would also seem to involve a species of self-hatred. Each of us has particular gifts and inclinations. Reading or study itself develops in us a *habitus*, a directed intention toward particular subjects. Should one simply disregard one's gifts and habitus as one stands before the library shelves? Would not one's doing so constitute something like an act of self-hatred? Should readers regard their inclinations or habitus as merely "arbitrary" or "contingent" as they pursue an education through reading? To do so would seem a sure prescription for boredom and the loss of self-respect that inevitably accompanies boredom.

Christian readers will, by contrast, understand themselves to be particular, situated, historical beings with particular talents, inclinations, and abilities that direct their consciousness toward certain objects. They would put their reading to the service of God and human beings by following these gifts rather than adopting the procedure of reading every fiftieth book along the library shelves out of the conviction that no one book has any greater claim than any other. I do not mean to make light of Miller's account of the reader's dilemma. I, too, have felt both enormously indebted to and miserably inadequate before the accounts of people's lives filling the library shelves. I have learned, however, to bring that feeling specifically under Christian reflection. I cannot do everything. I must do something. Perhaps in doing one thing, I will neglect to do something else that ought to have a greater claim on me, but focusing too much on what I might otherwise be doing will bring me to paralysis, endless deferral, leaving my life a void. I will read boldly what my gifts direct me toward and confess that in doing so I have not loved my neighbor as myself and that I have sinned in what I have left undone. Like Miller, I will "go to my grave still in debt and unable by the most heroic efforts to pay off my obligation." Nevertheless, I will go to my grave also knowing that Christ has been raised "for our justification" (Romans 4:25).

Nothing here should be understood as a suggestion that Christians should be content to read only what is familiar and intimate to them. Christian convictions will press readers strongly beyond their own preferences toward engagement with the stories of others. For Christians, this weighing of preference against a more universal calling might be reflected on as a problem in the proper relationship of *philia* and *agape;* it cannot be resolved by abstracting the reader from all history, asserting that all stories have an equal claim upon him or her, and arguing that all preference or inclination is merely arbitrary or contingent.

Miller writes confidently of guilt and justice in *Versions of Pygmalion.* He begins by locating his account within the *Metamorphoses,* noting that each of Ovid's individual stories "leads to the next and from the previous one in complex relations that are always part of the meaning of any given story." In the changes of shape that conclude each story, "justice is done, an account paid off, a case closed." Yet, for Ovid and apparently for Miller, "there is always a remnant, some residue of unassuaged guilt or responsibility that leads to the next story, the next metamorphosis literalizing yet another figure, then to the next, and so on." What we learn from Ovid's stories is "that you always get some form of what you want, but you get it in ways that reveal what is illicit or grotesque in what you want" (1). Blending an echo of the Old Testament with this account of Ovid's apparent relevance for us, Miller adds, "The sins of the fathers and mothers are visited on the children from generation to generation" (2).

The Christian reader must be troubled by Miller's account of the relationship between guilt and punishment. That account explicitly denies any possibility of atonement or the forgiveness of sins. Christians will find a sharp contradiction between Miller's argument that a "residue of unassuaged guilt or responsibility" is always left over from action and the language of I John 1:9: "If we confess our sins, he is faithful and just to

forgive us *our* sins, and to cleanse us from all unrighteousness." Perhaps I
am guilty of a mistake in reading, but the direct turn to the reader of
Miller's assertion that "you always get some form of what you want"
suggests to me that he is not simply making an interpretive point about
Ovid. I find myself wondering if he would want to apply this to people
suffering from serious disease. Miller's logic suggests that perhaps we
should read the sufferer's disease as the product even of the father's or
mother's sin. Christians will be unwilling to do this, for they will remember Jesus' breaking the ancient connection between sin and affliction
when his disciples ask him about a man blind from birth. "Rabbi, who
sinned, this man or his parents, that he should have been born blind?" the
disciples ask. "Neither he nor his parents sinned," Jesus answered, "he was
born blind so that the works of God might be revealed in him" (John 9:1–
3). The man's blindness is somehow related to the work of the sovereign
God, but it is not to be understood as a simple punishment for unassuaged
guilt or responsibility, either the man's or his parents'.

The biblically informed reader will insist also that Miller set his bor-
rowing of Old Testament authority in much more fully articulated contexts. In neither Exodus nor Deuteronomy does Yahweh say that He will
visit the sins of the fathers and mothers on the children in unlimited
fashion from generation to generation. He draws already a limit to the
way sin and guilt will continue to affect the future: He will punish the
"parent's fault" *to the third generation*: "the children, the grandchildren, and
the great-grandchildren." One must note, too, that Yahweh combines the
threat to punish with a promise to love: He will remember the parents'
fault to the third generation "among those who hate" Him but "act with
faithful love towards thousands of those who love [Him] and keep [His]
commandments" (Exodus 20:5–6). Moreover, as St. Augustine points out
in *The Enchiridion*, Ezekiel prophesies a new covenant of regeneration in
which "the sons should not in the future bear the sins of their fathers, and
that no longer should that byword apply to Israel, 'Our fathers have eaten
sour grapes, and the teeth of the children are set on edge.'"[3] Ezekiel is
absolutely clear on this matter: Yahweh is interested in repentance and
life. The son even of an evil father is able to turn from sin, and if he
"respects [Yahweh's] judgments and keeps [His] laws, he will not die for
his father's sins: he will most certainly live" (18:17). "The one who has
sinned is the one who must die; a son is not to bear his father's guilt, nor a
father his son's guilt" (18:20). Ezekiel closes Chapter 18 with words that
stand in sharp opposition to the Ovidian account of guilt or failed re-

sponsibility that keeps operating as a force in history: "Repent, renounce all your crimes, avoid all occasions for guilt. Shake off all the crimes you have committed, and make yourselves a new heart and a new spirit! Why die, House of Israel? I take no pleasure in the death of anyone—declares the Lord Yahweh—so repent and live!" (18:31–32).

Ezekiel's question "Why die?" must sound foreign to modern readers, accustomed to thinking about death as a temporal or biological event about which we have little choice. The prophet's question reflects the biblical understanding of death not only as an event in time but also as a power capable of reaching into, infecting, corrupting, and dominating life. Differences in the understanding of death are central to the way a Christian ethics of reading would depart from the account given by Miller. Miller argues that in "most of the metamorphoses, the dead do not completely die." They instead "remain to be memorialized in a work of mourning that may never be completed." Miller then follows with the seemingly opposing assertion that "the irreducible otherness of my neighbor or of my beloved may be expressed by saying that he or she may die." One's relation to another person "is always shadowed from the beginning by death." Prosopopoiea, the trope that "ascribes a face, a name, or a voice to the absent, the inanimate, or the dead" (4), is invoked by Miller as a model for literary creation or reading. Prosopopoeia is a "trope of mourning," of compensation for absence or death. The story of Pygmalion presents a strong example of prosopopoeia, for Pygmalion's creation of Galatea represents the giving of "life to the inanimate in a dream come true." The payoff in Miller's adoption of Pygmalion as the central figure of his book comes in the assertion, no doubt true of the story, that "for Pygmalion, the other is not really other." Galatea is instead "the mirror image of his desire"; Pygmalion's "relation to her is not love for another, in an attachment always shadowed by the certain death of the other." Instead, it is "a reciprocity in which the same loves the same" (5). Here are the central assumptions of Miller's ethics: literary creators and readers are involved in an endless task of incomplete mourning that compensates for the loss or absence of real others by revivifying or projecting figures of desire. Relations between readers and figures in a text, and perhaps between persons, are governed by the paradigm of sameness-otherness. Persons are really irreducibly other to one another because each is shadowed by death. Because none of us can quite face this, we pursue our work of continual mourning by reducing others to the same, to mirror images of our desire. "Ethical" acts of reading expose this error of mistaking images of our desire for irreducibly other figures shadowed by death. Whether an ethics of reading, on Miller's account, can do more than this in the way of specifying duties—whether it can be more content-full—is unclear.

Christian convictions about death will lead to quite different ways of reading. Perhaps the best way to illustrate these differences is by responding to one of Miller's readings of a "version of Pygmalion," Herman Melville's "Bartleby, the Scrivener." Miller calls "Bartleby" a text that "demands to be read" yet declares that "it cannot be read" (175). The text draws attention to the narrator's own attempts to place or account for the "unaccountable" scrivener. The narrator's attempts manifestly fail, yet readers repeat those attempts seemingly compulsively, perhaps because they "are institutionalized to do [this] work of policing for our society." For, in Miller's view, "all readings of the story, including [his] own, are more ways to call in the police . . . to put Bartleby in his place, to convey him where we want to put him" (174). How Miller would distinguish exercising responsibility from policing is unclear, for he also repeatedly argues that the former depends on our being able to tell the story of another completely, from beginning to end: "To name someone truly, to know who he is and therefore to know what our obligation to him is, we must be able to tell his story from beginning to end, as when I must sketch out my life in the witness box as a preface to answering questions or making a deposition" (143). Miller declares the end of Bartleby's story "appropriate" "because in death Bartleby becomes what he has always already been" (171). Bartleby's "I would prefer not to" is "strangely oriented toward the future. It opens the future, but a future of perpetual not-yet"—one might say, the future as that which is continually deferred. This future "can only come as death, and death is that which can never be present." Thus Bartleby is himself a kind of ghostly incursion of death into life, not from "outside life" but from within, as an "otherness that all along haunts or inhabits life from the inside" (172).

The Christian reader will object to Miller's analysis here on two important matters: that one needs to be able to tell the whole story of another's life in order to exercise responsibility toward that person and that the future is a continually deferred not-yet whose decisive coming can only be in the form of death as an otherness that haunts life. Insofar as Miller's intention is to prevent responsibility from becoming a tyrannical concept, one used, as Derrida seems to fear, to subsume absolute singularity within substitution and generality, then I am sympathetic to his argument.⁴ But the criterion for responsibility that Miller establishes would seem effectively to eliminate all responsibility, for it is impossible in principle, as well as certainly undesirable, to know all the details of another's life. One who remembers Augustine's dictum that God is nearer to one than oneself will respond further to Miller that it is impossible even to know all of what moves one's own action—and thus, on Miller's view, any notion of responsibility to oneself would be meaningless. I cannot tell the whole of either my own or my neighbor's story; that is part of what Christians mean when they refer to themselves as people on a way or journey, as pilgrim people.

I suspect Miller intends an ironic allusion to the story of the Good Samaritan in the title to his "Bartleby" chapter, "Who Is He?" The lawyer's similar question, "Who is my neighbor?" prompts Jesus' story. The Samaritan, we should remember, is not able to narrate the life of the man who falls among thieves and is left wounded and half dead. The parable's emphasis is quite otherwise: it narrates a moment in the middle of the life of both the Samaritan and the man he assists. That one is a Jew and the other a Samaritan further emphasizes their strangeness to one another. None of this precludes the Samaritan from becoming neighbor to the man, which he does through the exercise of mercy. By doing what the Jewish clergy of the story—who might be thought at least more likely than the Samaritan to recognize, to "know," the victim—conspicuously fail to do, the Samaritan fulfills the law. For Luke tells the story as an amplification of the great commandments. The lawyer has earlier asked Jesus, "What shall I do to inherit eternal life?" and Jesus has questioned him in turn, "What is written in the law? how readest thou?" The man's answer, which Jesus approves, is the double commandment, with its holding together love for God and the movement toward the neighbor: "And he answering said, Thou shalt love the Lord thy God with all thy heart, and with all thy soul, and with all thy strength, and with all thy mind, and thy neighbor as thyself" (Luke 10:25–27).

Translating the commandment to love the neighbor into the concrete structures of modern life is a difficult problem. The relationship between the Gospel and ethics has been the subject of centuries of Christian moral reflection, and different traditions—Catholic, Lutheran, Reformed, Free Church—have understood and approached the problem in different ways. Discussion of the issues raised by "Bartleby, the Scrivener" could be enriched by very specifically introducing the categories and ethical options worked out by the traditions. What Christian readers cannot accept is simply to be told that responsibility toward the other requires being able to tell the whole of his or her story. The double commandment's insistence that loving God and loving the neighbor are to be held together, the fact that Jesus has lodged forever in our minds the story of the Good Samaritan, will not allow Christians to rest in Miller's account of responsibility.

Christians live in a world that is already storied by Scripture. Although we cannot narrate the whole of our own or others' stories, we affirm in faith some decisive convictions about the narrative shape of our lives: that we are created by God in His image; redeemed by Jesus Christ, Who was both a particular itinerant Jewish rabbi and the Second Person of the Trinity; and headed toward definitive judgment by the God Who has revealed Himself decisively in the event of Jesus Christ. Christians live within the biblical narrative, which they grant the power to interrogate, interpret, and redescribe their lives. As Greg Jones explains, the "primarily claim" about narrative that "Christians are concerned to make" is not simply "that there is a narrative quality to human life that is morally significant." It is "rather that the biblical *narrative* seeks to incorporate all people into God's narrative."[5] Readers who have been "incorporated into the life of Christ" will encounter Bartleby as their neighbor. We could argue about what this means in terms of concrete responsibility to and for him, and part of this argument would have to engage Christian moral reflection on the relationship between the Gospel and everyday life. But the Christian cannot do otherwise than encounter Bartleby as neighbor, for he has already been identified by the One into whose life the Christian has been incorporated. As Luther argued in *The Freedom of a Christian,* "A Christian lives not in himself, but in Christ and in his neighbor. Otherwise he is not a Christian. He lives in Christ through faith, in his neighbor through love. By faith he is caught up beyond himself into God. By love he descends beneath himself into his neighbor."[6]

Christians will also bring to the reading of "Bartleby" a radically different sense of time from Miller's when he argues that the scrivener's "prefer" opens the future as "a perpetual not-yet" that "can only come as death, and death is that which can never be present" (172). Bartleby's "I would prefer not to" continually defers action, perhaps from the fear that to adopt one course is to preclude, perhaps even do violence to, all others. As Derrida says of it, Bartleby's peculiar locution "evokes the future without either predicting or promising; it utters nothing fixed, determinable, positive, or negative."[7] Seen as a way to keep the future perpetually open, it seems a way to continually defer death. Yet because the deferral of death is its aim, the refusal to act—the continual deferring of choice and action—remains completely, to use biblical language, under the dominion of death.

I have generalized here from Bartleby's specific case to a larger point about the relationship among choice, action, and death, but I have done so to respond to Miller's assumptions. In thinking about Bartleby, we must keep specifically in mind most of what he prefers not to do: to make or compare copies. While I am as reluctant as Miller to "account" entirely for Bartleby, I take it that Melville's story turns on an analogy between copies and human beings as they are conceived under intellectual and social forms gaining force in the nineteenth century: political economy, utilitarian ethics, bureaucratic rationalism. As these systems depend on regarding human beings as replicable units, they might be said to be under the dominion of death, to represent vast incursions of death's power into life. Thus, Bartleby's "prefer not" seems a resistance to the dominion of death rather than reason to regard him as, in Miller's phrase, "the invasion of death into life" (172). But perhaps so long as the terms are death's dominion and resistance to death, all action or resistance is still governed or determined by the horizon of death. Bartleby is not an "invasion of death into life" but the form of resistance to death under the dominion of death. To prefer not to comply is the way of resistance left to one considered by bureaucratic rationalism as being like every other.

But with all this the Christian reader simply has nothing to do. Christians do not believe that the future is a perpetual not-yet whose coming is in the form of "death," regarded by Miller as a "catachresis for what can never be named properly" (172). Christians are baptized into a death, and joined as well to the Resurrection, as Paul argued in Romans: "Know ye not, that so many of us as were baptized into Jesus Christ were baptized into his death? Therefore we are buried with him by baptism into death: that like as Christ was raised up from the dead by the glory of the Father, even so we also should walk in newness of life. For if we have been planted together in the likeness of his death, we shall be also *in the likeness of his* resurrection" (6:3–5). Christians confess that what is coming has been named properly: the Kingdom of God. Indeed, Jesus' first words in Mark announce that it is already with us: "The time is fulfilled, and the kingdom of God is at hand: repent ye, and believe the gospel" (1:15). Christians live in the time between the appearance of the Kingdom in Jesus and its future fulfillment. The consequences for action that flow

from our living between the already-present and the not-yet dimensions
of the Kingdom have themselves been the subjects of extensive Christian
reflection. What is vital to the argument here is that Christians live in a
time that is partially fulfilled, and they also live proleptically in a future
time. This is simply to say that Christianity is an eschatological faith, one
in which the end time has come forward in the life, death, and resurrection of Jesus. Death has, in a real sense, been put behind for Christians by
their baptism into Jesus' death and their being joined to the Resurrection.
This is not to make light of physical suffering or the bitter physical and
emotional agony of biological death. It is certainly not to present Christianity as offering a saving gnosis. Death is a real power not to be denied,
an enemy to be met daily through remembrance of one's baptism into
Jesus' death and Resurrection. Part of the daily overcoming of death is
recommitment to the community gathered around Jesus, for, as Stanley
Hauerwas has noted, the baptismal language of Romans 6 suggests that
the life "in Christ" is "fundamentally a social life": "We are 'in Christ'
insofar as we are part of that community pledged to be faithful to this life
as the initiator of the kingdom of peace."[8] That community is itself a
mortal, bodily, historical one, committed to cross carrying by its founder
and confessing that that founder Himself suffered death and was buried.
Thus Christians understand death as very much ahead both for themselves and for the other, but they know, too, that death has been named;
that it has been partly put behind, even for them; and that its power has
been forever circumscribed by the Word of God in Jesus.

Thus Christians cannot read "Bartleby" as Miller does, for they do not
share his basic assumptions about responsibility, temporality, and death.
Those formed by the community that confesses Jesus' Resurrection will
not need to know the whole of Bartleby's story to identify him as neighbor.
The Resurrection is part of what confirms Jesus' authority to identify the
neighbor as the one whom we, like the Samaritan, meet in the midst of life
and need. Those who confess the love of God and who understand themselves as participating in the story of God's love for the world will also be
unable to assent to the idea that in death Bartleby becomes what he has
always already been. Such death-essentialism is incompatible with any
doctrine of Creation, with its insistence on the person as an expression of
God's love, and with Christianity's basic eschatological affirmations.

For the Christian, the person is a creature, willed into existence by a
loving God yet finite, limited, committed to life as a *viator*, one on the way
between his or her own creation and a fulfillment that cannot be ade-

quately described in any earthly categories. Death is a real enemy, for it can prevent one from participating fully in that affirmation of creation that is God's love. Christians have thus often spoken of life as a process of learning how to die, but they mean something quite different by that from what Miller means when he says that Bartleby becomes in death what he has always already been. For Christians, learning to die means learning to live as a creature, joyfully, justly, and lovingly in a world understood as created, as God's gift—and it means learning to do so while being utterly honest about one's inevitable death. Miller's Bartleby seems so much death waiting to happen, perhaps in spontaneous combustion like Krook in Dickens's *Bleak House*, a well-established influence on Melville's story.[9] Or perhaps we could here give a theological turn of the screw to starvation in "Bartleby": that the person not fed from without will simply wither and die, as if death is what has been there from the beginning. Christians, however, are fed by the love of God, a love that has been there from the beginning. That is what Christians confess as part of the authoritative norm for faith and life; it is what they bring to their classrooms and interpretive communities.

In the rest of this chapter, I suggest how a community might reflect on "Bartleby" in relation to Scripture, tradition, and ways of doing Christian ethics. Perhaps we could imagine this community being in one of MacIntyre's "universities of constrained disagreement." My purpose is both to develop a Christian ethical reflection and a contribution to literary criticism. I place Melville in a variety of appropriate historical, literary, and ethical contexts and, in the last part of the chapter, use his insight to suggest the consequences of Kant's means-end distinction. Literary critics have frequently used philosophic arguments or positions to open up works of literature. Here, inspired by Nussbaum, I reverse the process, using Melville (and supplementary insight from Dickens) to read Kant.

Our imaginary community's reflection might focus productively on four areas of concern. First, the story's issues of responsibility might be addressed from within the tradition's basic options concerning the relationship between love and justice. Doing so opens up fascinating related questions, especially about the legitimacy of coercion and its relationship to anger. Second, we might see how interpretations that identify Bartleby as a "Christ figure" participate in the discourses of bureaucracy and utilitarianism that Melville satirizes. These discourses, based on the infinite substitutability of persons, depend on denying unique unsubstitutable identity to Jesus Christ. Their alternative is to affirm the insight of Pascal's that serves as an epigraph to this book: that Jesus Christ is not a figure but the very form of charity to whom each person is uniquely related. Third, "Bartleby" invites us to rediscover features of two central virtues, prudence and charity, specifically problematized by Melville. Prudence and charity were each, in a sense, primary for Aquinas, and it would be of immense value to students to explore the sea change in these virtues from Aquinas to Melville's lawyer. Fourth, the rediscovery of a more dynamic sense of prudence and charity might lead us to think about the story as a critique of the assumptions and consequences of liberal ethical systems, as articulated in Kant's means-end distinction.

II

Much criticism of "Bartleby" has been devoted to blaming the narrator. His list of sins is long: inhumanity, insincerity, sentimentality, self-deceit, hypocrisy, smugness, pomposity.[10] Behind the indictments lies the assumption that he should do more for Bartleby—though how one should do anything for Bartleby is difficult to discern—or, at least, that he should come to understand Bartleby. As anyone who has taught the story knows, many undergraduate students differ with the critics who blame the narrator for one failing or another. There is never any shortage of students who want to evict Bartleby the first time he utters "I would prefer not to." Such students draw an absolute separation between the world of business and private life. Bartleby contracts to work. When he no longer works, his employer's obligations to him cease. End of relationship, end of story.

Christian convictions might lead one to resist summary dismissal of Bartleby or rigid segmentation of public and private life. As H. Richard Niebuhr argued, we find ourselves always in a condition of response, always called on to act as if in response to God's action on us.[11] Melville places his narrator in a condition of response to Bartleby. It is important to remember that the two enter into a relationship before Bartleby first declares his "I would prefer not to." Bartleby's breaking with the assumptions of the workplace gives him the initiative, despite the lawyer's putative status as master of the office. Bartleby will not go away. His presence continually reminds the lawyer of his being in a position of response, of his needing to learn to live with others whom he has not chosen in advance. Despite his search for safety, the lawyer controls neither the beginning nor the ending of his story together with Bartleby. Niebuhr's ethics of the middle stresses the way we find ourselves always already enmeshed in a complex pattern of events and relationships. Like the Samaritan, we do not determine the conditions of our engagement with others. Christians are called to offer hospitality to the stranger, both for the sake of the stranger as a creature of God and because the offering of hospitality is part of that process by which we learn to trust in God and not in our own efforts to secure our lives.

"Bartleby" thus poses a rich opportunity for reflection to students formed by a tradition stressing creatureliness, response, neighbor love, and hospitality. If nurturance in these themes makes students unwilling to dismiss Bartleby summarily, it will, one hopes, also make them resistant to blaming the narrator. For the narrator does retain Bartleby in the office despite his preferring not to work. He offers to give the scrivener money, to help him find a more suitable job, and even to take him home. He does much more for Bartleby than the law requires. To judge him severely, one must invoke some standard higher than the law. Secular critics who invoke self-sacrificing love to judge the narrator are put in the curious position of advocating a standard whose background commitments they do not share. Their way out of this bind is to condemn the narrator for insincerity, inauthenticity, or hypocrisy. The narrator either fails to live up to some commitment or value that *he professes*, or he meanly represents himself in a self-justifying way as something other than his conduct warrants. Representative views are those of William B. Dillingham, who denounces the narrator as "a forger, a self-swindler"; Robert Weisbuch, who claims he "refuses authentic emotional commitment" to Bartleby; and Hershel Parker, who reads the narrator's "eloquent sequel" as merely an experience of "comfortable, self-indulgent" melancholy.[12]

The lawyer's responsibility to and for Bartleby can be clarified by thinking about it systematically in relation to several basic options for the correlation of justice and love. One classic way of relating the Gospel to the conduct of ordinary life has been to regard Jesus' rigorous commands as evangelical counsels fit for saints and heroes but not necessarily binding requirements on ordinary Christians. All are bound, however, by natural law, a morality evident to human reason from the very structure of human life and available to believer and nonbeliever. Another approach postulates an ethics of the Father, or the orders of creation, as a way of supplementing the ethics of the New Testament. God acts through the orders of creation—family, community, government—which have been established as the proper spheres for human flourishing. Readers

schooled in these traditions—one broadly Catholic, the other broadly
Lutheran—will be unlikely to judge the narrator of "Bartleby" harshly.
Surely the man does all that reason requires him to do. To ask that he love
one so resistant, a near enemy, or lay down his life for Bartleby—an act of
dubious efficacy—would be to insist on supererogatory behavior, to require sainthood or martyrdom from him. Before they attack the narrator,
Melvillean critics should ask themselves forthrightly whether they require supererogatory behavior of themselves.

A different Christian option stresses the "exemplary quality of Jesus'
social humanity," to quote John Howard Yoder. This option insists on
suffering servanthood, on the crucial force of New Testament language
about living in and dying with Christ, and on nonviolence. It argues that
the key concept of Jesus' ethic is not the Golden Rule. Rather, Jesus' fulfillment of the law leads to a "new commandment": "Do as I have done to
you" or "do as the Father did in sending his Son."[13] Historically, the position Yoder describes has been associated with the Free Church groups
who have rejected Constantinianism: Amish, Mennonites, Brethren,
Quakers. From within a position that assumes the inevitability of Constantinianism, they have been labeled, as by Ernst Troeltsch, "sectarian"
or "withdrawn," although the "apolitical" connotation of these labels has
been vigorously rejected by Yoder, who argues for the powerful "impact
on society of the creation of an alternative social group."[14]

Some evidence suggests that "Bartleby" bears a relation to an account
of an alternative group of Free Church Christians, probably Quakers,
presented by Lydia Maria Child in *Letters from New York* (1844).[15] Child's
book, composed of letters originally written for the *Boston Courier* and the
National Anti-Slavery Standard, urges her readers to adopt the "Law of Love"
that she sees in the New Testament. In her letter of June 23, 1842, she
tells the story of a group of New Englanders who move to the "western
wilderness" to establish a community based on New Testament principles, particularly the Pauline directive "to overcome evil with good"
(150). The community is harassed by "unprincipled adventurers," but
these are met only with the "gentlest remonstrance" and "unvarying kindness" by the practical Christians. Lawyers are specifically excluded, as the
community refuses to dispute. "To return good for evil," the community
believes, is both "the highest truth" and "therefore the best expediency"
(150). These are precisely the terms that haunted Melville, not only in
"Bartleby" but also in the "Chronometricals and Horologicals" section of
Pierre and in *Billy Budd*, where the "highest truth" must die precisely for the

"best expediency." This is not to say that Melville adopts the option Mrs. Child seems to favor, where the law disappears and love becomes a law. He does, however, think about moral problems in similar terms, as problems in the correlation of law and love.

For a time, the community is subject to depredations by those surrounding it, but as the years pass, the patient return of good for evil overcomes hostility, "till not one was found to do them wilful injury" (151). When the community is in danger of losing its land to speculators at public auction, the Christians observe, "with grateful surprise, that their neighbours were everywhere busy among the crowd," urging those in attendance not to bid on the lands of the community, to let them go at the government price. Even the "crowd of selfish, reckless speculators" honors the moral force of this appeal, as *not one bid over them!* (152). The fair acres return to the Christian colonists in a remarkable demonstration that "the wisest political economy lies folded up in the maxims of Christ."

Child represents this story as being told by a member of the community. She next engages him in dialogue, asking, "What would you do . . . if an idle, thieving vagabond came among you, resolved to stay, but determined not to work?" (152). Although Bartleby is no thief, the rest of Child's description of her hypothetical case applies very closely to him. Indeed, it seems no exaggeration to suggest that here is precisely the dilemma at the heart of Melville's story. The answer Child receives suggests the best of the lawyer's actions in "Bartleby": "We would give him food when hungry, shelter him when cold, and always treat him as a brother." When Child asks whether such charity might not attract a multitude of those unwilling to work, the man responds in language that stands in complex counterpoint to Melville's story: "Such characters would either reform, or not remain with us. We should never speak an angry word, or refuse to minister to their necessities; but we should invariably regard them with the deepest sadness, as we would a guilty, but beloved son. This is harder for the human soul to bear, than whips or prisons. They could not stand it; I am sure they could not. It would either melt them, or drive them away. In nine cases out of ten, I believe it would melt them" (152–153).

It would be helpful at this point to consider together Mrs. Child's story, "Bartleby," and an ethic that takes Jesus' social humanity seriously as a norm for Christians. A place to begin is with the emotion that Child's interlocutor specifically eschews: anger. Melville focuses very particularly on anger in "Bartleby." For the most part, the narrator avoids it in his dealings with his intractable scrivener. Nevertheless, the "passiveness" of Bartleby irritates him, and he confesses to feeling "strangely goaded on to encounter him in new opposition, to elicit some angry spark from him answerable to my own."[16] Quaker readers may well wonder if Melville is engaging their tradition directly, for he adopts here, and in the basic structure of the story, one of the central metaphors of Quaker ethics: answering. "Answering that of God in everyone" has, since George Fox, served as a central moral shorthand for Quaker Christians.[17] Melville's story turns on Bartleby's curious answer to the narrator's questions and commands, an answer that is itself strangely "unanswerable" in several senses: it does not meet the terms or assumptions of the narrator's questions, always turning them aside with that "prefer"; it does not really "answer," in the sense of giving an account, for Bartleby himself; and it literally remains "unanswerable" in giving the narrator no direction as to how to respond. The question that resounds throughout Melville's story is how to answer Bartleby, or perhaps, how to answer for Bartleby. Melville's narrator could solve these questions easily for himself if only he could elicit an "angry spark" from Bartleby "answerable" to his own anger. Angry opposition from Bartleby would justify the narrator's anger, and he would have no difficulty dismissing the scrivener from the office, by force if necessary. Bartleby's power over the narrator lies in his turning aside, or nullifying, the narrator's assumptions, his insistently suggesting that there is another way he and the lawyer could relate to one another, though the substance of this he never makes clear.

Advocates of natural law are likely to say that the story illustrates the futility of proceeding without some version of natural law: that the narrator and Bartleby cannot answer one another because they possess no common understanding of responsibility available to reason. They may argue additionally that the narrator is right to be angry at Bartleby, that the emotions have cognitive and moral value, and that anger specifically has value in directing our response to injustice. A critic of natural law assumptions, however, might respond that we must be very careful not to let an idea of natural law become merely a way of underwriting unjustified anger, violence, or coercion. The assumption that there is an account of morality evident to reason can lead to coercion against those who differ from us. If there is an account of morality or responsibility evident to reason, then "differences in principle should not exist" (*PK* 61). Complicating the matter for Christians, and for Melville, is Jesus' radical unmasking of anger with the brother in the Sermon on the Mount: "Ye have heard that it was said by them of old time, Thou shalt not kill; and whosoever shall kill shall be in danger of the judgment: But I say unto you, That whosoever is angry with his brother without a cause shall be in danger of the judgment" (Matthew 5:21–22). If anger can be the moving force needed to respond to clear injustice, as Aquinas would contend, so, too, it can be, at times, a sign of the will to kill, an indication of what Dale Aukerman calls "the dual drives to be rid of God and the countering brother."[18] From their double knowledge of anger, Christians might argue the need for a community of discernment devoted to sorting out justifiable anger from that which signifies the desire to be done with God and the brother.

Melville's narrator desires a justified anger, but the passivity of Bartleby's resistance prevents him from feeling it. Critics have been right to sense in "Bartleby" a connection to Thoreau's "Civil Disobedience" and Gandhi's *satyagraha* or soul force, even though direct arguments for Thoreau's "influence" on Melville seem unconvincing.[19] Melville presents the power of nonviolent resistance to disarm the anger of the oppressor, to call into question the moral force of his justification. Gandhi similarly understood truth's force to lie in its undermining the opponent's ability to justify to himself what he was doing. Gandhi argued that one had to renounce the response of hating the brother even as the brother was killing one. Melville places his narrator's dilemma within the context of hatred of the brother through his allusion to the Cain and Abel story, suggested by the narrator's own reflection on the spectacular Colt-Adams murder of 1841: "Bartleby and I were alone. I remembered the tragedy of the unfortunate Adams and the still more unfortunate Colt in the solitary office of the latter; and how poor Colt, being dreadfully incensed by Adams, and imprudently permitting himself to get wildly excited, was at unawares hurried into his fatal act—an act which certainly no man could possibly deplore more than the actor himself" (36).[20]

Dan McCall has suggested that Melville intends no allusion to Cain and Abel in his treatment of Colt and Adams. He does so to defend the narrator against critical arguments denouncing him by comparing him to Cain.[21] Although I applaud McCall's skepticism about the allusion hunting of the "Bartleby" industry, I suggest that what critics are responding to here is more than the parallelism of the murderers' and victims' initials. Critics sense the allusion because it has been prepared by Melville's problematizing the narrator's anger with his "brother," Bartleby. Where critics err is in identifying the narrator with Cain. He is neither a Cain nor a Colt, though the stories of these two murderers provide contexts within which Melville invites us think about his narrator. Melville's narrator would like to be done with Bartleby and yet he cannot be. He tries repeatedly after moving out of the offices to persuade others that he has no connection to the scrivener. He tells another lawyer, "I am very sorry, sir . . . but, really, the man you allude to is nothing to me—he is no relation or apprentice of mine, that you should hold me responsible for him" (39). On another occasion, he insists "that Bartleby was nothing to me—no more than to any one else" (40). Yet the narrator never succeeds in escaping Bartleby, even going to the Tombs after Bartleby is taken there by the police. The paradoxical way the narrator is bound to Bartleby is never better suggested than by his description of their leave-taking: "I tore myself from him whom I had so longed to be rid of" (39). Melville's narrator seems unlike Cain because he cannot be done with Bartleby. Yet we should remember that the marked Cain could never be done with Abel either.

III

Thus far I have suggested how readers might reflect on "Bartleby" in relation to two broad ways of doing Christian ethics, one based on natural law or the orders of creation, another based on Jesus' exemplary social humanity. As the conclusions these traditions lead to might seem at an impasse, perhaps what is needed is a third option, such as that offered by Paul Ramsey. Ramsey, whose works allude frequently to Melville, argues for "a dynamic ethic of redemption which does not simply build upon yet does not destroy the ethics of creation." He rejects the idea that ethics must either "remain wholly within the 'Egypt' of the natural law" or "pass wholly into 'Exodus,' taking note only of the demands upon men who live in the immediate presence of God."[22] The radical bifurcation Ramsey rejects here seems much like the gap between narrator and scribe that Melville fails to mediate in "Bartleby." Covenant is a key term for Ramsey's ethics, for it helps to reconcile creation and redemption, natural justice and Christian love. Men and women live with and for each other under rules and practices guided by covenant fidelity, whose model is "God's being for humanity."[23] Christian love will affirm and confirm natural justice where appropriate, but it also operates as a ceaselessly critical force "elevating, transforming, definitely shaping, and fashioning what justice may mean, if possible, more in the direction of the requirements of charity."[24]

Ramsey's understanding of love transforming justice might lead students to a critique of the practices operating in the narrator's office. Students might ask how the work could be organized to allow for Bartleby's preferences. They might ask simply how Bartleby could be encouraged to express his preferences. They might reflect on whether Bartleby could ever be helped to express a positive preference. They might ask why Bartleby seems able to express preferences only as negatives, as what he prefers not to do. They might then reflect on the relationship between Bartleby's defensiveness and the story's ruling metaphor of law. What has happened that the law here comes to be experienced only as demand and not as a positive guiding force directing people toward a good human life together?

"Bartleby" parodies the process by which a society might critique its own institutions on the basis of a principle such as agape. At several points, the narrator turns to Turkey and Nippers for their assessments of Bartleby; these seem places where an internal critique might develop. The narrator prefaces the first of these with a seeming admission of self-doubt: "It is not seldom the case that when a man is browbeaten in some unprecedented and violently unreasonable way, he begins to stagger in his own plainest faith. He begins, as it were, vaguely to surmise that, wonderful as it may be, all the justice and all the reason is on the other side. Accordingly, if any disinterested persons are present, he turns to them for some reinforcement for his own faltering mind." What Melville exposes here, much as he exposes Vere's manipulation of his jury in *Billy Budd*, is authority's use of the notion of disinterest to reconfirm its own practices. Turkey, Nippers, and Ginger Nut are not disinterested persons; they are employees of the narrator, dependent on him. Nor is the lawyer's question, addressed first to Turkey, asked in a disinterested manner: " 'Turkey,' said I, 'what do you think of this? Am I not right?' 'With submission, sir,' said Turkey, with his blandest tone. 'I think that you are.' " The narrator remains within a circle of self-justification. Turkey, Nippers, and Ginger Nut become enlisted to reconfirm the narrator's sense of his own rightness. The narrator turns to Nippers after his address to Turkey, and the younger clerk responds vehemently: "I think I should kick him out of the office." The lawyer then adds a depressingly predictable explanation of his copyists' different attitudes: "(The reader of nice perceptions will here perceive that, it being morning, Turkey's answer is couched in polite and tranquil terms, but Nippers replies in ill-tempered ones. Or, to repeat a previous sentence, Nippers's ugly mood was on duty, and Turkey's off)" (22). The lawyer understands his clerks' reactions through the stories he has already supplied for them. He can only repeat himself, for he perceives everywhere only confirmations of what he already believes to be true (later, Turkey and Nippers reverse roles in their responses to Bartleby, the scene taking place in the afternoon). It is unclear whether the narrator can ever truly meet another person or be surprised in any way. Bartleby disrupts his self-possession, but his psychological response to that disruption is to convert Bartleby into a double. Even in Bartleby he confronts only himself and not another.

IV

Communal process in "Bartleby" amounts to little more than the search for self-justification by the narrator, whose notions of "disinterest" blind him to his manipulation of his clerks. Christian interpreters should be sensitive to the lawyer's drive for self-justification, for they are formed by a narrative that attributes justification to God alone and calls into question all forms of human self-justification. Only Christ fulfills the law, and a Christian ethics of reading must begin by insisting on His unique particularity. No one should be more wary of the search for Christ figures in literature than the Christian interpreter. As Hans Frei has argued, "Jesus Christ is utterly unique in his particularity; his identity is uniquely given with his presence. His identity is unsubstitutable. There can be no Christ figures simply because there is no other like him."[25] David Yeago has made a similar point in his discussion of Hans Urs von Balthasar's Christological particularism: "Christian faith is centered on a particular person, Jesus of Nazareth, who is confessed to be of universal saving significance precisely *as* a particular person, in his singular, contingent concreteness. That is to say, Jesus Christ is not savingly significant because he symbolizes or mediates some more general truth, value, or dynamism; rather, it is just in the concrete *Gestalt* of his unique identity and the contingent singularity of his story that his all-encompassing redemptive significance is to be found."[26]

Von Balthasar has said that in attempting to grasp Jesus, "there is no place for abstraction, for disregarding particular cases, for bracketing off inessential accidentals at the historical level of his life, because it is precisely in this uniqueness that his essential, normative character lies."[27] Yet such abstraction, such bracketing of supposedly inessential particularities, is what literary critics do when they designate a Bartleby, a Billy Budd, or other character a "Christ figure." Christian interpreters must insist instead that they are formed by the story of the life, death, and resurrection of the particular man Jesus of Nazareth, Whose identity is singular and unsubstitutable. Jesus' identity is not available for assimilation to that of Bartleby or any other literary character.

The practical result for interpretation of insisting on the unique, unsubstitutable identity of Jesus can be seen by looking at the kind of use critics have made of the "Christ figure" strategy in past readings of "Bartleby." H. Bruce Franklin, for example, claims that the narrator's "language continually recognizes and defines the possibility that Bartleby may be Christ."[28] Franklin cites such passages as the narrator's Petrine triple denial of Bartleby, but bears hardest on what he considers an overall source for the story: the vision of the judgment in Matthew 25, especially Christ's statement, "Verily I say unto you, Inasmuch as ye did it not to one of the least of these, ye did it not to me." Franklin admits that the narrator follows the letter of Christ's injunctions—offering money to the stranger, taking him in, ministering to the sick, and visiting the prisoner—but argues that "he hardly fulfills the spirit of Christ's message" (127–128). The self-righteousness evident in Franklin's criticism depends on his being able to appropriate Jesus; he identifies Bartleby with Jesus and then criticizes the lawyer, and anyone sympathetic to him, for being insincere in love of Christ. Franklin's tone is actually much less self-righteous than that of many critics who denounce the lawyer for one or another form of insincerity or inauthenticity. But his approach is consistent with these in that it demands sincerity of love.

When Jesus, however, remains unsubstitutable, unavailable for any identification (except, in Matthew 25, *on his own terms and in his own voice*), He cannot be used to judge anyone insincere in the spirit of his or her love. Everyone, including Franklin and all others who judge the narrator's spirit, remains different from Jesus, the Innocent One whom we crucified. And no one has the authority to demand from the lawyer—or us—sincerity of love. This is not to say that sincere love of God is undesirable or that it does not have about it a kind of "necessity." Delight and love that issue in good works to the neighbor will flow from faith in the God who offers himself freely *pro nobis*, for us. But love must not become an oppressive requirement. At stake here is a matter of utmost theological impor-

tance, one that can be illumined by Yeago's discussion of the "necessity"
with which works of love follow faith. Yeago argues that the Reformers
understood "the theologians and preachers of their day" to be "telling
people, in effect: 'If you want to be saved, you must perfect your faith
with sincere love for God. And you must show your love by performing
these and these works of love with a pure intention." Thus, the "necessity"
with which love follows faith was "distorted into a necessity of condition"
and people were brought under the "oppressive demand" of sincerity.[29]
Franklin, and the narrator's other accusers, similarly say to him, and us:
Bartleby is Jesus and you must thus love him sincerely. The Christian
interpreter should say back to Franklin: Bartleby is not Jesus, for Jesus has
preempted the Christ figure, and while our faith in Him issues necessarily
in works of sincerest love, no one has a right to demand these from us as
proof of our love or sincerity of spirit.

A consciously Christian criticism might here point out how Franklin's
overriding the distinction between Bartleby and Jesus seems Neoplatonic
rather than Christian. Such identification seems to participate in Melville's central metaphor of "copying," which seems itself almost a representation of Neoplatonic emanation. The lawyer originates and the
scriveners copy, ideally producing replications of the original forms but
inevitably introducing corruptions. Bartleby, of course, refuses to copy,
offering what we might understand as a biblical kind of resistance, for it is
the God of the Bible who delights in creating what is other than Himself.[30] Bartleby prefers to be other than the narrator. But for Franklin,
Bartleby can substitute for Jesus and thus anyone can be substituted for
anyone else. There is no unique unsubstitutable identity who guarantees
the uniqueness of each person through his or her relationship to Him.
Thus Franklin's argument is captive to the discourses of bureaucracy,
utilitarianism, and political economy, which depend on the infinite substitutability of persons (and which Melville presumably is satirizing).
What Christians can learn from an encounter with the story is the degree
to which these discourses stand under the logic of death, whose aura
permeates the lawyer's work and office. Several critics have suggested the
connection between Melville's story and Dickens's *Bleak House*, especially
that between Bartleby and Nemo, the law-writer. His name means "no
one," and Dickens jokes grimly on his death that he had "established his
pretensions to his name by becoming indeed No one."[31] Similarly, the
very unspecific Bartleby seems to suggest no one in particular, and of
course no one in particular is the subject of the abstract rationalism of

liberal discourses. As seen by utilitarian morality, bureaucratic rationalism, or the languages of the social sciences, Nemo (or Bartleby) is a unit
like every other unit. Because he is like everyone, he is no one, a status he
confirms most fully in death. For Dickens, as for Melville, the world of
law copying might be said to stand under the horizon of death, where all
are regarded as copies, dead letters, infinitely substitutable. If the purpose
of Melville's story is, on one level, to expose this logic of infinite substitution, then that purpose can be called deeply Christian. For Christians
participate in a Trinitarian community whose unity is a unity of love that
never overrides the irreducible, concrete particularity of persons.

V

Melville problematizes the virtue that for Thomas Aquinas makes reasonable decision making possible in a world marked by "an infinity of singulars": prudence. Aquinas writes, "The infinity of singulars cannot be comprehended by the human reason. *Our counsels are uncertain.* Nevertheless,
they can be grouped and limited according to what usually happens, and
this approximation suffices for prudence."[32] As Josef Pieper remarks, for
Aquinas, "no moral virtue is possible without prudence"; prudence is the
"mold and 'mother' of all the other cardinal virtues, of justice, fortitude,
and temperance," dicta that must, in the primacy they assign to prudence,
strike a "note of strangeness to the ears of contemporaries, even contemporary Christians."[33] Prudence stands in a special relationship to charity,
the supreme theological virtue and the form of all the virtues: "Prudence
is called the form of all the moral virtues. But the act of virtue thus
established in the mean is, as it were, material in regard to the ordination
to the last end. This order is conferred upon the act of virtue by the
command of charity. In this sense charity is said to be the form of all the
other virtues."[34]

Melville, too, brings charity into close connection with prudence in
"Bartleby." The specific passage occurs when the narrator returns to his
office one morning after he has informed Bartleby the previous evening
that he simply assumes the clerk will leave the premises. When the narrator finds Bartleby still in residence, he goes into "a state of nervous resentment," which causes him to recall the murder of Adams by Colt, committed when the latter "imprudently permitt[ed] himself to get wildly
excited." But the narrator grapples with and throws "this old Adam of

resentment" in himself by the simple recall of "the divine injunction: 'A new commandment give I unto you, that ye love one another.'" The lawyer then begins an extraordinary musing on prudence and charity that deserves to be quoted at length:

> Yes, this it was that saved me. Aside from higher considerations, charity often operates as a vastly wise and prudent principle—a great safeguard to its possessor. Men have committed murder for jealousy's sake, and anger's sake, and hatred's sake, and selfishness' sake, and spiritual pride's sake; but no man that ever I heard of, ever committed a diabolical murder for sweet charity's sake. Mere self-interest, then, if no better motive can be enlisted, should, especially with high-tempered men, prompt all beings to charity and philanthropy. At any rate, upon the occasion in question, I strove to drown my exasperated feelings towards the scrivener by benevolently construing his conduct. Poor fellow, poor fellow! thought I, he don't mean any thing; and besides, he has seen hard times, and ought to be indulged. (36)

Critics have blasted the narrator here for bad faith: he uses what they consider the other-regarding virtue of charity to justify a decision that is really taken from the self-regarding motive of prudence. Such criticism reflects the diminution of prudence, considered to be little more than skillful self-defense, barely distinguishable from cunning and hardly a virtue at all. A more interesting strategy would be to look at both Aquinas's and Melville's conjunctions of charity and prudence—to see, first, what has happened to Aquinas's language under the epistemology of Melville's narrator, and second, to use Melville's own moral insight to suggest why we need to begin a return to Aquinas's grounding of the virtues. Along the way, we can consider the possibility of a richer understanding of prudence.

Pieper stresses the cognitive dimension of prudence within Aquinas's realism: "Prudence means . . . nothing less than the directing cognition of reality" (25). The prudent person must, in Aquinas's phrase, "know both the universal principles of reason and the singulars with which ethical action is concerned." The most important of these universal principles of reason—which for Aquinas means "nothing other than 'regard for and openness to reality'" (9)—is the dictate of natural conscience: "That the good must be loved and made reality" (11). Realization of the good depends on clear-sighted, objective perception of the concrete particulars of reality. Prudence is by no means narrowly self-regarding or defensive; indeed, it depends on a silencing of the "egocentric 'interests'" in order that one "may perceive the truth of real things, and so that reality itself may guide [one] to the proper means for realizing [a] goal" (20). Pieper calls attention to Aquinas's "astonishing" likening of "false prudences and superprudences" to covetousness—in doing so, providing an apt description of Melville's eminently safe lawyer: "Covetousness means an anxious senility, desperate self-preservation, overriding concern for confirmation and security." Such an attitude is fundamentally opposed to prudence, which depends rather on a "brave trust" and the "relinquishment of all egoistic bias toward mere confirmation of the self." The prudent person must be ceaselessly willing to "ignore the self" in order to see the truth of real things and persons. We can see how Aquinas would insist—quite paradoxically, to our way of thinking—that there can be no justice without prudence. Justice depends on prudence because it is the right judgment of prudence that allows one to properly estimate the due claims of others. Or, as Pieper puts it, "the foremost requirement for the realization of justice is that man turn his eyes away from himself" (21–22). Such turning is, for Aquinas, prudential.

Paul Wadell has stressed the quality of vision in prudence: "Not a stodgy virtue," prudence "looks through the immediate to the ultimate, and reads the everyday in the light of the future we want our behavior to achieve."[35] A prudence that looks to the ultimate is one informed and infused by charity, the end and mother of all the virtues, according to Aquinas: "Charity is called the end of the other virtues because it directs them all to its own end. And since a mother is one who conceives in herself from another, charity is called the mother of the other virtues, because from desire of the ultimate end it conceives their acts by charging them with life."[36] The infused virtue of charity directs us toward our end, which, in Wadell's reading of Aquinas's ethic, is friendship with God. Prudence, itself directed and empowered by charity, discerns the particulars of concrete ethical action in light of the ultimate end of one's life. In a way, then, prudence does serve a person's best "interest," but that interest is to be transformed into one who participates in the Kingdom of God's love. For Aquinas, charity is, as Wadell aptly puts it, "the comprehensive activity of our lives" (128). It includes a disposition of openness toward reality, a situated receptivity to being. We are incomplete creatures whose desire points us toward fulfillment in an ultimate end, the love of God, and as we are relational beings, the proximate goods of our lives along the way involve works of charity with and for others. A loving directedness toward others is part of the real structure of existence; the fulfillment of our lives lies in our becoming the love that we are through action with, among, and for real others.

My students have frequently felt a connection between "Bartleby" and Dickens's *A Christmas Carol,* a comparison also made by critics.[37] Perhaps what they have felt is the way both Scrooge and the narrator of "Bartleby" are covetous in the sense Aquinas applies to that vice. Both reveal an overanxious desire to secure their lives in worlds where everything seems already hopeless, fixed, and determined, at least before the ghosts' coming in *A Christmas Carol.* "Marley was as dead as a door-nail," and as Scrooge and Marley are so often mistaken for one another that Scrooge does not even bother to correct those who confuse them, he is as good as dead too. Indeed, "Marley," like Nemo of *Bleak House,* "was dead: to begin with."[38] Marley was dead to begin with because the logic of death dominated his life. The chains Marley forged are the result of his failures to love, the times he deferred works of love. The wailing phantoms that fill the air outside Scrooge's window lament their inability to do the good that they deferred in life: "The misery with them all was, clearly, that they sought to interfere, for good, in human matters, and had lost the power for ever" (38). Everything is, in a way, already over and done with for Marley, for Scrooge (before the interventions), and for Bartleby as J. Hillis Miller describes him—in death becoming what he always already is. Now, for Christians, there is a sense in which everything is already over and done with: God has acted in a decisive way in Jesus' life, death, and resurrection, and in doing so, has established His Kingdom as the end of history. But God's decisive action in the Cross and Resurrection does not paralyze Christians. Rather, it frees them to act in penultimate ways without anxiety or concern about the ultimate ends of things. Freed from the concern to make history "come out right," as Hauerwas puts it, the Christian acts from a freely offered gratitude and love and with a view toward the end of his or her life in God (*PK* 87). Everything is over and done with in the ultimate sense, but there are still plenty of things to enjoy, love, suffer, and do in the here and now—and perhaps even more to do, learn, and realize after death.[39] A liberal ethic effectively collapses this distinction between the already accomplished and the not-yet, and one consequence of this move is something Dickens and Melville help us to see.

Kant argued that persons are members of a realm of ends and expressed one of the formulations of the categorical imperative in ends-means language as well: "Act so that you treat humanity, whether in your own person or in that of another, always as an end and never as a means only."[40] The imperative surrounds the human person with an extraordinary dignity and respect and captures something of our ordinary sense of what distinguishes moral action specifically, as Kant set out to do. What interests me here, however, are the consequences of Kant's identification of rationality and personhood. If the distinguishing mark of personhood is rationality, then how do I regard another when he or she acts toward me in ways that seem distinctively irrational, if not positively evil? Or, to put the question more broadly, what is a person when the person is not acting rationally, that is, as a person necessarily does, according to Kant? Melville's narrator reveals one tendency of a Kantian or liberal ethic's approach to irrationality when he indulges in excuse making for Bartleby, as in the passage cited previously: "Poor fellow, poor fellow! thought I, he don't mean any thing; and besides, he has seen hard times, and ought to be indulged." Behind this judgment is something like the following loose syllogism: Persons are marked by rationality; Bartleby is here acting in a manifestly irrational way but is still just as clearly a "person"; therefore, Bartleby must not be acting as himself—hence the construction of excuses to explain why Bartleby is not acting as he manifestly should be (which can mean, in real terms, as I think he should be). Melville intends a hard pun here on "he don't mean any thing." The primary sense is that Bartleby does not intend the narrator any wrong, but he also "don't mean" anything in the sense that he does not count for anything. He has been rendered "unaccountable" by the equation of rationality with personhood. For when Bartleby acts in seemingly irrational ways, the narrator "discounts" his actions, excusing them as not representing him: Bartleby is "barred from being," ceases to be.

The narrator further discounts Bartleby in his benevolent construal of the scrivener's motives: "At any rate, upon the occasion in question, I strove to drown my exasperated feelings towards the scrivener by benevolently construing his conduct." Charity ceases to be real and often difficult action on behalf of another and becomes instead the mildly pleasant exercise of attributing benevolent motives to one who is fundamentally just like oneself: the possessor of that singular mark of moral action, the good will. Here the loose syllogism, with perhaps an added premise, would look something like this: What distinguishes the moral action of persons is a good will; Bartleby seems to be acting here without a good will, but he is clearly a person; I, being without doubt a moral person, am actuated by a good will; therefore, Bartleby must really be a person of good will, though he is at present unable to act on that will because of circumstances. I exercise charity toward him by "benevolently construing his conduct." Melville's narrator has locked himself in moral solipsism, freeing himself from any self-scrutiny, and made of Bartleby a mirror image of himself. How truly alone he is emerges starkly from his self-reflection on the fate of Colt, who murdered Adams: "It was the circumstance of being alone in a solitary office, up stairs, of a building entirely unhallowed by humanizing domestic associations—an uncarpeted office, doubtless, of a dusty, haggard sort of appearance;—this it must have been, which greatly helped to enhance the irritable desperation of the hapless Colt" (36). Colt was not, of course, "alone in a solitary office"—he was with Adams! But this obvious fact seems utterly overlooked by the lawyer. And perhaps it is this primary fact—the ever-mysterious presence of others—that is overlooked by the moral style of one who regards himself as an end in himself and whose primary moral focus is on the maxim of his own will.

Prudence and charity are, for Aquinas, exercised in pursuit of goals that are "not yet" realized. Pieper emphasizes the way the prudent person "fixes his attention precisely upon what has 'not yet' been realized, what is still to be realized" (17). Prudence requires foresight, *providentia*, "the capacity to estimate, with a sure instinct for the future, whether a particular action will lead to the realization of the goal." The best counsels of prudence are wise estimates. Because prudence deals with "things concrete, contingent, and future (*singularia, contingentia, futura*), there cannot be that certainty which is possible in a theoretical conclusion." When he ponders whether prudence might not arrive at "the certitude of truth," Aquinas asserts, "*non potest certitudo prudentiae tanta esse quod omnino solicitudo tollatur*": "the certitude of prudence cannot be so great as completely to remove all anxiety" (18).[41] In this orientation to the future lies the deep complement between prudence and charity. We love because we have been loved by God and because we are caught up in that movement of love that directs us toward God. Agape involves loving the other as he or she is in God, and this involves a certain kind of foresight, the ability to envision the other in the process of becoming what he or she is, of finding himself or herself in God. Love causes us to see ourselves too as we might come to be, for love actively transforms us as we love others. Love directs and informs prudence, and prudence serves love in turn. Together they make judicious decisions, informed by experience, on concrete and contingent matters and without any pretense of final certainty. Because prudence and love know not to expect certainty where it cannot exist, they are open to grace.

Prudence and charity exist for Aquinas within a structure of experience and understanding that is radically different from the world in which Melville's lawyer appeals to those virtues. The words "open" and "closed" perhaps capture that difference as well as any others. Aquinas's prudence and love are profoundly open to the concrete particularities, however irregular, in experience, open to human beings in their singularity, open to the uncertain future, open, of course, to God. Melville's world is closed: by walls, by the office, by the screen the narrator uses to surround himself, by the ready-made, invariable narratives he uses to account for his scriveners, by the nature of the work itself, the replication of documents, mostly having to do with the dead. Aquinas's prudent lover necessarily opens himself to anxiety, to the risk of action; Melville's lawyer, and Bartleby himself, seek safety and security. Bartleby's search for security involves purging himself of needs, becoming self-enclosed, even finally to the point of starvation. Melville seems almost to have designed Bartleby's declaration of nonpreferences as a parody of Kant's insistence that the rational person will attempt to purge himself of needs: "The inclinations themselves as the sources of needs, however, are so lacking in absolute worth that the universal wish of every rational being must be indeed to free himself completely from them" (45).

VI

If Bartleby's drive is suicidal, Kant would have opposed it, for suicide is inconsistent with the idea of humanity as an end in itself. To commit suicide is to dispose of oneself as a thing, to use oneself as a means and thus to violate a duty to oneself. But, as the human being is a needy creature, is there not a kind of suicidal possibility built into the argument that to be rational is to free oneself as much as possible from "inclinations as the sources of needs"? Does the drive to be free of inclination and need not lead to extreme self-enclosure? Is one who conceives of himself as an end in himself likely to end by himself? Such seems the frightening deathbed vision of Scrooge when he glimpses his untended body covered only by a ragged sheet: "a something covered up, which, though it was dumb, announced itself in awful language" (124). Scrooge watches the charwoman, the laundress, and the undertaker's man negotiate with old

Joe over the plunder they have stripped from his room and body. What has happened to Scrooge is precisely what the categorical imperative seems designed to prohibit: he has been regarded as utterly lacking in dignity or respect, quite literally treated as a means, a thing. One of Dickens's old women suggests that Scrooge has been brought to this point by acting too rigorously as an end in himself: "This is the end of it, you see! He frightened every one away from him when he was alive, to profit us when he was dead!" (124).

Melville seems to have Scrooge's deathbed vision specifically in mind when the narrator discovers that Bartleby has been living in the office. Struck by his "fraternal" bond to Bartleby as a "son of Adam," the narrator declares, "For the first time in my life a feeling of overpowering stinging melancholy seized me. Before, I had never experienced aught but a not-unpleasing sadness." In a passage reminiscent of Dickens's spirits, the narrator recalls a vision of Bartleby, his own doubled self, laid out like Scrooge: "These sad fancyings—chimeras, doubtless, of a sick and silly brain—led on to other and more special thoughts, concerning the eccentricities of Bartleby. Presentiments of strange discoveries hovered round me. The scrivener's pale form appeared to me laid out, among uncaring strangers, in its shivering winding-sheet" (28). This, then, is the end of it, for Bartleby and Melville's lawyer as well as for the Scrooge who may have come to be. Particularly striking is Melville's joining of this solitary death with the narrator's unconscious revelation of his own extreme self-possession. It seems astonishing that "a rather elderly man" could confess to never having experienced "aught but a not-unpleasing sadness." The confession seems tantamount to saying he has never loved, for he has certainly never grieved.

Melville and Dickens suggest imaginatively the consequences of one's conceiving oneself as an end in oneself. Dickens's old woman suggests that death was not just the temporal end of Scrooge's life but its telos. Being laid out among uncaring strangers is the end, in both senses, of one whose primary expression concerns what he would prefer not to do. The key moral insight lies in what the end-in-itself language represents in the way of temporal understanding. Establishing persons as ends in themselves collapses the difference between the now, the already accomplished, and the not-yet. Prudence and charity, as Aquinas understood them, become impossible, for they are oriented toward the not-yet, toward a future that is, at least in the near term, inherently uncertain (though ultimately secure in God). Prudence instead becomes self-regarding, concerned primarily with protecting its possessor from risk and anxiety, with attempting to make the future either as much like the present as possible or as predictable as possible. Ideally, the currently safe prudential person would prefer a future whose every moment repeated or copied the present.

Alasdair MacIntyre has argued that the moral content of Kant's ends-means formulation seems to be something like the following: "I may propose a course of action to someone either by offering him reasons for so acting or by trying to influence him in non-rational ways. If I do the former I treat him as a rational will, worthy of the same respect as is due to myself, for in offering him reasons I offer him an impersonal consideration for him to evaluate. What makes a reason a good reason has nothing to do with who utters it on a given occasion; and until an agent has decided for himself whether a reason is a good reason or not, he has no reason to act. By contrast an attempt at non-rational suasion embodies an attempt to make the agent a mere instrument of *my* will, without any regard for *his* rationality."[42] The Kantian scheme isolates the agent in a moment of time: if I wish to influence another, I am asked to make an argument that will appeal to his or her rationality now. Any *relationship* between the other and myself, any history that might bind us or be a source of trust, is irrelevant, for a good reason has nothing to do with who utters it. The Kantian scheme will press agents toward making impersonal (one might say, disembodied) arguments that are perfectly and immediately compelling. Arguments about the shape of the future—of the direction, for instance, of social policy—will have to claim great authority for themselves: they will have to be presented as certain predictions or solutions capable of compelling all rational minds. The need to present rationally compelling solutions, as opposed to good prudential judgments, contributes, no doubt, to what MacIntyre argues is the tendency of sociologists and bureaucrats to claim far more predictive value for their research and policy decisions than is reasonably plausible.

We typically associate bureaucracy with utilitarianism rather than Kantian liberalism; "Bartleby" may help us to see the connection between bureaucracy and Kant's establishing human beings as ends in themselves. The obsession with security and safety in "Bartleby," as well as the story's central metaphor of copying, suggests the need to render the future predictable. Bartleby's withdrawal represents a way of controlling the future, for nothing is more predictable than that not eating will lead to death (note how the at first surprising "I would prefer not to" becomes

utterly predictable as the story proceeds). Bartleby ends in himself, hud-
dled in the fetal position against the wall of the Tombs. The narrator
supplies an appropriate gloss on the scrivener's retreat from history to the
"heart of the eternal pyramids": when asked by the turnkey whether
Bartleby is asleep, the narrator quotes Job, "With kings and counsellors"
(45). The line is from Job's tremendous curse on the days in which he was
conceived and born: "Let the day perish wherein I was born, and the
night *in which* it was said, There is a man child conceived. Let that day be
darkness; let not God regard it from above, neither let the light shine
upon it" (Job 3:3–4, 14). Here lies the appropriate conclusion to the
narrator's and Bartleby's insistence on controlling the future: How better
to be utterly safe, how better to render the future completely predictable,
than to never be born?

Bartleby's "I would prefer not to" is the appropriate expression of the
liberal agent who conceives of himself as an end in himself and for whom
actions are sharply delineated by the opposition of autonomy and heteronomy. As MacIntyre remarks, "Until an agent has decided for himself
whether a reason is a good reason or not, he has no reason to act" (46).
The lawyer does not offer Bartleby good reasons to act, and Bartleby
seems concerned above all to remove the possibility that he will act
heteronomously, in part through the Kantian policy of denying his inclinations. The result is inaction, marked by a static and defensive "I
would prefer not to" directed against force. What Bartleby would prefer
remains unknown, for even expression of a positive preference would
imply action toward a goal, movement toward a future—and thus Bartleby would no longer be an "end" in himself. Force meets preference:
thus Melville frames the terms that seem increasingly to dominate political discussion in liberal states.

VII

Bartleby has been figured as many things by critics: from Charles Dickens
to Thoreau to Jesus to an anorexic.[43] I would like briefly to add to this list
by figuring him as a student. We who teach literature meet increasingly
with students whose characteristic response is "I would prefer not to";
they are generally too polite to say this directly but communicate as
much by inattentive reading or infrequent attendance. I have been struck
lately, too, by my younger colleagues' passion for Paolo Freire's pedagogy

of liberation, with its simple binary opposition of "banking" education—in which reified content is deposited into the students' heads—and problem-solving education, in which the teacher serves as facilitator for groups of students as they pursue education in the process of world-transforming praxis.[44] Banking education mirrors the realities of Melville's office: everything has already been determined; it is now left simply to students to become copies of what is fixed in advance. (Again Dickens is marvelously anticipatory; Freire's banking pedagogue resembles no one so much as Mr. Gradgrind attempting to pour imperial gallons of facts into so unlikely a vessel as Sissy Jupe.) Particularly striking is the way suburban American students, arguably the freest in history, identify with Freire's depiction of education as oppression and manipulation from which they must be liberated. Missing from Freire's characterization of traditional teaching—and apparently from my colleagues' experience as students—is love, the idea that teachers could transmit content to students not to enslave them to the masters or the past but to empower them by giving them something others had considered worth knowing. I am suggesting that the problem in our schools and colleges is a crisis of love caused by erosion of the telos of education by the liberal self's understanding of itself as an end in itself.

Regarding students as "ends" in themselves leaves one the option only of accepting students just as they are. Unconditional acceptance is what parents should offer their children, but it is antithetical to education. For education—and this is the painful truth we too often omit—involves moving students from one point to another; it involves change and work. One hopes such change will take place in a community guided by love, where the ends of education are matters of constant concern, debate, and at least loose consensus. Where there is no community, where debate about the good is, as in liberal polities, officially bracketed, education seems increasingly coercive (especially in a welfare state where even children's supposed advocates argue that we need "world-class" education to guarantee the future level of productivity needed to support the entitlement budgets). Teachers will, and do, feel guilty about participating in this universal reign of coercion, guilt that they confuse with love and that takes the form of accepting the student just as he or she is. Thus the cult of self-esteem, the way a culture guilty about itself fails to pass on the very means for its survival (while, at the same time, leaving students uneducated). What we need is clearly a way to *both* love the student and press him or her to learn, to take risks, to achieve. To rework an old Augustinian formula, students need to know we love them while at the same time we deplore, for instance, their lack of knowledge of eighteenth-century texts. Short of a serious change toward more intentional communities of learning, however, those of us who teach literature in the postliberal classrooms of the welfare state face an increasingly Melvillean future where the terms are those of "Bartleby": force and preference.

I do not mean to sound cynical about today's students. I am not. I think real teaching and learning do occur in literature classrooms, particularly when students are able to see that they and the instructor are engaged together in an inquiry about the good. Students want to know and understand texts that others before them have valued and loved. Teachers' ability to communicate their own love for the texts is critical: when students see that a text has modified the life of one who exhibits concern and respect for them, they want to understand that text. Thus, teachers might best love their students by loving and honoring the works they treat, thereby offering them as worthy candidates to modify the students' lives. To say this is to argue that teaching literature is a profoundly *moral* enterprise. Following Stanley Fish, we should argue that it is necessarily moral, for we continually enact value in everything we do. Even choices of texts are made with some idea in mind of the ends of life. What is needed, then, is a reimagining of the communities in which we study literature so that frank and ongoing debate about the ends of life can be conducted. Christian communities of interpretation—open, hospitably, of course, to others—might develop across disciplinary boundaries along the lines followed by departments of women's studies or African American studies. Whatever shape such institutions take, literary education for Christian students should be guided by the conviction that education involves helping unique and unsubstitutable persons to be open to reality in such a way as to see, prudentially, how to move toward their own proximate ends in light of the ultimate end of their life in love—the love revealed to us by Him in the form He chose to take, that of the Jew Jesus of Nazareth, crucified under Pontius Pilate.

chapter 3

THE "BEST BLESSING OF EXISTENCE":

"CONSCIOUS WORTH" IN *EMMA*

Lionel Trilling's remarks on Jane Austen's irony reveal the difficulties of the liberal critic in reading a writer who was not a liberal: "What we may call Jane Austen's first or basic irony is the recognition of the fact that spirit is not free, that it is conditioned, that it is limited by circumstance."[1] Such remarks seem strongly Gnostic in their hypothesizing a spirit that would somehow be free of all conditioning or circumstance, a spirit presumably free of embodiment. It is hardly surprising that Trilling would "respond to Jane Austen with pleasure" when he is able to "recognize in her work an analogue with the malice of the experienced universe, with the irony of circumstance" (208). For one who seeks freedom from all conditioning, any experience of resistance or binding circumstance will inevitably seem to be evidence of malice. Trilling instinctively prefers Mary Crawford, representative of "spiritedness, vivacity, celerity, and lightness," to Fanny Price, whom "Nobody . . . has ever found it possible to like" because she "is overtly virtuous and consciously virtuous" (211–212). Trilling reveals the liberal imagination's uneasiness with virtue. For him, the primary problem involves the self's or spirit's maintaining its integrity against all that seeks to shape or limit or restrain it. The title of the book in which his essay on *Mansfield Park* appears is, significantly, *The Opposing Self*. Yet developing the virtues always involves acts of self-submission and transformation, as well as the giving of trust to others who seek to school one in the practice of virtue. Schooling in the virtues necessarily involves accepting the authority of the standards that govern a practice, being willing to be judged inadequate according to those standards, and "subject[ing one's] own attitudes, choices, preferences and tastes to the standards which currently and partially define the practice."[2] The liberal, or opposing, self defined by Trilling will have difficulty accepting the notions of self-transformation, discipline, and authority presupposed by the language of the virtues.

Difficulties caused by liberal presuppositions are evident in the criticism of *Emma*. A case in point involves the crucial role of Knightley's rebuking Emma for insulting Miss Bates at Box Hill. One way critics have sought to establish Knightley's authority to reprove Emma has been by appealing to his supposed objectivity. Alastair Duckworth calls him, for instance, "the reader's objective point of reference within the novel."[3] Underlying Duckworth's comment is the liberal assumption that authoritative moral judgments must be independent of particular standpoints and interests. Feminist critics have quite properly responded to the assertion of Knightley's "objectivity" that he is not objective but rather interested in forming Emma in particular ways. Thus, Alison Sulloway speaks of "the pedagogical Knightley disciplin[ing Emma] to his satisfaction."[4] Judith Wilt argues that several of the relationships between Austen's men and women, including Knightley and Emma, represent Gothic-like "sequences of the deliberate manipulation, almost terrorization of the lover-student by the lover-mentor." We might think that Emma's being made to cry by Knightley is deserved, Wilt remarks, before hinting otherwise: "Knightley, we want to say, has no manipulation in mind but is acting in pure rectitude. Let us see."[5]

Noteworthy is Wilt's antithesis of "manipulation" and "pure," presumably disinterested, "rectitude." If Knightley can be shown to be not disinterested, then he must be guilty of manipulation and even psychological terror—precisely the direction of Wilt's argument. One "can then detect in Knightley's outburst [at Box Hill] a special personal sting and a tinge of personal despair"; therefore, his reproving Emma "is not a neutral rational moment." Rather, it is an act of "mentorlike punishing" that derives from "his dread—at his plight, at his risk," and whose effect is to "finally make dread a fully embodied part of Emma's world" (159). Evident again is the liberal assumption that rationality must be "neutral"—independent of all particularity. Any reproof or attempt to discipline that cannot justify itself by an appeal to "neutral" rationality will seem a punishment. Little wonder that the liberal self of Trilling, likewise assumed by Wilt, encounters "malice" throughout the "experienced universe." As any appeal to a "neutral" or "encyclopedic" rationality will always be subject to genealogical critique, the liberal self will be unlikely to encounter good reasons to change, accept shaping or discipline, or assent to the need for transformation. It will turn instead to Gnostic escape, as in Trilling's remarks, from everything that conditions "spirit."

The difficulty of the liberal critic in accepting changes in the self is illustrated by responses to the ending of Emma. Edmund Wilson and Marvin Mudrick reject the novel's ending as false and claim the marriage between Emma and Knightley will be unhappy. Wilson thinks Emma will find another Harriet in order to continue her "infatuations with women," and Mudrick maintains that Emma remains a habitual "exploiter."6 Both critics take a static view of the novel. Although they project a future beyond the novel's end, it simply represents a repetition or mirroring of what happens in the novel's own time. Emma cannot change, develop, or be transformed: the Emma who lives on in marriage to Knightley will be exactly like the Emma who begins the novel. Against Wilson and Mudrick, Wayne Booth has defended the novel's happy ending by arguing that "all is finally well for Emma and George Knightley, in their fairy-tale world."7 For Booth, it will "be a happy marriage because there is simply nothing left to make it anything less than perfectly happy."8 Interestingly, Booth's analysis transports Emma and Knightley to a world that is just as static as that of Wilson and Mudrick, a world that bears little relation to ordinary time. Booth offers a fully realized eschatology: "All is finally well"; "nothing"—not even the continuing sinfulness of Knightley and Emma or the hard resistance of the world—remains to make them "anything less than perfectly happy."

Booth is aware that the "fairy-tale" ending troubles feminist readers because it seems to endorse the romantic ideology whereby a woman finds supreme happiness in a relationship of willing subordination to a man. In The Company We Keep, he defends the novel against this charge by insisting that we incorporate "an ironic vision of the ending" into our reading. "We are to enter with absolute wholeheartedness" into the romance plot, according to Booth, and to believe that all is well for Knightley and Emma. At the same time, however, Austen so insists "that all is far from well in the real world implied by the book" that the attentive reader knows not to simply accept the fairy tale ending as the truth about men and women. If we fail to incorporate irony along with our enjoyment of the fairy tale, then "we are indeed confirming its capacity to implant a harmful vision of the sexes" (CK 435). Such a reading seems impossibly schizophrenic in its call for both a "wholehearted" and an ironic response to the romance plot and ending. Moreover, it asserts a complete discontinuity between the world of Knightley and Emma and the rest of the novel's world (as well as our own). Knightley and Emma's marriage can, then, have no effect on the rest of Highbury. The lovers are not so much changed or transformed as transported into another world, perhaps something like the Kantian realm of ends in which nothing is left to interfere with their free development.

Wilson, Mudrick, and Booth reveal the way "the encyclopaedists' narrative reduces the past to a mere prologue to the rational present."[9] Wilson and Mudrick predict unhappiness for the marriage because Emma, judged in light of present rationality, remains irrational. Booth answers by transporting Emma and Knightley to the rational present. He does not successfully answer the feminist charge because his reading remains vulnerable to the claim that the romantic mythology of his happy ending has contributed to the oppression of women in that "real world implied by the book." The problem with Booth's approach lies in its ahistorical character, one signaled by his encyclopedic methodology and his subtitle, *An Ethics of Fiction*, with its suggestion that "ethics" can be done apart "from the practices of communities of people who carry forward relatively thick notions" of "how life should be lived."[10] Booth assumes that we now know how men and women ought to relate to one another, and then proceeds to examine *Emma*, in our present light, to determine whether we can still justify reading it. The approach is "moralistic" in the narrow sense, as is much current criticism. It is not enough to enjoy *Emma*, as Booth clearly does: we had also better be able to prove that the novel is good for us. We must prove that Jane Austen shared our enlightened view of gender relations, in which case, she can be enlisted as a forebear "in the progress of reason" (*TRV* 78). The liberal encyclopaedist's reduction of the past to mere prologue inevitably undermines the study of literature. For if we always already know the answer to Martha Nussbaum's question "How should one live?" on the basis of an enlightened reason available in the present, then why should one bother to study past literature at all?[11] The Jeremiahs who lament our lost literature focus on the wrong villains when they attack relativism, postmodernism, and multiculturalism. It is the ahistorical model of liberal rationality that erodes the kinds of community needed for the meaningful study of literature.

If reading literature is not to become merely an antiquarian study or the purely private pursuit of pleasure, we must reconfigure reading communities in accord with the Thomist narrative defined by MacIntyre. In contrast with the encyclopaedist and genealogist's narratives, the Thomist "treats the past neither as mere prologue nor as something to be struggled against, but as that from which we have to learn if we are to identify and move toward our *telos* more adequately and that which we have to put to the question if we are to know which questions we ourselves should next formulate and attempt to answer, both theoretically and practically" (*TRV* 79). Here is a model for treating a text like *Emma* as a living entity, one with a real and present capacity to modify our lives. It depends, of course, on the assumption that human life has a telos, one shared to a significant degree by Austen and her readers. Otherwise, there is no particular reason to believe that Austen's questions bear on our own. Once again we can see how fully at odds are the assumptions underlying the communal study of literature and those of liberal ethics. The genius of liberal ethics has been to provide procedures by which societies of strangers can negotiate life in the absence of a shared account of the good. Meaningful study of the moral dimension of literature could go on among those strangers as long as they implicitly shared enough sense of the good life for human beings to make discussion possible. The atomizing effects of liberal culture have eroded that shared sense dramatically. Individuals who look on society simply as a set of procedures designed to facilitate the pursuit of individual ends, or who reject the idea of an "end" altogether, will be unlikely to care seriously about reappropriating either the past or its texts in the living way of MacIntyre's Thomism.

The reappropriation of *Emma* that I propose takes seriously Gilbert Ryle's and MacIntyre's placing her within the Aristotelian tradition of thinking about the virtues and also C. S. Lewis's reminder, reiterated by MacIntyre, that Jane Austen was a Christian.[12] Emphasizing the virtues means "to adopt a stance on the narrative character of human life"; it is to see life as a "progress through harms and dangers, moral and physical." The virtues are "those qualities the possession and exercise of which generally tend to success in this enterprise," whereas the vices are those that "tend to failure" (*AV* 144). Focusing on the virtues directs our seeing to growth, development, and transformation in character—in Emma as well as other figures in the novel. Accepting the need for transformation is central to *Emma,* for its heroine is one who has a strong desire to be, or be regarded as, "perfect," an illusion that, in Austen's Christian view, must be broken—as it is at Box Hill and afterward—before she can begin to lead a real moral life among others worthy of respect. Emma's development is guided by several figures, notably Mrs. Weston and Mr. Knight-

ley, who is himself neither an objective observer educating Emma in
moral truth nor a sinister male forming Emma according to his own
interests. Knightley is a Christian friend of Emma's who comes also to
realize his own erotic love for her. Knightley does not, indeed cannot,
speak from some moral point of view abstracted from all particularities.
Austen does put questions of moral partiality in *Emma*, but what she offers is not a move toward a "mid-air" position—identifiable, as Bernard
Williams says, with anyone and no one[13]—but the creation of relationships and communities that balance partiality with love and respect for
others. One of the advantages for moral education of reading a Jane
Austen novel lies in its offering an extended and systematic experience in
assuming various viewpoints—the partialities of different characters, one
might say. We try on different roles in reading *Emma* and, in the process,
learn to recognize how partiality works, why we ought not to will a world
in which it would disappear, and why it yet must be checked by respect
for others. One reason we ought not to will the disappearance of moral
partiality is that we are erotic beings who wish to stand out from creation
in our uniqueness. *Emma* poses the question throughout of the role of eros
in knowing, presenting the marriage of Emma and Knightley ultimately
as one that best balances eros with mutual respect.

Emma puts several other questions about the good life for men and
women. One is concerned with what it means to be good. Does it involve
primarily learning the requirements of particular social roles, or is it a
matter of learning to direct the will in particular ways? Closely related are
the questions of what it means "to do good to" another or "to be good for"
another. The novel addresses, too, a question that has fascinated Martha
Nussbaum, that of "moral luck."[14] To what degree does the living of a
good life depend on luck, on factors largely independent of one's character? The novel's justly famous first sentence establishes Emma as one
blessed with an enormous degree of luck: "Emma Woodhouse, handsome,
clever, and rich, with a comfortable home and happy disposition, seemed
to unite some of the best blessings of existence; and had lived nearly
twenty-one years in the world with very little to distress or vex her."[15]
These evidences of favorable fortune contribute to Emma's flourishing,
but insofar as they facilitate her project of perfection, they also present a
real danger. That danger lies in her missing her need for others, missing
the richness that real others provide one's life. One of the novel's major
ironies is that Emma's ultimate happiness depends on others having
qualities that can be trusted. Thus Austen would seem to say too much

good fortune can lead away from human flourishing, especially if it encourages a kind of invulnerability. Becoming invulnerable is to ignore and lose the real "blessing" that others are for us.

A seemingly minor remark of Harriet's early in *Emma* poses rich questions about moral partiality and what it means to be good. Harriet reports to Emma what Robert Martin's mother told her: "It was impossible for any body to be a better son; and therefore she was sure whenever he married he would make a good husband" (58). To a contemporary reader, it must seem far from obvious that a good son will become a good husband. Might it not be that precisely what makes one a good son will prevent one from being a good husband? Certainly, marriages have gone awry because a son was too loyal to his mother (or the mother too possessive of the son). The passage problematizes something Austen ponders throughout *Emma*: whether goodness is primarily a matter of learning what is appropriate in particular roles or whether it is a quality of character and will that inheres in the person independent of his or her skill at particular roles. Mrs. Martin's logic seems open to two interpretations. On the one hand, it might mean that Robert has so thoroughly learned the requirements of being a good son that he will have little difficulty in understanding similarly what is appropriate in the role of husband. On this view, being good seems primarily a matter of habituation and insight, learning to perform appropriately in well-defined roles. Or does the statement mean that the qualities of kindness and affection, of good humor and the willingness to oblige that Robert has always displayed toward his mother have persuaded her that he possesses a goodness of character and willing that will move his actions in any role?

We might be tempted to dismiss Mrs. Martin's comment as the testimony of one obviously partial to her son. But Austen will not allow this dismissal. She returns to the question of Robert's goodness when Harriet receives his letter proposing marriage. Harriet gives the letter to Emma and stands anxiously by while her friend and advocate reads it. Finally, Harriet asks whether it's a "good letter" (78), a phrase again open to more than one construal. Is a "good letter" a skillful expression of sentiment, evidence that the writer understands the conventions of the genre? Or is a good letter—and it is not only good but better than Emma has expected—the expression of a good man, testimony to qualities of character evident in the language and style? The letter gives us a more direct form of evidence about Martin than his mother's testimony. Emma's recognition of its goodness suggests that Mrs. Martin's earlier comment to

Harriet cannot simply be dismissed as the biased judgment of one emotionally and morally partial to her son. Perhaps Mrs. Martin is simply best positioned to see the goodness in her son, goodness likewise perceived by Harriet and even grudgingly recognized by Emma, who is, however, at this point able to explain it away. Perhaps we might even ask whether Mrs. Martin is largely responsible for the goodness of her son. Her comment about him exhibits a trust noteworthy for its sharp contrast with the attitudes of the novel's two most important parental figures of her generation: Mr. Woodhouse and Mrs. Churchill. Both these figures attempt to keep the young people under their care in roles of childhood or dependency. Neither is able to see the appropriateness of the people they cherish moving from one role to another. Both exhibit a strong resistance to time and death and seem to assume that their dependents exist primarily for them. Neither shows any faith in the right order of the world. Indeed, the universal adoption of Mr. Woodhouse's attitude toward marriage would mean the end of humanity. In contrast to Mrs. Churchill and Mr. Woodhouse, Mrs. Martin affirms Robert's movement from being primarily her son to being primarily the husband of another. Her affirmation suggests a trust in the good order of creation, a trust that has perhaps itself been important to the formation of goodness in her son Robert.

Harriet's report of Mrs. Martin's comment about her son's becoming a good husband occurs in Chapter 4 of *Emma*, the receipt by Harriet of Martin's letter and the discussion of its goodness in Chapter 7. Between them, in Chapter 5, Austen presents an extended conversation between Mrs. Weston and Knightley about the friendship of Emma and Harriet, a conversation that is crucial to the moral thinking of the novel as a whole. Chapter 5 amplifies Mrs. Martin's preceding remarks about her son and provides additional context for the following discussion of his letter's goodness. It represents Austen's most sustained contemplation of the relationship between learning to be good at particular roles and a more generalized quality of goodness, and it asks further about the relationship between "doing good to" another and "being good for" another.

Knightley begins the conversation bluntly by saying, "I do not know what your opinion may be, Mrs Weston . . . of this great intimacy between Emma and Harriet Smith, but I think it a bad thing." Mrs. Weston seems shocked by Knightley's frankly moral appraisal of the friendship and by the notion that Emma could do anything "bad": "A bad thing! Do you really think it a bad thing?—why so?" Knightley's response frames the subject of the conversation clearly: "I think they will neither of them do the other any good" (65). What it means to do good to another, or perhaps to be another's good, occupies much of Austen's attention throughout this remarkable chapter. Noteworthy is Knightley's framing the issue primarily as one of "doing" directed toward one who is separate from, and potentially in opposition to, oneself; for him, the matter of goodness is primarily one of doing toward others (and, consequently, a matter of right intentions and good willing). For Mrs. Weston, however, there is no question that Emma will do Harriet good: "Emma must do Harriet good," she claims (65). Mrs. Weston makes this point because she, as a former member of the household, has similarly experienced the good that familiarity with Emma and Hartfield can bring. As governess to Emma, she has learned qualities of taste, social grace, and the arts of conversation. Mrs. Weston's "must" also encompasses her sense that friendship is a good, that intimacy is itself a good, that being in an environment like Hartfield gives one a sense of human care about beauty and order. Mrs. Weston claims that Emma must do Harriet good simply by being with her and by being Emma. Harriet, complementarily, "may be said to do Emma good" by "supplying her with a new object of interest" (65). Mrs. Weston understands that boredom, and a too exclusive focus on her father, are real problems for Emma; she needs to be engaged in promoting the good of another person. In a near reversal of Knightley's sense of "doing," she suggests that Harriet will "do" Emma good simply by being, and being Harriet.

Knightley argues that Emma's "doctrines" may at best "only give a little polish" to Harriet without producing any real "strength of mind" or ability to "adapt herself rationally to the varieties of her situation in life" (67). Harriet is likely to acquire only so much of Emma's finish as to become "uncomfortable with those among whom birth and circumstances have placed her home" (67). Likewise, Harriet will have deleterious effects on Emma's character by reinforcing her worst features. She's "the very worst sort of companion that Emma could possibly have," one who "knows nothing herself, and looks upon Emma as knowing every thing" (67). Such flattery will confirm Emma's tendencies toward willfulness and exaggeration of her own talents relative to those of others. Knightley argues that Emma needs subjection, discipline, limits; she needs to meet the hard resistance either of particular tasks or of other persons. Developing steadiness, patience, and industry depend on learning to direct the will with persistence. Emma may "mean," as Mrs. Weston puts it, to do more reading, but she has, as Knightley skeptically replies, taken this resolve numerous times in the past. The net result has been a number of well-chosen and "neatly arranged" alphabetical lists of books still waiting to be assayed. Knightley has "done with expecting any course of steady reading from Emma. She will never submit to any thing requiring industry and patience, and a subjection of the fancy to the understanding" (66). In losing her mother, she "lost the only person able to cope with her" (66)—with the exception, of course, of Knightley. Knightley's language throughout suggests that to "do good" for oneself or others requires acquiring a set of virtues that depend on disciplining one's own desires, submitting one's judgment to that of others who are more experienced or knowledgeable, recognizing real conflicts in the world, and establishing hierarchies of value.

Mrs. Weston's confidence in Emma's "excellence" derives from her thinking about conduct primarily in terms of the ability to be good at doing what is appropriate in particular roles. "Where," she asks Mr. Knightley, "shall we see a better daughter, or a kinder sister, or a truer friend?" (68). The conclusion she draws from this rhetorical question adumbrates concerns of the rest of the novel: "No, no; she has qualities which may be trusted; she will never lead any one really wrong; she will make no lasting blunder; where Emma errs once, she is in the right a hundred times" (68). Even to "lead wrong" here contains unintended irony: Does it mean to lead with a wrong heart or wrong intention or, more simply, to lead into a mistake? Obviously, much of the novel is concerned with whether Emma will lead Harriet wrong.

It does seem possible that Emma's turning Harriet from Martin could become a "lasting blunder." Why this does not happen is crucial to the novel's ethical vision, especially in the way it suggests how skill at the requirements of certain roles must be supplemented by a more generally directed goodwill. Emma is, to use Mrs. Weston's language, a good daughter, a kind sister, a true friend, and none of these should be discounted in their ethical significance. But even her virtuous proficiency in these roles does not guarantee her the level of insight necessary to understand what is good for Harriet. She underestimates the freedom of other persons, their separateness. Emma directs Harriet away from Martin toward Elton and seeks to move Elton to marry Harriet. She fails to perceive that Elton's attention is actually focused on her, and we see clearly that Martin would be better for Harriet than Elton. Emma laments her "error" and "blunder"—her language this time (155–156)—and resolves to do no more matchmaking. Soon she is, however, mistakenly pondering Frank Churchill's possible intentions toward her, inventing a scandalous relationship for Jane Fairfax, and failing to see what is before her eyes between Frank and Jane—a series of errors treated again by Austen as "blunders," the word Frank places before Jane in the alphabet game played at Hartfield, during which Knightley senses "disingenuousness and double-dealing" at every turn (344). Emma is similarly mistaken in her campaign to interest Harriet in Frank, again because others are not transparent to her, as she assumes. Here she comes perilously close to doing lasting harm to herself in the process of doing good to Harriet. Emma has continually directed Harriet's attention to what she regards as better objects, thereby elevating Harriet's self-esteem. Harriet is no fool: she accepts the spirit of Emma's direction, absorbs Emma's influence in manners, and begins to admire the best available man, Knightley.

The nature of Emma's erring here seems problematic. She errs in scheming for Harriet, but she can hardly be said to err insofar as she empowers Harriet to recognize Knightley's superiority to both Churchill and Elton. In arguing that Austen's ethical vision is basically Aristotelian, Ryle suggests that a fitting title for *Emma* might be *Influence and Interference*, for the novel's main concern was to define a proper mean between appropriate and inappropriate influence.[16] Following on Ryle's insight, I would suggest a distinction between direct and indirect influence. Emma tries directly to influence Harriet to desire Elton, and under this influence Harriet sometimes seems pretty silly, as in the saving of the court plaister. She again tries to directly influence Harriet to love Frank, without success. But her indirect influence on Harriet bears out Mrs. Weston's statement to Knightley that "Emma must do Harriet good." Being with Emma does Harriet unquestionable good, recognized by Knightley in a series of remarks late in the novel on how much Harriet is improved and evidenced by Harriet's own firm, clear judgments about men. Readers who diminish Harriet need to reckon with such judgments as this expression of surprise that Emma could ever have thought her interested in Churchill rather than Knightley: " 'I should not have thought it possible,' she began, 'that you could have misunderstood me! I know we agreed never to name him—but considering how infinitely superior he is to every body else, I should not have thought it possible that I could be supposed to mean any other person. Mr Frank Churchill, indeed! I do not know who would ever look at him in the company of the other' " (396).

Harriet has similarly recognized Knightley's superiority to Mr. Elton, a recognition that leads to her destroying her *"Most precious treasures"* (335), chief among them, "envy" of Mrs. Elton (334). The critical incident in Harriet's estimation of Knightley has been his standing up to dance with her when Mr. Elton has so conspicuously refused to do so. Harriet refers to this moment in her climactic conversation with Emma, who has assumed, wrongly, that Harriet's earlier references to her beloved's "service" were meant to indicate Frank Churchill's aid during the incident with the gypsies: " 'Oh, dear,' cried Harriet, 'now I recollect what you mean; but I was thinking of something very different at the time. It was not the gipsies—it was not Mr Frank Churchill that I meant. No! (with some elevation) I was thinking of a much more precious circumstance—of Mr Knightley's coming and asking me to dance, when Mr Elton would not stand up with me; and when there was no other partner in the room. That was the kind action; that was the noble benevolence and generosity; that was the service which made me begin to feel how superior he was to every other being upon earth'" (397). Harriet speaks here as if with a solidly Aristotelian sense of the virtues. The contrast between Churchill's and Knightley's service is particularly instructive: Churchill's takes place almost accidentally, whereas Knightley's springs from the settled disposition of the man. Harriet sees correctly that this act of generosity and kindness reveals the man, in Aristotle's terms, as one who does the right thing at the right time and for the right reason.

Emma cries out at Harriet's estimation of Knightley's superiority: "Good God! . . . this has been a most unfortunate—most deplorable mistake!— What is to be done?" (397). But where is the "mistake"? Surely not in Harriet's judgment of Knightley, here so much in line with that Austen has been forming in us. Surely not in Emma's being responsible, however indirectly, for helping to form in Harriet the kind of judgment that recognizes Knightley's superiority and the kind of self-esteem that leads her to think herself worthy of his regard. Perhaps the line is directed back at "Good God" himself, Who has formed those like Harriet—whom Emma desires to help but whom she wishes to regard as inferior—with the capacity for judgment that is every bit as good as Emma's own. (It would not be beyond the endearing arrogance of Emma to inform God that he had made a most unfortunate mistake!) Emma herself has made the two clearest mistakes. The first is that she has been looking at Frank Churchill when Knightley is one of the company, that she has not frankly recognized his superiority. The second, closely related to the first, is that she has been investing her emotional life in Harriet, to the point where she has almost brought about Knightley's marriage to the wrong person—a worthy one indeed, but not the uniquely right one. Emma has erred in both cases from a lack of proper self-regard, a lack she disguises from herself through the fantasy of her own perfection, one aided and abetted by her father.

Perfection for her father is an important concern of Emma's; she "would not have him really suspect such a circumstance as her not being thought perfect by every body" (42). Such a passage should be read together with Austen's saying of Mr. Woodhouse that he was "never able to suppose that other people could feel differently from himself" (39). Emma and her father form a narcissistic circuit. She compensates him for the loss of his wife by being perfect in his eyes. In the process, he is enabled to avoid the real confrontation with otherness that the death of his wife, and his own mourning, should bring him. Of course, in one area, the erotic, Emma cannot be her mother to her father: thus the desexualization of Mr. Woodhouse and Emma's own indefinite postponement of marriage. Emma's compensation for her own erotic denial comes in the form of her matchmaking fantasies. Knightley threatens the whole system from the beginning: "few people" even "see faults in Emma Woodhouse," and he is the "only one who ever told her of them" (42). If Emma has faults, then she cannot be perfect for her father and he will have to face and mourn the loss of his wife. Emma will have to abandon the impossible project of compensation, feel the perhaps suppressed grief of being without her mother, and face the inevitable death of her father. Given the painfulness of these alternatives, is it any wonder that Emma gives herself so seriously to being perfect in her father's eyes?

Emma specifically thematizes the relationship between particularized and more general loves, between eros and agape. The most erotic relationship in the text is between John Knightley and Isabella, a couple strongly focused on their own life together and on their children. Isabella has truly left her father, in a way Emma cannot, even at the end of the novel, to cleave unto her husband. John Knightley's irritation at Mr. Woodhouse's crotchets is telling: he wants no advice from a hypochondriacal old man who looks at life as a series of disasters to be avoided. John Knightley is hopeful, oriented to the future, actively engaged in extending his life in time through his family. Little wonder that he is described by Emma as having "penetration" (shared here by his brother) after she learns just how accurate he has been in sizing up Elton's intentions toward her: "To Mr John Knightley she was indebted for her first idea on the subject, for the first start of its possibility. There was no denying that those brothers had penetration" (153–154). In this word, "penetration," Austen captures the whole incisive, active, directed, intelligence—grounded ultimately in erotic efforting in the world—of the Knightleys. John Knightley has this quality in a way that is both more intense and more narrowly focused than his brother, as Austen suggests through the difference in what each perceives about Elton. Knightley warns Emma that Elton "will not do" for Harriet Smith, that "he knows the value of a good income as well as anybody," and that he "may talk sentimentally, but he will act rationally" (92) in marrying. Unlike his brother, he does not see that Elton's intentions are directed toward Emma, an oversight explainable in one of two ways. Either Knightley, who has known Emma since she was a child, has not yet recognized that the mature Emma can be of erotic interest to men (including himself), or he is acting on some yet subconscious assumption parallel to what Emma herself verbalizes in the novel's climax: Emma must marry no one but himself.

Knightley can see where Elton is *not* interested: in Harriet. But he cannot see where Elton is interested, something his more erotically focused brother perceives in a matter of minutes. As the group discusses who will go to the Westons, John Knightley offers Elton a spot in the carriage, causing the latter to glow with pride: "It was a done thing; Mr Elton was to go, and never had his broad handsome face expressed more pleasure than at this moment; never had his smile been stronger, nor his eyes more exulting than when he next looked at her" (132). John Knightley knows what such looks mean. In one sense, he and Elton are nearly complete opposites. John Knightley mostly goes his own way, follows his own purposes, cares too little, if anything, about pleasing others. Elton is studiously agreeable and, in this quality, rather feminine (Mr. Woodhouse later mistakes his "prettily" written charade for Emma's work). With some amusement, John Knightley notes Elton's efforts to please: "I never in my life saw a man more intent on being agreeable than Mr Elton. It is downright labour to him where ladies are concerned. With men he can be rational and unaffected, but when he has ladies to please every feature works" (133). Elton is not strongly erotic, but there is enough in him for the penetrating John Knightley to see his attraction to Emma. After Emma lauds Elton's "perfect good temper and good will," John Knightley adds, meaningfully, "Yes . . . he seems to have a great deal of good-will towards *you*" (133). The suggestion that Elton might be in love with her astonishes Emma, who is unprepared to think of herself as the "object" of desire. John Knightley presses on to offer her good, rational advice: "I speak as a friend, Emma. You had better look about you, and ascertain what to do, and what you mean to do" (133). The advice, characteristic of the man, reveals Austen's sensitivity to the gendering of moral or ethical language. Here is a good, firm masculine approach to problem solving: look about, determine a course of action, and then follow through with will and purposiveness. But such open, direct pursuit of one's purposes may not be available to a woman in anything like the same degree.

The role of eros in knowing others is played out by Austen through Emma's comments on drawing the members of Isabella and John Knightley's family. Austen's language insinuates the erotic quality of "taking" another's image, of producing a representation that captures another as object. Four times in her paragraph-long artistic history, Emma uses some version of the verb "to take" in regard to portraying a likeness, at least twice in such a way as to make her seem a huntress seeking prey. Pointing to a study of her father, she remarks, "The idea of sitting for his picture made him so nervous, that I could only take him by stealth" (72), and later she applies similar language to doing a likeness of Isabella's youngest child, the baby George, bearer, not so incidentally, of Mr. Knightley's name: "Here is my sketch of the fourth, who was a baby. I took him, as he was sleeping on the sofa, and it is as strong a likeness of his cockade as you would wish to see. He had nestled down his head most conveniently. That's very like. I am rather proud of little George" (73). Noteworthy is Emma's pride in her strong likeness of little George's "cockade," that piece of ribbon or bow on his hat worn as a badge of his knightly quality, both in nobility and cockiness.

Several points need to be made here. I do not wish to suggest that Emma is aware of the erotic innuendoes of this language of "taking" likenesses. Nor do I wish to imply that Austen was not quite aware of the conventional sense of "taking" a likeness, as we today speak of "taking" a picture in a way synonymous with "producing" or "creating." Rather, Austen's language communicates nuances in the process of capturing another's image that Emma does not consciously understand. Austen does suggest, however, that Emma's drawings serve as erotic displacement. Emma's eros is blocked, above all by her trying to be perfect for her father—in other words, her trying to be all things for him, including a substitute for his lost wife—and by the very skittishness in him that fears being captured, either in a likeness or ultimately by death. Writing before photography's mass production and resultant commodification of images, Austen still shares the sense that to "take" another's likeness or image is to possess the spirit, to reduce to dead stillness the living, moving quality of the person. Emma's history of her own drawing comes round finally to precisely this point. She reports that she has given up taking likenesses, her "last and best" having been of John Knightley. She, and Mrs. Weston, considered it "a very good likeness"—only, if anything, "too handsome— too flattering"—but Isabella offered merely the "cold approbation of— 'Yes, it was a little like—but to be sure it did not do him justice'" (73). Isabella knows John Knightley in a way that Emma does not; she knows him as a distinct, particular person in a way that the less interested observer simply cannot capture. That "knowing" is, in part, erotic, and it is precisely the erotic knowing of others as particular beings that is denied Emma. Austen emphasizes particularity in knowing earlier in the passage, through Emma's appraisal of her drawings of her nephews and niece: "Then, here come all my attempts at three of those four children;— there they are, Henry and John and Bella, from one end of the sheet to the other; and any one of them might do for any one of the rest" (73). Isabella makes no comment on these likenesses, but her remark about Emma's not doing "justice" to John Knightley suggests what she would say. Emma has not done justice to the children, as even her own assessment acknowledges. The children are interchangeable to her in a way that they cannot be for the mother who knows them intimately. Perhaps Emma's failure to capture specific differences in the children results from her own "indistinct remembrance of her [mother's] caresses" (37): without the clear memory of an absolute love directed to her in her utter uniqueness, she is unable to see and represent the uniqueness of each of Isabella's children.

Austen foregrounds particularity in knowing and concern through its contrast with goodwill. We have seen the tension between these concepts in John Knightley's insight into Elton's designs on Emma: Emma characterizes Elton as a man of "good will," amusing her brother-in-law, who responds that the young clergyman evinces a "great deal of good-will towards [her]." One character "whom no one named without good will" is Miss Bates, also described as a "happy woman" despite her misfortunes and relative poverty. What works these "wonders" in Miss Bates are the qualities of her character: "It was her own universal good-will and contented temper which worked such wonders. She loved every body, was interested in every body's happiness, quick-sighted to every body's merits; thought herself a most fortunate creature, and surrounded with blessings in such an excellent mother and so many good neighbours and friends, and a home that wanted for nothing" (52). This passage, the novel's opening note about Miss Bates, is critical to an understanding of the weight of Emma's insult at Box Hill. Emma's victim is a woman whose primary quality is the possession of "universal good-will" (in Kantian terms, the only thing wholly good). She also breaks from the way all others regard Miss Bates. "No one name[s]" Miss Bates "without good-will" except Emma, who, at Box Hill, is doing what she does so often, distinguishing herself from all others (52).

Perhaps Emma's real need at Box Hill is to distinguish herself from Miss Bates. Austen uses the innocent questions of Harriet early in the novel to propose the possibility that Emma may become like Miss Bates. Harriet professes her wonderment that one so charming as Miss Woodhouse should not be married, prompting Emma to explain that she is unlikely ever to marry. She offers several reasons: not being in love or expecting ever to be; having no need of fortune, consequence, or employment; being already mistress of Hartfield. Her final reason is especially interesting: "Never, never could I expect to be so truly beloved and important; so always first and always right in any man's eyes as I am in my father's" (109). Emma is aware here of being seen by men. The only gaze that would look at her as "always first and always right" is the de-eroticized one of her widowed, hypochondriacal father. Later, when she marries Knightley, she accepts being regarded as "always first," though not "always right." But here she contents herself with being under her father's gaze and with the fantasy of being perfect for him. In doing so, she conveniently avoids the threatening erotic gaze of men who would look at her as both an object of attraction and an imperfect being.

When Harriet hears Emma explain that she will probably never marry, she blurts out, "But then, to be an old maid at last, like Miss Bates!" The comparison must seem surprising at first, but two things Emma says in response indicate that she has pondered this fate. She says to Harriet, "That is as formidable an image as you could present, Harriet," suggesting by the use of "formidable" that the comparison is not trivial or simply stupid but rather worthy of consideration, if only to be dismissed. Emma then argues that she could never be like Miss Bates, "so undistinguishing and unfastidious." If she ever came to think this a serious possibility, she "would marry to-morrow." "But between us," Emma adds, "I am convinced there never can be any likeness, except in being unmarried" (109). The word "convinced" here implies that she has pondered the problem, argued it within, and persuaded herself she has nothing to fear. Her very need to do so, however, as well as her passion for "distinguishing," suggests her worry that the likeness may come to pass.

One likeness between Miss Bates and the way Emma imagines her future self lies in their childlessness. Miss Bates is an aunt who talks endlessly on the minutiae of her niece's existence; indeed, the flow of talk about Jane Fairfax is what Emma finds most irritating about her elderly neighbor. But perhaps that irritation should be read as, in part, a sign of Emma's fear that she may some day have little else to do except bore others with accounts of her own nieces and nephews. For she contemplates satisfying her need for "objects for the affections" through aunthood, as she explains to Harriet in developing her reasons for not marrying: "And as for objects of interest, objects for the affections, which is in truth the great point of inferiority, the want of which is really the great evil to be avoided in *not* marrying, I shall be very well off, with all the children of a sister I love so much, to care about. There will be enough of them, in all probability, to supply every sort of sensation that declining life can need. There will be enough for every hope and every fear; and though my attachment to none can equal that of a parent, it suits my ideas of comfort better than what is warmer and blinder. My nephews and nieces!—I shall often have a niece with me" (110). This rich passage invites several comments. The first concerns the confidence with which the youthful Emma projects what she will need in "declining life." The passage should be read, too, together with Emma's account of her drawings of Isabella's children, where she reveals that she does not know them intimately enough to produce portraits in which they can be distinguished. Austen again thematizes the tension between knowing others in their unique particularity and knowing them only in a more distanced and general way. The first, whose paradigm is the mother's love of a child, is "warmer and blinder"; the second, less threatening, more "comfortable." Emma, with only an indistinct remembrance of her own mother, contemplates knowing and loving as she has been known and loved; the comfortable, distanced affections of aunthood will suffice. Significantly absent is the sense that one of the evils of "*not* marrying" is the loss of an intimate, passionate relationship to a man or, concomitantly, the possibility of being known herself in an erotic way.

Austen later comically reintroduces Emma's commitments as an aunt when Mrs. Weston "make[s] a match between Mr Knightley and Jane Fairfax" (232). Taken aback, Emma exclaims, "Mr Knightley must not marry!—You would not have little Henry cut out from Donwell?—Oh! no, no, Henry must have Donwell. I cannot at all consent to Mr Knightley's marrying; and I am sure it is not at all likely. I am amazed that you should think of such a thing" (232). Of course, this speech of Emma's points directly to her climactic exclamation that "Mr Knightley must marry no one but herself!" (398). Unpacking the earlier speech with this counterpoint in mind will help us to see how Emma uses her role as aunt to compensate herself for what she forgoes: an erotic life in which she would be known and loved as a unique, particular person.

Why "must" Mr. Knightley not marry? By the novel's climax, we understand that Knightley "must" not marry because he and Emma are well suited for one another in a marriage that combines desire and respect. Here, then, Emma's concern for her nephew's claims serves to block from herself her own need for Knightley and for the kind of love he can give her. Why cannot Emma "consent" to Knightley's marrying? Because Knightley's marrying would mean change, the passing of time, the end of their relationship in the form she has known and believed would always continue. Emma's inability to "consent" to Knightley's marrying is closely related to her inability to consent to other eventualities. She cannot consent to being less than perfect in the eyes of a father whose opposition to marriage represents deep opposition to the passing of time and the generational process. She has perhaps never really consented to the loss of her mother, or to her father's loss of her mother, a loss she tries to compensate by being perfect for him. If Mr. Knightley can marry, then time is passing and Emma must face the eventual death of her father and, with it, the disappearance of a gaze that finds her faultless.

The novel's resolution suggests how closely all these matters are bound to one another. After Box Hill, Emma comes to recognize that she is less than perfect, and with Harriet's profession of love for Knightley, she realizes that she can lose him. When the character who serves as a parallel to Mr. Woodhouse, the "great Mrs Churchill," suddenly "was no more" (379), the thought of death very much enters Emma's world, as is evident from her reaction when Mr. Weston comes to Hartfield to tell her of Frank Churchill's marrying Jane Fairfax. When Weston arrives on that occasion, he tells Emma he wants to take her to Randalls because his wife can "break it to [Emma] better" than he, language that moves Emma to fear not that someone intends to marry in a way at odds with her fantasies but that "Something has happened in Brunswick Square" (384). Weston assures her specifically to the contrary, but nevertheless Emma assumes that someone close to her is threatened by illness or death: "Mr Weston do not trifle with me.—Consider how many of my dearest friends are now in Brunswick Square. Which of them is it?—I charge you by all that is sacred, not to attempt concealment" (385). With the loss of her own sense of perfection comes the clear sense, and fear, that she can lose others. Austen's next chapter underscores that sense and fear as Emma learns that the object of Harriet's desire is Mr. Knightley, not Frank Churchill, the recognition that leads directly to her insight-cum-resolution that "Mr Knightley must marry no one but herself!" Part of the force of Austen's "must" lies in Emma's implicit recognition of time and her own finitude, her creaturely status, to use traditional Christian language. To recognize necessity is to recognize that one is not perfect, that one cannot have all that one desires, that one is a limited, particular being given a finite amount of time within which to act—a creature, in short, as distinguished from the Creator. Being a creature means that one must focus on particular objects of desire, although doing so inevitably involves sin, and one must be content also to be an object of desire for others. Being "perfect in her father's eyes" has been Emma's way to avoid both desiring and being desired: her way, in short, of remaining in a deathless, sexless, changeless world.

The trouble at Box Hill begins in the tension between good-will and Emma's need to distinguish herself. She has planned her own expedition to Box Hill, involving the Westons and "two or three more of the chosen only," a drive to be made "in a quiet, unpretending, elegant way, infinitely superior to the bustle and preparation, the regular eating and drinking, and pic-nic parade of the Eltons and the Sucklings" (348). Mr. Weston, however, proposes a united party of the Eltons and Emma's group, an arrangement that offends Emma, as it "expose[s] her even to the degradation of being said to be of Mrs Elton's party!" She conceals her offense while inwardly railing against "the unmanageable good-will of Mr Weston's temper." Thus, from the party's inception, Emma engages in deception: she must appear to be something she is not; her manners must cover a lack of inner assent to Mr. Weston's scheme. When he argues that "one could not leave [Mrs. Elton] out," Emma "denied none of it aloud, and agreed to none of it in private" (349).

The Donwell and Box Hill party labors under another deception as well: the hidden engagement of Jane Fairfax and Frank Churchill. At

Donwell, all await the delayed arrival of Frank, wondering whether he
has been detained by some sudden variation in Mrs. Churchill's health.
Finally unable to endure the tension, and perhaps Mrs. Elton's patronage,
any longer, Jane goes to Emma, requesting her to inform the rest of the
party that it has been necessary for her to start homeward. Jane's parting
words—"Oh! Miss Woodhouse, the comfort of being sometimes alone!"—
elicit pity from Emma, who mistakenly reads them as referring to Miss
Bates: "'Such a home, indeed! such an aunt!' said Emma, as she turned
back into the hall again. 'I do pity you. And the more sensibility you
betray of their just horrors, the more I shall like you'" (358). This interpretation is already, as Knightley says to her after the Box Hill insult,
unworthy of Emma, who here engages in a transference of anger and
scapegoating. She cannot speak the anger she harbors at Mr. Weston; she
cannot ensure that others will recognize her superiority to the rival, Mrs.
Elton (toward whom Emma ought not to feel the slightest rivalry if she
had a proper, and assured, sense of self-respect). Blocked from expressing
her anger, she directs it at the one least able to defend herself, the
innocent Miss Bates, whose only crime is the remarkable good-will she
directs toward all. Moreover, Emma resolves that she will like Jane more
not because she has come to respect what Jane is, and has accomplished,
in herself, but because she imagines Jane moving toward her own mean-
spirited attitude toward a woman who loves Jane deeply. Would Emma
really have Jane come to look on her aunt with "horror"? Not, one suspects, if all were open and plain at Donwell, but where "disingenuousness
and double-dealing" (344) prevail, someone usually pays—and the one
who pays is typically the one least powerful, least able to defend herself.
Emma is no different from the rest of us in this willingness to satisfy the
anger of her own heart by turning on the innocent.

The rivalry of Emma and Mrs. Elton shadows the Box Hill excursion.
The party is marked by a "want of spirits, a want of union, which could
not be got over" despite all the good-natured attempts of Mr. Weston
(361). Deception reigns, with Frank paying such exclusive attention to
Emma that she fears they are laying themselves open to being described
thus in a letter to Maple Grove or another to Ireland: "Mr Frank Churchill
and Miss Woodhouse flirted together excessively" (362). Austen frames
Emma's insult to Miss Bates by using the surrounding gaming to call
attention to central features of Emma's character. To break up the dull-
ness, Frank declares himself "ordered by Miss Woodhouse (who, wherever she is, presides), to say, that she desires to know what you are all

thinking of" (363). Emma laughingly distances herself from Frank's remark, because she does not wish to reveal the degree to which her
feelings are at cross-purposes with the spirit of the occasion. Frank suggests both Emma's desire to "preside" and her assumption that the minds
and lives of others are transparent to her. Having failed in his first sally,
Frank announces himself again "ordered" by Miss Woodhouse to ask for
"one thing very clever," two "moderately" so, or "three things very dull
indeed" from each member of the group. Again he defines a feature of
Emma's habitual way of being with others: if she cannot know what they
are doing and thinking, she will engage "to laugh heartily at them all"
(364).

Emma's insult of Miss Bates follows immediately. Miss Bates makes
light of herself, saying that three very dull things will "just do for me, you
know," while she looks "round with the most good-humoured dependence on every body's assent." Emma cannot resist replying, "Ah! ma'am,
but there may be a difficulty. Pardon me—but you will be limited as to
number—only three at once." Two motifs that follow are extremely important to evaluating the weight of what Emma has done. Austen says
first of Miss Bates's response, "When it burst on her, it could not anger,
though a slight blush showed that it could pain her" (364). Austen's
"could not" here roughly parallels the expressions of necessity she packs
into the crucial word "must": Emma's remark "could not anger" Miss Bates
because, on one construal, she is so thoroughly good-willed, but on
another, the phrase marks Miss Bates's social inferiority, her dependence
on Emma, and her defenselessness. It could not anger her because an
angry standing up for her claims is not within the range of responses she
can direct at Emma. Such defenselessness ought to make Emma extremely careful not to offend Miss Bates, but it has not—and it is a
measure of her moral failure that she has allowed herself the freedom to
attack the defenseless. Contemporary post-Nietzscheans, or all those
trained in the hermeneutics of suspicion, might argue that Miss Bates's
universal good-will cloaks resentment, that it represents merely the supreme strategy by which the weak assert their will to power against the
strong. They will be tempted, I suppose, to applaud Emma's putting Miss
Bates in her place as an assertion of the truly noble over against the
hidden mean-spiritedness of the meek. Readers formed by the Christian
story, however, are more likely to identify Emma's action as one that veers
back across the centuries toward the crucifixion. Emma here does not
assail just anyone: she assails precisely that one who has been identified

by Austen as the bearer of universal good-will, that quality Christians will identify with the God who is no respecter of persons. In one sense, Emma is right to attack Miss Bates, for it is that quality of equal regard for all persons that cuts against the social and class distinctions that uphold Emma's sense of herself. But clearly, Austen rebukes Emma for her insult to Miss Bates, which is to say that Emma is not simply a conservative fiction nor Austen simply a conservative writer. Rather, Emma is a Christian fiction that seeks to balance the claims to value of a particular way of life, inevitably bound up with class, and those of a God who is no respecter of persons.

In his bringing home to Emma the full weight of what she has done, Knightley shatters her illusion of perfection, in the process driving her from the haven where she has enjoyed that perfection: her father's eyes. Mr. Weston's conundrum, offered to the group after the insult to Miss Bates, reintroduces the theme of perfection: "What two letters of the alphabet are there, that express perfection?" (364). Too impatient to wait for guesses, he reveals his answer, "M. and A.—Em-ma. Do you understand?" Knightley responds with measured praise for Mr. Weston's efforts but closes with a "grave" reservation: "Perfection should not have come quite so soon" (365). Austen alludes here to the perfection Emma has treasured in her father's eyes, a perfection she has had, in a way, at the beginning of life—too soon. Perfection ought to be the goal of the well-directed life, even if one perennially unattainable, rather than the starting point.

Knightley makes two distinct, though related, arguments in his criticism of Emma's treatment of Miss Bates. The first addresses her special obligations as a member of the gentry. She has forgotten that her duties toward the poor woman are quite distinctly different from those toward one more nearly her social equal: "Were she a woman of fortune," Knightley remarks, "I would leave every harmless absurdity to take its chance, I would not quarrel with you for any liberties of manner." Knightley undertakes his defense of Miss Bates from what he understands to be his responsibility to protect one less fortunate than himself. His second argument is less specifically bound to Emma's class- and role-specific obligations. It goes rather to the heart of her self-understanding as a Christian: "She is poor; she has sunk from the comforts she was born to; and, if she live to old age, must probably sink more. Her situation should secure your compassion. It was badly done, indeed!—You, whom she had known from an infant, whom she had seen grow up from a period when her notice was an honour, to have you now, in thoughtless spirits, and the pride of the moment, laugh at her, humble her—and before her niece, too—and before others, many of whom (certainly *some*,) would be entirely guided by *your* treatment of her" (368). Emma has ignored the role of Providence, failed to have proper gratitude for her own abilities and favored circumstances, and mistaken the nature of power. Once, the relationships of dependence and favor were quite the opposite: Emma was an infant, Miss Bates the occupant of a privileged position. Yet Miss Bates conferred honor on Emma, the honor due to one simply as a member of this order of creation that the good God condescended to share. Now that their circumstances have been reversed, Emma has assumed that Providence has singled her out for favor and given her license to laugh at and humble the needy Miss Bates, even to humiliate her before others. The "pride of the moment" involves an error in reading that identifies the way things are at a particular moment with the workings of Providence. The Christian who has been trained to see the power of God not in dominative control but in self-expending service will identify the will revealed here in Emma with that of the Gentile lord of Scripture (Mark 10:42–45). Implicit throughout Knightley's rebuke of Emma is an understanding of power that informs the best traditions, if not the practice, of the Christian knight: that power is given to be exercised in service, especially to those most vulnerable.

In the midst of his rebuke, Knightley pays Emma a supreme compliment. Telling her truths is not "pleasant" either to her or to him; he does so because he "must": "I will tell you truths while I can, satisfied with proving myself your friend by very faithful counsel, and trusting that you will some time or other do me greater justice than you can do now" (368). Knightley places faith here in Emma's ego strength and judgment; he counts on her being strong enough and honest enough to recognize eventually that, in acting against her, he has truly acted for her good. What he has done is tantamount to a confession of love, for he has risked his own good—her love—for her sake; he has trusted his own good to her ultimate good-will and judgment. In Chapter 5's conversation with Mrs. Weston, Knightley closes by saying, "It would not be a bad thing for her to be very much in love with a proper object. I should like to see Emma in love, and in some doubt of a return; it would do her good" (69). The conclusion of the Box Hill episode recalls those lines of Knightley's. As Emma's carriage pulls away, she "looked out with voice and hand eager to show a difference; but it was just too late. He had turned away, and the horses were in motion. She continued to look back, but in vain" (368–369). Emma must look forward, not back at a fantastic perfection; here she is in love, though not yet fully aware of it, and in some doubt of a return. The doubt does her good.

The good for Emma after Box Hill begins in mortification and grief. Her feelings after Knightley's rebuke are "of anger against herself, mortification, and deep concern"; after her carriage has pulled away, "and every thing left far behind," she acknowledges having never "felt so agitated, mortified, grieved, at any circumstance in her life" (368–369). Knightley has begun the process, which she must continue, of causing her pride to die; she grieves both for the fantasized self that she must give up and for what she has revealed herself capable of doing. The language Austen uses here is not that of committing errors, blunders, or mistakes. Rather, Emma "felt" the truth of Knightley's representation "at her heart," causing her to ask, "How could she have been so brutal, so cruel to Miss Bates!" She has not erred or blundered; she has been cruel, and in a way that she cannot fully account for—in both senses of that phrase. The passage stands in contrast to Emma's earlier remorse over leading Harriet wrongly to believe that Elton loves her. Emma there treats her manipulation of Harriet as a blunder at worst, imposes on herself a penance she cannot seriously believe in—that of thinking Harriet better than she—and soon allows time to restore her sense of herself. After Box Hill, however, she seems unable to avoid the mystery of what the alien will can do: "Time did not compose her. As she reflected more, she seemed but to feel it more. She never had been so depressed." She sits in silence, feeling "the tears running down her cheeks almost all the way home, without being at any trouble to check them, extraordinary as they were" (369). Those "extraordinary" tears are for the fantasized perfect self being put to death here by the light shed by Knightley on what Emma has done. Her tears are truly mysterious, and yet we can begin to suggest their source: the knowledge of what she is capable of doing and yet the extraordinary counterfact that she is loved.

Contra Wilson and Mudrick, Emma does exhibit a significant change in conduct after the Box Hill episode, one that suggests she will not return to old habits after marriage. Her moral vocabulary changes; her action descriptions change. She makes increasing use of the category of respect, that attitude or emotion that recognizes others as independent sources of worth; she begins to understand that her actions sometimes bring real evil to others whose interests are not simply the same as her

own; with this increasing sense of conflict comes resolution, the will to
act from duty and against inclination when necessary, and the need to
hierarchize claims and duties, recognizing some as inevitably more pressing or valid than others.[17] During the evening of her return from Box Hill,
Emma resolves to begin "a regular, equal, kindly intercourse" with Miss
Bates, and she is "just as determined when the morrow" comes. She sets
out early, "that nothing might prevent her," her eyes directed "towards
Donwell" (370), a phrase that recalls her last perception of that place
from the excursion just before Box Hill: "It was just what it ought to be,
and it looked what it was—and Emma felt an increasing respect for it, as
the residence of a family of such true gentility, untainted in blood and
understanding" (353). Emma seeks to be what she ought and to bring
what she feels into line with her actions; indeed, what she feels most
distinctly is the previous sharp disparity between her inner and outer
regard for Miss Bates. On hearing the "ladies were all at home," Emma
reflects, "She had never rejoiced at the sound before, nor ever before
entered the passage, nor walked up the stairs, with any wish of giving
pleasure, but in conferring obligation, or of deriving it, except in subsequent ridicule" (370). Now she seeks a pleasure greater than that of using
others to confirm her sense of superiority: the pleasure of being with
them in mutual respect.

The change in Emma is evident in her conduct toward Jane Fairfax.
Emma's complaint about Jane has been that she cannot love a reserved
person, but now she attributes the "coldness" in their relationship to
herself rather than to Jane. When it seems that Jane must be off to
employment as a governess, Emma feels "scarcely a stronger regret than
for her past coldness; and the person, whom she had been so many
months neglecting, was now the very one on whom she would have
lavished every distinction of regard or sympathy. She wanted to be of use
to her; wanted to show a value for her society, and testify respect and
consideration" (380). The desire to "testify respect" suggests a new commitment to recognizing Jane as a center of worth in herself and not
simply as a player in Emma's idle fantasies. Emma, at this point, offers
Jane an excursion in the carriage, but Jane refuses, prompting Emma to
conclude "that Jane was resolved to receive no kindness from *her*" (382).
Already the suspicious critic may hear Emma's characteristic self-concern
in this reflection, an impression her following thoughts will likely confirm: "She was sorry, very sorry. Her heart was grieved for a state which
seemed but the more pitiable from this sort of irritation of spirits, incon-

sistency of action, and inequality of powers; and it mortified her that she was given so little credit for proper feeling, or esteemed so little worthy as a friend" (382–383). Sorrow, grief, and mortification that one is not credited properly or esteemed sufficiently worthy: such emotions necessarily seem full of excessive, even unhealthy self-concern to readers steeped in one version or another of a liberal ethics in which the turn to impersonality is a primary move. I would argue, however, that Emma's self-esteem here is the necessary condition of her grief and mortification: that what she feels is regret and sorrow that the whole state of her relationship with Jane is so different from what it could be, or ought to be, if she, Emma, had acted in ways truly worthy of her. Emma could now be given credit for proper feeling, if she had showed it; she could now be regarded as a valued friend, if she had conducted herself as one; an equality of powers could now exist between the women, if Emma had not been so intent on directing her envy of Jane into the harboring and promotion of damaging fantasies about her. Emma has failed herself in the way she has acted toward Jane: she has acted, in a way, irrationally by indulging her envy of Jane. What she needs is to have her desires corrected in such a way that she recognizes it to be a good thing for her to act toward Jane as a friend worthy of equal regard and respect.

The agent who corrects Emma's desires is Knightley. At the conclusion of the passage cited above, Emma finds "consolation" in "knowing that her intentions were good" and in "being able to say to herself, that could Mr Knightley have been privy to all her attempts of assisting Jane Fairfax, could he even have seen into her heart, he would not, on this occasion, have found any thing to reprove" (383). Emma exhibits here a more promising kind of movement away from egoism than that required by the assumption of the moral point of view as defined by liberal ethics. Emma remains herself; she does not seek to imagine herself as if she were anyone. She subjects her own motives, her own heart, to the judgment of one whom she recognizes to be both trustworthy and judicious. We might say she is coming to learn to look at herself as if she were an other, but she is doing so not by assuming an impossible, impersonal point of view but rather the very personal point of view of one whom she respects. Earlier she has masked an occasional bad will, even from herself, by remaining perfect in the eyes of her father, who is utterly unaware of any disparities between her outer and inner selves. Now she contents herself with the possession of a good-will and seeks the penetrating gaze of one who knows her to be quite imperfect. She has begun the process, too, of moving toward a condition in which everything can be open and plain. When Jane eventually assures Emma of the imminence of her marriage to Frank, Emma heartily thanks Jane, declaring "Oh! if you knew how much I love every thing that is decided and open!—Good bye, good bye!" (443). Students angry at Emma's manipulation of Harriet and her duplicity in dealing with Jane invariably scoff at what they here regard as Emma's hypocrisy. Such a reading misses the change in Emma after Box Hill, a change toward bringing her inner and outer lives into harmony—in order that she need not conceal anything. We have come to place an almost supreme value on privacy in a liberal society—precisely, I would argue, because we feel ourselves to be constantly manipulated by the regulatory and therapeutic powers needed to keep a society going in the absence of any real discussion about the good. We perhaps find it difficult to understand Emma's professed love for the "decided and open" because we fear that being too "decided and open" is to be vulnerable to others, to risk the loss of a self whose autonomy consists in treasuring its inner life against those who might violate it. But *Emma* envisions a different possibility: a group of friends, however small, where one can be decided and open because one trusts others to be likewise and because one recognizes that to deal in deceptions is irrational.

Emma's sense of the near violence she has done to Jane Fairfax reflects the new prevalence in her language, after Box Hill, of expressions that recognize conflict. Austen continues her meta-discussion of propriety and duty when Mrs. Weston tells Emma about Frank's secret engagement to Jane. As she has earlier with Knightley, Mrs. Weston focuses on propriety in her assessment of Frank's conduct; the present crisis in his relationship with Jane, she indicates to Emma, "might very possibly arise from the impropriety of his conduct." Emma reacts vehemently, reflecting a very Knightleyan sense that duty ought to have overridden Frank's desire for secrecy in the whole affair: "Impropriety! Oh! Mrs Weston—it is too calm a censure. Much, much beyond impropriety!—It has sunk him, I cannot say how it has sunk him in my opinion. So unlike what a man should be!—None of that upright integrity, that strict adherence to truth and principle, that disdain of trick and littleness, which a man should display in every transaction of his life" (388). Frank has not simply done something inappropriate: he has failed to act against his own inclinations for the sake of the superior claims of Jane Fairfax (as well as the claims of his friends to open and honest relationships). In the scene immediately following, Emma herself acts very specifically from a new sense that duties themselves can frequently be in conflict and that one must determine ways to arrange them in some sort of hierarchy. Mr. Weston has asked Emma that she keep confidential the new revelation about Frank and Jane, backing his request both with Mr. Churchill's desire for secrecy "as a token of respect to the wife he had so very recently lost" and with an appeal to "due decorum" (394). "Emma had promised," Austen tells us, "but still Harriet must be excepted. It was her superior duty" (394). Full of anger at herself for promoting Harriet's attachment to Frank, Emma tells her friend of his engagement.

Emma's anger is a healthy development, for it marks her ability now to judge her own actions, to carry on a dialectic within herself about what she can and ought to do. In Emma's reflections before going to speak to Harriet, Austen specifically recalls another moment early in the novel when Harriet has been the subject of discussion between Mr. Knightley and herself: "Poor Harriet! to be a second time the dupe of her misconceptions and flattery. Mr Knightley had spoken prophetically, when he once said, 'Emma, you have been no friend to Harriet Smith.'—She was afraid she had done her nothing but disservice" (393). In one sense Knightley has spoken prophetically but wrongly, and Emma is herself wrong in judging that she has not been a friend to Harriet: she has done Harriet good, but *indirectly*, as I argued earlier and as Mrs. Weston claimed she "must." She has contributed to the formation of judgment in Harriet that recognizes the superiority of Knightley to both Elton and Churchill and apparently to enough raised self-esteem in her friend that she considers herself a possible object of interest to Knightley. I want to stress a different point here about Emma's anger. Knightley's earlier insistence that Emma has been "no friend" to Harriet occurs in Chapter 8; its influence on Emma is emphasized by Austen in the opening words of Chapter 9: "Mr Knightley might quarrel with her, but Emma could not quarrel with herself" (95). To be unable to quarrel with oneself is to be incapable of repentance, regret, or change. After Box Hill, Emma can be angry with herself, she can conduct an internal quarrel, she becomes aware of real regrets—that she and Jane, for instance, have not been the friends they ought rightly to have been. Being angry at oneself is an essential feature of the awareness of the moral agent, for it derives from the recognition that one could have acted otherwise.

The primary conflict toward which the narrative moves is that between Harriet and Emma over Knightley. When Harriet discloses her love for Knightley and her hope of a return, Emma asks two questions I wish to explore, and comes to a recognition that is the climactic moment of the novel: "Why was it so much worse that Harriet should be in love with Mr Knightley, than with Frank Churchill? Why was the evil so dreadfully increased by Harriet's having some hope of a return? It darted through her, with the speed of an arrow, that Mr Knightley must marry no one but herself!" (398). The easy answer to Emma's questions is that Harriet will be disappointed, even broken-hearted, because Knightley will not marry her—primarily because of their difference in class. Emma will thus again have contributed to her friend's devastation. Emma, however, does not really believe it to be impossible that Knightley should marry Harriet; she thus, implicitly, pays Harriet a supreme compliment and acknowledges that Knightley possesses sufficient confidence in his own judgment to make a match involving some social "disparity." Emma remembers distinctly two occasions on which Knightley has seemed to exhibit a preference for Harriet: "The first, was his walking with her apart from the others, in the lime walk at Donwell, where they had been walking some time before Emma came, and he had taken pains (as she was convinced) to draw her from the rest to himself." The second took place during his moments at Hartfield before leaving for London; Knightley sat a half hour with Harriet while Emma went on a visit, telling Harriet that "it was very much against his inclination that he left home at all." This "was much more (as Emma felt) than he had acknowledged to *her*" (400). Only when Emma, as Austen begins the following chapter, seemed "threatened with its loss" did she begin to know "how much of her happiness depended on being *first* with Mr Knightley, first in interest and affection" (404). In reckoning her losses near the end of that chapter—of Mrs Weston's "heart and time" that will now be directed to the daughter at Randalls, of Frank Churchill's society, and of Jane Fairfax—Emma takes seriously the possibility that now Harriet will be first with Mr. Knightley: "If Harriet were to be the chosen, the first, the dearest, the friend, the wife to whom he looked for all the best blessings of existence; what could be increasing Emma's wretchedness but the reflection never far distant from her mind, that it had been all her own work?" (410–411).

Emma's thoughts suggest the reason Knightley *must* marry no one but herself: surely Austen does not want to leave her heroine with a perpetual grudge against Harriet or with the implicit self-hatred of being wretched over having done her friend good. In one sense, the "evil" Emma alluded to earlier is not an evil at all. Harriet tells her regarding Knightley that she has followed Emma's advice, letting "his" behavior be "the rule" of her own; now she adds, "I seem to feel that I may deserve him; and that if he does choose me, it will not be any thing so very wonderful" (400–401). This speech occasions "bitter feelings" in Emma, a bitterness that both we readers and Austen herself must want to see eliminated by the end of the novel. For who could love or admire an Emma who felt bitterness at having helped Harriet to regard herself as deserving of Knightley? Thus the paradox at the heart of Emma and Harriet's conflict: by doing Harriet good, Emma has raised her to the status of rival and now must either do her evil or be done evil in turn. For there is only, at the moment, one Knightley. When Emma asks why the evil is so dreadfully increased by Harriet's expectation of a return of affection from Knightley, one must ask, Evil to whom? For clearly, what is evil to Emma is not so to Harriet, and vice versa. After Box Hill, Emma has fallen into the realm of evil and, with it, one might say, into the realm of ethics, for there is only one Knightley and two contenders with competing claims. Some way must be found to rank the competing claims. Emma thinks about the dilemma in these terms as Knightley proposes to her. As she listens to him, she resolves that she will not let Harriet's secret escape her. In thus resolving, she does not indulge in any fantasy that she can somehow make things right for Harriet or save her pain by redirecting her toward some other lover. (After all, Knightley is the best available; where else would Harriet look?) Instead, she exhibits a chastened sense of what she can do for Harriet: not revealing her secret "was all the service she could now render her poor friend." Moreover, she will not pretend, as she has earlier when going contritely to Harriet after Elton's proposal, that Harriet is her superior: "As to any of that heroism of sentiment which might have prompted her to entreat him to transfer his affection from herself to Harriet, as infinitely the most worthy of the two—or even the more simple sublimity of resolving to refuse him at once and for ever, without vouchsafing any motive, because he could not marry them both, Emma had it not" (418).

Emma refuses to value herself falsely, and she recognizes that to sacrifice her own happiness will do nothing for Harriet. Knightley has indicated that he desires her, not Harriet. To attempt in some self-sacrificing way to establish her own perfection by manipulating him toward an interest in Harriet would perhaps be the response of Emma before Box Hill, but she has not that "sublimity" any longer. What her full response indicates is a maturing sense in Emma of the separateness of other persons. Knightley loves her, not Harriet, and she must recognize that she is better suited for marriage to him; she is, in that regard, more worthy. She has further, of necessity, had to wish what could only bring pain to Harriet and now must acknowledge that she cannot remedy that pain, cannot compensate for Harriet's loss. "Mr Knightley must marry no one but herself" because she is, at this particular historical moment, the one most worthy of him. Feminist arguments notwithstanding, Emma is not dependent on Knightley to confer worth upon her. Rather, she consciously recognizes her own worth and asserts its binding force on Knightley. He "must" marry her. Immediately after that famous "must," Emma goes on to use a crucial word, "blessed," to denote her insight into the rightness of Knightley's marrying her: "Her own conduct, as well as her own heart, was before her in the same few minutes. She saw it all with a clearness which had never blessed her before" (398). Clarity of insight into her own worth, her conduct, and her heart is given as a blessing. The sentence begs to be read in relation to the novel's opening insistence on Emma's good fortune: "Emma Woodhouse, handsome, clever, and rich, with a comfortable home and happy disposition, seemed to unite some of the best blessings of existence; and had lived nearly twenty-one years in the world with very little to distress or vex her." These blessings mentioned are real and substantial ones, by no means simply to be negated by Emma's later blessing of insight. On the other hand, we must recognize that the later blessing derives largely from her being distressed and vexed—first by Knightley's rebuke at Box Hill, then by her own reflections on her conduct, then by Harriet's emerging as a rival. What Austen regarded as the "best blessing" is suggested by a poem she wrote to her brother Frank on the birth of his son:

> Then like his Father too, he must,
> To his own former struggles just,
> Feels [sic] his Deserts with honest Glow,
> And all his self-improvement know.—
> A native fault may thus give birth
> To the best blessing, conscious Worth.—[18]

"Conscious worth" is what Emma recognizes when she sees that "Mr Knightley must marry no one but herself." It derives not from the impossible project of perfection, but from feeling her deserts honestly, along with her self-improvement, after coming to an awareness of her native faults. Knightley's role in assisting Emma to a conscious sense of her own worth has been crucial. He is not, as many critics of Austen have argued, an objective observer and moral guide. He is, as feminist readers have stressed, an interested participant in Emma's development. How could he be otherwise? He has known Emma since she was a child; his family and hers are related by marriage; Emma and he share status as aunt and uncle to the children of John and Isabella; they have long been friends. Only if we assume that the moral point of view involves objectivity, freeing oneself from one's particular history, will we be troubled by Knightley's guidance of Emma. The reading of such critics as Sulloway and Wilt is dependent for its force on the assumptions that it overturns. On one view, Knightley is an objective observer educating Emma in moral truth; on the other, he is a sinister male forming Emma according to his own interests. On the view being developed here, he is a Christian friend of Emma's who comes also, during the course of the novel, to realize his own erotic love for her—in part, by sensing the possibility that he may lose her to Frank Churchill (the process being obviously analogous to Emma's fearing the loss of Knightley to Harriet). Knightley proves himself worthy of Emma when he risks losing her for her own sake by rebuking her at Box Hill, at the same time trusting that she will understand the way she has betrayed her true telos in insulting Miss Bates. If he were simply forming her for himself, he could have overlooked her treatment of Miss Bates. Knightley acts against Emma, for Emma, out of the conviction that it is better for him to lose her than for her to not recognize her own cruelty to the one whose universal good-will comes closest to the heart of a God who is no respecter of persons.

If this seems too explicit a Christianizing of Miss Bates's significance, I invite the reader to return to Emma's comments to Harriet about why she is convinced she will never be like Miss Bates. Emma argues that "a single woman, with a very narrow income, must be a ridiculous, disagreeable, old maid! the proper sport of boys and girls." "A single woman, of good fortune," on the other hand, as Emma fully intends to be, "is always respectable, and may be as sensible and pleasant as anybody else." Emma grounds this "distinction" in "the candour and common sense of the world," for a "very narrow income has a tendency to contract the mind, and sour the temper. Those who can barely live, and who live perforce in a very small, and generally very inferior, society, may well be illiberal and cross" (109–110). Emma's disquisition sounds a bit like a brief essay on "moral luck," much as Bernard Williams or Martha Nussbaum might present it. If the primary ethical question is the Aristotelian one with which

Nussbaum begins—"How shall one live?"—then one is likely to conclude that possession of a good income and exposure to "superior" society will help one to greater *eudaemonia*, fuller human flourishing. A narrow income and inferior society will make one pinched and crabbed. As Emma is thinking here about how one grows old, it might be instructive to set her comments next to a favorite passage of Nussbaum's from Aristotle's *Rhetoric*. "Because they have lived many years and have been deceived many times and made many mistakes, and because their experience is that most things go badly," the old, Aristotle writes, become "malignant," lacking in trust, and "small of soul (*mikropsuchos*) because they have been humbled by life." They are "ungenerous" because they know how hard it is to get property "and how easy to lose it"; they are cowardly, fearing everything beforehand; they are "chilly" in ways quite opposite to the young; and they are "self-loving more than is appropriate; for, this, too, is a kind of smallness of soul." They "live for advantage" and "feel pity," for "they think every suffering is waiting for them"; they are "given to grieving, and are neither charming nor fond of laughter."[19]

Nussbaum says of the passage that its "observations show us clearly to what extent Aristotle is willing to acknowledge that circumstances of life can impede character itself, making even acquired virtues difficult to retain" (*FG* 338). Aristotle represents what Emma calls the commonsense view of the relationship between circumstances and the virtues, especially insofar as these are thought of as our "acquisitions." As Emma describes her, however, Miss Bates represents an exception to the moral luck thesis. She is "too good natured and too silly" to "suit" Emma, but "she is very much to the taste of everybody, though single and though poor. Poverty certainly has not contracted her mind." Miss Bates differs from Aristotle's description at every point. Despite her loss of fortune, she remains trusting, generous, loving, and not without a certain charm: "I really believe," Emma says of her, "if she had only a shilling in the world, she would be very likely to give away sixpence of it; and nobody is afraid of her: that is a great charm" (110). Again Emma's remarks point beautifully to motifs developed in the Box Hill episode. The Emma who presides everywhere, the perfect Emma who regards other minds as transparent, would very likely develop into one to be feared—if not for her experiences at Box Hill and afterward.

Aristotle's old person loses his charm and fondness for laughter; Emma will not lose hers, we feel, perhaps because she "really" does "believe" in her heart what she says about Miss Bates: that "if she had only a shilling in the world, she would be very likely to give away sixpence of it," or half. Miss Bates reminds one of the widow in Jesus' story of the widow's mite, she who, in "her penury" casts into the treasury "all the living that she had" (Luke 21:1–4). Her antithesis in the Austen canon is Mrs. Norris of *Mansfield Park,* who is forever declaring her generosity while consistently withholding her mite.[20] Mrs. Norris seeks always to call attention to her own goodness while living without love or trust; Miss Bates bears goodwill toward all without distinction while living from a trust so comprehensive that she would give away half her substance despite her poverty. Emma's seeing Miss Bates's faith is an important fact about Emma, for much of her experience has the potential to militate against the development of fundamental trust or to cause a kind of untrusting retrospective orientation: the loss of her mother, her father's narcissism, her own impossible, related projects of replacing her mother for her father and of being perfect in his eyes. The comic opening motif of the novel is deeply telling: "poor" Miss Taylor has gone away to marry Mr. Weston. In Mr. Woodhouse's view, it is always a bad idea for young ladies to do this, a position that, if universalized, would have disastrous consequences for human survival. Fortunately, Emma also possesses some fundamental trust, some willingness ultimately to relinquish her own Mrs. Norris–like "love of directing" and move into the future.[21] That trust is evident initially in her ability to "really believe" in the story of the widow's mite, as it is refracted through Miss Bates. Common wisdom may suggest that poverty contracts the mind, but the Gospel story works otherwise. Neither Aristotle nor moral luck thinking can account for the widow of Jesus' story or for Miss Bates.

Surely MacIntyre is right in calling Jane Austen "an Aristotelian," but it is important to remember, as he does, that she is a Christian. As a way of nuancing MacIntyre's account of Austen, I think it should be added that *Emma* reveals her to be a more specifically Protestant Christian than he allows. MacIntyre stresses Austen's "uniting of Christian and Aristotelian themes in a determinate social context," calling this quality that which makes her "the last great effective imaginative voice of the tradition of thought about, and practice of, the virtues" (*AV* 240) that he identifies in *After Virtue.* The word "uniting" here, consistent with MacIntyre's generally Thomist sense that "supernature redeems and completes nature" (*AV* 184), underestimates the degree to which an Aristotelian understanding of the virtues is in tension with Protestant Christianity in Austen. MacIntyre says of Miss Bates, for example, that "she is *exceptionally* favored because she is *exceptionally* good" (*AV* 240), but I would argue that Miss Bates is exceptionally favored because she is exceptionally faithful or trusting. One who seeks *to be seen as* "exceptionally good" is Mrs. Norris. MacIntyre is aware of the degree to which Austen is preoccupied "with the counterfeit," with the assumption of virtues by those who have them not. He also places appropriate stress on her praise for humility. What perhaps needs greater stress is her insistence on humility about the source of virtue itself. Austen illumines the counterfeit benevolence and humility of Mrs. Norris by pointing us to the New Testament's reading of those who make great show about their works and by setting up the implicit contrast with the widow who throws in her mite to the treasury—not because she has acquired great virtue but because she has great faith. Likewise, the humility Emma attains after Box Hill derives from her recognizing in herself a capacity for cruelty toward the innocent so seemingly unaccountable that it seems the product of an alien will ("How could she have been so brutal, so cruel to Miss Bates!" [369]). Emma's moral education is not simply a matter of developing what is hers by nature, of her realizing a telos that she has by nature; she must become aware of the degree to which she can lose herself—becoming one who presides everywhere, the incarnate perfection, a Gentile lord—and then be redirected toward her true telos.

MacIntyre argues that "morality in Jane Austen is never the mere inhibition and regulation of the passions"; rather, morality is "meant to educate the passions," while the "outward appearance of morality may always disguise uneducated passions" (*AV* 241). He cites Henry and Mary Crawford as examples of this latter phenomenon, and we might add Mrs. Norris to this list. What I want to insist on, however, is that the process of educating the passions for Emma means recognizing honestly a kind of negative limit on them. Pursuing her passion for distinction to its extreme leaves her unrecognizable to herself. MacIntyre's point about Austen's never favoring "the mere inhibition" of the passions helps to clarify the oft debated matter of Austen's relationship to Evangelicalism, in its narrower sense. Critics have often expressed puzzlement about a series of comments on Evangelicalism in Austen's letters. On January 24, 1809, she writes to Cassandra, who has recommended Hannah More's *Coelebs in Search of a Wife*, "You have by no means raised my curiosity after Caleb;— My disinclination for it before was affected, but now it is real; I do not like the Evangelicals.—Of course I shall be delighted when I read it, like other people, but till I do, I dislike it" (*Letters* 169–170). Dislike of the

Evangelicals seems almost a matter of policy, as well as of some humor, with Austen, the humor based at least in part on the recognition that such dislike depends on a measure of willed ignorance. On November 18–20, 1814, she writes a straightforwardly positive comment on the Evangelicals in her advice to Fanny Knight regarding a possible marriage to Mr. J. P. Plumtre:

> Mr. J. P.—has advantages which do not often meet in one person. His only fault indeed seems Modesty. If he were less modest, he would be more agreeable, speak louder & look Impudenter;—and is not it a fine Character, of which Modesty is the only defect?—I have no doubt that he will get more lively & more like yourselves as he is more with you;— he will catch your ways if he belongs to you. And as to there being any objection from his *Goodness,* from the danger of his becoming even Evangelical, I cannot admit *that.* I am by no means convinced that we ought not all to be Evangelicals, & am at least persuaded that they who are so from Reason & Feeling, must be happiest & safest. (*Letters* 280)

Austen's critics have created much of their own puzzlement by citing only the dislike of the Evangelicals—without the qualifying, self-reflexive humor—expressed in the letter to Cassandra, together with the latter part of the letter cited just above. Austen herself clarifies the matter by implicitly indicating, later in the letter to Fanny, what she means by saying that we perhaps ought all to be Evangelicals.[22] Fanny has apparently observed that her brothers have more wit than Mr. Plumtre, to which Austen responds by comparing the worth of wit and wisdom: "Wisdom is better than Wit, & in the long run will certainly have the laugh on her side; & don't be frightened by the idea of his acting more strictly up to the precepts of the New Testament than others" (*Letters* 280). Here, then, is the sense in which we ought all to be Evangelicals: in taking the New Testament seriously as a guide for action. Surely Austen is aware, too, of the root sense of *evangelion,* proclaiming the good news of the Gospel.[23]

Austen suggests that those will be happiest who live seriously to the New Testament precepts as a matter of both reason and feeling. She resists the strong separation of nature and grace on which Evangelicalism typically insists. The passions must not simply be inhibited or suppressed but educated, disciplined by reason and by the scriptures, as the person moves toward the telos of good human life. One way for this disciplining to occur is to submit the passions to the historic forms of human existence: MacIntyre stresses this process when he says that Austen's "hero-

ines seek the good through seeking their good in marriage" (*AV* 240).
Surely Emma does seek the good through marriage to Knightley, but she
arrives at a recognition of the "best blessing," "conscious worth," before
her marriage. Perhaps this is to argue again that Austen is somewhat more
Protestant, feminist, and individualistic than MacIntyre allows. Emma
discovers her own capacity for cruelty against the innocent and loses the
illusion of perfection, but in the process comes to recognize herself as a
moral agent who finds pleasure in showing respect to others, regarded
now as centers of worth in their own right; in a real knowledge of her
own heart; and in consciously improving her conduct, if only by reducing
the occasions for regret. Blessed with clarity about her own worth,
"blessed" because this is what the good God wills for all, she sees the
rightness, the near necessity, of Knightley's marrying her. He can then
pursue his own good in marriage to one who is not only the object of his
love but also worthy of his respect.

Austen reintroduces consideration of how one does another good in a
conversation between Knightley and Emma occasioned by the birth of
Mrs. Weston's daughter. Knightley observes that Mrs. Weston will "indulge" her daughter even more than she has Emma "and believe that she
does not indulge her at all"; that "will be the only difference" in her
approach to rearing the two.[24] After Emma asks, "What will become of
her?" Knightley offers a reading of Emma's moral experience: "Nothing
very bad.—The fate of thousands. She will be disagreeable in infancy, and
correct herself as she grows older. I am losing all my bitterness against
spoilt children, my dearest Emma. I, who am owing all my happiness to
you, would not it be horrible ingratitude in me to be severe on them?"
(444). Emma laughingly replies that she had the "assistance" of his "en-
deavours to counteract the indulgence of other people," adding her
"doubt" that her "own sense would have corrected [her] without it."
Knightley's response relates closely to several themes of this chapter: "Do
you?—I have no doubt. Nature gave you understanding:—Miss Taylor
gave you principles. You must have done well. My interference was quite
as likely to do harm as good. It was very natural for you to say, what right
has he to lecture me?—and I am afraid very natural for you to feel that it
was done in a disagreeable manner. I do not believe I did you any good.
The good was all to myself, by making you an object of the tenderest
affection to me. I could not think about you so much without doating on
you, faults and all; and by dint of fancying so many errors, have been in
love with you ever since you were thirteen at least" (444–445).

Knightley has here adopted a point of view on the good strikingly like that advocated by Mrs. Weston in Chapter 5 and, at that point, rejected by him. He now sees a necessity about Emma's doing well, just as Mrs. Weston argued that Emma "must do Harriet good." He seems also to reject his earlier sense of "doing good to" others, adopting instead the idea that Emma *has been* his good. Mrs. Weston had claimed that Harriet would do Emma good by providing her "an object of interest"; now Knightley sees that Emma has done him good by being "an object of tenderest affection to" him.

Austen does not simply abandon the point of view advocated by Knightley in Chapter 5. She now gives Knightleyan arguments to Emma, who uses his language of "doing good to others": "'I am sure you were of use to me,' cried Emma. 'I was very often influenced rightly by you— oftener than I would own at the time. I am very sure you did me good'" (445). Just as Knightley earlier worried that association with Harriet would reinforce Emma's "spoiled" qualities, now Emma urges him to exercise corrective influence on little Anna Weston if she should become "spoiled": "And if poor little Anna Weston is to be spoiled, it will be the greatest humanity in you to do as much for her as you have done for me, except falling in love with her when she is thirteen" (445). Emma and Knightley's exchange argues the wisdom of a synthesis of the views of "being good for another" and "doing good to others" first adumbrated in Chapter 5. One must have both an object of tenderest affection and a source of discipline that insists on the respect due to others in their difference. Interestingly, for Christians that object of supreme affection and ultimate disciplinary authority is the same Person.

Remaining is the question of how to evaluate the relationship between Emma's own tendencies, her nature, and Knightley's corrective influence in the development of her character. In coming round to Mrs. Weston's earlier view that Emma "must do well," he now sees it as "natural" that she should have seen his interference as disagreeable lecturing. His love leads him to suggest that the simple development of Emma's own nature would have corrected her faults in time. Emma, however, argues that being spoiled and indulged has caused her to need correction from without. Again, a synthesis does most justice to what happens at Box Hill and to the changes in Emma thereafter. Being indulged contributes to Emma's insulting Miss Bates, but insofar as it has also contributed to her self-esteem it gives her the strength she needs to bear Knightley's criticism and the knowledge of what she has done without withering altogether.

Knightley appeals to her strength when he reproves her at Box Hill, saying, in effect, This kind of conduct is not worthy of you; you have betrayed what you are and are directed to be, your telos. Even her project of perfection, however impossible, seems necessary to her sense that her cruelty to Miss Bates is uncharacteristic of her. If she had been reproved continually in childhood, reminded constantly of her sinfulness—a rough model of Evangelical child rearing—she would have been less disturbed by her insulting Miss Bates. It would not have seemed alien to her in the way it does. Its very unaccountability leaves her in tears, yet the understanding she has been given by nature and the ego strength she derives from the love that has surrounded her are what allow her to incorporate real self-knowledge, give up the false search for perfection, and realize that a graced existence with fellow creatures whom she can love and respect is preferable to solitary presiding over others seen as objects of one's fantasies.

Through Knightley's loving remark that Emma "must have done well," Austen recalls Mrs. Weston's early prediction that Emma "has qualities which may be trusted; she will never lead any one really wrong; she will make no lasting blunder." We have seen how this language has been tested throughout the novel, and I have argued for the manifold ironies surrounding judgments of right and wrong in Emma's leading Harriet. We can now see the ironies of Mrs. Weston's last phrase as well. Emma's blunders have not been lasting, for they can be corrected. But at Box Hill she has committed something more serious than a blunder that will, we hope, be lasting—at least in memory—for it has been essential to her arriving at the truer self-estimation that leads to her recognizing the rightness of marriage to Knightley. The more obvious sense of Mrs. Weston's language, however, seems inaccurate: at the time of her betrothal, Emma has very possibly done lasting harm—to Harriet and Robert Martin, who might be happily married if not for her interference.

Fortunately for Emma, Martin and Harriet also have "qualities which may be trusted." Martin "means" to marry Harriet just as much at the end of the novel as he has at the first. He remains constant throughout all of Harriet's misdirection by Emma, and his constancy saves Emma from making "a lasting blunder," from doing real harm. By the novel's conclusion, Harriet has been recognized by Knightley as "an artless, amiable girl, with very good notions, very seriously good principles" (456). She bears these judgments out by her acceptance of Martin, a man of "good sense and good principles," whom Knightley honors as "my friend" (453–

454). Mrs. Weston's prediction that Emma will "never lead any one really wrong" is borne out only because others can be trusted. The good for Emma depends not simply on her own efforts or even her virtues. Rather, the good for each of us depends very largely on others, specifically on their having qualities of character that "may be trusted." Thus the critical importance, for Austen, of the virtue of constancy, as MacIntyre has noted. The degree to which our good is dependent on others suggests, too, why the Christian must be skeptical of the moral luck conundrum of Nussbaum. Christians will reject, for reasons *Emma* shows, the assumption on which the conundrum rests—what Nussbaum describes as the Platonic project of isolating the good from harm.[25] Christians know that their good is always vulnerable, for it lies, to great extent, in the hands of others. Moreover, the very project of isolating the good from harm is likely to lead away from the relations of interdependence that are central to our realizing the good. Christians are paradoxically empowered to reject invulnerability in favor of a vulnerability that nevertheless trusts.

Austen returns to the matter of moral partiality in the novel's final pages. She does this again by depicting a pair of characters reflecting on a letter. John Knightley has written to offer congratulations on the engagement of his brother and Emma, who comments on the letter, "He writes like a sensible man . . . I honour his sincerity. It is very plain that he considers the good fortune of the engagement as all on my side, but that he is not without hope of my growing, in time, as worthy of your affection, as you think me already." Emma recognizes the rightness of John's partiality to his brother: "Had he said any thing to bear a different construction, I should not have believed him." She indicates her growing maturity by not being offended by John's remarks, which she parries to Knightley by reminding him that her father is yet to be heard: "If you fancy your brother does not do me justice, only wait till my dear father is in the secret, and hear his opinion. Depend upon it, he will be much farther from doing *you* justice" (446–447). Knightley thinks that John has not done Emma justice; Emma knows her father will not do justice to Knightley. Emma's love for Knightley enables her to see the rightness of John's partiality for his brother and the too great partiality for her of Mr. Woodhouse. Knightley's loving ability to put Emma before himself similarly allows him to see John's too great partiality for him. For each, love enables a recognition of both the rightness and the limits of partiality.

Emma's reading of John Knightley's letter stresses the way she might *grow* to become worthy of Knightley's affection. Marriage, on this view, is a matter of development, of becoming worthy of one whom one has come to regard as more worthy than oneself. Perhaps this is a way of understanding more specifically what MacIntyre means when he says that Austen's heroines "seek the good through seeking their own good in marriage." Perhaps the same telos moves Austen's heroes. We should remember that one's telos is not simply out in front of one like the finish line in a race: one's good is already with one, but it needs to be realized for what it is. Knightley's experience is that of realizing a good that has been present to him all along. He recognizes, at last, that he has been in love with Emma since she was thirteen at least. We might even wonder whether his seeming near perfection throughout the novel derives from the attempt to be worthy of Emma—his real, though largely unrecognized, good.

Jane Austen closes *Emma* by emphasizing the importance of realizing the good, of making it real. She does this through her brief, simple narration of Emma and Knightley's wedding, linked first in the penultimate paragraph with that of Harriet and Robert Martin: "Mr Elton was called on, within a month from the marriage of Mr and Mrs Robert Martin, to join the hands of Mr Knightley and Miss Woodhouse." As Emma's happiness has depended on Martin and Harriet's having "qualities that may be trusted," so now her destiny is connected to that of the Martins through their participation in the historic form of Christian marriage. The beginning of the novel's final paragraph reiterates the similarity of the marriages; indeed, the style of Emma and Knightley's wedding seems almost a kind of tribute to the virtues of Robert Martin: "The wedding was very much like other weddings, where the parties have no taste for finery or parade" (464). Taste for parade is the province of Mrs. Elton, who predictably "thought it all extremely shabby, and very inferior to her own" (464–465). For Mrs. Elton, whom Emma considered a rival at Box Hill, a wedding is an opportunity for ostentatious social display, a chance to be seen in a way that marks her supposed superiority to others. The last sentence of the novel stresses a different kind of seeing: "In spite of these deficiencies," remarked by Mrs. Elton, "the wishes, the hopes, the confidence, the predictions of the small band of true friends who witnessed the ceremony, were fully answered in the perfect happiness of the union" (465). The sentence balances the good of the band of true friends and the good of the couple, stressing the way each reinforces and strengthens the other. Especially significant are the words "witnessed" and "answered." "Witnessed" here is not meant to suggest seeing from a spectatorial point of view, as if watching some parade of passing finery; rather, it connotes the act of making real, of realizing a good in one's own life that one has seen or glimpsed. This is bearing witness in the sense of being faithful. The true friends' hopes are answered because Emma and Knightley regard themselves as answerable, in the sense of being accountable, to the hopes and confidence of those who wish and will them good. The last lines of the novel work out further the implications of Emma's recognition that Knightley must marry no one but her. Knightley must marry no one but Emma because, at this particular moment in history, theirs is the marriage that best balances not only love and respect between the partners but also their need, as particular individuals, for erotic love, with a wider communal good.

Austen promises "perfect happiness" for Emma and Knightley, but that perfection lies in their "union" within a form, Christian marriage, that itself involves its participants in a process of realizing the good, that of becoming increasingly worthy of one another. The perfection of this union depends on its answering the witness of true friends, themselves engaged in making the good real in their own lives. The language of Austen's final paragraph seems to preclude Booth's suggestion that we transport Emma and Knightley to a fairy tale world that has little to do with "the real world implied by the book" (CK 435). Also militating against Booth's reading is Mrs. Weston's prediction that the marriage of Emma and Knightley will bring "increased happiness for all." Perhaps one must believe in Providence to accept the possibility of Mrs. Weston's prediction coming true. If one believes that God is the lord of history, and that He is working through such forms as Christian marriage, then one can say that "increased happiness" *must* redound to all when two people like Emma and Knightley unite love and respect in a form that answers to the witness of true friends. We may not understand, at present, how this can be, but we look to see it accomplished further on in the story. Paradoxically, the understanding that we are living the narrative of a journey depends on one thing that does not change. We must all lose the illusion of perfection, as Emma does at Box Hill. For if we are already perfect, and without need of transformation, then surely the "experienced universe" will come to seem "malicious" to us, as Trilling says. We will seek Gnostic escape, the preservation of "spirit" from all that limits or bears us down.[26] Fortunately, we know, with Knightley, that it is best for perfection not to "come quite so soon" (365).

chapter 4

HONOR, FAITHFULNESS, AND COMMUNITY IN

ANTHONY TROLLOPE'S *THE WARDEN* AND

HE KNEW HE WAS RIGHT

Stanley Hauerwas begins an essay, "On Honor," with the curious assertion that "Karl Barth's main problem is that he did not read enough
Trollope." Hauerwas notes that he has no evidence that Barth ever read
any Trollope, grants the strangeness of comparing people as different as
Barth and Trollope, and wonders whether juxtaposing theologians and
novelists is of much value anyway.[1] Of course, Hauerwas does believe
there is much to be learned by getting theologians and novelists to talk to
one another. He has used novels in several theological essays, reflecting,
for example, on *Watership Down* as a way of showing how "every social
ethic involves a narrative"[2] and retelling sections of Peter De Vries's *The
Blood of the Lamb* to show how philosophical answers to the "problem" of
evil can never do justice to actual narratives of suffering.[3] Hauerwas's use
of literature is related to his contention that Christian convictions require
narrative display. Christians are formed by the narrative of Israel, Jesus,
and the Church. They come to self-understanding within the community
formed by that narrative, whose *"primary social task"* is to *"be itself"*—a body
of people faithful to the story of Scripture and thus able to *"negotiat[e] the
danger of this existence"* (CC 10) without engaging in self-deception, idolizing the powers, or resorting to violence. His focus on the formation of
the virtues is another reason for Hauerwas's fondness for narrative. The
presentation of a virtue such as honor requires not just a powerful conceptual description, as Barth admittedly offers, but also the extended
concrete display we find in a Trollope novel.

Barth's central contention is that human honor rests in God's condescension. God does human beings the "unsurpassable honour" of calling
them to Himself; it is their task to accept this recognition and to enjoy the

"freedom" that comes with "limitation." God also calls to obedience, and there is no contradiction between freedom and obedience nor any dishonor in obedience. Rather, "the one summoned by God to obedience is as such one who is honoured and magnified and respected by God."[4] All human honor "is always God's honour," in which we participate as part of His grace (DC 654). The "superfluity of grace" consists in God's "will[ing] to need man and his witness, even though He does not really need him" (DC 657). Grace is superfluous, an overflowing through which God wills not to be absolutely self-contained and isolated, like some perfect geometric figure in the highest heavens. Rather, God wills to be with human beings, to confront them as their Commander, thus honoring them, and also "to stand on [their] level" as Partner. "God could also be a God enthroned high above man," omnipotently running everything in the human world like some perfect manager or technician who never needed even to consult with those he manipulates. And, Barth suggests, it "might be asked whether it would not be better for all concerned if God were to act in this manner" (DC 649). But He has not done so. He has willed to honor human beings as our commander and partner, and in His grace He wills to need us "truly and seriously" (DC 657), though this need must be construed as part of His freedom and not as a lack or imperfection.

Hauerwas pays tribute to the "extraordinary imagination" of Barth in treating honor, for honor is, as Peter Berger has argued, an increasingly "obsolescent" quality, one associated with aristocracies or with particular institutional roles or obligations—all of which are undercut by egalitarian emphasis on dignity or rights.[5] Even from my brief summary above, however, one can see why Barth would treat honor, for honor defines the very relationship human beings have with God by virtue of His condescension. Thus it is "the supreme earthly good," which, if lost, may well mean "to lose everything" (DC 663). Barth's account has its own potentially egalitarian consequences: honor, for him, is not a matter of role or rank but of every person's participation in the honor of God. Barth's translators sometimes use the word "dignity" almost synonymously with "honor" for what God confers on human beings, but Barth's difference from egalitarian accounts of dignity lies in the way he insists always that honor is not something human beings have in themselves but a quality conferred by God and defined by His relationship to us (and ours to Him, the *relationship* being central). Indeed, so that honor might not be lost, "it must be supremely true of it that it is secured, protected and guaranteed to man in such a way that it does not fall out of the hand of God and pass into the hands of man, to become something for him to possess, guard and administer, but that it remains in God's hand as His honour, as a gift the reality of which remains bound to the Giver and His giving, thus being genuinely guaranteed in Him and His action" (DC 663).

"To possess, guard, and administer"—is it possible to find three better verbs for the way contemporary persons regard their dignity and rights? I ask this question by way of beginning a partial answer to Hauerwas's objection that Barth's account of honor is insufficiently concrete in specifying ways that honor should be displayed in everyday life. In large part, I agree with Hauerwas's claim, though I wonder whether we should expect the level of specificity from a systematic theologian that we do from a novelist. On the other hand, certain concrete consequences for action do follow from making honor a matter of relationship to God rather than something one guards and administers in one's own right. Those who regard honor in the Barthian sense will be less likely to enter into conflicts or wrangling over what is due them. They will be less likely to be defensive under attack, for they will recognize that their honor depends not on their own efforts but on acts already accomplished by a gracious God. They will also be more likely to act politically—in the broad sense—in ways that accrue to the honor of all rather than in those that set group against group, individual against individual.

Rather than setting Barth and Trollope in opposition, I want to have them speak to one another on the matter of honor. My hope is that Barth's conceptual account will help to illumine Trollope's novelistic one, and that Trollope will, in turn, provide contexts in which we can see the specific consequences of something like Barth's idea of honor. I do not want to overemphasize the degree to which Trollope's and Barth's accounts of honor resemble one another. They are, in many ways, very different. Nor do I wish to suggest that honor is the only, or even the most important, concern of the two novels I focus on here, *The Warden* and *He Knew He Was Right*. Both novels are concerned with honor, however, and with attacks, either real or perceived, on honor. "What is going on" in both can be opened up by the understanding of honor presented by Barth. This is especially true of *He Knew He Was Right*, which, I argue, is a richly theological novel.

Hauerwas has also pointed Trollope's readers to two prominent theological concerns of the novels, each closely related to honor: constancy and forgiveness. He builds his account of constancy in Trollope on MacIntyre's case for its centrality to Jane Austen.[6] Constancy, or integrity, is that virtue by which the unity of a human life is affirmed. Because it has less to do with actions within concrete practices than it does with the telos of a whole human life, it is difficult to describe formally and must be displayed through the unfolding of a character's life. Hauerwas connects constancy in Trollope with the ideal of the gentleman, an ideal that involves not simply living in accord with a code of conduct and manners but with possessing individuality in a particular way. What marks the gentleman is an individuality that yet knows itself "made from the materials provided by . . . communal life," an individuality that "emerges . . . from society with other selves and can be expressed only by the means provided by that society" (*DF* 36). For Hauerwas, the gentleman offers an alternative to the individualism of liberal societies, where individuals are conceived as ends in themselves and, in the process, convert others into means.

Constancy stands in a problematic relationship to change and depends on forgiveness. As Hauerwas notes, "Constancy seems to suggest a sense of being set, of being a person who can be trusted not to change." Yet sometimes persons of constancy or integrity must change; sometimes "there are aspects of our selves, past commitments we have made, that ought not to be honored" (*DF* 33). That this is true might be taken to mean that MacIntyre and Hauerwas are asking too much of the virtue of integrity or constancy, that the way the self affirms a unity within the complex, fragmented encounters and reversals of experience involves a more flexible and creative stance than constancy suggests. *The Warden* and *He Knew He Was Right* provide a test of this hypothesis, for they foreground matters of constancy and change. Mr. Harding of *The Warden* and Jemima Stanbury of *He Knew He Was Right* undergo major changes, even reversals, in their lives, yet in doing so, arguably return to themselves. Louis Trevelyan of *He Knew He Was Right* is easily the most constant character, in a sense, in the two novels, and yet his very constancy, his continual reaffirming the truth, erroneously, of his singular conviction leads to his madness. Hauerwas seeks to incorporate change within constancy, quoting Shirley Letwin on the particular "moral excellence" of the gentleman: "It is a conquest of mutability not by renouncing or trying to overcome or stifle it, but by developing a steady way of dealing with it. This manner of conducting himself constitutes the moral excellence that defines a gentleman and is called 'integrity.'"[7] Later, in addressing the complexity of the theme of constancy in Trollope, Hauerwas argues that "change is as much necessary for constancy as loyalty is to past decisions"

(*DF* 43). Here, perhaps, "constancy" is being asked to do more conceptual work than it can by itself. What would be useful is a fuller account of the relationships among faithfulness, the unity of the self, and change in Trollope. To offer something like that fuller account is one of the purposes of this chapter.

Constancy depends on forgiveness because forgiveness makes possible the sustaining of the communities necessary for constancy. Forgiveness allows communities to affirm the standards by which they define themselves while also permitting the reintegration of those who sometimes fail the standards. "No more easily defined than constancy," forgiveness, too, "requires display through the temporal narration of lives" (*DF* 52). Hauerwas's focus on forgiveness in Trollope's fiction will come as no surprise to readers of his work in Christian ethics, for forgiveness is as central to that work as it is in Trollope's fiction. Both men focus not only on our willingness to forgive others, but on the difficult yet necessary work by which the Christian learns to live as the forgiven: "We must remember that our first task is not to forgive, but to learn to be the forgiven. Too often to be ready to forgive is a way of exerting control over another. We fear accepting forgiveness from another because such a gift makes us powerless—and we fear the loss of control involved."[8] Noteworthy is the conceptual similarity between Hauerwas's suggestion that we must "learn to be the forgiven" and Barth's idea that our honor lies in God's honoring us. Barth might well say that we must learn to accept being the honored. Both men are working out specific descriptions of a broadly Protestant understanding of justification. The critical point is our learning to accept what Barth calls "freedom in limitation," our freedom within the specifically created realm that God makes possible through our justification in Christ. We no longer need to justify ourselves, to prove ourselves free of the need to be forgiven, or to insist on our honor as a possession to be guarded. We have been justified, forgiven, and honored by God's condescension in Christ. Our task is to accept these gifts, "letting God," as Luther put it, "be God," while living freely in the realm He has opened for us as His children.

He Knew He Was Right offers a particularly rich display of the use of forgiveness as a power, the refusal to forgive or be forgiven, the drive of characters to justify themselves, and, in one splendid case, the acceptance of forgiveness. Before turning to Trollope's novels, I would like to raise one further conceptual matter regarding constancy and integrity, by way of nuancing Letwin's excellent account of the gentleman's integrity. She suggests that the gentleman "might be said" to be "self-possessed, self-determined, self-contained, well-regulated, or collected." Granting that each of these terms carries "distracting connotations," she argues further, "It is perhaps less misleading to see a gentleman as the opposite of someone whose steadiness depends on conformity to something outside himself and, where such a support is missing, contradicts himself and fragments his life. When a man contradicts himself, he becomes an adversary of himself." Letwin wants to insist that the gentleman's steadiness is not a matter of heteronomy or conformity to external standards. Rather, it derives from an awareness of "himself as engaged in shaping a coherent self" (65). It is important, however, not to conceive all response to "something outside himself" as heteronomy or to conceptualize the process of shaping a self as something done only from within. Mr. Harding's steadiness depends not simply on himself but on faithfulness to others and a particular way of understanding his relationships to others. He is involved in shaping a coherent self, but that coherence is made possible, paradoxically, by his fidelities. On the other hand, the attempt to be entirely "self-determined" contributes to Louis Trevelyan's madness, and the self-containment of Jemima Stanbury must be broken by her love for Dorothy in order for her to return to herself. Surely Trollope would not want to advocate one's becoming the "adversary" of oneself; with its Satanic suggestions, the word has rich possibilities for exploring what goes wrong in Trevelyan. But to never be in contradiction to oneself is to be incapable of change, incapable of self-criticism or repentance.

Hauerwas insists on the importance of repentance to Trollope's gentleman, linking the self-knowledge necessary to repentance with the ability to forgive and suggesting that repentance is primarily "a set of skills formed by a life open to others" (*DF* 53). He is reluctant, however, to too directly theologize Trollope's writings, saying that he has "thought it inappropriate to attribute to Trollope a sense of forgiveness that required theological backing." Hauerwas notes that Trollope "was a member in good standing in the Church of England," but that he "seems not to have thought very much about religion one way or the other" (*DF* 56). *The Warden* and *He Knew He Was Right* suggest otherwise, for both do invite theological reading. I suspect that Hauerwas overemphasizes the implicit or unconscious quality of Trollope's religion to make the point that a good culture can carry a great deal of moral wisdom through habits, conventions, rituals, and practices. Hauerwas wants to stress the power of conventional Christianity as it is lived out through the gentleman in Trollope's fiction. But as he also recognizes, the world of the English gentry was, in Trollope's times, very much "in danger of being lost under the onslaught of the new commercial culture" (*DF* 40). Gentlemen no longer dealt only with other gentlemen or with others who could be counted on to act in certain ways. Their ideals of conduct were not necessarily shared by others, even by those who seemed to be gentlemen—a problem at the heart of *He Knew He Was Right*. My purpose here is again to suggest that we need to ask whether constancy can capture the kind of virtue exhibited by a Mr. Harding or Jemima Stanbury. The gentleman could be constant to his own ideal because he moved in a circle where the "others" he encountered were likely to be quite similar to himself. Letwin grants this point when she says, "A gentleman understands himself as one among others like himself . . . He will think of others in the same way as he thinks of himself" (67). This must give Christians pause, for we are called to be open not only to those who are much like ourselves but also to the stranger. We must also question ideals of integrity that put too much emphasis—as in Letwin's description of the gentleman quoted earlier—on self-determination and self-possession. For again, we follow a God whose integrity consists not in His being absolutely self-contained, but Who moves out of Himself toward His creatures, willing Himself in His freedom, as Barth put it, to need us. I am in full sympathy with Hauerwas's and MacIntyre's desire to hold up constancy to moderns caught in a fragmented existence that often seems just one damn thing after another. Emphasizing constancy seems a way to stress the centrality of virtue in assuring the narrative unity of a life directed toward the good. But even in Trollope's day, the kind of coherent culture needed to make constancy sufficient to ensure the narrative unity of a life was breaking down. In *The Warden* and *He Knew He Was Right*, he seeks a more specific kind of faithfulness.

The attraction of a novel like *The Warden* for Hauerwas is easy to understand. In *The Peaceable Kingdom*, he stresses the need for Christian ethics to "begin in the middle." We are "historic beings who must begin our ethical reflection in the midst of history," he argues, for "there is no point outside our history where we can secure a place to anchor our moral convictions." Beginning in the middle means beginning "within a narrative," for Christians, the narrative of "God's relationship to creation that gives us the means to recognize we are God's creatures" (*PK* 62). Trollope likewise begins *The Warden* in the middle, specifically locating his narrative within a longer history. This longer history involves the force of a document, succeeding interpretations of the document made in adaptation to changing historical circumstances, and various communities of interpretation. John Hiram's fifteenth-century will reflects feudal arrangements: the wool-stapler guarantees charitable provision for twelve of those men to whom he has been personally bound, wool-carders born, bred, and laboring in Barchester. By the nineteenth century, wool carding is no longer practiced in Barchester, and the church administrators have extended the charity to men of other occupations in keeping with the spirit of Hiram's original intention. Fifty years prior to Mr. Harding's tenure, they have additionally modified the original arrangements to reflect a profound change in the hospital community's self-understanding. Originally, the men had received only sixpence a day "and their breakfast and dinner was found them at a common table by the warden." This arrangement had come to seem inconvenient to both the warden and the bedesmen, and thus, by "common consent of all parties," a larger daily stipend had been substituted for the common table.[9] With this change, the warden has become less immediately responsible for the sustenance of the men, and their communal bond is loosened. The change suggests the beginning of a shift from a feudal polity of lord and wards to a nascent modern one in which the bedesmen begin to think of themselves as autonomous bearers of rights and claims.

Trollope's crucial point is that John Hiram's will is a document whose meaning has been, and will continue to be, in need of interpretation. Its primary community of interpretation has been the church, though the definition of who counts as an interpreter has varied somewhat from decision to decision. The novel also offers two interpretations of the will by agencies other than the church: the law, operating through Sir Abraham Haphazard, and the press, operating through Tom Towers's seemingly omnipotent *Jupiter.* Although both of these rival interpretations are important to Mr. Harding, his doubts about his compensation and his decision to resign the wardenship arise most clearly from an understanding of his duties shaped by the church. Trollope complicates the matter of churchly interpretation, of course, by using Archdeacon Grantly to present a different understanding of Harding's duties and loyalties. At stake between Grantly and Harding, as I will show, are quite different understandings of church.

Before looking specifically at Harding's integrity and faithfulness, his reasons for leaving the wardenship, it will be helpful to introduce an account that stands at great variance to my own. In a far-ranging interpretation of moral choice in Trollope, J. Hillis Miller claims that "the novels are all versions of an ever-renewed, ever-unsuccessful attempt to demonstrate that moments of moral decision on the part of Trollope's invented characters are securely grounded in a demonstrable right to act as they do act." Harding's relinquishing the wardenship is merely "an ungrounded act of self-affection like Trollope's act of creating characters out of nothing but his unaided 'moral consciousness.'"[10] This solipsistic conclusion is, however, the result of the assumptions of Miller's *Ethics of Reading*. Miller argues that reading has within it an "ethical moment" in which the reader recognizes the claim of a text in a way analogous to the self's recognition of the law as such in Kant's *Foundations*. Ethical action involves response to the law as such, and yet the law can never be known directly. Any narration or story will always fall short of closing the gap between the law as such and the particular example. Because we cannot know whether an action has been done out of obedience to the law as such, we are left with the possibility that any act is really one of "self-affection." Miller finds himself left, then, with the need to invent the curious notion of "right" mentioned above: that Harding must demonstrate a right to resign his position (or, in another example he cites, that Nora Rowley of *He Knew He Was Right* must demonstrate a right to refuse Mr. Glascock). Surely it runs counter to our ordinary moral language to expect a person to demonstrate a right to resign a position or refuse a marriage proposal. To be asked to do so would seem tantamount to a kind of slavery. Because Harding cannot demonstrate such a right—which, in my view, he is certainly not required to do—Miller judges him "lawless," an expression of the "subversive" in Trollope. These judgments are generated simply by Miller's premise that "ethical" action must derive from respect for the law as such.

The way out of Miller's self-created dilemma is easy: it is to insist that there is more to the moral life for Mr. Harding or Trollope than the ever-present demand of the law, the constant failure to meet that demand, and the agonizing recognition that one's ethical acts may be grounded in no more than personal preferences. In short, I want now both to explore the reasons behind Harding's decision to give up the wardenship and to argue that his action is well-grounded. Doing so involves two general interpretive moves: one, stressing explicitly the warden's involvement in an interpretive community, the church, as it struggles to give living embodiment to a will expressed in a quite different past; and two, bringing into focus much of the novel's material and even one pretextual circumstance that a dilemmatic approach to ethical decision making might not even consider.

I refer to his relations to his daughters and son-in-law, his devotion to sacred music, and the loss of his wife—all of which Trollope shows to be quite pertinent to his decision to leave the wardenship.

Mr. Harding's resignation must not be regarded as simply hetero-nomous, a mere caving in to pressure from Bold and the *Jupiter.* He first changes the bedesmen's stipend before receiving anything that could be considered pressure. On becoming warden, he declares "his intention of adding twopence a day to each man's pittance, making a sum of sixty-two pounds eleven shillings and fourpence, which he was to pay out of his own pocket" (4). Harding insists that the men understand that this change does not bind the next warden. This is not a matter of determin-ing an amount to which the bedesmen are entitled: Harding is moved by his sense of fairness and by a desire to alter the relationship between himself, as warden, and the men. His gesture suggests that he will not relate to the men simply as an overseer or member of the hierarchy. His being given the opportunity to serve in the position implies his need to give something from his own substance to those he is to serve. How Trollope regards the action of this "open-handed, just-minded man" (4) is suggested by two biblical contexts surrounding the dilemma Harding faces. The number of the bedesmen, twelve, reminds us of the apostolic community gathered around Jesus, which remains as a memory and crit-ical standard for forms of churchly community. Noteworthy, too, is the very way the problem of the warden's income arises from the "almost fabulous" (3) increase in value of Hiram's butts and patches—increase that recalls the sense-defying multiplications of New Testament miracles such as that of the loaves and fishes. These allusions enrich our sense of the question facing Harding. A resource left for the sustenance, at common table, of twelve poor and elderly men has multiplied to an extraordinary degree. Should all of the benefit of this increase go to one supervisor, or is a different sort of distribution more appropriate, particularly in a commu-nity founded on the memory of one who came in the form of a servant, one who taught his own twelve that he who would be first must "be last of all, and servant of all" (Mark 9:35)? Or, to put the question another way: If one, such as the warden, is to receive all the benefit of an extraordinary, even providential, increase of resources, can the community still be said to be consistent with the will of its founder, one who not only distributed his own fabulous increases so broadly but also gave of his own substance in those distributions?

To put the ethical questions in this way is to use a language of fairness and relationship within a particular community rather than the language of rights and claims. Rights language is used by many of Trollope's figures: Bold, Towers, the elderly claimants, even Harding himself when he asks whether he has a right to his income. Surely Trollope is reflecting the increasing dominance of rights language as the currency of moral discourse in the nineteenth century. Much of Harding's moral action and reflection have more to do with relationships within a specific kind of Christian community than with establishing or adjudicating rights and claims. As we have seen, his initial gift of the twopence per man represents a way of diminishing the difference between the bedesmen and himself, a way of giving from his own substance. Similarly, one of his earliest and clearest reflections on the dilemma emphasizes fairness and the nature of the hospital community. After a troubling conversation with Bold, Harding finds "the question . . . arise within his heart: Was that will fairly acted on? Did John Hiram mean that the warden of his hospital should receive considerably more out of the legacy than all the twelve old men together for whose behoof the hospital was built?" (22). Obviously, these questions cannot be answered except from within a community that understands itself in particular ways.

Complicating matters for Harding is that John Bold is his accuser. Although he dislikes the arrogance of Bold's investigations, he has liked Bold since the latter was a child. Moreover, Bold loves Eleanor, Eleanor loves Bold, and Harding wants to think well of the young man for her sake. Harding is thus in the extraordinary position of being assailed by one whom he has all sorts of reasons to love and respect. He is forced to do, and remarkably able to do, what no one else in the novel could even conceivably do: to look at himself through the eyes of another, to question his own self-justification. This ability derives from the fact that his identity is never exhausted by his institutional role, that he is always more than even the English church defines him to be. Harding's freedom from the drive for justification that marks someone like Archdeacon Grantly comes from his nearly erotic engagement in a love that he knows most positively through sacred music. He is always simultaneously a member of two communities: one, that of Barchester society and the English church of his own particular day, and two, that of the church and the love it represents, present most fully to him, sometimes in its absence, through music.

Trollope defines Harding's love by contrasting the warden with Dr. Grantly. The men differ in their sense of "church," Grantly identifying with the hierarchy while Harding takes a more inclusive view. Never is this difference more apparent than in Grantly's visit to the hospital, his intrusion into those grounds where Harding finds his greatest pastoral happiness in simply playing the violoncello for the twelve men under his care. As one who "did not believe in the Gospel with more assurance than he did in the sacred justice of all ecclesiastical revenues," Dr. Grantly comes to the hospital "to defend the holy of holies from the touch of the profane" (36). He has no hesitation in defining Hiram's will to the bedesmen; his hectoring them reflects his assurance that he is empowered to offer the church's interpretation. The "archdeacon militant" peppers his speech with ecclesiastical grapeshot: "I'll tell you what John Hiram meant . . . That was what John Hiram meant . . . I know what his will was; and I tell you that that was his will, and that that was his intention" (43). Full of his supposed success, the archdeacon tells the warden that he has been "plain" with the bedesmen, for "that's everything: with those sort of people one must be plain, or one will not be understood. Now, I think they did understand me—I think they knew what I meant" (44–45). Reflected here is Grantly's sense of class and the church, the bedesmen being simply "those sort of people" whom one must direct from above and with whom one has no essential connection. The scene defines a very different sense of church in Mr. Harding. Though pained by Grantly's treatment of the men, he contains himself through most of the scene. When Grantly threatens the men, however, by insinuating that the warden may change their condition for the worse, Harding breaks in, "No, my friends. I want no changes—at least no changes that shall make you worse off than you now are, as long as you and I live together" (44). For Harding, the men are "friends," and the hospital and church that have made it possible are places where people "live together," where the substance of life lies in community and dialogue, where questions and conversations are kept open rather than concluded authoritatively in the manner of Dr. Grantly.

Trollope repeatedly stresses Grantly's tendency to close questions definitively and silence others. Suggestive of Grantly's sensibility is his friends' judgment on his "Sacerdos" pamphlet regarding the Earl of Guildford and St. Cross: they consider "that his logic is conclusive and has not, in fact, been answered" (8). Later, Harding feels that "the archdeacon's speech had silenced him—stupefied him—annihilated him" (80) after Grantly has enumerated the manifold obligations that point to Harding's retaining the wardenship. Grantly is a warrior for whom the world is divided into opposing parties, and he is at his best when he puts "on his good armour" (36) to defend the church against those he deems enemies. Mr. Harding's difference from Grantly is never more apparent than in his simple reflection on his anxiety about the archdeacon's visit to the hospital: "he was most anxious neither to accuse them [the bedesmen] nor to defend himself" (40). Harding seeks peace, the maintenance of continuing dialogue within a community, rather than angry polarization into self-justifying factions.

There is something erotic about conversation in *The Warden*, as Trollope first suggests through the comic bedroom scenes of Dr. Grantly. The only place that Grantly "unbends," comes down "to the level of a mortal man," and ceases being archdeacon is "within that sacred recess formed by the clerical bedcurtains at Plumstead Episcopi" (11–12). "'Tis only" when he puts his armor off to don his "tasselled nightcap" and *"robe de nuit,* that Dr. Grantly talks, and looks, and thinks like an ordinary man" (12). In bed, his clerical hectoring, angry epithets, and expressions of horror are no match for the good sense of his wife, as she argues, for instance, the advantage to her father of a match between Eleanor and John Bold. Grantly is left sputtering "Good heavens!" as she closes the conversation by turning "herself round under the bedclothes, in a manner to which the doctor was well accustomed, and which told him, as plainly as words, that as far as she was concerned the subject was over for that night" (13). The archdeacon's bedroom scenes, made doubly amusing by his furtive reading of Rabelais, help to define by contrast the more serious conversations of Mr. Harding. Whereas Grantly seeks to silence others, Harding seeks to hear the voices that speak in silence. Whereas Grantly seeks to close questions with unanswerable arguments or expressions of authority, Harding engages in the continuing conversation that is carried by his sacred music. Harding's absent violoncello is "his constant consolation in conversational troubles." When the words of others such as Grantly pain him, he turns to the instrument, beginning with short and slow passes, then slowly "warm[ing] to the subject," "ris[ing] to a higher melody," and finally "creat[ing] an ecstatic strain of perfect music, audible to himself and to St. Cecilia, and not without effect" (39).

Trollope emphasizes the erotic movement of Harding's violoncello playing during the tea party scene following Grantly's visit to the hospital. The scene's organizing metaphor is the battle of the sexes: "the muslin frocks," who await "the battle," draw up in "semicircular array"; the warden endeavors "to induce a charge" but fails signally, "not having the tact of a general"; Eleanor tries to comfort her "forces" but has little spirit for the work, for "the only enemy whose lance she cared to encounter was not there" (51). The musicians begin with hesitant scrapings and tunings before "the crash begins" and "they go in full flow of harmony together," alternately "loud, as though stirring the battle; then low, as mourning the slain." The metaphor of conversation in music is central, with the saddest voice belonging to Harding's violoncello: "Now alone that saddest of instruments tells its touching tale. Silent, and in awe, stand fiddle, flute, and piano, to hear the sorrows of their wailing brother." But "before the melancholy of those low notes has been fully realized," an "impetus of passion" flows from the full force of the band. Now the skirmish begins, the "black-coated corps" leaving their retreat to advance on the muslin ranks. Soon there is full engagement of opposing regiments and "hand to hand, and foot to foot" encounters between "single combatants." Then, "in corners, and under the shadow of curtains, behind sofas and half hidden by doors . . . are blows given and returned, fatal, incurable, dealing death" (52). Eros deals death as the couples unite in love that leads to fulfillment in marriage, time, and children. Fortunately moved by passion, none of the lovers quite realizes the full melancholy of eros, to be heard by those with ears to hear in the low notes of Mr. Harding's violoncello. Eros wounds too in its opening the lover to the loss of the beloved. If Harding fully understands the lowest tones of his conversation partner, it is perhaps because he has been so many years a widower, wounded in losing his wife.

The full force of eros in *The Warden* is revealed through Eleanor's attraction to John Bold. Clearly her father's favorite, Eleanor senses his dismay after the accusing article in the *Jupiter* and urges him to share his sorrow with her. Indeed, Trollope delicately suggests at this point that she is acting almost as a substitute for the wife he has lost. Pressing him to speak of his unhappiness, she declares, "We are all in all to each other now." He "squeeze[s] her hand as a lover might" while she lies "upon his bosom, and comfort[s] him as a woman only can do." Harding speaks to Eleanor in lines that resonate with his sense of loss: "My own, own child, why should you too be unhappy before it is necessary . . . ?" (87). The immediate reference here is to Harding's giving up his position and to the losses that will mean for Eleanor. But in the context of Eleanor's seeming substitution for her mother, what we hear is Harding's asking his daughter why she, in losing Bold, should be unhappy, as he has been unhappy in losing his wife. Unhappiness will come of necessity, Harding tells her; one need not court it beforehand.

Despite her father's pleas, Eleanor resolves to give up Bold, to act the part of Iphigenia, to sacrifice herself for her father. Eros intervenes, with Bold promising to give up his suit out of love for Eleanor even as she insists that "there can be no talk of love" between them (98). Her attraction to Bold, her failure as Iphigenia, represent one important stage in her breaking away from her father. Another comes when she discovers Harding seems bent on relinquishing the wardenship despite Bold's dropping the suit. Eleanor "had looked forward to much delight from the knowledge that she had freed [her father] from his sorrows," but "now such hopes were entirely over" as she discovered that "the evil was utterly beyond her power to cure!" (113). A difficult problem for parents is to let their children go into their own lives, but perhaps sometimes it is equally difficult for children to recognize their parents' separateness. What Eleanor discovers here is nothing less than her father's individuality, his separateness from her as a person whose ills and sorrows cannot be cured by any degree of magical thinking or dutiful acting on her part. She cannot replace her mother. She cannot compensate, or console, him for his afflictions. She and her father cannot be "all in all" to each other: he has his own life and now she must have hers. Mr. Harding begins the novel with one daughter safely married to an ecclesiastical ally and another dedicated to him at home. Insisting on his integrity alienates his ally and one daughter while the pressure of eros causes the other to move away from him. Yet Trollope finally brings all together in relative harmony and within the church, which supplements the family as the locus of a good community capable of affirming time and the generational process.

Harding's most impassioned playing of his imaginary violoncello accompanies the resolution of his ethical dilemma at Sir Abraham's chambers. As Harding affirms his decision to resign—after listening to Sir Abraham's counterarguments—"he played up such a tune as never before had graced the chambers of any attorney-general. He was standing up, gallantly fronting Sir Abraham, and his right arm passed with bold and rapid sweeps before him, as though he were embracing some huge instrument, which allowed him to stand thus erect." Sir Abraham can only listen and look "in wonder" as the "gentleman who had a few minutes since been so subdued as to be unable to speak without hesitation, was now impassioned—nay, almost violent" (155). Harding's playing recalls his playing for the bedesmen at Hiram's Hospital and for the lovers wounding one another at the tea party; it also connects this moment of decision with his role as precentor at the Cathedral, which, he has been careful to inform Sir Abraham, he intends to keep. The playing of the absent violoncello suggests Harding's participation in those communities of love gathered in the embracing form of the church. Even as he is again being told that a question is closed, settled, dead—this time by Sir Abraham—his actions indicate that the question remains open for him because he participates in a conversation that includes voices not heard by the lawyer or the law. He has ears to hear what others do not. And perhaps the opening of his ears derives from the wound he has received, first in love and then in the loss of his love. Harding's playing the absent violoncello seems an uncanny example of "turning toward the one who is not seen," as Kierkegaard, himself thinking musically, put it in *Works of Love*: "Does the dance end because one of the dancers has gone away? In a certain sense. But if the other remains standing in the position that expresses bowing toward the one who is not seen, and if you know nothing about the past, then you will say, 'The dance will surely begin just as soon as the other one, who is awaited, comes.'"[11] Mr. Harding's playing embodies faithfulness and expectation: faithfulness to what he has been, to what he knows himself to be, and to how he is known in that community of love toward which he turns in expectation—a community to which he has been opened by the death of the other and whose earthly form is the church. The positive shape of his duty is unclear, but he knows with clarity what he must not do or be: he must not be a "despoiler of the poor." As he tells Sir Abraham, it is better that he and Eleanor "should both beg, than that she should live in comfort on money which is truly the property of the poor" (154). This affirmation should be set within its churchly context, for Mr. Harding's role is not just any role but that specifically of pastoral caregiver in an institution whose founding memory is of God's becoming poor in order to serve the poor in love.

Harding seems surest that he must not do harm, as he stands in danger of doing if he continues in the sinecure. In philosophic terms, he gives priority to nonmaleficence. The distinction between nonmaleficence and benevolence is confused by Miller in his analysis of an important statement on the morality of Trollope's fiction from the *Autobiography.* Trollope writes, "I do believe that no girl has risen from the reading of my pages less modest than she was before, and that some may have learned from them that modesty is a charm well worth preserving. I think that no youth has been taught that in falseness and flashness is to be found the road to manliness; but some may perhaps have learned from me that it is to be found in truth and a high but gentle spirit. Such are the lessons I have striven to teach; and I have thought it might best be done by representing to my readers characters like themselves,—or to which they might liken themselves."[12] Trollope here rigorously maintains the distinction between nonmaleficence and benevolence: he has done no ill, made no girl less modest or any youth false. He hopes that he has also done some good, perhaps taught the value of modesty or truth. But this latter result depends on the freedom of his readers, who "may perhaps" learn something from the novels.

Trollope's distinctions are overridden by Miller, who sees, in the passage cited above, the claim that the "novels have a good moral effect because they return the same to the same, that is, they are modeled on social reality and reflect back to his readers themselves" (85). Miller repeatedly slips from Trollope's suggestion that his characters are those to whom his readers "might liken themselves" to the Hegelian language of "sameness." The rhetorical effect is to depict a Trollope who sought calculatingly to enforce a middle-class Victorian morality by creating characters who would exactly mirror his readers. A favorite related metaphor of Miller's involves coins and coining. Trollope's characters are said to "pay [his] readers back in their own coin, so to speak or, to follow the image of impregnation, are children who bear a family resemblance to the character traits of those who read the novels. Coining is like impregnation in that it is the passing on of a preexisting pattern" (86). One should note the sleight of hand by which the general resemblance of family likeness gets palmed off as the exact replication of coinage. One should also note the inapplicability of this notion of children as coins to *The Warden*, where Harding's experience causes him to turn his face away, so to speak, from one child while the other must learn to turn hers away from him.

Trollope presents the complex play of likenesses and differences within the "family" dynamics of society and church, play that Miller's binary modes of thinking cannot help but distort. For Miller, Trollope mints a character like a coin to "be homogeneous to the value system of the society within which it circulates, recognizable within it and measurable in worth by it, not heterogeneous, incommensurate, and therefore inassimilable" (87). Here are simple, binary options: one is either a coin, a mirror of others and completely assimilable, or one is inassimilable, utterly alien. Such binarism precludes the distinction between nonmaleficence and benevolence on which Trollope insists. On Miller's view, one must either do good, by reflecting society's values to itself, or harm, by undermining those values. There seems no possibility of simply writing one's tale, with the confidence that one is doing no harm and the hope that one may perhaps do good. Trollope, Miller argues, sought through novel writing to be assimilated into the society from which he felt outcast as an unhappy boy at Harrow and Winchester. He never really was assimilated, remaining "an island of heterogeneity," a "subversive," a counterfeiter who sought to "grow rich through the manufacture of counterfeit coin so expertly made and so apparently genuine as never to be found out, since it causes no more than an imperceptible inflation in the general currency" (95). Miller bases this last argument on a highly strained reading of a passage in the *Autobiography* in which Trollope writes of being able at times "to imbue" himself "thoroughly with the characters [he has] had in hand" and to feel as if he has been "impregnated with [his] own creations" (132). Creation here, as Miller sees it, becomes a process of self-doubling, and Trollope's characters "have no authority other than himself and no other source than himself." The "text of the novel" is the "illicit or illegitimate birth" of a "strange act of auto-insemination," a "counterfeit production . . . then passed off as legitimate coin" (95).

Miller's language obscures the way characters are created from observation, experience, and memory as well as imagination. Miller's is a desperate attempt to free Trollope from a social production that Miller imagines as endless replication of human simulacra, but in the process Trollope becomes a solipsist, left only to endlessly recreate himself. The moral actions of his characters are analogously only ungrounded acts of self-affection, as much self-authorized as his acts of creation. Miller creates these dilemmas for himself through the very un-Trollopean ideas that underlie his analysis: the Hegelian opposition of the same and the other and the reduction of ethics to Kantian respect for the law as such. The binarism of sameness-otherness will not capture the balance of experience and imagination that went into Trollope's creation of characters that were both like and unlike his readers. Nor will the universalizing moves of Kantian ethics do much to explain Harding's resignation as warden. Miller's work suggests the solipsistic dead end to which a rigid opposition between autonomy and heteronomy leads. For the shape of Harding's constancy, we have to look elsewhere than to a model of integrity that does not allow for self-contradiction or influence from "outside."

Mr. Harding is embroiled in self-contradiction through much of the text, and he is able to hear, and give real credence to, the way others regard him, even the *Jupiter,* which Trollope obviously abhors. Hauerwas has given a better description of the fidelity of Harding in another context, when he describes "discipleship," a concept that could hardly have been far from Trollope's mind when he created the community of twelve at Hiram's Hospital: "Discipleship is quite simply extended training in being dispossessed. To become followers of Jesus means that we must, like him, be dispossessed of all that we think gives us power over our own lives and the lives of others. Unless we learn to relinquish our presumption that we can ensure the significance of our lives, we are not capable of the peace of God's kingdom" (PK 86). In its overall design, Harding's experience throughout *The Warden* is dispossession, a self-emptying. He gives up status, advantageous social connection, closeness to his children, financial security, his socially authorized justification for being. If he is a disciple, he is also a man of peace. Explaining the relationship between being dispossessed and being freed from violence, Hauerwas argues first generally that "our possessions are the source of our violence" and then goes on to give a specific example that sounds almost exactly like Mr. Harding—but with an important difference: "Stung by the seldom acknowledged sense that what we have we do not deserve, we seek self-deceptive justifications that mire us in patterns of injustice which can be sustained only through coercion" (PK 86–87). The correspondence to Mr. Harding lies in the description here; the difference, in the response to being undeserving. Harding refuses the justifications others provide him; refuses to be sustained through coercion, even though he can arguably do much good by remaining warden. He prefers dispossession in the search for peace. He is a man of integrity, but of a sort that must be carefully distinguished from liberal autonomy. His integrity does not need endless defense, for it does not depend strictly on himself; rather, it lies in his fidelity to the story that animates his sacred music, makes possible his continuing conversation with his wife, and gives form to the Church.

Harding knows he is right, and we agree, though a significant number of my students disagree, most arguing in a utilitarian way that he can do more good in his wardenship than he can by leaving it. Nevertheless, I take it that, for Trollope, Harding is correct in knowing that he is right.

The powerful *He Knew He Was Right* works in the opposite fashion, relentlessly presenting the self-justification of a mind moving into madness
in defense of the rightness of convictions that we know to be wrong, both
empirically and morally. First published serially from October 1868 to
May 1869, some fourteen years after *The Warden,* the novel focuses on the
bitterness in marriage between Emily and Louis Trevelyan caused by
Trevelyan's irrational suspicions that Emily is too willing to allow the
attentions of the rakish Colonel Osborne. While the novel's primary
focus is on Trevelyan, it provides four intricately developed and successfully concluded romances as well as the redemption story of an elderly gentlewoman, Miss Jemima Stanbury, whose family becomes enmeshed in the drama of Emily and Louis Trevelyan.

Hauerwas has commented that "Trollope is certainly not satisfying as
an explicitly religious novelist, but then few writers are" (*DF* 57). *He Knew
He Was Right* is not "satisfying," to be sure; its "brilliance" is far too "fragmented," to use Elizabeth Epperly's terms.[13] But it does come close to
being an explicitly religious or theological novel, one that explores from
beginning to end what it means to live under wrath. Trollope presents a
systematic, religious critique of liberal autonomy as he sees it being lived
out in a society where people are increasingly anonymous, where honor
has no force, and where moral questions are largely understood as clashes
of rights. He presents with special acuteness the way rights language is
deployed by way of justifying the self against others. The novel presents,
too, an extended treatment of the problem of forgiveness, specifically of
the difficulty of forgiveness for those who have come to think about
morality as a matter of rights and claims. At the novel's center is the need
to learn to live "as one of the forgiven," something to which Trevelyan
never consents. Jemima Stanbury, on the other hand, does learn to live a
forgiven life. Her plot takes up the same issues as the main one to a
greater degree than critics have recognized. Trevelyan knows he is right
and lives in narcissistic self-justification under wrath, admitting fallibility
only on his deathbed, and then in an ambiguous way. During the course
of his life, he progressively alienates himself from everyone around him.
Miss Stanbury also knows she is right about most everything and runs the
risk of driving everyone from her as well. At a certain point, however, she
turns about, comes to herself, and begins to live again in relationship to
others. The experiences of Trevelyan and Miss Stanbury can be read, too,
as further attempts toward a definition of constancy or integrity. For
Trollope, these virtues cannot mean self-determination, self-possession,

self-containment: a too rigid commitment to self-consistency can make one mad, as we see in Trevelyan. Rather, the drive toward self-possession must always be disciplined by dispossession, which means coming to rest in one's need and recognizing the other as a gift and call to living beyond oneself, in relationship and love.

He Knew He Was Right opens with a chapter title that seems designedly allegorical and archaic, a suggestion that the drama to be played out will be influenced by larger than human forces. Just under that chapter title, "Shewing How Wrath Began," Trollope alludes in his first sentence to Milton's Adam and Eve as they leave the Garden of Eden after bearing the divine wrath: "When Louis Trevelyan was twenty-four years old, he had all the world before him where to choose."[14] Thus Trollope begins where Milton ends *Paradise Lost:*

> The World was all before them, where to choose
> Thir place of 'rest, and Providence thir guide:
> They hand in hand with wand'ring steps and slow,
> Through *Eden* took thir solitary way.[15]

Louis Trevelyan "chose to go to the Mandarin Islands, and there fell in love with Emily Rowley" (1), whom he marries, but their union unfortunately does not reflect the patient mutual support, and dependence on Providence, of Milton's Adam and Eve as they leave the Garden. Rather, through most of the novel, Trevelyan seems more like the Adam of Book 10, experiencing God's wrath and refusing consent to his own creation:

> Did I request thee, Maker, from my Clay
> To mould me Man, did I solicit thee
> From darkness to promote me, or here place
> In this delicious Garden? (ll. 743–746)

With this rejection of his creation in clay comes Adam's blaming Eve for their plight. Why, he asks, could God not have filled "the World at once / With Men as Angels without Feminine, / Or find some other way to generate / Mankind?" (ll. 892–895). *He Knew He Was Right* includes a Satan figure, too, within its pattern: Colonel Osborne. The tempter of Emily Trevelyan, though different from Satan in his lack of success, Osborne is frequently described as a serpent, the possessor of a sting. That "sting" suggests death to Trevelyan, the conspiracy between death and the woman to bring on him what he consistently refuses to accept: the rightness of his own death.

Wrath begins with a man who is free from nearly every constraint. Trevelyan might have done just about anything he wished. As a result, he "liked," as Lady Rowley observes, "to have his own way" (3). Perhaps Lady Rowley sees this tendency so quickly because she is apprehensive about Trevelyan's marriage to one whom she knows "also liked to have her own way." Clearly, their ways clash, for Trollope comments ominously that after the couple has become established in London and baby Louis has been born, "Mr. Trevelyan had begun to think that he should like to have his own way completely." Trevelyan's "suspicion" about Emily's attentions to Osborne surface, and she declares to her sister, Nora, "that life will not be worth having" (4) under such conditions. After Trevelyan angrily tells Nora that he "did not wish Colonel Osborne to come so often to his house," he briefly considers apologizing to her. He does not apologize, however, for "he could not bear to have to own himself to have been wrong." Immediately he turns to self-justification. As he cannot bear to own being wrong, he discovers that he was not; the fault lay in her being "most provoking in her manner to him" (8). Having "spoken those words which he could not recall," Trevelyan "almost" feels he should "beg his wife's pardon." He believes "he knew his wife well enough to be sure that she would not forgive him unless he did so" (9). What he really knows is his own mind and the fact that he would never forgive without a full confession from the other, one that left his self-justifications intact.

The third figure in the beginning of wrath, Colonel Osborne, is a bachelor somewhat past fifty, and, like Trevelyan, one who possesses extraordinary freedom in all the worldly senses. "A man of fortune to whom the world had been very easy," Osborne had "no burdens but those imposed upon him by his position as a member of Parliament" (5). In politics, he "was supposed to be a Conservative, and generally voted with the conservative party; but he could boast that he was altogether independent, and on an occasion would take the trouble of proving himself to be so" (11). Trollope's suggestion seems to be that Osborne's independence has less to do with the affirmation of any particular political principle than with the demonstration of his being free from determination by anyone else. What such entire autonomy leads to is wittily suggested by Trollope: "It was generally thought of him that he might have been something considerable, had it not suited him better to be nothing at all." Vain and possessed of "a free and pleasant way with women" (11), he draws the ire of many London ladies for being the proverbial snake in the grass. But even his attentions to women such as Emily Trevelyan are based less on passion than on the vain desire for pleasure, the need to fill his empty self. Seemingly detached from everyone, Osborne has been a friend in youth to Sir Marmaduke Rowley, Emily's father, though the two men have not seen one another for many years. Osborne knew Emily when she was a baby, and it is on this familial connection that he grounds his attentions to her, even well after he is aware of Trevelyan's objections.

Trollope uses the triangle of Osborne, Emily, and Trevelyan to pose a complex problem of honor. Trevelyan considers himself to be dishonored by Osborne's attentions to Emily and by her receiving them, especially after he has forbidden her to see or correspond with the Colonel. But it seems clear that Emily is not unfaithful to Trevelyan. As she regards herself to be innocent, she interprets his suspicions as dishonoring her. Trollope causes us to trust Emily and to see Trevelyan's fears as irrational, at least in regard to her. His expository remarks about Osborne, however, suggest that Trevelyan's suspicions of him do possess some justification. Osborne delights in upsetting Trevelyan, not because he cares about Emily, but because Trevelyan's taking notice of him confirms his sense of himself. "Being nothing at all," Colonel Osborne seeks to be something in somebody's eyes; he seems already the kind of modern self that performs for others in a search for confirmation. As he is a gentleman, we would expect him to cease his attentions to Emily after he learns they are dishonoring her to Trevelyan, however unjustified such dishonor might be. But he does not cease. Instead, he uses what ought to make him most concerned about her honor, his friendship for Sir Marmaduke and relationship to the family, to justify continuing to see her. Indeed, Colonel Osborne exhibits a remarkable capacity to deceive himself about his own intentions. When Emily removes to the Clock House of Mrs. Stanbury at Nuncombe Putney, he resolves to visit, but he does so under the guise of going to see an "old schoolfellow" of his, the Vicar of Cockchaffington, a nearby village. As he explains in a letter to her, he goes, too, to see the religious antiquities: "There is something in his church which people go to see, and though I don't understand churches much, I shall go and see it" (188). Being in the neighborhood, he must of course see his old friend Emily. At least, that is how he explains himself to himself, and the most dreadful thing is that he does not know he is lying. When Bozzle later confronts him with the mischief he has done, Osborne defends himself with the justifications I have laid out here. Trollope's comment illumines the closed circle of self-justification: "Let the charitable reader suppose that Colonel Osborne did not know that he was lying,—that he really thought, when he spoke, that he had gone down to Lessboro' to see the remarkable piece of antiquity" (217). The irony here has been prepared by Osborne's actual meeting with Emily, during which she begins "to think that he certainly had not come to see her" (199). Indeed, he has not; he has come to see a "remarkable piece of antiquity": himself.

The closest thing to Trollope's view of Colonel Osborne's conduct is spoken by Lady Milborough in the chapter called "A Real Christian," near the end of the novel. By this time, Trevelyan's descent to madness and death is nearly complete, and the romance of Hugh Stanbury and Nora Rowley has resulted in their engagement. As the Rowleys are to depart for the Mandarins, the problem is to find a place for Nora to live, one solved when Lady Milborough asks Nora to live with her. That action accounts for Trollope's chapter title and gives the lady authority to speak on the matter of Osborne's conduct. Nora argues that the Colonel "meant not the slightest harm,—no more than she [Emily] did," but mere non-maleficence is not enough for Lady Milborough: "He was old enough, and ought to have known better. And when the first hint of an uneasiness in the mind of Louis was suggested to him, his feelings as a gentleman should have prompted him to remove himself. Let the suspicion have been ever so absurd, he should have removed himself. Instead of that, he went after her,—into Devonshire." When Nora offers one of the Colonel's own defenses, that "he went to see other friends," Lady Milborough responds with an echo of some of the harshest words of the Sermon on the Mount: "I hope it may have been so;—I hope it may have been so. But he should have cut off his hand before he rang at the door of the house in which she was living" (891). Lady Milborough's judgment here will hardly make sense to one accustomed to thinking about ethics in terms of rights. They depend, rather, on a much deeper sense of social solidarity than rights language can support. She argues that Osborne should have taken into account the weakness of his brother, Trevelyan. What must appall the reader is the gap between her way of setting the problem and Osborne's level of moral reflection. Osborne could never even begin to think of his conduct in the terms Lady Milborough applies. What Trollope sees happening to the ideal of the gentleman can perhaps best be illumined here by considering the Colonel in light of Shirley Letwin's description: "A gentleman understands himself as one among others like himself, his respect for his own integrity entails respecting the integrity of others. He will think of others in the same way as he thinks of himself. He will recognize them as personalities, as characters, whose distinctiveness he is obliged to respect, and whom he must treat as he wishes himself to be treated" (67). Osborne could perhaps be said to understand himself as being among others like himself, not so much because they all have been shaped by some coherent body of values or social order but because he is a narcissist who can hardly imagine anything other than his own desire. The very idea of "integrity" seems inapplicable to one who has chosen "to be nothing at all." The willful demonstrations of his independence for which he is known seem rather a kind of self-indulgence than evidence of true integrity. Letwin's final standard above echoes the Golden Rule, but Lady Milborough has referred to a higher standard, one that imposes the most rigorous control over oneself and insists that the Christian always take into account the brother's or sister's weakness.

Trollope gives the ability to define what it means to be a gentleman to a woman and a "real Christian." Perhaps this represents his sense that much of what was good about the ideal of the gentleman must now, in the world of increasingly urban and commercial society, be carried by people other than the traditional gentleman, by women like Lady Milborough and by those who impose on themselves a higher standard even than the Rule. It would be a mistake to suggest that Trollope presents no traditional English gentleman in *He Knew He Was Right:* Mr. Glascock, owner of the splendid estate Monkhams, represents the values Letwin attributes to the gentleman. The closest thing to an urban hero in the novel, however, is neither Colonel Osborne nor Louis Trevelyan but Hugh Stanbury, journalist for the *Daily Record,* regarded as such a "filthy" and radical paper by his Tory aunt that it leads to their alienation. No appeal to the proper integrity or constancy of the gentleman can restore the bonds of honor between a Colonel Osborne and a Louis Trevelyan. The ideal of the gentleman, as Letwin describes it, could actually be of force when one could truly assume that others shared one's basic commitments. This seems no longer true, however, among the London gentlemen of *He Knew He Was Right.* Osborne is, to adapt a Barthian phrase, an "administrator" of his own empty dignity, his right to do as he pleases. No bond to Trevelyan is of any importance to him. Honor as Barth understood it might recreate the sense of social solidarity on which meaningful ideals of honor depend, the solidarity Trollope shows in the process of erosion. This is not to say that Barth's reflection is directed to the purpose of rebuilding social solidarity: he is attempting to offer a description of what the doctrine of creation means for the honor of creatures. But the creature who knows his honor to derive from God's condescension to him, who knows that it need not be asserted as a right over against others but rather consented to as part of a gracious gift to all, will not act like either the self-justifying Colonel Osborne or Louis Trevelyan.

In Trevelyan's history, Trollope depicts the frightening self-destruction of one who liked to have his own way, of one who, as Barth might gloss Adam's lines from Book 10 of *Paradise Lost*, refused to assent to being created, to having his honor rest in his relationship with God rather than himself. The novel shows Trevelyan becoming increasingly deluded, self-pitying, shrill in his efforts at self-justification, and isolated. His habitual good fortune has caused him to believe in his own desert, and he resents even the care of others who try to assist him. His early response to Lady Milborough's caution about Osborne's tendency to "mischief" is instructive. Trevelyan recognizes that she has acted as a friend and acknowledges the truth of what she has said, which merely echoes what "he had said to himself more than once." Still, "it was intolerably bitter to him that he should be warned about his wife's conduct by any living human being; that he, to whom the world had been so full of good fortune,—that he, who had in truth taught himself to think that he deserved so much good fortune, should be made the subject of care on behalf of his friend" (26–27). Unwilling to become "the subject of care," Trevelyan refuses the help of one friend after another. He prefers an alliance with the ex-policeman, now private investigator, Bozzle. Attachment to Bozzle allows Trevelyan to indulge simultaneously his self-hatred and his wounded sense of being wronged: he hates Bozzle, hates himself for being reduced to employing Bozzle, but clings to Bozzle because the man's experienced cynicism confirms his need to believe that he is the one wronged.

Bozzle combines universal suspicion with a love of power that delights in using the law to convict people of transgressions. He bills himself as a man of "facts," seemingly employable for a value-free inquiry into the truth. One of his assumptions is that appearances and reality must always be at odds with one another. Thus Trollope intuits the connection between the claim to finding facts, independent of any description, and the universal reign of suspicion: "Men whose business it is to detect hidden and secret things, are very apt to detect things which have never been done. What excuse can a detective make even to himself for his own existence if he can detect nothing? Mr. Bozzle was an active-minded man, who gloried in detecting, and who, in the special spirit of his trade, had taught himself to believe that all around him were things secret and hidden, which would be within his power of unravelling if only the slightest clue were put in his hand. He lived by the crookedness of people, and therefore was convinced that straight doings in the world were quite exceptional" (267–268). Bozzle is one justified by the law. His reason for existence lies in his ability to prove how others have sinned and fallen short of the law. Trevelyan comes to "believe in Bozzle" despite hating the detective and despite the fact that he must put aside all that "chivalry, and love, and sense of woman's honour" tell him about the impossibility of his wife's "hav[ing] sinned." He believes in Bozzle because Bozzle "had no interest in the matter, one way or the other," and thus "would find out facts" (363). Trollope everywhere shows Bozzle to be interested, despite his pretensions otherwise. His interest lies in justifying himself as the one who proves people to be other than they seem. He has a deep interest in power, which he exercises by convicting people of falling short of the law: "He was a man loving power, and specially anxious to enforce obedience from those with whom he came in contact by the production of the law's mysterious authority. In his heart he was ever tapping people on the shoulder, and telling them that they were wanted" (492).

By depending on Bozzle, Trevelyan also seeks justification through the law. What would justify his belief in Bozzle, and in his own sense of being wronged, is Bozzle's discovering that Emily has been unfaithful, that she has fallen short of the law. As Trevelyan comes increasingly to feel wronged and to depend on Bozzle alone, he envisions all whom he has previously regarded as friends or well-wishers as now his enemies. Mrs. Stanbury had "been false to him and to her trust"; Mr. and Mrs. Outhouse "were, of course, his enemies"; his "old friend, Hugh Stanbury, had gone over to the other side"; his "own lawyer had refused to act for him"; and even "his fast and oldest ally," Lady Milborough, "had turned against him." Employing Bozzle allows Trevelyan a delicious self-punishment. Bozzle "made suggestions to him which were as bad as pins stuck into his flesh," suggestions Trevelyan seeks as a way to feed his melancholy sense of betrayal: "From morning to night he sang to himself melancholy silent songs of inward wailing, as to the cruelty of his own lot in life;—and, in the mean time, he employed Bozzle to find out for him how far that cruelty was carried." The one thing that "never occurred to him" was "to inquire of himself whether it might be possible that his old friends were right, and that he himself was wrong" (317–318). In a real way, others have ceased to exist for him.

Trevelyan seems most deluded in his obsessive, misogynist fantasies about Emily's supposed unfaithfulness: "His mind was at work upon it always. Could it be that she was so base as this—so vile a thing, so abject, such dirt, pollution, filth? But there were such cases. Nay, were they not almost numberless?" (363). The emphasis on filth and pollution suggests the degree to which Trevelyan projects on Emily, and women more generally, his sense of embodiment as betrayal. When he learns of Colonel Osborne's appearance at the parsonage of the Outhouses at St. Diddulph, Trevelyan casts himself as Othello, announcing his mingled self-pity and sense of betrayal to an imaginary Iago: "Iago;—oh, Iago! The pity of it, Iago!" (422). He walks nearly all night on the piazza of St. Mark's, thinking of "it," the shape that Emily's meeting with the supersubtle Osborne has taken: "Of course she had seen him. He walked there nearly the whole night, thinking of it, and as he dragged himself off at last to his inn, had almost come to have but one desire,—namely, that he should find her out, that the evidence should be conclusive, that it should be proved, and so brought to an end. Then he would destroy her, and destroy that man,—and afterwards destroy himself, so bitter to him would be his ignominy. He almost revelled in the idea of the tragedy he would make" (422–423). The allusion to Othello's murder of Desdemona continues here, but also revealing is the emphasis on bringing everything—his own life as well as Emily's and Osborne's—to an end. The desire for an end, a conclusion, a judgment, a place in which all veils will be lifted and all secrets known—this is to deny living in history, living in narrative. This is to live under wrath, like the Adam of Book 10 in *Paradise Lost*, angrily noting that he had not asked to be created from "clay" and wondering why God could "not fill the World *at once* / With Men as Angels without Feminine" (italics added). Trevelyan would like to be done with living in the body, living with women, living under the slow, sure pain of dying. Kierkegaard's paradoxical analysis of suicide perfectly describes Trevelyan's desire to destroy himself: he would die the death so as not to die. By taking his own life, he would cheat death, for he would avoid the process of subjection to necessity that is death itself.

Although Trevelyan's madness has perplexed readers, Kierkegaard's analysis of "infinitude's despair" offers clear insight into it. For Kierkegaard, the self is a "synthesis of which the finite is the limiting and the

infinite the extending constituent. Infinitude's despair, therefore, is the
fantastic, the unlimited."[16] "Fantastic," with its fine Shakespearean feel,
describes quite well the exaggerated and self-conscious theatricality of
Trevelyan, who not only plays Othello but is aware of himself playing
Othello. At Casalunga, Trevelyan plays King Lear, speaking to Stanbury
in echoes of Lear's inspired madness as he is led away to prison with
Cordelia. When asked by Stanbury if he sees Emily, Trevelyan responds
with grim comedy, reflecting the same desire to be "done with it" that he
has earlier expressed in figuring himself as Othello: "Wives, Stanbury, are
an evil, more or less necessary to humanity, and I own to being one who
has not escaped. The world must be populated, though for what reason
one does not see. I have helped,—to the extent of one male bantling; and
if you are one who consider population desirable, I will express my regret
that I should have done no more" (869). Trevelyan would be done with
the whole farce of humanity as it struts and frets in a self-importance
based on denying meaninglessness and death. He has not developed a
healthy balance between realistic grounding in everyday experience and
the desire for self-transcendence, Kierkegaard's motion toward the infinite. Kierkegaard's language about the self's needing to be grounded in
necessity uncannily describes Trevelyan: "But if possibility outruns necessity so that the self runs away from itself in possibility, it has no necessity
to which it is to return; this is possibility's despair" (35–36). When Stanbury suggests that Trevelyan return to England, Trevelyan informs him
that he has chosen a new country and made Casalunga his home: "I have
no tie, sir;—no tie anywhere. It has been my study to untie all the ties;
and, by Jove, I have succeeded. Look at me here. I have got rid of the
trammels pretty well,—haven't I?—have unshackled myself, and thrown
off the paddings, and the wrappings, and the swaddling clothes. I have
got rid of the conventionalities, and can look Nature straight in the face"
(869). Here is Kierkegaard's despair of possibilities, the despair of a self
that "leads a fantasized existence in abstract infinitizing or in abstract
isolation, continually lacking its self, from which it only moves further
and further away" (32). Trevelyan never really becomes a self, for "to
become oneself is a movement" in a place, and "necessity is literally the
place where it is" (36). From the beginning of the novel, Trollope has
emphasized the apparently limitless number of Trevelyan's possibilities:
he has had all the world before him where to choose. As the untrammeled
self confronting limitless possibilities seems very like the autonomous self
of liberalism, Trollope's account of Trevelyan suggests that liberal auton-

omy is really a formula for despair, a despair usually unrealized because of the self's dispersion in the mundane.

Trevelyan resembles Ernest Becker's "full-blown schizophrenic," whose symbolic self "splits away from the body," leaving him "abstract, ethereal, unreal." Such a figure "billows out of the earthly categories of space and time, floats out of his body, dwells in an eternal now," and essentially vanquishes death and destruction in his fantasies by "quitt[ing] his body, renounc[ing] its limitations."[17] The drive to live "in an eternal now" stands in opposition to living in narrative, in story, an opposition that offers a way to understand Trollope's extraordinary, and very disciplined, devotion to writing fiction. Miller explains Trollope's immense "production" primarily in psychological and materialist terms: Trollope compensated for his youthful sense of exclusion from society by offering back to society a huge quantity of works seemingly reflecting Victorian values but actually subverting them. Such a view explains Trollope as a revenger engaged, like Trevelyan, in acts of self-justification against others. An alternative explanation might see in Trollope's continual storying of experience precisely the disciplined attempt to remain living in narrative, in history, in time—in that freedom within limitation opened to us by God's condescending to honor us, as Barth might put it.

Trevelyan remains committed to bitter self-justification until the last moments of his life, when he seemingly gestures his trust to Emily by kissing the fingertips she has placed at his lips. The novel's other major story, that of Jemima Stanbury, suggests, however, that it is possible to turn from self-justification, even for one deeply committed to knowing she is right. Like Trevelyan, Miss Stanbury "likes her own way" (72), as we learn from her nephew Hugh, who is well positioned to know. After quarreling with her brother's family, she has proposed to her brother, Hugh's father, to undertake her nephew's education. She sends Hugh to Harrow and Oxford, then to training for the bar in London, but when he decides instead to write for the *Daily Record*, she severs their relationship altogether, closing a letter to him by pronouncing, "I will have no connection that I can help, and no acquaintance at all, with radical scribblers and incendiaries" (62). After Miss Stanbury dismisses Hugh, she makes another attempt to do her duty toward her brother's family by inviting Hugh's sister, Dorothy, to come live with her. Trollope stresses the comic quality of Miss Stanbury's willfulness, the naïve assumption that she can change her life at will, in her reflections on receiving Dorothy: "She was going to change the whole tenour of her life for the sake,—as she told herself,—of doing her duty by a relative whom she did not even know. But we may fairly suppose that there had in truth been a feeling beyond that, which taught her to desire to have some one near her to whom she might not only do her duty as guardian, but whom she might also love" (73–74). Here Trollope suggests the ironic shape of Miss Stanbury's experience from this point forward. Dorothy does "change the whole tenour" of Miss Stanbury's life but not because the old woman wills it so from a sense of duty. Dorothy changes Miss Stanbury's life by being one whom her elderly aunt cannot help but love. When Dorothy first arrives, Miss Stanbury is on her guard against any show of weakness or need. She goes to meet her guest "looking sternly," from the conviction "that she must initiate her new duties by assuming a mastery at once" (74). As she directs operations at the dinner table that evening, she declares that if she can't have "English green peas" she won't have any, all the while "standing up as she said this,—as she always did on such occasions, liking to have a full mastery over the dish" (76). As Dorothy goes to bed, Aunt Stanbury lays down her version of the unforgivable sin: "If you read in bed either night or morning, I'll never forgive you" (78).

The serious aspects of Miss Stanbury's liking to have her own way involve the distribution of her wealth. She has received her wealth through romance, her own father being a parish vicar, a position to which her brother succeeded on their father's death. When she was twenty-one, Miss Stanbury "became engaged" to Mr. Brooke Burgess, a wealthy banker in Exeter. He subsequently quarreled with Miss Stanbury's family, and then she quarreled with her own family, leaving the parsonage when her father died and remaining alienated from her brother. After she moved to lodgings in Exeter, where she "lived on the smallest pittance," Burgess was "untrue to her and did not marry her." He, at last, died "and left her every shilling that he possessed"—leaving her alienated from his family and still, of her own will, alienated from her own (61). Miss Stanbury's most cherished resolve, then, has been to make sure that every shilling she has received from Burgess is to return to the Burgess family at her death. She has made provisions for small bequests to members of her own family, but she is careful to let them know that these come only from her own savings, not from any money that has come to her from Burgess. Miss Stanbury has willed all the inherited money to the current Mr. Brooke Burgess, the son of one of her fiancé's brothers and a favorite of hers. Meanwhile, she continues to be hated by the rest of the Burgesses, especially the younger Brooke's Uncle Barty, who has always insisted that his brother's will was not freely made but the work of Miss Stanbury herself.

As her once-affianced had neared death, Miss Stanbury returned to nurse him, because, as she explains to the young Brooke, she "considered it [her] duty to do" so (328), an explanation that perhaps uses duty to deny her own need and love in much the same way as she does in her relationship with Dorothy. Her nursing had nothing to do with the will, which had already been made. Indeed, "the will was no great triumph" to her; she "could have done without it" (329)—expressions tantamount to saying that she could have done without the evidence of Burgess's continuing love for her that the will made manifest. Jemima evinces, at times, a deep sense of being unlovable, unworthy to be loved; it surfaces, for instance, when she suspects Dorothy of being ungrateful, of expecting to get something from her. When Dorothy says she does not expect anything, Jemima bristles, "No; and I don't expect anything. What an old fool I am ever to look for any comfort. Why should I think that anybody would care for me?" (347). In effect, what Jemima says is that she is not worthy of anyone's care or love. Thus, the only justice she can render for the curious fact that Burgess has continued to love her is a kind of Lambert Strether–like renunciation: "not to have got anything for" herself, to use James's line.[18] She has gotten something for herself, despite not wanting it, but she can at least make sure that none of it ever passes to one of her own. She cannot "compromise" the will, as the Burgesses have pressured her to do, because that would allow the appearance of her complicity in writing it and would also represent unfaithfulness to the dead. She knows, as she tells her nephew, that "if ever there was a good will in the world, the will of your Uncle Brooke was good" (329). Hers is the paradoxical position of being faithful to the clearest example she has ever seen of "a good will in the world" and yet having that very faithfulness continually reemphasize her unworthiness of the good fortune she has received. No wonder she tells young Brooke, "The romance of a life is always a melancholy matter" and "they are most happy who have no story to tell" (328). Those with no story to tell are without a history, without a self: dead. Trollope's problem becomes, then, restoring Jemima to life by restorying her, by giving her a way to be released from her admirable faithfulness to the dead. She must be given a new way for her story to resume, consistent with the past yet not bound by it, a way that will defy the closure she seeks to impose on her own story.

Dorothy's coming to stay marks the beginning of a new thing in Aunt

Stanbury's life. Part of Jemima's motive in bringing her niece to her is to arrange a marriage for Dorothy to the clergyman Mr. Gibson. The first crisis in the relationship between Dorothy and her aunt occurs when Dorothy fails to develop appropriate affection for Gibson. As Miss Stanbury understands herself primarily "as one who, from the peculiar circumstances of life, was bound to do much good for others," she interprets Dorothy's failure to love Gibson as a betrayal. Trollope's comment on Miss Stanbury suggests the comic and pathetic quality of the way the dutiful doing of good substitutes in her life for relating freely to others: "There was no end to her doing good for others,—if only the others would allow themselves to be governed by her" (345–346). Dorothy offers to return home, a gesture Miss Stanbury reads as evidence of ingratitude and confirmation of her own fear that she is unlovable. Indeed, it is because Miss Stanbury regards herself as unlovable that she must "govern" others: for if she were to relate to them as free beings, one of them, like Dorothy, might do the truly unaccountable and love her! Being loved would destroy Miss Stanbury's whole self-understanding, based as it is on proving herself not guilty of influencing Burgess's will— which, as we have seen, paradoxically amounts to proving herself undeserving of the love he has shown her through the bequest. We can now also see that she rejects freedom. Burgess has imposed no conditions on his gift to her but has trusted her to dispose of the money as she sees fit. She has imposed the conditions on herself, preferring unfreedom to the recognition that she has been loved and trusted. In her own unfreedom, she cannot grant freedom to others but must "master" and "govern" those who might otherwise love her: Hugh, Dorothy, the young Brooke. The conclusion is clear: Trollope links the desire to be master with the need to justify oneself in the eyes of others, and relates both the drive for mastery and for justification to the deep sense that one is unloved and unlovable.

A crisis occurs between Dorothy and Miss Stanbury when Brooke Burgess falls in love with Dorothy and proposes marriage. The match is anathema to Miss Stanbury, for it defeats all her plans: she has willed her inherited money to Brooke, and no Stanbury is to have any of it. If Brooke and Dorothy marry, then anything passing to Brooke will also go to Dorothy and to their children. Brooke and Dorothy's marriage threatens the story of Miss Stanbury's life as she has willed it to be written to the end. Their love threatens her narrative control. Complicating the matter is Miss Stanbury's seeing something of her own young self in her niece, and, of course, Trollope has stressed the similarity of the current Brooke to

Miss Stanbury's lost fiancé through their names. Brooke's loving Dorothy reminds Miss Stanbury that she was once loved too, despite her self-protective efforts to believe herself unlovable. This crisis between Dorothy and Miss Stanbury leads to a break and Dorothy's returning to Nuncombe Putney. Especially hurtful to Dorothy are her aunt's accusations that she has been "immodest" in receiving Brooke while Miss Stanbury has been ill and that she has cunningly refused Mr. Gibson because she had set her mind on Brooke. Neither of these accusations contains even the slightest truth, but the latter confirms Miss Stanbury's self-estimation. It explains her niece's apparent love for her without her having to believe herself lovable: Dorothy has merely been scheming, from the first, to get Brooke and his intended inheritance.

What saves Miss Stanbury is the love Dorothy has aroused in her. When she dispatches Martha to Nuncombe Putney with a gift "of a quarter of lamb," the letter she sends Dorothy speaks with near pathetic indirection of the old woman's yearning for reconciliation and her niece's return:

> As Martha talks of going over to pay you a visit, I've thought that I'd just get her to take you a quarter of lamb, which is coming in now very nice. I do envy her going to see you, my dear, for I had gotten somehow to love to see your pretty face . . .
>
> I am very desolate and solitary here. But I rather think that women who don't get married are intended to be desolate; and perhaps it is better for them, if they bestow their time and thoughts properly. (627)

Trollope indicates that Miss Stanbury loves Dorothy even more than she recognizes, and yet she considers herself "bound not to . . . suggest an unconditional return" (628). With the gift of lamb, she does, however, empower Martha to speak for her, telling the servant, "Do it out of your own head, just as it comes up at the moment" (626). When Martha is greeted by the unexpected news that Brooke has proposed to Dorothy and been accepted, she finds it difficult to know how to speak, for she knows very well that the marriage contravenes Miss Stanbury's will. Martha's reserve, however, breaks down and she "expresse[s] herself in strong language," speaking as one who knows Miss Stanbury better than the old woman knows herself: "There was nothing on earth her mistress wanted so much as to have her favourite niece back again" (677).

Having cued the reader toward biblical contexts through the offering of the lamb, Trollope sets his narration of Dorothy's return to her aunt in relation to the parable of the prodigal son. Lest we miss the point, Trollope has Dorothy remark, "You see I didn't stay to eat any of the lamb," and her aunt respond, "You shall have a calf instead, my dear . . . because you are a returned prodigal" (681). But surely Dorothy is a curious prodigal: she has not asked Miss Stanbury for her share of the inheritance nor "wasted [her] substance with riotous living." Nor does she undergo a reversal in returning to Miss Stanbury. She is motivated rather by the same uncomplicated affection she has always felt for her aunt and a recognition of the old woman's need. If there is truly a prodigal in the story, one who reverses the direction of a life in an act that seems a "coming to oneself," it is Miss Stanbury. Her *metanoia* resembles the prodigal son's in the way it combines this coming to herself with a return to living in relationship to others and to the unconditional love of God. She must, like the prodigal, give up the desire to justify herself, a desire that dies hard in her. The reconciliation scene begins with Miss Stanbury's eager reception of her niece, but when Dorothy tells her aunt that Brooke is to be with her tomorrow, "the whole colour and character of Miss Stanbury's face was changed in a moment." She turns immediately to interpreting Dorothy's return in the self-punishing yet self-justifying way that has come to be habitual for her: "She, in the fulness of her heart, had written words of affection to Dorothy;—and both Dorothy and Brooke had at once taken advantage of her expressions for their own purposes." Trollope, ever aware of the way people continually story experience, glosses this reaction immediately: "Such was her reading of the story of the day" (682).

The ensuing conversation between Dorothy and her aunt challenges Miss Stanbury's authorial control. After Miss Stanbury declares that Brooke "need not come," Dorothy pleads to be allowed to continue her story: "Aunt Stanbury, you must let me tell it you all." "There is no more to tell, I should think," her aunt responds, unintentionally suggesting the way she has closed her own life story. "But there is more," Dorothy insists and goes on to remind her aunt that she has known of Brooke's love. What follows is an interchange that bears on Trollope's understanding of narrative, his critique of liberal autonomy, and the relation of the ongoing stories of Dorothy and Miss Stanbury to the parable of the prodigal son:

"He is his own master, my dear;—and you are your own mistress."
"If you speak to me like that you will kill me, Aunt Stanbury. I did not think of coming;—only when Martha brought your dear letter I could not help it." (682–683)

Self-mastery, exerting narrative control over one's own existence as if one is outside or above it, amounts to death, for it precludes one's being led beyond oneself in response to others and in acknowledgment of one's own love and need. The prodigal is dead when he seeks to sever the relationship with his father and be his own master; he comes to life again when he returns to the unconditional love and acceptance of his father. No longer is there struggle for mastery, for the very term has no application to a relationship understood as mutual love.

Jemima Stanbury gives up her own struggle for mastery when she comes to Dorothy that night, wakes her niece from sleep, and says to her, in response to the question whether it is morning, "No;—it is not morning. You shall sleep again presently. I have thought of it, and you shall be Brooke's wife, and I will have it here, and we will all be friends" (687). The moment signifies Miss Stanbury's metanoia, her turning about, and in a way that Trollope's framing the whole episode within Jesus' parable has prepared us to see. Miss Stanbury has come to herself by allowing herself to return to a bond of unconditional love and acceptance with Dorothy. One must not underestimate what she has done. She has given up trying to determine the end of her life, given up, in authorial terms, narrative control over the way her story will go. She has given up the attempt to justify herself in the eyes of others and opened herself to precisely the charge she has always feared, that of manipulating her fiancé into leaving her money for her own selfish ends. She has decided to trust instead to what has always seemed most improbable to her: that Dorothy and young Brooke love her, as that earlier Brooke had also, not from any motive of gain, but simply because she is lovable. She accepts herself, consents to others' loving her, and can thus relate to them as free beings capable of making their own choices. One suspects that she will continue to stand over the victuals, but she need no longer be master in relation to Dorothy and Brooke; they can "all," instead, "be friends." As the novel moves toward its conclusion, that "all" becomes increasingly more extensive, including, most significantly for Aunt Stanbury, her previously alienated nephew Hugh.

Jemima Stanbury's experience thus stands in dialogic relationship to Trevelyan's. He continues in self-justification to his dying moment, alienated from nearly all who show concern for him, schizophrenic in his ability to accept embodied life in time. Miss Stanbury makes Kierkegaard's "movement in the place," an act of repentance that signifies the acceptance of justification from without, return to life-in-relationship with others, and a consent to, perhaps even an affirmation of, time and finitude. On one construal, all of Miss Stanbury's effort to ensure Burgess's money would never pass to her family has been a way to deny his death: If I do not accept any of this, she seems to reason, it will be as if Burgess had never died. If I can prove myself sufficiently unlovable, then the whole thing will have been a kind of mistake: Burgess could not have loved me, the money can go back to where it came from, and it will be as if we never existed, the series of stupid quarrels and mistakes never occurred. Allowing the money to pass to Dorothy is tantamount to Jemima's affirming that Burgess has died, that one cannot make a kind of gap or bracket in history, that the money and the love it represents and enables must be passed to others for it to have force. For Jemima has actually been blocking, denying, trying to control from her own narrative point of view, the good that her lover willed to do, the way he wanted his love known in history. She must let Burgess go. However honorable it is to bury the dead, one must turn from continually burying them or one becomes dead oneself. And they, paradoxically, remain dead, for their way of living must be in our own living—or, better yet, in the great narrative that embraces us all—and not in the dying we would do, like Jemima, to prevent ourselves from acknowledging that they have died.

Hauerwas's analysis of forgiveness applies very closely to Jemima Stanbury. He stresses the importance for Christians not only of learning to forgive, which can too often become "a way of exerting control over another," but also of "learn[ing] to be the forgiven." Learning to live as one of the forgiven involves a loss of control, which is why we fear it; it means ultimately "that I must face the fact that my life actually lies in the hand of others" (*PK* 89). Before her metanoia, Jemima, with no sense for irony, proclaims, on the occasion of altering her will after Dorothy's refusal of Mr. Gibson, "I'm not going to have mistakes when I'm gone" (475–476). Her own love and need for Dorothy thwart this attempt to control history, to make things turn out as she would have them, and she must learn to be accepted, to give the ending of her story over into other hands, and to stop attempting to justify her own version of the past. Trollope gives serious consideration to forgiveness throughout *He Knew He Was Right*. Neither Trevelyan nor Emily readily asks the pardon of the other, and each is willing to use the hint of forgiveness to exercise control over the other rather than to heal the relationship. They consistently reject repentance because they pridefully see it as humiliation before the other, who, in assuming the right to forgive, uses the offer of forgiveness to justify his or her own rightness.

Two passages in particular pose the relationship between forgiveness and forgetting. The first occurs soon after Trevelyan has first "cautioned" Emily against Colonel Osborne. As he and Emily walk home from church, his heart is "filled with returning gentleness towards his wife," for "he could not bear to be at wrath with her after the church service which they had just heard together." Trevelyan suggests to her, "Let all this be . . . as though it had never been." Emily's response stresses the impossibility of what he has asked: "That will hardly be possible, Louis . . . I cannot forget that I have been—cautioned" (52–53). Later, in a parallel passage, Jemima Stanbury gives succinct expression to a problem at the heart of accounts of forgetting or forgiveness. Young Brooke urges her to "forget" the malignity directed at her by the Burgesses over his namesake's will. She responds, much as Emily to Trevelyan, "Forget it! How is that to be done?" and then goes on to distinguish between forgetting and forgiving: "How can the mind forget the history of its own life? No,—I cannot forget it. I can forgive it." To what degree Miss Stanbury has forgiven is the subject of the conversation that follows; she argues that she has forgiven, pointing to her nephew's presence with her as evidence, but it is also clear that she has not forgiven entirely because she has not relinquished the desire to impose conditions. She tells Brooke, for instance, "You shall have it all when I'm gone, if you don't turn against me" (329–330).

Forgiving seems possible to Miss Stanbury in a way that forgetting does not, because it allows her mind to retain "the history of its own life." Forgetting would leave a blank or a gap in her narrative, a discontinuity in her life. Forgiveness, on the other hand, seems to involve a double motion: an affirmation that these things have been, that wrongs have been done to one or by one, and yet they will not determine the future. Forgiveness is thus essential to affirming the narrative continuity of the self. It bears a close, yet paradoxical relationship to constancy. If one is in process of learning to be forgiven, this implies some change in course from past actions, past wrongdoing, hence a kind of "inconstancy." But the acceptance of forgiveness allows one constancy of a different sort, for it allows one to honestly own—because one is freed from the need to justify—one's wrongdoings. One of the "chief obstacles" to forgiveness, as Greg Jones has shown, is "the tendency to see one's own life as some-

thing to be either possessed or simply given over to another's possession."[19] Jemima Stanbury's story reveals the way these tendencies depend
on one another: she has attempted to rigidly possess her own life because
she has actually been possessed by her history with the Burgesses. She is
enabled to forgive when she is reconciled with Dorothy, a reconciliation
Trollope sets within the parable of the prodigal son. She reads Dorothy's
return in terms of the parable while the parable reads Miss Stanbury
herself as a returning prodigal. What we see is Miss Stanbury's coming to
herself, her turning about, and her releasing the need to control the
future, which can now take another shape because she no longer needs to
justify a particular version of her past.

Forgiveness is crucial to constancy and the narrative continuity of life
because it enables one to affirm the truth of memory, of evil done and
suffered, without its determining the future. Constancy should not be
confused with absolute self-consistency, which knows no need for forgiveness. *He Knew He Was Right* is particularly effective in showing how an
absolute self-consistency leads to experiencing life essentially as repetition. Trevelyan lives continually under wrath, experiencing over and over
the basic wound to his desire for immortality and trying futilely to prove
himself undeserving of death. To use the common phrase, he is "stuck,"
unable to move in time. Being able to return continually to the source
of forgiveness—God's justification of sinners in Christ—paradoxically
makes movement in time possible. The vertical movement of God's seeking us in Christ must always be thought together with our horizontal
movement through time; we return continually to the source of forgiveness that enables our maintaining the continuity of self through time—a
continuity of self needed, too, to give meaning to sanctification. Only
that ability to "let the past be," and yet, "*as though* it were not," to quote
Trevelyan's request to Emily, can allow us the openness to the future
needed to live beyond ourselves.

Jemima Stanbury makes one observation that might have drawn the
full agreement of Karl Barth. When she first learns that Colonel Osborne
has visited Emily at the Clock House, she proclaims, "I shall begin to
believe that the Evil One has been allowed to come among us in person
because of our sins" (146). Osborne is, as we have seen, one who has
chosen to be nothing in particular but who parades about as a kind of
administrator of his own dignity. He lives in such entire illusion, and with
such little respect for the solidarity of human relationships, that he is able
to persuade himself that his connections to the Rowleys justify actions

that he knows to be destructive of their family. Barth once wrote that the Evil One had himself brought ethics: when the Serpent promised Adam and Eve that they would become as God, he had in mind "the establishment of ethics."[20] Reacting to this seemingly bizarre and counterintuitive claim, Nigel Biggar argues that it is "clear from the context of [Barth's] provocative interpretation of Genesis 3:5 that he uses 'ethics' to refer to the subjective idealist conception of the making of moral judgments as an autarkic process; that is, as a process in which the human subject is absolutely self-determinative."[21] "Absolutely self-determinative" describes rather well both Osborne and his own adversary, Louis Trevelyan, who, as we recall, begins the novel with "all the world before him where to choose." Barth's "theological version of ethical realism" (Biggar 8), including his account of honor, is meant to counter an approach to ethics that would establish it as an autonomous realm of human discourse concerned primarily with the adjudication of rights and claims. Barth's description of the relationship between honor and service to God reflects his deep concern for human solidarity. In service, men

> learn to know and respect one another, not by simply observing or thinking about one another, or even by living with one another, however great their concord or even friendship, in indolence or caprice, self-will or arrogance. So long as it depends on these factors, they can only underestimate or overestimate one another and miss the real honour which they both have, since each can only miss his own honour. Mere companions and comrades cannot appreciate either their own honour or that of the other. The honour of two men is disclosed and will be apparent to both when they meet each other in the knowledge that they are both claimed, not by and for something of their own and therefore incidental and non-essential, but for and by the service which God has laid upon them. (DC 659)

Hauerwas has expressed his "unease" at the "peculiar 'abstractness' to Barth's ethics that gives his account of the moral life an aura of unreality" (*DF* 61). Thus he turns to Trollope for the "kind of concrete account of honor that Barth's method seems to prevent," and asks the pragmatic question of whether a Trollope novel or Barth's account would provide a better introduction "to a young person beginning to think about honor" (*DF* 77). Defending Barth, Biggar grants that the Trollope novel would be "more useful in the moral education of the young" but argues that such education was never the point of Barth's critical work of systematic theological redescription (139). Biggar's defense is well taken, but even he grants some force to Hauerwas's general objection to Barth's abstractness. Hauerwas's best formulation of his reservation occurs when he speaks of how we read Barth; the danger of the abstract account lies in our filling "up the formal analysis with our own categories without knowing how those categories are to be theologically controlled" (*DF* 67). Because honor has traditionally depended on very specific codes, practices, forms, and social arrangements, we tend to pour all kinds of concrete content into Barth's account without examining that content in any significant theological way.

But *He Knew He Was Right* and *The Warden* have given us some very specific content to bring under ethical and theological reflection. *He Knew He Was Right* shows, above all, how meaningless honor becomes for those like Osborne and Trevelyan, who seek always to procure respect for themselves without first respecting others or recognizing that their honor lies in realizing a deeper call to service. Because they miss their own honor, or lack all significant call to anything in particular, they miss the honor of others as well. The questions Barth raises about honor at the end of his account in *The Doctrine of Creation* seem astonishingly pertinent to *He Knew He Was Right*. Consider the following, for instance, as a question directed to Colonel Osborne: "Do you not see how much dishonour is continually done to your fellows, and perhaps not completely without your participation?" Similarly, it would be completely appropriate to ask either Osborne or Trevelyan, "What are you doing to help others to their honour? Are you mobilising the same zeal and deploying the same weapons of irony and anger as if your own honour were at stake?" (*DC* 684). One who does mobilize the weapons of irony and anger is Dr. Grantly of *The Warden*. But I think we might say of him, from within Barth's terms, that he too zealously defends Mr. Harding and the church's honor, thereby revealing that he is not really sure of it. Some of Barth's most specific passages on honor depict the honorable man instead as one rather like Mr. Harding, who accepts being honored by God in simplicity, modesty, and humor: "The modesty about which man is sharply asked . . . consists in the simplicity with which he is quietly and unassumingly pleased to have the honour (no greater and no less) which is really allotted to him. Negatively, therefore, it consists in an absence of the pride in which he would lay hands upon it, proclaim it as his own honour, and like to see it proclaimed as such by others, fighting for it as for himself and meeting any threat upon it as though he himself were threatened. Were he to do this, he would simply demonstrate that he is not sure of it, forfeiting it to his pride and in any case betraying that he has not yet properly recognized or affirmed or grasped it" (*DC* 666). That Mr. Harding has properly recognized and grasped his honor is indicated, paradoxically, by his willingness to relinquish its earthly sign, the wardenship, and rest in the honor God has conferred on him.

Most Christians would, I suspect, agree with Hauerwas that "any people who seek to live worthy lives require an account of honor" and that we now live in "a world that no longer honors honor" (*DF* 60). As worldly honor derives from, or signifies, some particular form of distinction, it will necessarily come under suspicion in an age increasingly dominated by egalitarianism and resentment. As Barth's account of honor would surely, if taken seriously, diminish resentment, perhaps we can reconcile Barth and Hauerwas by suggesting that Barth's account provides the necessary theological context for the more specific accounts of human honor that Hauerwas maintains we need. This would be to perform a kind of Hauerwasian move with Barth's account of honor, for it is one of the permanent contributions of Hauerwas's theological ethics that it reminds us repeatedly of the contexts within which Christian virtues are formed, displayed, and transmitted.

Barth anchors human honor in God's honor. Human beings are honored by God's condescension; their primary problem lies in assenting to be honored. If they could consent to being honored by God, then they would not need to defend their dignity and rights at every turn. Standards of honor could develop within particular practices precisely because no one who knew his or her honor to lie in God's condescension would ever resent the success of another within the practice. Distinction would not inevitably create resentment. Failing a standard of honor could be treated not as resentment-creating evidence that one is less worthy than another, but rather as one's missing one's own telos. Barth's account of honor contains a powerfully antitotalitarian emphasis. Much resentful insistence on dignity and rights today derives, quite understandably, from the bureaucratic state's continual overriding of individual distinctions in the name of social utility. Barth's sense of honor is powerfully antistatist in its insistence that God honors human beings in their unique, irreducible particularity: "God has created every man. He gives him his time and his vocation. He it is who limits him. He wills and supports and rules him in this limitation as He causes him to be only this and not something else, only this person and not another—all through Him and from Him, all according to His good-pleasure, and all to His praise. This is the honour of every man" (DC 651). We cannot decide, on Barth's view, to be, like Colonel Osborne, "nothing at all," because we have already been honored by God in our particularity, as the particular person that each of us is "and not something else." Taking particularity as part of the way they are honored will inevitably lead Barthians to serious critique of bureaucratic utilitarianism. The freedom from resentment, derived from the sense that one has been honored as the person one is, should also lead Barthians into practices with clearly defined standards of honor (ones that could very likely be subject to continual upward revision). Those assenting to being honored by God would see participation in such practices always as ways of ever more deeply realizing their vocations for service rather than as ways to competitively demonstrate their worth. Hauerwas is rightly concerned about Barth's lack of a "conceptual or empirical" description of the communities necessary to sustain a sense of honor. But I suspect that any reconstruction of communities of honor in this day will have to be by people who assent to something like Barth's account and, infinitely more important, to being honored by God.

chapter 5

THE "VERY TEMPLE OF

AUTHORISED LOVE": HENRY JAMES AND

THE PORTRAIT OF A LADY

In *Notes of a Son and Brother,* Henry James remarks the near complete disjunction of sensibility between his Swedenborgian theologian father and himself: "I couldn't have framed stories that would have succeeded in involving the least of the relations that seemed most present to *him,* while those most present to myself, that is more complementary to whatever it was I thought of as humanly most interesting, attaching, inviting, were the ones his schemes of importances seemed virtually to do without."[1] James intriguingly puts his difference from his father in terms of what he could or could not narrate: he could not "frame" narratives (or portraits, perhaps) of the very relations that seemed most present to his father. On the other hand, all those human relations that so engaged James— relations he devoted more than fifty years to embodying in narrative— seemed to have no place in his father's "schemes of importances." We might say that, for James, his father's world appeared nonnarrated or nonnarratable.

Elsewhere in *Notes,* James playfully hedges the matter of his grasp of "Father's Ideas." Through a contrast with William, James claims that his father's speculations were beyond his ability to put into clear formulation: "Of this vast and interesting conception, as striking an expression of the religious spirit surely as ever was put forth, his eldest son has given an account—so far as this was possible at once with brevity and with full comprehension—that I should have been unable even to dream of aspiring to" (164). On the other hand, James writes that his father's philosophic and theological notions so "pervaded and supported" the man's existence that they provided the very atmosphere of the James household. He remarks that he "easily and naturally lived with" his father's ideas and with "the colour and savour they gave to his talk." He "breathed them in and enjoyed both their quickening and their embarrassing presence." Somewhat comically, he figures his father's faith as so many "poured-out cups [standing] about for our either sipping or draining down or leaving alone," and then "freely confess[es]" that "so far as the taking any of it all 'straight' went, my lips rarely adventured." But this rarely taking the cup, James adds, "was doubtless because we drank so largely at the source itself, the personally overflowing and irrigating" (156–157).

William James said of his father's "whole view of things" that its "centre" was an "intense conception of God as a creator. Grant it, accept it without criticism, and the rest follows."[2] The senior James sought to correct what he regarded as the abjectly childish idea of Creation as an event in time and space, insisting that creation be understood instead as *giving being.*[3] "To create a thing," James Sr. argues in *Christianity the Logic of Creation,* "means to give it inward or substantial being; he who creates a thing *himself constitutes the substance of that thing*" (CLC 176). To say that human beings are created is to say that "He who is infinite Love and wisdom constitutes their spiritual and invisible being: that He stands to them in the eternal relation of inward genetic source or object, and they to Him in the eternal relation of outward derivative stream or subject" (CLC 178). "Creating or giving being," in this view, is quite specifically different from making; indeed, it "is an exactly inverse process to that of making or giving form" (CLC 176–177).

The Incarnation is "involved" in Creation for the elder James. Summarizing "the whole problem of creation," he writes: "The natural man (or man in a state of nature simply, without historic experience) is a form of supreme self-love, and thus presents an exactly opposite aspect to the Divine Love which is incapable of selfish regards." In this state of affairs, "creation must remain an eternal possibility unless some middle term can be projected capable of reconciling or fusing these inveterate opposites" (CLC 199–200). Jesus provides this "middle term." He brings "the infinite creative love into perfect harmony with the individual bosom of man." This Jesus is not the unique, particular, itinerant rabbi from Nazareth. Rather, James Sr.'s Jesus "unfalteringly renounc[es] His own sacred writings, in so far as they were literal, personal, and Jewish, and accept[s] them only in their spiritual, universal, or humanitary scope" (CLC 198–200). His idea of the Incarnation introduces a radical split between Jesus' particular humanity and his spiritual role: "In the historic position to which he found himself born, he was exposed on the one side to the unmeasured influx of the Divine Love, and on the other to the equally unmeasured influx of every loathsome and hellish lust of personal aggrandizement. The literal form of Christ's pretension was profoundly diabolic. View his personal pretension as literally true and just, as having an absolute basis, and you can imagine no more flagrant dishonour to the Divine name" (CLC 214). James Sr. does exactly what Hans Urs von Balthasar warns against: he brackets off many supposedly "inessential accidentals at the historical level of [Jesus'] life."[4] Faith in James's Jesus is not centered on a particular person "confessed to be of universal saving significance precisely as a particular person, in his singular, contingent concreteness."[5] Rather, his Jesus is the "middle term" of creation, the one who carries the divine love to the supremely self-loving natural man in order to liberate his essential being as created.

"Society," for the elder James, provides the redeemed form of mankind. God's "becoming actually what He is potentially, or outwardly what He is inwardly, depends entirely upon His being creative and thus having a sphere of actual or outward manifestation put within His grasp." It is God "who is real or inward and essential man" and Who is in the process of "becom[ing] actual or outward and existential man only through His creature."[6] The creature seems little more than the vehicle or vessel through which God loves or realizes Himself. The creature "seems to himself to be a most veridical actual man," but this is "all a seeming." He is only "a mere finite form or image of humanity" and "even as such form or image can only reproduce the human type in so far as he is freely united to his brethren"—which he "selfishly loathes to be." "In truth," then, "God alone is both real, or inward and essential man, and actual, or outward and existential man. In short, He alone is man in substance, and man in form" (SRF 445–446). Clearly, William James was accurate in saying that the "negativity and dearth of the creature" plays "an active and dynamic part" throughout his father's pages. William refers to the "hegelian" quality of his father's depiction of the "creative drama," recalling that "Hegel sometimes speaks of the Divinity making an illusion first, in order to remove it; setting up his own antithesis in order to the subsequent neutralization thereof."[7] Particular human beings do seem to be illusions or mere negatives for the elder James. God is in the process of loving Himself by realizing Himself through creatures, who are to recognize that they are not unique identities or individualities but "form[s] or image[s] of humanity" whose redemption lies in the race's becoming "fused within itself—that is, so constituted in felt or conscious unity with itself—as to form a perfect society, brotherhood, or fellowship of its particular and universal elements" (*SRF* 446, 449).

I have presented the theology of Henry James Sr. at some length because I wish to suggest a way of reading *The Portrait of a Lady* in response to it. One can see how Henry Jr. would have sensed the exclusion of the rich drama of human relations from his father's "schemes of importances." In the elder James's theology, the human being's purpose is to be entirely transformed, to be negated entirely as a being other than God and "cre-ated" as what one essentially is: God Himself, now living in perfect social fellowship. One can see why James Jr. would find it difficult to narrate the relations most present to his father, for the creation conceived by the elder James requires no temporal process. The gradual transformation of a being other than God into one more godly would require time and narrative display. The liberation of the real substance of a being, itself God, from within the shadowy nonreality of its existence requires no more than a moment.

Although the elder James identifies redemption with fusion into a per-fect society rather than with possession of a special saving knowledge, his theology seems otherwise Gnostic. He emphasizes what Harold Bloom has identified as a feature of the widespread Gnosticism of the "American Religion": a drive in the individual toward unity with the uncreated, with spirit that antedates Creation.[8] This may seem strange to say of a theolo-gian who so emphasized Creation, but it is not. For the elder James's theology of Creation is quite antithetical to an orthodox understanding of Creation or the creature. James's God does not "make" something other than himself; rather, he is "real or inward and essential man." The ortho-dox sense of the creature's contingency and dependence is entirely lost. Indeed, James describes "God's true creature" as "bound above all things to exhibit that power of self-derived or spontaneous action which con-stitutes our idea of the divine personality."[9] James simply calls "creation" that process by which what is already God returns to Himself in a form of divinized human society. What Bloom says of Jesus' role in the American Gnostic religion describes his role in the elder James's theology with extraordinary precision. God or Jesus "will find the spirit" in the American Gnostic "because there is something in the spirit that already is God or Jesus" (32).

Bloom has made an important claim: that the American religion is a post-Christian Gnosticism that "masks itself as Protestant Christianity yet has ceased to be Christian" (32). If he is right, even in small measure, it behooves us to understand the work of American theologians of Gnostic tendency like Henry James Sr. Giles Gunn has called James Sr. an "American original" and related his theology to the religious convictions of progressivism as defined by Daniel Aaron: that Christ should be understood "as a symbol of humanity itself"; that human beings are saved or damned collectively; that they enter "into communion with God when they shed their selfish personalities and unite with one another in a confederation of love"; and that the "social good" can be attained only "through the organized clemency of man to man."[10] Aaron's polarization of selfish personality and loving unity mirrors the elder James's way of setting "the natural man," characterized by "supreme self-love," over against "the Divine Love which is incapable of selfish regards" (CLC 199– 200). James's theology represents an extreme example of the polarizing of nature and grace, a post-Reformation development whose worst theological consequence has been the tendency, evident in James, to isolate nature as a realm entirely apart and wholly intelligible in itself. "Nature," for James, is not theological shorthand for "human beings in their contingent historical complexity, always already caught up in a drama whose real resolution" is grace.[11] Rather, James's "man in a state of nature" is "without historic experience" (CLC 199–200): he is outside history, outside narratability, outside contingency.

James's theologizing about an independent "Nature" results in two critical differences from a Trinitarian account of Creation and creatures. First, because Nature seemingly precedes Creation, it is, at once, apparently intelligible in itself and entirely to be escaped (through Gnostic liberation of the real self within the shadow self).[12] The Trinitarian account insists that Creation is partially, though not exhaustively, intelligible precisely because it is Creation permeated by the Logos. Creation is certainly not to be escaped, for it is the realm within which the contingent creature moves toward fulfillment. Second, James's idea of Creation leaves out the otherness of creatures, their difference from God. What seems "other" in human beings is defined as unreal: God Himself is "man in substance, and man in form." The God of the Trinity, however, according to David Harned, "wills what is other and distinct from himself, not merely a replication or reflection or shadow of his own reality. He does not repeat himself in some radically diminished mode, but summons into existence creatures who are entirely different."[13] The nature of God's love lies in willing into existence, taking delight in, and deciding for that which is other than Himself. He is not simply realizing Himself through a set of replicable forms destined for redemption in some form of divinized humanity. As David Yeago puts it, "The doctrine of creation . . . celebrates our otherness from God as proceeding from God's own will and goodness. It is the high mystery of God's creative love that he wills and loves the being of creatures who are entirely different from himself." The doctrine of the Trinity, with its insistence that the Father exists in the giving of Himself to the Son, means that "there is, from all eternity, otherness in the life of God."[14] God creates, from sheer generosity and love, beings other than Himself. It is the nature of love to reaffirm that goodness originally spoken by God in the Creation. Love, as Josef Pieper has put it, takes the form of the affirmation, "It is good that you exist."[15] Love modeled on the divine love affirms the goodness of the other.

The God of Henry James Sr. is a loveless God who does not will into existence creatures other than himself. We might say about Him what the Countess Gemini says about her brother, Gilbert Osmond: "He can't love any one."[16] Part of what the Countess means has been recognized by Isabel Archer in the great vision scene that James Jr. regarded as "obviously the best thing in the book."[17] Her "real offence" to Osmond, Isabel "ultimately perceived, was her having a mind of her own at all. Her mind was to be his—attached to his own like a small garden-plot to a deer-park" (2:200). Isabel's very existence, her being as an other, is, to Osmond, an evil, the source of the hatred for her that becomes "the occupation and comfort of his life" (2:201). What I contend is that Gilbert Osmond should be read as the very antithesis of the Trinitarian love, love that includes otherness within itself from all eternity. Rather, he represents something very like the God of Henry James Sr., one for whom creatures are not truly "other" but only vessels or material through which He realizes himself. I wish to leave moot the question of whether *Portrait* is specifically intended as a criticism of the elder James's theology. We have seen how James Jr. disclaims much conceptual understanding of his father's ideas while also affirming that they provided the atmosphere in which he grew up. It seems reasonable to suggest, then, that *Portrait* is his attempt to "frame" a response to those ideas by showing how they play out in Osmond.[18] To the extent that Henry Sr.'s theology retained some orthodox sense that Creation was dependent on a ground of being outside itself, the novel could be said to reflect a positive appropriation of his ideas. For *Portrait* offers a rich sense of the doctrine of Creation's importance in human lives and compelling insight into the consequences of its absence or rejection. But the son's theology, whether he understood it to be so or not, is more orthodox and Trinitarian than the father's. *Portrait* points, in many ways, to the rightness of Trinitarian love.

Henry James links Osmond's inability to love to three specific vices: envy, a distorted eros, and a curiosity akin to that censured by Augustine as "ocular desire." Although not a romantic possibility for Isabel, Ralph Touchett provides an alternative to Osmond's lovelessness. His generosity, even at the point of death, affirms the goodness of Isabel's existence in a way that enables her to retrieve her earliest convictions about the world's created goodness. Unfortunately, Isabel has preferred Osmond's "disinterested" presentation of himself as a suitor, ignoring Ralph's reservations about the marriage on the grounds that he is not "disinterested." Isabel marries in a curiously disinterested fashion, an act James places at the center of the novel's extended interrogation of the notion of "disinterestedness." Liberal notions of disinterest tend to foster a split between "good reasons" on the one hand, and "love" on the other, a split reflected by Isabel's remark to Lord Warburton: "Love has nothing to do with good reasons" (2:220). "Good reasons" presumably can be offered by anyone to anyone, whereas "love" names precisely that emotion devoted by and to unique particularities. The whole of *Portrait*, however, suggests a different relationship between "love" and "good reasons" than Isabel describes. If love leads to patterns of reciprocity and mutuality in which human beings can be more "for" one another than they can be alone, then one would have good reasons to love. In her work on ethics and literature, Martha Nussbaum emphasizes the tension between love and the moral point of view. I offer a brief engagement here with Nussbaum's work on Henry James, one that focuses especially on the tension between her point of view as a philosophical ethicist and a Jamesian understanding of point of view. "The whole of anything is never told," James wrote, in defending the notoriously unresolved ending of *Portrait*.[19] His statement should be read, I believe, as a moral one reflecting insights carried for Christians by a Trinitarian understanding of Creation and the creature: that Creation is intelligible but not exhaustible in its meaning; that creatures point to a fulfillment beyond themselves, yet anticipated now in patience, courage, and hope; and that the kind of resolution possible for the novelist dealing with figures of finite freedom is a dramatic one. Finally, I suggest that the openness of James's "portrait"—a form never entirely detachable from the person who is its subject—may derive from the novel's relation to James's loss of his cousin Minny Temple.

We have seen how Isabel recognizes that her real "offence," for Osmond, was "her having a mind of her own at all" (2:200). This insight represents perhaps her clearest recognition of Osmond's inability to will and love the being of one entirely different from himself. Another name for this inability is envy, Osmond's most significant vice, noted by Isabel in a scene at the opera as the two discuss Lord Warburton:

> "How detestably fortunate!—to be a great English magnate, to be clever and handsome into the bargain, and, by way of finishing off, to enjoy your high favour! That's a man I could envy."
>
> Isabel considered him with interest. "You seem to me to be always envying some one. Yesterday it was the Pope; to-day it's poor Lord Warburton."
>
> "My envy's not dangerous; it would n't hurt a mouse. I don't want to destroy the people—I only want to *be* them. You see it would destroy only myself." (2:5–6)

The distinction at the end of Osmond's comment here seems suspect: Can one become or be another without destroying the other? Envy here, although masked by Osmond's false humility, seems aimed at the very being of others.

James's treatment of envy resembles that of Kant, who gave his attention to the vice in several works. Distinguishing among jealousy, envy, and grudge in one lecture, Kant found the distinctive quality of envy to lie in the envious person's desire to be the only one happy. Grudge consists "in wishing to be more happy than others," Kant writes, but envy wishes "to be the only one to be happy." The envious man "is not happy unless all around him are unhappy; his aim is to stand alone in the enjoyment of his happiness."[20] The envious man's desire to be "the only one," to "stand alone," suggests why Kant judged envy to be "satanic" and "devilish." James similarly suggests that there is something "satanic" about Osmond, most particularly through a description of Isabel's from her vigil: "He took himself so seriously; it was something appalling. Under all his culture, his cleverness, his amenity, under his good-nature, his facility, his knowledge of life, his egotism lay hidden like a serpent in a bank of flowers" (2:196).

Particularly relevant to James is Kant's insight into the way envy functions to protect one from any need to be transformed, hence from the passage of time: "To be envious is to desire the failure and unhappiness of another," Kant writes, "not for the purpose of advancing our own success and happiness but because we might then ourselves be perfect and happy as we are" (*JEG* 217). It would be difficult to better characterize Osmond's basic strategy of life. He has renounced any possibility of success or happiness in terms understood by the world, preferring to seem perfect above the fray. He "envie[s] the Pope of Rome—for the consideration he enjoys" (1:382). The strategy Osmond and Madame Merle adopt to reinforce their superiority is precisely that Kant condemns: endless comparison to others. For Kant, envy involves systematic lying or self-deception supported by comparison to others rather than to an absolute standard. The dynamic of envy involves "a reluctance to see our own well-being overshadowed by another's because the standard we use to see how well off we are is not the intrinsic worth of our own well-being but how it compares with others."[21] "The Idea of perfection is a proper standard" for us, because "if we measure our worth by it, we find that we fall short of it and feel that we must exert ourselves to come nearer to it." We generally reject comparison to an Idea of perfection, however, preferring instead to leave our self-worth intact by using comparison to "arrive at a result favourable to [our]selves" (*JEG* 215).

Comparing themselves to others serves as the religion of Osmond and Madame Merle. Ralph speaks of Osmond's too exclusive insistence on "taste" as he warns Isabel against her husband-to-be: "He judges and measures, approves and condemns, altogether by that." Isabel defends Osmond by arguing that his taste is "exquisite," but Ralph maintains that such exclusive devotion to the life of comparative judgment, measurement, and criticism leaves Osmond a "sterile dilettante" (2:71). Osmond himself outlines the "right" kind of methodology for evaluation in a conversation with Madame Merle. When she remarks that "Society is all bad," Osmond responds: "Pardon me. That is n't—the knowledge I impute to you—a common sort of wisdom. You've gained it in the right way—experimentally; you've compared an immense number of more or less impossible people with each other" (1:343). Especially interesting, in Kantian terms, is the way Madame Merle, later in the scene, specifically eschews any notion of a telos or intrinsic worth for human beings. Sensing that she has something in mind for Miss Archer, Osmond inquires of Madame Merle: "What do you want to do with her?" Her response heightens the suggestion of Isabel's being a thing at their disposal: "What you see. Put her in your way." When Osmond asks whether Isabel is not "meant for something better than that," Madame Merle links the refusal to speculate about ends with an instrumental approach to others: " 'I don't pretend to know what people are meant for,' said Madame Merle. 'I only know what I can do with them'" (1:345). In Kantian terms, the scene brings together two related attitudes: devotion to endless comparative valuation and the tendency to regard others as means, of no intrinsic worth, rather than ends in themselves.

Madame Merle employs comparative judgment as a strategy of aggression, a truth the young Isabel blunders on without knowing it. When she is first "dazzled" by Madame Merle at Gardencourt, Isabel finds herself knowing, but "for reasons she could not have defined," that her American journalist friend, Henrietta Stackpole, "would not at all subscribe to Madame Merle." But Madame Merle would know how to estimate Henrietta, for "she appeared to have in her experience a touchstone for everything, and somewhere in the capacious pocket of her genial memory she would find the key to Henrietta's value." The conclusion Isabel naïvely draws from her observation applies brilliantly to Madame Merle, even though Isabel lacks any sense of its darker implications: " 'That's the great thing,' Isabel solemnly pondered; 'that's the supreme good fortune: to be in a better position for appreciating people than they are for appreciating you.' And she added that such, when one considered it, was simply the essence of the aristocratic situation. In this light, if in none other, one should aim at the aristocratic situation" (1:271).

"Appreciation" here, in reference to Madame Merle, loses its fullness as an expression of admiration, of attention directed to one superior to oneself in some regard; instead, it suggests the aggressive action of "placing" another person, of valuing another and estimating the degree of attention he or she deserves before the other can do that to oneself. Turning life into endlessly comparative appreciation paradoxically creates the other-directed self, as Isabel recognizes about Osmond, who, despite his contempt for others, is utterly dependent on them for his sense of himself. His view of himself "as the first gentleman in Europe"

> implied a sovereign contempt for every one but some three or four very exalted people whom he envied, and for everything in the world but half a dozen ideas of his own. That was very well; she would have gone with him even there a long distance; for he pointed out to her so much of the baseness and shabbiness of life . . . But this base, ignoble world, it appeared, was after all what one was to live for; one was to keep it for ever in one's eye, in order not to enlighten or convert or redeem it, but to extract from it some recognition of one's own superiority. On the one hand it was despicable, but on the other it afforded a standard . . .

indifference was really the last of his qualities; she had never seen any one who thought so much of others. (2:197)

James comes close to Kant in two points about envy: the link between envy and the desire to be "first," distinguished from all others, and the use of comparative evaluation to reflect one's sense of superiority. What James depicts in Osmond is a narcissistic circuit where others are used as a mirror to reflect the self to itself.

The nearest Osmond approaches to comparing himself to a perfect standard occurs in St. Peter's, when Isabel asks his "opinion" of the great cathedral. "It's too large; it makes one feel like an atom," he responds. When Isabel suggests that this is the way one ought to feel "in the greatest of human temples," Osmond responds, "I suppose it's the right way to feel everywhere, when one *is* nobody. But I like it in a church as little as anywhere else." James exploits the irony here to suggest the way Osmond masks supreme arrogance in supreme humility. Does he mean it's the right way to feel, and he himself is nobody? Or does he mean it's the right way to feel for a world full of nobodies but not for that one who is different, himself? Isabel's response, with its recognition of his drive for singular distinction, is more accurate than she realizes: "You ought indeed to be a Pope!" She is "remembering something he had referred to in Florence" (1:427): his envying the Pope for the "consideration he enjoys" (1:382). Even here we see the degree to which Osmond's is a life played for others: he would be Pope not for any intrinsic quality in the man or power of doing good—or even, apparently, for infallibility on matters of faith and morals—but because the "consideration" of others would reflect his holiness to him.

Reading Kant's and James's treatments of envy together opens one further insight into Osmond, specifically, into his collecting. Kant suggests that the envious person succeeds in persuading himself that he is perfect as he is, that he need not change or be transformed. Envy involves a resistance to time, to finitude. James makes the connection between envy and resistance to time explicit when Isabel returns to Gardencourt to see the dying Ralph. As she strolls through the picture gallery, she finds that she "envied the security of valuable 'pieces' which change by no hair's breadth, only grow in value, while their owners lose inch by inch youth, happiness, beauty" (2:403). James indirectly comments here on the motivation for Osmond's collecting, his surrounding himself with a museum of beautiful "pieces," with Isabel the crowning acquisition. The passion for collecting is another manifestation of envy. The envy that seeks security by diminishing all others as a way of self-confirmation seeks also to surround itself with valuable pieces, unappreciated by the "vulgar"—one of Osmond's favorite phrases—and impervious to time.

If we accept Ernest Becker's definition of eros as the desire "to stand out as something different and apart" from creation,[22] then it is possible to see the erotic quality of Osmond's envy in his desire to be "the first gentleman of Europe," the one distinguished from all others. Osmond's scenes with Madame Merle are redolent with distorted eroticism suggested by James through motifs involving knowledge and possession. The scene in which Madame Merle first proposes to put Isabel in Osmond's way resonates with a sense that the two conspirators know one another in a way that is simultaneously unpleasant and empowering. Rather than forgetting themselves in the presence of one another, Madame Merle and Osmond seem only "to intensify to an appreciable degree the self-consciousness of the other" (1:346). James emphasizes the narcissistic tendencies of both to refer everything, in a mirroring way, to themselves. In this instance, Madame Merle, ordinarily so flawless in performance, fails to cover her embarrassment entirely: she "had not on this occasion the form she would have liked to have—the perfect self-possession she would have wished to wear for her host." Nevertheless, James notes, with heavy intimation of the pair's previous relationship: "At a certain moment the element between them, whatever it was, always leveled itself and left them more closely face to face than either ever was with any one else. This was what had happened now. They stood there knowing each other well and each on the whole willing to accept the satisfaction of knowing as a compensation for the inconvenience—whatever it might be—of being known" (1:346). Being known seems a matter of profound fear, to be compensated only by the power involved in knowing the other. The passage echoes what Isabel earlier thinks she has learned from Madame Merle: that "supreme good fortune" consists in being "in a better position for appreciating people than they are for appreciating you" (1:271). Just as "appreciation" seems a matter of competitive valuation, of learning to place people better than they can place one, so, too, knowledge for Osmond and Madame Merle involves competition and control, knowing others better than one allows oneself to be known. Thus "knowing," with its sexual suggestion, becomes closely related to possession. The game, to recur to Madame Merle's language, is to be in "perfect self-possession" so as not to be vulnerable to possession by the other. In either case, one becomes a thing, at one's own disposal or another's. What seems impossible is a relationship of mutuality in which one's knowing another includes, within it, a knowledge of the other's otherness.

If desire is for "possession" of the other, it seems reasonable to ask whether what one desires is truly an "other" or oneself. Osmond actually desires himself, mirrored by others. He enjoys titillating the curiosity of others, only to deflect their efforts to know him—a habit recognized by Ralph: "[Osmond's] tastes, his studies, his accomplishments, his collections, were all for a purpose. His life on his hill-top at Florence had been the conscious attitude of years. His solitude, his ennui, his love for his daughter, his good manners, his bad manners, were so many features of a mental image constantly present to him as a model of impertinence and mystification. His ambition was not to please the world, but to please himself by exciting the world's curiosity and then declining to satisfy it. It had made him feel great, ever, to play the world a trick" (2:145). James makes clear the narcissistic loop of curiosity: Osmond, the seeker of curiosities, enjoys exciting the curiosity of others only to deny their satisfaction. Because he cannot actually have himself, he engages in endlessly stimulating a desire whose fulfillment is endlessly deferred. Curiosity plays over surfaces, and Osmond becomes an elegant provider of ever-shifting surfaces. The reward is power, exercised in playing the world the trick of reflecting him to himself.

James's treatment of curiosity in *Portrait* recalls Augustine's discussion of the vice in Book 10 of *The Confessions*.[23] Augustine understood curiosity as "ocular desire," or concupiscence of the eyes. His "central concern," Gilbert Meilaender argues, focuses on "curiosity as 'the empty desire to possess.'"[24] The eyes seem implicated, for Augustine, in a dialectic of possession: on the one hand, things can take possession of the soul; on the other, the desire to see and to know can itself become an act of taking possession. The only freedom from this dialectic lies in being possessed by God: "The eyes delight in beautiful shapes of different sorts and bright and attractive colours. I would not have these things take possession of my soul. Let God possess it, he who made them all. He made them all very good, but it is he who is my Good, not they."[25] Especially noteworthy here is the emphasis on the goodness of Creation, which is good precisely as Creation, that is, insofar as it has been "made" by the Creator, who is the source of its good. Remembering that creatures are always good in their createdness, in their relation to the Creator, means that they can never be fully possessed, never fully known or exhausted in their depth and richness. Augustine's examples of unhealthy curiosity are very instructive. He notes the tendency of people to be drawn to "the sight of a mangled corpse, which can only horrify," and he remarks similarly curiosity's attraction to "freaks and prodigies [who] are put on show in the theatre" (242). In both cases, satisfaction of fantasy seems more important than the desire for any real knowledge of the object. For Augustine, curiosity seems to connote a kind of narcissism, a look that seeks to discover something about itself—how the self is like/unlike the freak— rather than anything truly about the object.

Gilbert Osmond's evil is in his eye, in his watching others to see himself. In Isabel, Ralph remarks, Osmond "at last . . . had material to work with. He always had an eye to effect, and his effects were deeply calculated." Osmond "lived with his eye on [the world] from morning till night, and the world was so stupid it never suspected the trick" (2:144). During the vision scene, Isabel recognizes that Osmond "spoil[ed] every-thing for her that he looked at"; "it was as if he had the evil eye" (2:188). She sees that, for him, the great thing is ever to keep the world "in one's eye" in order to "extract from it some recognition of one's own superi-ority" (2:197). The perversion of the mind's orientation toward knowl-edge and the light is evident in the imagery of darkness with which James continually surrounds Osmond. Osmond's "rigid system close[s] about" Isabel, a "sense of darkness and suffocation [taking] possession of her" (2:199). Osmond tells Goodwood that he and his wife are "as united, you know, as the candlestick and the snuffers" (2:309). Osmond seeks to put out Isabel's lights, one by one. His deeds, and those of Madame Merle, must remain masked, veiled, for they cannot come to the light. Slowly Isabel comes to understand the way she has been used by Madame Merle and Osmond. A key moment involves her sense that Madame Merle's request about Lord Warburton ("Let him off—let us have him!") betrays an inappropriate degree of collusion with Osmond and an unaccountable degree of interest in Pansy's marriage. When it "come[s] over" Isabel "like a high-surging wave" that Madame Merle had married her, she looks to her companion for enlightenment. Isabel's face "was almost a prayer to be enlightened," but Madame Merle's mask is intact: "The light of this woman's eyes seemed only a darkness" (2:326–327). James's phrase beau-tifully contrasts Madame Merle's ocular desire with two traditional ways of figuring the eyes. Her eyes are neither oriented toward reality as light, nor are they windows to her soul; rather, they are the self-darkened instruments by which she manipulates others, denying them access to the self she has carefully shrouded in response to previous losses and defense against the further wounding of being known.

Osmond and Madame Merle reject creaturely life with others regarded as partially knowable but ultimately inexhaustible because of their created depth. They present themselves as perfect objects for the appreciation of others while regarding others as objects of their own designs. James stresses these objectifying habits through a strong pattern of language emphasizing finishing, completion, perfection, and possession. Madame Merle remarks that Osmond's "rooms at least are perfect," a judgment she's again reached by comparative evaluation: "I know none better anywhere. You understand this sort of thing as nobody anywhere does. You've such adorable taste" (1:348). Adding to Osmond's perfections is his little daughter, Pansy, introduced by the nuns from the convent school with the remark, "She's perfect. She has no faults" (1:332). When Osmond first displays his things to Isabel, she senses that Pansy forms part of the design: "Even Mr. Osmond's diminutive daughter had a kind of finish that was not entirely artless" (1:367). Later, Isabel is impressed by Osmond's artistic or "plastic view" of Pansy's innocence (2:84), as if that innocence were a resource to be molded into a fine object. Osmond's success in his project is noted by his fellow connoisseur, Edmund Rosier, who devoted his time "in vain to finding a flaw in Pansy Osmond's composition. She was admirably finished; she had had the last touch; she was really a consummate piece" (2:90). The sinister feel of James's language here lies in the deathlike suggestions of finishing, consummation, flawlessness; these are not the qualities of a real and living creature but those of an inanimate object. In an even more sinister figure, James likens Pansy to a blank page either to be filled with text by Osmond or stamped with his imperial image. Pansy was "like a sheet of blank paper—the ideal *jeune fille* of foreign fiction," Isabel reflects, hoping "that so fair and smooth a page would be covered with an edifying text" (1:401). When she goes, at Osmond's request, to visit Pansy in Florence, Isabel sees the girl as "really a blank page, a pure white surface, successfully kept so." At this point, Isabel is unaware of what threatens Pansy, but she sees that the girl will have little power to resist: "She would have no will, no power to resist, no sense of her own importance; she would easily be mystified, easily crushed" (2:27). Pansy is already "mystified," a fact we, like Isabel, do not understand until much later. She says to Isabel, innocently, of her father, "If he were not my papa I should like to marry him; I would rather be his daughter than the wife of—of some strange person" (2:28). The disquietingly incestuous suggestion here seems consistent with James's depiction of Osmond. He has been loving himself through his daughter, creating in her a desire for him, finishing her as a piece that will reflect his own glory to himself.

Osmond closely resembles the "Perfect Man" described by Henry James Sr. in *Moralism and Christianity*. James Sr. begins with several "fundamental axiom[s]" about Creation, each at odds with the Trinitarian conception of creatures as beings other than God and loved in their otherness. "The creature of God" has "no being or substance in himself," asserts James; "the substantial being or life of every creature is God." "The creature is but a form or image of God"; "the creature is not another being than God" (MC 124). Creatureliness does not mean, then, that the human being is always in a condition of response and is to act in all things as if in response to God.[26] Rather, the perfect man, the creature, acts in an entirely spontaneous way, as a self-caused, self-originating source of his own being: "God's true creature or image is bound above all things to exhibit that power of self-derived or spontaneous action which constitutes our idea of the divine personality" (MC 126). The lecture abounds in similar formulations: "personality impl[ies] the power of self-derived or spontaneous action"; personality "affirms . . . the subject's entire sufficiency unto himself"; personality "attest[s] the subject's self-sufficiency or perfection by exhibiting in him the power of self-derived action" (MC 127–129). Insisting so radically on the creature's self-sufficiency means that he will experience his natural, civil, or moral life with others as alienation. Moral life becomes unlimited heteronomy, for "moral life displays me in subjection not to God, but to society or my fellow-man, and thus equally with nature denies me proper personality" (MC 129). Even benevolence cannot confer personality because it originates outside the subject in the sufferings of those with whom the benevolent man sympathizes.

"Who, then, is the perfect or divine man?" James Sr. asks. "We find him in the aesthetic man, or Artist" (MC 130). This person is not to be confused with any specific poet, painter, musician, or artisan, whose work is alienated by its arising from necessities outside himself. Indeed, in language suggestive of Osmond, James Sr. asserts that "this man may indeed have no technical vocation whatever" (MC 131). The Artist is not marked by any specific skill or craft but by the principle of his action, which "obeys his own internal taste or attraction, uncontrolled either by necessity or duty" (MC 130). The Artist is a priest of taste, a "law unto himself," "who in every visible form of action acts always from his inmost self," bringing an "exquisite" attention to beauty to all the details of life. He is the "only adequate image of God" because "he alone acts of himself, or finds the object of his action always within his own subjectivity" (MC 133). This last statement provides the appropriate context, I would argue, for an especially curious remark of Osmond's to Isabel: "The events of my life have been absolutely unperceived by any one save myself; getting an old silver crucifix at a bargain (I've never bought anything dear, of course), or discovering, as I once did, a sketch by Correggio on a panel daubed over by some inspired idiot" (1:382). The "events of my life" here seem to be only those known by my own subjectivity: all else, anything perceived by an other, is not "my life." The point might seem at odds with Osmond's other-directedness, which we saw earlier. But actually it is not. Osmond's radical subjectivity fears alienation, fears falling into the world; therefore, he must stimulate the world's curiosity about him but continually deny its satisfaction. He is dependent on the world's attention to reconfirm his difference from it, his existence as a subject.

James Sr.'s understanding of the "perfect life" of art leads to a gendering of the elements in action that his son reproduces in Portrait. The "spontaneous production" of art involves a "certain generative or paternal end" realized "through a certain formative or maternal means."[27] Similar language occurs in Christianity the Logic of Creation, where James Sr. polarizes God and nature, inward generative principle and experiential ground, as male and female. "The sensible world" is a "realm of shadow, not of substance; of seeming, not of being": "Nature is a purely experimental world, and experience is a first-rate mother, but a most incompetent father." Divine Creation involves a kind of "procreative action" in which "the father is generative, the mother simply prolific or productive: the former gives life or soul, the latter existence or body: the one is creative, the other formative" (CLC 183–184). Here are the terms of Osmond's relationship to Pansy: he, creative, she, merely the form or body molded to the form he desires. She is a blank page to be filled by Osmond's text or image, a metaphor James reintroduces in the bitter scene between Osmond and Isabel that precedes her leaving for Ralph and Gardencourt. Entering Osmond's room, Isabel finds him copying a drawing from a folio propped before him: "This volume was open at a page of small coloured plates, and Isabel presently saw that he had been copying from it the drawing of an antique coin. A box of water-colours and fine brushes lay before him, and he had already transferred to a sheet of immaculate paper the delicate, finely-tinted disk" (2:352). The image perfectly suggests the paternal "generative" action associated with the divine Creation by James Sr. The creation is "sterile," however, as Ralph remarks of Osmond's dilettantism. Osmond can do no more than copy an antique form. As we have been well prepared to associate Pansy with that "sheet of immaculate paper," we see here what she is ultimately to be for him: the means to a certain quantity of coin of the realm, the means by which he will acquire a certain number of replicated images reflecting his glory to himself. Like the loveless God of James Sr., Osmond takes no delight in what is other than himself; Pansy is merely vehicle, medium, or body through which he loves himself.

The alternative to Osmond in *Portrait* is Ralph Touchett, who expresses ultimately a love for Isabel that affirms the goodness of her existence. Ralph's love takes the form of love as Pieper defines it; he expresses to Isabel directly the truth carried in the Trinitarian love: "It is good that you exist." His love is directly opposed to the hatred Osmond conceives for her, hatred directed at her very being. Yet Ralph's difference from Osmond is not always clear in the novel. Recognition of their difference is a hard-won insight on Isabel's part. Ralph's detachment from life, his rumored love of Madame Merle, and his vicarious living through Isabel all have parallels in Osmond. Madame Merle compares the men to Isabel in the text's first mention of Osmond. She begins with a sardonic description of Ralph, who, in her view, has relied on his illness for an identity and self-justification: "Look at poor Ralph Touchett: what sort of a figure do you call that? Fortunately he has a consumption; I say fortunately, because it gives him something to do. His consumption's his *carriere*; it's a kind of position. You can say: 'Oh, Mr. Touchett, he takes care of his lungs, he knows a great deal about climates.' But without that who would he be, what would he represent?" (1:280). Important to note is the identification by Madame Merle of being and representation, an identification reinforced by her contrast of Ralph with his father: "With the poor old father it's different; he has his identity, and it's rather a massive one. He represents a great financial house, and that, in our day, is as good as anything else." From her description of Ralph's ennui, his inability to do anything, Madame Merle moves to a comparison with Osmond: "The worst case, I think, is a friend of mine, a countryman of ours, who lives in Italy (where he also was brought before he knew better), and who is one of the most delightful men I know. Some day you must know him. I'll bring you together and then you'll see what I mean. He's Gilbert

Osmond—he lives in Italy; that's all one can say about him or make of him" (1:281).

How to distinguish Ralph from Osmond is an important question of *Portrait*, made additionally problematic by suggestions of Ralph's vicarious participation in Isabel's life. His father, Daniel Touchett, raises ethical concerns about Ralph's gift to Isabel when the two men renegotiate the elder's will. Daniel would like to see Ralph marry Isabel; his son's idea of putting "wind in her sails" and then watching her go makes Ralph "very different" from what Daniel was as a young man: "When I cared for a girl—when I was young—I wanted to do more than look at her. You've scruples that I should n't have had, and you've ideas that I should n't have had either" (1:262–263). Some of those ideas seem downright bad to Mr. Touchett. He doubts whether it's good to make things "so easy for a person" (1:264), observes that Ralph speaks as if the proposal to enrich Isabel "were for [his] mere amusement" (1:262), and objects that Isabel may fall victim to a fortune hunter rather than being freed by the gift. Ralph's imaginative appropriation of Isabel's life is suggested by his response to this last objection of his father's: "That's a risk, and it has entered into my calculation. I think it's appreciable, but I think it's small, and I'm prepared to take it" (1:265). One is tempted to observe that taking risks with one's own life is one thing, taking them with the lives of others, quite another—and that Ralph has not adequately weighed the difference. When Ralph urges her to "take things more easily," to question her conscience less, and to let her character form without so much active shaping, Isabel asks whether he has thought about the responsibility that comes with intervention in the life of another, though she, of course, does not know of his role in providing her inheritance: "I wonder if you appreciate what you say. If you do, you take a great responsibility" (1:319).

A classically liberal way to defend actions that intervene in the life of another is to argue that these are "disinterested," done without regard for the good of the agent. James seems to have ruled off this defense in Ralph's case from the first. Ralph seeks to empower Isabel, to "put wind in her sails," yet he is undeniably seeking imaginative satisfaction of his own in watching her course. Ralph will never be in a position to take up the "logic" with which Lambert Strether famously justifies himself at the end of *The Ambassadors*: "Not, out of the whole affair, to have got anything for myself."[28] From the moment of his father's revising his will, Ralph has begun to get pleasure from his speculations about Isabel's future.

James does, however, interrogate the word "disinterested" throughout the novel. Indeed, it is Osmond who presents himself in a curiously disinterested manner in his courtship of Isabel. He makes no strong case for his abilities, his interests, his passions or desires, but stresses the things he has not done. It is his supreme genius to recognize that Isabel will be moved by the opportunity to admire what he describes as "my studied, my wilful renunciation" (1:381). He pitches his announcement of love "in a tone of almost impersonal discretion, like a man who expected very little from it but who spoke for his own needed relief." His superb strategy is to "offer nothing," thus allowing Isabel maximum freedom to exercise her generous imagination while seeming to make no claims upon her: "I've neither fortune, nor fame, nor extrinsic advantages of any kind. So I offer nothing. I only tell you because I think it can't offend you, and some day or other it may give you pleasure" (2:18–19).

It seems odd to marry a person who offers one nothing. To do so would seem to marry out of Strether's logic, to get nothing for oneself. Such a marriage seems an act of perfect self-sacrifice or pure disinterestedness. Mrs. Touchett understands Isabel's motivation in just this way, as in the following warning to Ralph: "She wants to be disinterested: as if she were the only person who's in danger of not being so! Will *he* be so disinterested when he has the spending of her money? That was her idea before your father's death, and it has acquired new charms for her since. She ought to marry some one of whose disinterestedness she shall herself be sure; and there would be no such proof of that as his having a fortune of his own" (1:396). Mrs. Touchett sees acutely how Isabel is in danger of being the only one acting from disinterested motives in a game where everyone else is decidedly interested. She makes a strangely Kantian argument that what would best guarantee disinterestedness in a suitor for Isabel is his having no needs, his possession of a large fortune of his own.

James continues the consideration of disinterestedness during Ralph and Isabel's conversation about her engagement. Understandably finding Ralph's warnings about Osmond incomprehensible, Isabel takes "the heroic line": "I see you've some special idea; I should like very much to hear it. I'm sure it's disinterested; I feel that" (2:67). Later, when Ralph tells her she is "meant for something better than to keep guard over the sensibilities of a sterile dilettante," he confesses,"I've said what I had on my mind—and I've said it because I love you!" Isabel's reaction is to discount Ralph's advice because "[he's] not disinterested" (2:71–72). Here is one way to pose sharply the differences between Ralph and Osmond. Ralph is clearly interested in the shape of Isabel's career, and yet he combines "interest" with love for her. Osmond, on the other hand, has persuaded Isabel of his heroic disinterest, his indifference to all worldly distinction. He has also confessed his love to her, but that love seems rather an "impersonal" tribute to an ideal than a passionate commitment to another human being.

If James asks us to choose between the combination of frank interest together with love on the one hand, and disinterestedness on the other, then clearly the choice must be for interest and love. For Isabel's bitter realization is that she has only been dealing with supreme interestedness masking as disinterestedness in both Osmond and Madame Merle. By the time Warburton is ready to leave Rome after deciding not to propose to Pansy, Isabel has come to understand her husband's ability to feign perfect charity:

> It was indeed a part of Osmond's cleverness that he could look consummately uncompromised. His present appearance, however, was not a confession of disappointment; it was simply a part of Osmond's habitual system, which was to be inexpressive exactly in proportion as he was really intent. He had been intent on this prize from the first; but he had never allowed his eagerness to irradiate his refined face. He had treated his possible son-in-law as he treated every one—with an air of being interested in him only for his own advantage, not for any profit to a person already so generally, so perfectly provided as Gilbert Osmond. He would give no sign now of an inward rage which was the result of a vanished prospect of gain—not the faintest nor subtlest. (2:268)

Osmond's unsatisfied desire does not show in his masked face. What lies behind such habitual disinterestedness, James suggests, is narcissistic rage, which should perhaps be thought of as a response to a morality insisting on a too complete suppression of self and orientation to the other.

The "morality" of the senior James polarizes "the natural man" and "Divine Love." The former is "a form of the supreme self-love, and thus presents an exactly opposite aspect" to the latter, "which is incapable of selfish regards" (CLC 200). Elsewhere, James Sr. describes the "universe of the human mind" as split into spiritual spheres, one the "external principle (self-love, or hell)," the other "its internal principle (which is brotherly-love, or heaven)" (CLC 204). The Divine acts on the mind to effect conversion from the hell of complete self-regard to the perfect other or universal concern of heaven. All private interest or right seems suspect to James Sr., who looks to the day when men will cease being "such arrant idiots spiritually as to deem ourselves God's true creatures in our own private right, or out of social solidarity with all other men." On that day, "the great phenomenon of human society" will be accomplished: "men made social out of . . . their extreme and inveterate selfishness" (*SRF* 449). What such language actually prepares for is Osmond, masking "supreme self-love" under apparent incapability "of selfish regards." One can readily see how Osmond's careful protection of his private life represents a recoil action against the devaluing of private right in James Sr. The self told that it is of no intrinsic worth, that it can strive only to renounce its own shadowy nonbeing for the true "created" being of universal concern, will likely respond by protecting itself, encasing its own wounded self-esteem within a mask of disinterestedness. The wisdom of the Trinitarian love, with its affirmation of the creature's goodness in otherness from God, should be apparent.

Christianity understands the human creature to be sinful and in need of having his or her love redirected toward God. But this does not require annihilating the irredeemably selfish creature and replacing him or her with a spiritual being devoted to universal love. Kierkegaard, who understood that no struggle is "so protracted, so terrifying, so involved as self-love's war to defend itself," argued that Christianity sought not to annihilate self-love or to direct one "to love a person more than oneself," as poetic enthusiasm might insist. Christianity "master[ed] self-love" in a single wonderful stroke by granting it, yet turning it to the neighbor, in the second part of the Great Commandment: You shall love your neighbor as yourself. Self-love will "be broken" if it once seriously "struggle[s] with this phrase, which nevertheless does not seek to teach a man not to love himself but in fact rather seeks to teach him proper self-love." Training in Christianity involves learning to love the self "in the right way," that is, "in the same way as you love your neighbor when you love him as yourself."[29]

James's critique of disinterest involves not only Osmond but also his associate, Madame Merle. As Osmond is able to prevent desire from irradiating his "refined face"—suggesting the imperial physiognomy on some well-worn antique Roman coin—Madame Merle consistently masks the light of her intentness behind her seemingly impenetrable performance. Under the guise of disinterestedness, she marries Isabel and seeks to marry Pansy. Indeed, she remains supremely interested even to her last act vis-à-vis Isabel, her revealing that Ralph, not his father, has been the author of Isabel's fortune:

> Madame Merle appearing to see herself successful, she went on more triumphantly: "He imparted to you that extra lustre which was required to make you a brilliant match. At bottom it's him you've to thank." She stopped; there was something in Isabel's eyes.
>
> "I don't understand you. It was my uncle's money."
>
> "Yes; it was your uncle's money, but it was your cousin's idea. He brought his father over to it. Ah, my dear, the sum was large!"
>
> Isabel stood staring; she seemed to-day to live in a world illumined by lurid flashes. "I don't know why you say such things. I don't know what you know." (2:388)

I have quoted at length to catch the motifs of light and the eyes, the wonderful opening description of Madame Merle's narcissistic playing for herself, and the ironies of Isabel's final sentences. Perhaps Isabel really does not know why Madame Merle says such things, but revenge seems her motive, continuing revenge for an unhappiness that seeks to make others unhappy. Isabel does not know what Madame Merle knows: the rage of an unsatisfied desire that seeks triumph over others in revenge. But Isabel does fathom Madame Merle's logic, when she says—and "it was her only revenge"—"I believed it was you I had to thank!" (2:389). In her unhappiness, and her supreme self-protective self-interest, Madame Merle seeks to spoil Isabel's affection for Ralph by suggesting that he, not she, be held responsible for Isabel's unhappiness with Osmond. Isabel, however, refuses to read her own history in that way.

The day of Isabel's confrontation with Madame Merle brings Isabel two critical, and related, recognitions: that the gift of her inheritance has been Ralph's doing and that Madame Merle is the mother of Pansy. We are prepared, at last, to understand the reason for the deep unhappiness that is Madame Merle's final confession to Isabel and also to see the connection between her denial of Pansy and seeming need to avenge herself on others, even to poisoning Isabel's relationship with her dying cousin. Madame Merle's ever-shifting performance of self, her continual being for others, is thus related to the disruption of her relationship with Pansy, the relationship in which she could have loved and known another in her particularity and been loved and known uniquely herself. The Jamesian conclusion for liberal ways of doing ethics might be that divorcing agents from their particular histories and connections is likely only to create unsatisfied desire, or interest, masking itself as disinterestedness. James's treatment of Madame Merle might suggest to the Christian ethicist the wisdom of a communal form in which particular loves can be disciplined—without being denied or lost—into more inclusive ones. Dispensing with that form, the disciplinary process, and, above all, the One who provides the loving discipline, is likely not to produce persons capable of universal concern but those who pursue their own interests under masks of disinterestedness and who are really moved by narcissistic rage, unsatisfied desire, and deep unhappiness that enviously seeks to spoil the happiness of others.

If Ralph is, in some ways, reminiscent of Osmond, so, too, he has acted in parallel fashion to Madame Merle. Both have been unrecognized agents in Isabel's career. The difference between Ralph on the one hand and Osmond and Madame Merle on the other lies simply in Ralph's love. Isabel understands this plainly during the vision scene: "It was simply that Ralph was generous and that her husband was not. There was something in Ralph's talk, in his smile, in the mere fact of his being in Rome, that made the blasted circle round which she walked more spacious. He made her feel the good of the world; he made her feel what might have been" (2:203). Ralph "made her feel the good of the world," the goodness of Creation, the goodness she has felt originally at Gardencourt. The "generosity" James attributes to Ralph is worth pausing over for a moment. The word derives from *gene,* or giving birth, and thus suggests how Ralph's magnanimity affirms in a way that is generative, life-giving, capable of passing on the original flow of love from creation in a way that the "sterile" Osmond cannot. Ralph's affirmation of goodness takes form again in his final words to her, words that again distinguish him from the husband who has made hatred of Isabel "the occupation and comfort of his life" (2:201). "Remember this," Ralph says to Isabel, "that if you've been hated you've also been loved. Ah but, Isabel—*adored!*" (2:417).

The goodness of Creation, as Creation, has been implicit in an early Gardencourt conversation between Ralph and Isabel on the matter of suffering. Isabel remarks, "It's not absolutely necessary to suffer; we were not made for that" (1:65). Her sense of the likelihood of suffering seems empirically naïve, but her theology is quite orthodox. We were not made to suffer, but brought that upon Creation in the wounding of the Fall; neither is suffering an absolute necessity, though it is likely to occupy a significant part of our existence. We know, however, that we were not made simply to suffer, and we retain some memory of "what might have been," the goodness we were made for and that yet will be. This early conviction about suffering reemerges powerfully in Isabel during her journey from Rome to Gardencourt. At times on that journey, she feels "almost as good as being dead," sitting "in her corner, so motionless, so passive, simply with the sense of being carried, so detached from hope and regret, that she recalled to herself one of those Etruscan figures couched upon the receptacle of their ashes." Struggling with this sense of herself as a passive, even dead, object is a deeper conviction: "Deep in her soul—deeper than any appetite for renunciation—was the sense that life would be her business for a long time to come . . . It was a proof of strength—it was a proof she should some day be happy again. It could n't be she was to live only to suffer; she was still young, after all, and a great many things might happen to her yet. To live only to suffer—only to feel the injury of life repeated and enlarged—it seemed to her she was too valuable, too capable, for that" (2:391–392). James insists on the dimension of depth in Isabel, so different from Osmond's and Madame Merle's infatuation with surfaces, finish, image, representation, impression, and masking. Osmond and Madame Merle manage surfaces exquisitely as part of their strategies of manipulation and possession. Isabel has about her the depth of the creature, inexhaustible, incapable of being possessed or known precisely because she is created and thus in relation to the ungraspable Creator.

Isabel soon wonders, however, if it is not "vain and stupid to think so well of herself" as to believe she is "too valuable" to "live only to suffer." James closes the scene of her travel in the railway carriage with a covering, shrouding image reminiscent of Madame Merle: "The middle years wrapped her about again and the grey curtain of her indifference closed her in" (2:392–393). Isabel's orientation toward happiness is only reconfirmed in her last scene with Ralph, where, having forgiven one another, she and Ralph reach "the only knowledge that was not pure anguish—the knowledge that they were looking at the truth together" (2:414). Here is knowledge that lies beyond the will to power, knowledge that is outside of them, ahead of them. Their facing the truth together contrasts directly with the way Madame Merle and Osmond face one another, each knowing, and known to, the other, each willing to accept the inconvenience of being known only because the knowing brings with it power over the other—the power to triumph, to vindicate oneself.

For Ralph and Isabel, there is no question of triumph; death is imminent for Ralph and must be faced. He seems to Isabel almost beyond pain, which prompts her to ask, "In such hours as this what have we to do with pain? That's not the deepest thing; there's something deeper." Ralph makes clear that the "deepest thing" is love, which "remains" for him even on the other side of pain, but James leaves both Ralph and Isabel too with a sense of that other feeling he brackets with pain: wonder, the original motive for philosophizing, a motive perhaps, after all, not separable from love. "I don't know why we should suffer so much," Ralph says, leaving open the possibility of yet more light. "Perhaps I shall find out." He predicts that Isabel will "grow young again," so young as to embrace that deep youthful feeling of hers that we are not made to suffer. That seems to be Ralph's logic, for James inserts again that word "generous" that has come to mean the affirming, begetting, strengthening, life-giving love that moves Creation. "I don't believe that such a generous mistake as yours can hurt you for more than a little," Ralph says to Isabel, who responds, "Oh, Ralph, I'm very happy now" (2:416–417). Near death, Ralph speaks a fundamental Yes to his existence, his status as a creature, for he says, in effect, to Isabel, Your goodness, your love cannot hurt you ultimately; the way of generosity cannot lead ultimately to suffering. To make those affirmations is to affirm the goodness of Creation.

Ralph's affirmation contrasts starkly with a remark of his mother's to Isabel made as she sits "motionless and upright beside the couch" of her dead son. Mrs. Touchett "submit[s]" to a caress, for once, from Isabel, but immediately distances herself even from Isabel's expression of care: " 'Go and thank God you've no child,' said Mrs. Touchett, disengaging herself" (2:419). Here is a direct repudiation of the goodness of Creation, of the ontological weight in the affirmation of love, as we have seen in Pieper's phrasing, "It is good that you exist." Mrs. Touchett urges Isabel to give thanks for what is not, apparently because the threat of suffering and death is so fearful to her, so threatening to her characterological armoring, that it seems better for Ralph never to have lived than to have lived, died, and caused her the pain of loss. To live so fearfully is to live under the power of death, and it becomes, at last, possible to see Mrs. Touchett's rigid independence as only a way to avoid all risk of suffering, a strategy of constant "disengagement."

If one is to thank God that a child has not been, perhaps it is because one, above all, fears regret. For a child to be, and then to die, is to be left with a strong sense both of what might have been and of what else one might have done but failed to do. The most touching moment regarding Mrs. Touchett involves Isabel's perception, on returning to Gardencourt, that her aunt senses the failure of a life whose plan has been to be without regret: "Her old pity for the poor woman's inexpressiveness, her want of regret, of disappointment, came back to her. Unmistakeably she would have found it a blessing to-day to be able to feel a defeat, a mistake, even a shame or two. She wondered if she were not even missing those enrichments of consciousness and privately trying—reaching out for some aftertaste of life, dregs of the banquet; the testimony of pain or the cold recreation of remorse" (2:406–407).

It would be valuable here to work out the difference between two senses of regret. During his last illness, Thoreau wrote a young poet who had inquired about his health, "I am enjoying existence as much as ever, and regret nothing." One hears in this his vigorous Stoic insistence on conforming his will to the order of nature, the insistence evident in his remark that "it was just as good to be sick as to be well."[30] Affirming what has been, and is now, requires, for Thoreau, being without regret; his comments suggest his determination to live in the very "nick of time," to live deeply in the moment where eternity intersects the present and to let the past and future take care of themselves. His example illustrates, by contrast, the danger of living too much in regret. Too much focus on the might-have-been devalues the present, leading to the empty, desiring self's quest to be filled in consolation, compensation, or vindication for what has not been.

It seems difficult to imagine, however, how a meaningful life with others could be entirely without regret. Surely we fail continually to meet both our own and others' expectations. And how can we be without disappointment in others unless we give up having any expectations of, or for, them? Mrs. Touchett perhaps indicates the only way to completely eliminate regret: to insist, with absolute rigidity, that others will never impinge on her obligations to herself. When it is time for her visit to America, she goes, even though her son is dying. It is best to give no thought to what one might miss.

To be without regret is to be without a source of creativity in the present and future. Seeing what might have been can lead to making things different, that is, if the might-have-been does not itself become so overpowering as to cause us to repeat, perhaps from the need to justify, the past. What is needed is a creative way for us to carry regret over into the present and future. Making regret creative depends on forgiveness, by which we affirm that the past, with its failures and missed opportunities, has really been and therefore needs no denial. Furthermore, because they do not need to be justified, we can avoid repeating the mistakes, errors, crimes of the past. As it becomes available to us at a certain distance, the past can become a creative source of action in the present: we can see what might have been, regret it, yet avoid the paralysis of regret by doing what we can to make things different. Forgiveness seems central to the narrative unity of the self, for it allows the past to be without its determining the shape of the future. As Ralph leaves Rome to return home, Isabel feels the sacredness of Gardencourt, for "no chapter of the past was more perfectly irrecoverable" (2:296). Here James intimates the way the novel will end: Isabel cannot return to Gardencourt to stay, because to do so would be to try to repeat the past, to live in regret for what Ralph justifiably makes her feel: "the good of the world . . . what might have been" (2:203). Rather, Isabel must return to Gardencourt, recognize what might have been, recognize further that the past is freeing precisely because it is "perfectly irrecoverable," and then carry forward into the future her renewed sense of the good of the world.

Isabel's relationship to Pansy offers her the best opportunity to be free for, and good for, another in a relationship of mutuality. Isabel returns to Rome because she "must," but this "must" should not be understood to mean either constraint from outside or from some perverse inner compulsion. Goodwood makes the case for Isabel's absolute freedom from constraint: "We can do absolutely as we please; to whom under the sun do we owe anything? What is it that holds us, what is it that has the smallest right to interfere in such a question as this? Such a question is between ourselves—and to say that is to settle it! . . . The world's all before us—and the world's very big" (2:435). Pansy "holds" Isabel, though in a way that Goodwood cannot understand because it does not involve the assertion of a right to interfere in Isabel's life or the imposition of an obligation on her. Pansy holds Isabel through an offer she has made, on the day of their conversation in Florence before Isabel first goes on tour. As their interview ends, Pansy presses on Isabel an extension of faith. Asking when Isabel will come again, Pansy closes, "As soon as you can, I hope. I'm only a little girl . . . but I shall always expect you" (2:30). Pansy's language—her intention to expect, await, look out for—constitutes an extraordinary commitment of fidelity to Isabel together with a belief in Isabel's own faithfulness. After the Osmonds' marriage, Pansy becomes increasingly "dear" to Isabel, who recognizes that "nothing else in her life" has "the rightness of the young creature's attachment or the sweetness of her own clearness about it." Pansy offers "more than an affection" for Isabel; hers is "a kind of ardent coercive faith" in her stepmother. Isabel experiences a direct appeal, a call, from Pansy; the young girl's dependence "operated as a definite reason when motives threatened to fail her" (2:161).

James describes Pansy's "sympathy" as both "a direct admonition" to Isabel and "an opportunity, not eminent perhaps, but unmistakeable." Isabel cannot supply in advance the specific nature of the opportunity or precisely what it will entail. But she does characterize it, "in general," as the chance and call "to be more for the child than the child was able to be for herself" (2:161). James plays here with the word "for," whose nuances he exploits throughout his fiction. Madame Merle has spoken of her self "for other people," meaning by it the constant acts of representation by which she performs a self. Clearly, Isabel does not intend being "for Pansy" in Madame Merle's sense. Isabel means something more like being available to Pansy, putting herself at the disposal of Pansy—yet these descriptions suggest the degree to which Isabel risks being used as a thing, for the quality of a thing is to be available, at hand, and disposable. What makes it possible for Isabel to risk "being for Pansy" is the prior faith Pansy has confessed: faith in, and fidelity to, Isabel. Isabel and Pansy form an intersubjective unity in which each can be available to the other without fear of being used as a thing, a unity in which the polarity of subject and object ceases to be meaningful. This seems to involve something like modeling the Trinitarian love, in which the goodness of the other as other is included within the very movement of love. Perhaps we can gloss Isabel's sense of "being for" Pansy by saying that she knows her own good and Pansy's to be inextricably linked: what is good for her must somehow be involved in her own being more for this child who has so appealed to her than the child can be for herself.[31]

Isabel's return to Rome must be understood, too, in light of the strong pattern of detail linking Ralph to Pansy in the second half of the novel. Isabel's recognition of the opportunity of "being for" Pansy takes place at a moment James marks, simply and unobtrusively, as occurring "one day about a month after Ralph Touchett's arrival in Rome" (2:161). After Lord Warburton gives Pansy up and takes his leave, the girl surprises Isabel by saying, "I think you are my guardian angel!" (2:272). Unknown to Pansy is that Ralph has also acted the part of guardian angel, for he first suggested to Warburton that perhaps the "leading" merit he has seen in Pansy is her being "so near her stepmother" (2:153). Warburton vehemently denies Ralph's intimation, but later recognizes its rightness. Later, the "rupture" between Osmond and Isabel caused by her decision to go to Ralph at Gardencourt leads to the Countess Gemini's revelation that Pansy's mother is Madame Merle. After that revelation, Isabel closes Chapter 51 of the novel with a "must" that signifies both imperative and deep need: "'Ah, I must see Ralph!' Isabel wailed; not in resentment, not in the quick passion her companion looked for; but in a tone of far-reaching infinite sadness" (2:373). Chapter 52 opens by repeating that "must" in the first paragraph: Isabel has made her arrangements for England, but she continues to think "(except of her journey) only of one thing. She must go and see Pansy; from her she could n't turn away" (2:374). Isabel's scene with Pansy at the convent closes with a reminder of the earlier scene at Florence in which Pansy pledged always to expect Isabel. "In a voice that Isabel remembered afterwards," Pansy asks, "You'll come back?" To which, Isabel responds, "Yes—I'll come back" (2:386).

Isabel must see Ralph; she must see Pansy. After she has seen Ralph, she retraces this movement: she must again see Pansy. Freedom for Isabel lies in consenting to this must, together with the faith, reinspired by Ralph, that such "generous" actions as her promise to Pansy cannot hurt her "but for a little." James knew that his ending would be criticized as unsatisfactory and incomplete, as is evident from his *Notebook* entry on *Portrait*: "With strong handling it seems to me that it may all be very true, very powerful, very touching. The obvious criticism of course will be that it is not finished—that I have not seen the heroine to the end of her situation—that I have left her *en l'air*.—This is both true and false. The *whole* of anything is never told; you can only take what groups together. What I have done has that unity—it groups together. It is complete in itself—and the rest may be taken up or not, later."[32] James makes a moral argument for truth's dramatic force. The truth of Isabel's experience lies not in his, or our, being able to give a complete account of it but in its making a kind of dramatic sense. We can see that the story has about it a kind of unity that draws our assent. The assertion that "the whole of anything is never told" is a moral one rooted in the assumption that the created human being can never be exhausted, used up, or disposed of precisely because she lives from a depth of love that is not something possessed in herself but that she has only in relation to her Creator. James's refusal of totalizing vision contrasts very specifically with the language of Caspar Goodwood in the final scenes of *Portrait*. We have seen his telling Isabel they can do "absolutely as we please" and his claim that "the world's all before us" (2:435). The same rhetoric is evident when he tells Isabel about her marriage, "I see the whole thing," and then asks, "It's too late to play a part; did n't you leave all that behind you in Rome? Touchett knew all about it, and I knew it too—what it would cost you to come here. It will have cost you your life?" (2:432–433).

James revised the portrayal of Goodwood significantly for the New York edition. Whereas the Goodwood of the earlier edition is a rather earnest late-Puritan businessman, the Goodwood of the New York text is a proto-fascist for whom others represent pure material to do his will: "There were intricate, bristling things he rejoiced in; he liked to organise, to contend, to administer; he could make people work his will, believe in him, march before him and justify him. This was the art, as they said, of managing men—which rested, in him, further, on a bold though brooding ambition" (1:164). Isabel senses that the appropriate sphere of action for such a man is war. The spirit evident in those "clear-burning" eyes could never rest "in harmony with mere smug peace and greed and gain, an order of things of which the vital breath was ubiquitous advertisement"; rather, "it pleased Isabel to believe that he might have ridden, on a plunging steed, the whirlwind of a great war—a war like the Civil strife that had overdarkened her conscious childhood and his ripening youth" (1:164). From being merely "the strongest man she had ever known" in 1880–1881,[33] the revised Goodwood has become a mechanical product of human fashioning: "He was of supremely strong, clean make—which was so much: she saw the different fitted parts of him as she had seen, in museums and portraits, the different fitted parts of armoured warriors—in plates of steel handsomely inlaid with gold" (1:165).

Goodwood seems a consequence of the Gnostic denial of Creation we have seen in Henry James Sr. He seems pure spirit encased in a mechanical body or, to borrow the language of James Sr., "personality" seeking to "affirm the subject's infinitude or perfection" through the "power of originating his own action." Such a man lives under subjection to nature and his fellow man unless he is capable of being "lift[ed] . . . entirely beyond the sphere of necessity or duty" (MC 128). James Sr.'s perfect man "finds the object of his action always within his own subjectivity" (MC 133). To act in relation to others, then, must always be to act as if on objects of one's own will. The alternative is to become the object of others, a thing, ready-to-hand, disposable. James Jr. captures this either-or of pure subjectivity, pure thinghood in his description of Goodwood, insightfully suggesting that war is the proper expression of a spirit that must either drive others before it to justify it or lose itself by being subjected to another will. The difference between such Gnosticism and the Trinitarian doctrine of God can be seen by comparing James Sr.'s conception of the perfect man to the working of Trinitarian love. The Gnostic perfect man "finds the object of his action always within his own subjectivity"; the Trinitarian love includes within it, from all eternity, the goodness of the creature as other from God.

James Jr.'s statement that "the whole of anything is never told" is worth pondering in relation to his role in Nussbaum's work on ethics and litera-ture. Nussbaum has written repeatedly on James, enlisting him in support of her Aristotelianism and posing him sharply against Kantian alterna-tives. For Nussbaum, the Aristotelian inquiry begins with the question "How should one live?" rather than with a more Kantian question focused on understanding moral duties. Nussbaum finds especially congenial James's attention to particularity, his stress on responsiveness and a wise passivity, and his giving "priority" to perception.[34] Surely James is com-mitted to the importance of discriminating perception, but one might just as well argue, as a number of fine critics have, that the second formu-lation of Kant's categorical imperative forms the chief moral maxim of his fiction.[35] James describes one of Isabel's clearest moments of ethical per-ception in terms reminiscent of Kant's "means-ends" distinction. Having just learned the real relationship between Madame Merle and Pansy, Isabel saw "the dry staring fact that she had been an applied handled hung-up tool, as senseless and convenient as mere shaped wood and iron" (2:379). Similarly, in *The Ambassadors*, the subject of Nussbaum's "Percep-tive Equilibrium: Literary Theory and Ethical Theory," Strether recog-nizes finally that Chad's "famous knowing how to live" consists largely in knowing how to use others "to turn his wheel" (2:278). It seems mistaken, then, to read James in such a way as to break down the distinction between the moral and the nonmoral as categories of experience (*LK* 25, 169, n.2). Although James is certainly interested in how human beings might live well, he also marks off a realm of experience defined by the maxims one adopts in relation to others. Osmond, Madame Merle, and Chad Newsome suggest that there is no necessary relationship, for James, between having learned "to live well" and regarding others as ends in themselves. Indeed, Strether muses about how Madame de Vionnet and he have conspired in creating Chad as a polished work famously incar-nating how to live: "She had made him better, she had made him best," and he, Strether, "had made him too; his high appreciation had, as it were, consecrated her work." Nevertheless, it comes "to our friend," Strether, "with supreme queerness that he was none the less only Chad"

(2:284)—for which read "cad," one most of all able to make others turn his wheel.

If James maintains a sharper sense than Nussbaum of the distinction between "knowing how to live" and "treating others as ends in themselves," it is perhaps because he is less confident than she in the possibility of characterizing all available ethical positions from a single vantage point. Nussbaum sometimes seems to think that the whole of things can be told. In "Perceptive Equilibrium," she argues that the "central procedural idea" of her Aristotelian inquiry is to "work through the major alternative views about the good life, holding them up, in each case, against our own experience and our intuitions" (*LK* 173–174). The "first step" in the "procedure" is to "get a perspicuous description of these alternatives (though we should bear in mind that these descriptions will already contain an element of evaluation and response)." Nussbaum's phrase "perspicuous description" is revealing; "perspicuous," meaning clearly presented or lucid, derives from Latin *perspicere*, to see through. Thus, a "perspicuous description" would in no way be opaque or obscured by language; we would simply "see through" to a reality described as it is. The next step in Nussbaum's procedure is to "notice and clearly describe the conflicts and tensions among the views that we find." What follows is a methodology for resolving tensions:

> Where there is inconsistency or irreconcilable tension—and where this tension corresponds to something that we notice in our own experience and thought (individually or communally)—we aim to revise the overall picture so as to bring it into harmony with itself, preserving, as Aristotle says, "the greatest number and the most basic" of the original judgments and perceptions. There is no rule about how to do this. Individuals simply ask what looks deepest, what they can least live without—guided by their sense of life, and by their standing interest in consistency and in community. That is, they want to arrive at a view that is internally coherent, and also at one that is broadly shared and sharable. (*LK* 174)

Unclear here is how "irreconcilable tension"—by definition, that which cannot be reconciled or brought into harmony—is brought into "harmony with itself." Moreover, the position that is irreconcilable is in tension with something else. Presumably, it's already in harmony with itself. Nussbaum's procedure is not dialectical, as the metaphor of "the overall picture" also reveals. It assumes one pictorial point of view from which one can cast all major alternative "views" of the human good in a neutral "perspicuous" language—and then, when it sees "tension," to bring it into harmony with the one view it has already chosen as most worthy. Nussbaum claims that the procedure considers "nothing unrevisable" but brings her description to a conclusion strongly emphasizing consistency: the procedure "seeks for coherence and 'fit' in the system as a whole" (*LK* 174). A "system" that seeks coherence will place little value on a prophetic criticism that calls into question its major assumptions.

The totalizing language of "procedure," "system," "coherence," and "fit" seems quite alien to James. I doubt there is anything, except at the highest level of abstraction, that one could characterize as James's major "view" of the good life for human beings. The famous "house of fiction" that he describes in the preface to *Portrait* offers no single vantage point from which one can characterize all competing views. It "has in short not one window, but a million—a number of possible windows not to be reckoned, rather; every one of which has been pierced, or is still pierceable, in its vast front, by the need of the individual vision and by the pressure of the individual will." These windows do not allow for "perspicuous" descriptions: they "are but windows at the best, mere holes in a dead wall, disconnected, perched aloft; they are not hinged doors opening straight upon life." No "straight" description of "life" is available, only so many "impression[s]," each "distinct from every other" because it is the product of the "unique instrument" of the "person making use of it" (1:x–xi).

Nussbaum takes very seriously the tension between human uniqueness and the moral point of view. She has argued forcefully that love's focus on unique and particular beings is at odds with the universalizing emphases of modern ethics (*LK* 67–68, 335–363). Nussbaum might well assent to a statement of Isabel's to Warburton made when he asks about Pansy, "Could any one in the world be more loveable than Miss Osmond?" "No one, possibly. But love has nothing to do with good reasons," Isabel responds (2:220). The context James has created for Isabel's remark provides an opening into the relationship between love and rationality. Warburton is attempting to persuade himself to engage in a substitution: Pansy for Isabel, the one to whom he "really" wishes to be close. James's context, together with Isabel's remark, suggests that love has nothing to do with this kind of substitution. Love is directed toward, or elicited, by a person in his or her uniqueness and unsubstitutability. "Good reasons," on the other hand, are those that can be offered to, or by, anybody. Unpacking the moral content of Kant's means-end distinction, Alasdair MacIntyre writes, "What makes a reason a good reason has nothing to do with who utters it on a given occasion; and until an agent has decided for himself whether a reason is a good reason or not, he has no reason to act."[36] Kant's conception of rationality, then, seems to depend on substitutability: any reason giver can substitute for any other reason giver; the identity of the reason giver is irrelevant to the force of the reasons. In one sense, then, love seems to have nothing to do with good reasons, for love is directed at particular persons; one cannot bracket the particularity, the identity of the beloved, from one's love. Yet, in another sense, the conception of love articulated by Isabel does seem linked dialectically with rationality conceived along Kantian lines. When rationality becomes the sphere of infinite substitutability, then love becomes the refuge of uniqueness and particularity.[37]

James thematizes the relationship between love and reason throughout *Portrait*. Isabel's remark to Lord Warburton is undoubtedly a response, in part, to her own experience. She has supplied herself with all kinds of good reasons to marry Osmond, even defending her matrimonial choice to Mrs. Touchett by saying, "Whatever I do I do with reason" (2:57). She has tried to love where it seemed reasonable to do so, and the experience has been a failure—from which we might conclude that James thinks it best to keep reason and love entirely separate. But one who defends that kind of separation is the Countess Gemini, whose marital failure and adultery suggest the isolation of one who never brings feeling into discourse with reason. After declaring to Isabel that she "detested arguments," she says, "One should like a thing or one shouldn't; one can't like everything, of course. But one shouldn't attempt to reason it out—you never know where it may lead you" (1:369). The notion of reason's "leading" one richly foreshadows the way "reasons" ultimately lead Isabel both to Pansy and to Ralph. Where reasons "may lead" one is to a real encounter with other persons, but perhaps that kind of encounter is precisely where one fears going if one is committed to always doing what one "likes."

James frames the question of Pansy's love and marriage within a notion of reasonableness. During their visit in Florence, Isabel tells Pansy she will be right to always obey her father, for "he'll never ask you anything unreasonable" (2:30). The line prepares us to see the unreasonableness of Osmond's design of marrying Pansy to Warburton. It is unreasonable of Pansy to dispose of herself where there is no love. What is reasonable, for Pansy, must be to follow love, to be oriented toward love. James underscores that kind of connection between love and reason when he describes Pansy's "ardent coercive faith" in her stepmother as a "definite reason when motives threatened to fail her" (2:161). For Isabel, the commitment to being more for Pansy than the child can be for herself is a matter of both love and rationality. It would be unreasonable not to be led where Pansy's prior love and trust have invited Isabel.

James brings the matter of love and good reasons to a climax in the scene that marks Isabel and Osmond's "rupture." That bitter scene begins with the description of Osmond making his perfect copy of an antique coin on a sheet of "immaculate paper." After learning of her husband's determined opposition to her going to see the dying Ralph, Isabel says, "You've no reason for such a wish . . . and I've every reason for going. I can't tell you how unjust you seem to me" (2:354). Osmond takes up the matter of reasons specifically: "You say I've no reason? I have the very best. I dislike, from the bottom of my soul, what you intend to do. It's dishonourable; it's indelicate; it's indecent. Your cousin is nothing whatever to me, and I'm under no obligation to make concessions to him" (2:355). Later, Osmond reiterates his emphasis on Ralph's nothingness, insisting to Isabel: "Your cousin's nothing to you; he's nothing to us. You smile most expressively when I talk about *us*, but I assure you that *we, we,* Mrs. Osmond, is all I know. I take our marriage seriously; you appear to have found a way of not doing so. I'm not aware that we're divorced or separated; for me we're indissolubly united. You are nearer to me than any human creature, and I'm nearer to you. It may be a disagreeable proximity; it's one, at any rate, of our own deliberate making" (2:355–356).

Osmond asks Isabel to negate her whole history with Ralph. When she speaks of having "every reason for going," she points to the interconnectedness of Ralph's and her lives: their being cousins, their time together at Gardencourt, the Touchetts' generosity to her, their mourning together the death of Ralph's father, Ralph's being a comfort at Rome during her most despairing hours. All these count as "good reasons" for Isabel to go to England. Perhaps we should understand James to be defining, in Osmond, the point of view from which it would make sense to say that Isabel has no reason to go to England. That point of view seems utterly detached from "natural" experience (even to denying the family connection between Isabel and Ralph), committed to regarding human beings as so many interchangeable images, and devoted entirely to techne, to the idea that nothing is given, that the form of marriage, even the form of one's child—which Osmond is metaphorically copying on that sheet of immaculate paper—are matters only of "our own deliberate making." Fortunately, Isabel follows where "every reason" leads her: to Gardencourt, where, as we have seen, Ralph affirms his love for her and her goodness as a creature. And she returns ultimately where she, too, has "definite reason" to be—with Pansy—in order to be more for the girl than Pansy can be for herself in the same way that Ralph has been more for her than she could be for herself. Thus James suggests that love and good reasons are bound up together, for if love leads to patterns of reciprocity in which everyone becomes more for one another than they can be for themselves, then how can it be unreasonable, irrational, to love?

Isabel's return to Rome means a return to Osmond and the unhappiness of their marriage, an outcome deemed deeply unsatisfactory by many critics. Dorothea Krook and others suggest that sexual fear of Goodwood motivates Isabel's return to Rome.[38] Virginia Fowler argues that the limitations of James's socially realistic novel constrain Isabel's possibilities: "the consciousness" of the American girl is "inevitably limited by the world the fiction forces her to inhabit." What, for Fowler, is particularly painful about James's ending is his showing "us that behind the 'cage' of Isabel's marriage is the cage of her own mind, for she has unconsciously internalized those values of the male world which function to keep her an imprisoned and unquestioning victim."[39] Also reading *Portrait* in relation to "nineteenth century Realist/humanist ideology," Priscilla Walton advances a different objection. She argues that *Portrait* raises questions about "subjectivity" throughout, explicitly "proffer[ing] the idea of freedom," conceived as liberal autonomy, while actually "dramati[zing] the extent to which society limits and thus forms all its 'free' subjects (both male and female)." Thus, although James might seem to be offering a critique of realist/humanist ideology, his ending conforms to the conventions of realism by attempting, despite his *Notebook* comment, to effect closure. The novel's ending invites readers to ignore its paradoxes and to "believe that both they and Isabel are autonomous and free agents": "Isabel's autonomy should be apparent in her 'free' choice to return to Rome, the readers' in their acceptance of the inevitability and rightness of this decision; yet by inviting readers to effect closure, the text (as a form) again negates any possibility of freedom for the reader, since it dictates the way in which it should be read."[40]

Several textual points need to be made here. First, readings that stress Isabel's return to victimization tend to ignore the "tough honorableness"[41] she exhibits throughout Pansy's courtship. She resists Osmond's pressure to influence Warburton; she aligns herself with Rosier, of whom Osmond disapproves; and she defies Osmond in returning to Gardencourt. Isabel possesses courage, as Pansy recognizes when she tells the crestfallen Rosier that she will enlist the help of her stepmother in forwarding their romance: "She's not afraid of any one. We must have patience" (2:134). Readings critical of James's revictimizing Isabel tend to ignore Pansy. The Roman chapters suggest Pansy's development of a difference with her father, at least to the extent of her preferring Rosier to Warburton. She reveals a quality of independent perception, unsuspected even by Isabel. When Pansy correctly reads both Warburton's lack of interest in her and his real nobility, Isabel is "touched with wonder at the depth of perception of which this submissive little person was capable; she felt afraid of Pansy's wisdom—began almost to retreat before it" (2:260). In short, there is more in Pansy for Isabel to return to than is commonly acknowledged by the ending's detractors.

Nevertheless, there is much to be said for the criticisms summarized above. To the degree that Goodwood's sexuality is part of his claim to know Isabel totally, she is right to fear it. As Fowler rightly points out, real-life Isabels have been victimized, particularly in marriage, by accepting something like the ideology of suffering the novel might seem to uphold: "that suffering is the necessary condition of being fully human" (80). To the degree that a Christianized ideology has underwritten that suffering, especially for women, it must be repudiated. Finally, Walton's point about the novel's critique of realist/humanist ideology brings us back to where we began, with *Portrait* as a response to the theology of Henry James Sr. and its radical emphasis on the autonomy of the "created" subject. Walton's paradox of the "subject" mirrors the way the elder James sees all moral life as heteronomy. To the extent that an unstoried, autonomous self is set over against the world, engagement with that world will likely appear as determinism and necessity. Suffering, as that which blocks the will, must seem particularly intolerable. Or, as the will must always find itself determined, suffering will become the whole of life.

Christian readers of James's text should be grateful for the laying to rest of realist/humanist ideology. A case in point is Fowler's contention about suffering. As long as people believe that "suffering is the necessary condition of being fully human," they will never hear the more complex, sustaining, and liberating Christian good news about suffering. Christians know that suffering is real and unavoidable, that one must learn to live into and with it, and that engagement with it will very largely affect the shape of one's character. They know, too, that they are part of a story that declares suffering not simply "necessary"; as we have heard the young Isabel Archer put it, "we are not made for that." At the heart of that story is the self-emptying of God in order to participate in human suffering and reveal that its reality is not final. Christians do not seek escape from suffering, as in Gnostic removal to the uncreated; rather, they seek to actively limit it while, at the same time, recognizing that attempts to eliminate it altogether risk seriously distorting our nature as creatures. Christians can suffer, and combat suffering, with eschatological hope, knowing both that suffering is not final and that they are not finally responsible for eliminating it. Sustaining this kind of hope is one task of the eschatological community that is the church.

Freed from the sense that suffering is necessary, Christian readers will see in Isabel's return to Pansy the response of love to love. Aware of the paradox of the subject, Christian readers will not look to James's text for an impossible version of unstoried autonomy. Neither will the Christian reader reject all "form," as Walton seems to, from the sense that it is necessarily "dictatorial." The Christian reader will see in Isabel's return a pattern of freedom within the form, a form that remains itself partially open from the conviction that "the whole of anything is never told." *Portrait* makes no claim to being a final statement about how things are. Rather, it offers, in dramatic fashion, what "groups together," calls attention to its own artfulness in its title, and points beyond itself.

The way particular beings point to a freedom beyond themselves is suggested throughout the text by James's habit of situating his characters at doorways or thresholds. Two examples are particularly noteworthy. The first involves Pansy's invitation to Isabel in Florence. The scene is Osmond's villa, with its beautiful empty rooms kept "dusky" by "half-darkened" windows. As their interview concludes, Isabel and Pansy move "together through the vestibule, to the door that opened on the court." Pansy stops at this door, though she "look[s] rather wistfully beyond," as she tells Isabel, "I may go no further. I've promised papa not to pass this door." She makes her extraordinary offer of fidelity to Isabel, then, while standing within the doorway that Papa has defined as her limit but looking beyond: "'I'm only a little girl,' said Pansy, 'but I shall always expect you.' And the small figure stood in the high, dark doorway, watching Isabel cross the clear, grey court and disappear into the brightness beyond the big *portone*, which gave a wider dazzle as it opened" (2:30).

My second example involves a scene meant to work specifically in relation to Pansy and Isabel's parting at Osmond's villa. During his last conversation with Isabel regarding Pansy, Warburton contrasts himself with Rosier: "I'm not like the young man in the doorway. I admit that. But what makes it so unnatural? Could any one in the world be more loveable than Miss Osmond?" (2:220). Someone in the world is, of course, more loveable to Warburton than Pansy: his question, his own seeing the difference between himself and Rosier, leads to his recognizing that his unacknowledged motive is to be close to Isabel. Rosier still stands framed by the doorway when Isabel decides to help him: "What has suddenly brought you round?" he asks her, and she responds, "The sense that you are an inconvenience in doorways!" (2:222). James has prepared the moment through an earlier description of Rosier's first opportunity to be alone with Pansy. The two stand together looking into "another room beyond the one in which they stood—a small room that had been thrown open and lighted, but that, the company not being numerous, had remained empty all the evening. It was empty yet; it was upholstered in pale yellow; there were several lamps; through the open door it looked the very temple of authorised love" (2:109). Thus James establishes the contexts within which to understand Isabel's return to Rome: to help Pansy and Rosier through the doorway—beyond the limits established by the loveless god Osmond—and into the "very temple of authorised love." Doing so will be a way of responding to the unlimited fidelity Pansy has opened to Isabel as she looks through the big portone of her father's house and into the "wider dazzle beyond."

A New York edition revision, "the very temple of authorised love" suggests at once a house of worship, the work of fiction itself, and the name of James's beloved cousin, Minnie Temple, whose death in 1870 has been called "the death of deaths" for Henry James.[42] Many critics have addressed the relationship between Minnie and Isabel Archer, and I do not want to enter into that complex discussion here. I am willing to accept James's account of the matter when he told Grace Norton that "there is in the heroine a considerable infusion of my impression of [Minnie's] remarkable nature," but "the thing is not a portrait."[43] I want simply to conclude by looking at two Jamesian passages, both involving houses as temples or places of authorized love, that may stand in relation to Minnie's death. The first involves the ambiguity of within and without in the windows of James's house of fiction, "every one of which has been pierced, or is still pierceable, in its vast front, by the need of the individual vision and by the pressure of the individual will" (1:x). "Pierced" seems out of place as a description of window construction: bodies, not houses, are pierced. Piercing is done to the body from without, outside, and thus seems to stand in tension with "individual vision" and "individual will," which we ordinarily think of as working somehow from the inside outward. Yet perhaps James is suggesting that individual vision derives from being pierced from without, from having one's "vast front" penetrated by the death of the other. Later in the passage, he suggests the fullest possible interpenetration of "subject" and "form," of consciousness and field: "The spreading field, the human scene, is the 'choice of subject'; the pierced aperture, either broad or balconied or slit-like and low-browed, is the 'literary form'; but they are, singly or together, as nothing without the posted presence of the watcher—without, in order words, the consciousness of the artist. Tell me what the artist is, and I will tell you of what he has *been* conscious. Thereby I shall express to you at once his boundless freedom and his 'moral' reference" (1:xi). The artist's "boundless" freedom lies not in anything he is in himself, or for himself, but in what he holds in consciousness and is able to shape into literary form—a form defined by the particular shape of his own "pierced aperture." As a perpetual watcher, the artist seems somewhat like Osmond, with his eye obsessively on others and with his argument that others can be "nothing" except insofar as they are something in, and for, his consciousness. The difference between Osmond and James is that Osmond watches others always for the way they reflect himself to himself or the way they confirm his own difference from them. The Jamesian artist, on the other hand, watches the human scene from the conviction that his freedom and his moral commitment lie in giving form or body to as much of the lives of others as his consciousness can hold. Perhaps we should think of James here as defining an "authorising love" much as he defines Isabel's commitment to Pansy: as a way of being "for" the other that enables the other to be more than she can be for herself.

My second passage brings us back to a comment of James's on his father's faith, made in *Notes of a Son and Brother*: "In fine I should have been thankful for a state of faith, a conviction of the Divine, an interpretation of the universe—anything one might have made bold to call it—which would have supplied more features or appearances. Feeling myself 'after' persons so much more than anything else—to recur to that side of my earliest and most constant consciousness which might have been judged most deplorable—I take it that I found the sphere of our more nobly suppositious habitation too imperceptibly peopled" (309). James's father's house simply contained too many suppositions and too few persons. James felt himself "after" persons in two senses. Persons provided the "relations . . . most present" to him, those "most interesting, attaching, and inviting"—and those most simply left out of his father's "schemes of importances." He was also "after" persons in a narrative, temporal way: he came after others, followed upon them, knew himself in relation to those who were before him. He could never be "the self-sufficient subject" that his father associated with God's "true creature" or the "perfect man." This double sense of being "after" persons—together with the death of the other, most sharply felt in the loss of Minnie—leads in James to a sense of contingency reflected in Isabel's beliefs that we are not made simply to suffer and that the "good of the world" is what might have been. To adapt the language of theologian Rowan Williams here, such statements as Isabel's point "to a deeper ground and context which . . . cannot be conceived as necessity." To be so intensely and ineluctably "'after' persons" as James is to experience being as participation in a world; to experience the death of the other is to be aware that we are "unique, non-necessary" beings "distinct from the 'necessity' of the world around."[44] To experience oneself and others as "non-necessary" opens the possibility of gratuity, a sense of ourselves as gifts and of others as gifts to us.

It is this sense of the other as gift that Harold Bloom misses when he claims that, for Isabel, "love entails her conferring of esteem upon others, and accepting back from them only her own authentic self-esteem." "No shadow of the object can fall upon her ego," he maintains.[45] This interpretation presses Isabel too far in the direction of Emersonian self-reliance while unintentionally suggesting the connection between that hallowed American Gnostic ideology and a lonely narcissism. The shadow of the object does fall on Isabel in, for example, Mr. Touchett's death, which James narrates in such a way as to invite specific contrast with Bloom's thesis. James frames Isabel's experience of Mr. Touchett's death to contrast specifically with her first youthful Emersonianism. When Mrs. Touchett discovers Isabel in the library at Albany, she is marching her mind through pages of German philosophy, but on the day of Mr. Touchett's death, Isabel's "attention [is] not fastened" on her volume as she sits in the library at Gardencourt. Unable to will her mind to grasp what she wishes it to grasp, she has "placed herself in a deep window-bench" where she can look out at the entrance of the house. She suspects the thing has happened when she sees—through the window that defines her own limited, embodied point of view—the great doctor Sir Matthew Hope come through the door at the entrance and get into his waiting brougham. But as she "turn[s] quickly away from the window," she sees Ralph standing there with his hands in his pockets, his habitual sign that there is nothing to be done. "Ah, my poor Ralph!" Isabel gently "wail[s], putting out her two hands to him" (1:293–294), less to confer esteem than in recognition of how important Ralph, and his father, have become to her. Here, in the limited experience of the self-reliant will—the death of the other—Isabel and Ralph confirm a bond that not even Osmond can undo when he later forbids Isabel's return to Gardencourt on the grounds that Ralph is "nothing" to her. Finally, neither is Isabel simply receiving back her own self-esteem when the dying Ralph says to her, "I don't believe that such a generous mistake as yours can hurt you for more than a little" (2:417). That, as we have seen, bears the authentic form of love, wherein an I addresses a Thou directly with the affirmation, "It is good that you exist."

chapter 6

A LIGHT THAT HAS BEEN THERE

FROM THE BEGINNING: STEPHEN CRANE

AND THE GOSPEL OF JOHN

Near the end of "The Monster," Stephen Crane gestures twice unmistakably toward the Gospel of John. He first introduces Martha Goodwin as one who takes exception to the communal fear of the "monster" and anger at Dr. Trescott. After Henry Johnson has escaped from the Williamses, been chased through Whilomville by a stone-throwing crowd, and reapprehended, Crane begins Chapter 19 with a description of this woman who recalls her biblical namesake, "cumbered about much serving" in Luke (10:40), and present again in John 11 and 12 during the story of her brother Lazarus's being raised from the dead by Jesus: "Martha Goodwin was single, and well along into the thin years. She lived with her married sister in Whilomville. She performed nearly all the house work in exchange for the privilege of existence. Every one tacitly recognized her labor as a form of penance for the early end of her betrothed, who had died of small-pox, which he had not caught from her."[1] Crane seems especially interested in placing his story in relation to the twelfth chapter of John. When a delegation of well-wishers visit Trescott in the story's penultimate chapter, Crane gives their leader the suggestive name John Twelve. He reiterates the name throughout the chapter, and lest we miss its biblical suggestion, he has Twelve represent the thinking of a group: "about a dozen of us," as he puts it.

By this time, Henry Johnson has come to live at the Trescotts, and Dr. Trescott has lost nearly all his patients. Twelve, a wealthy "wholesale grocer," offers to help Trescott by providing Henry "a little no-good farm up beyond Clarence Mountain" (63). The offer is difficult to evaluate, for, as Trescott makes clear, Henry cannot take care of himself and no one seems inclined to care for him: "You don't know, my friend. Everybody is

so afraid of him, they can't even give him good care. Nobody can attend
to him as I do myself." After this response by the doctor, Twelve makes
a more mysterious suggestion: "And if you—and if you—through your
house burning down, or anything—why, all the boys were prepared to
take him right off your hands, and—and—" (63). The "boys" seem prepared to kill Henry. Earlier in the text, Judge Hagenthorpe, now one of
Twelve's twelve, has argued that the horribly burned Henry "ought to die"
(31). The silence and prolonged stillness that follow Twelve's suggestion
add to the sense that an ultimate solution has been proposed, as does
Trescott's eventual response: "It can't be done."

Allusions throughout Crane's oeuvre have led some critics to read his
works in close allegorical relationship to the Gospel of John. Undoubtedly, some of the New Critical attempts to trace Johannine or biblical
allegories in Crane's works were excessively ingenious. Nevertheless,
critics such as R. W. Stallman, Daniel Hoffman, and Daniel Knapp are
right, I believe, to read Crane's work in a Christian, and more specifically
Johannine, light.[2] To demonstrate this claim, I propose to look carefully
at two of Crane's works, "The Blue Hotel" and "The Monster," in which
Knapp and others have identified motifs from John. My concern is not to
draw close, parallel by parallel, connections between the stories or to explain details in "The Monster" through allegorical correspondence to biblical texts. Rather, I wish to suggest how Crane's understanding of a
constellation of matters—violence, the scapegoat function, glory, war,
hospitality, and lying—can be read from a perspective formed by John.
Crane's broad gestures toward John in "The Monster" suggest that his
understanding of his material was specifically related to John. Thus I offer
my interpretations as contributions to our understanding of Crane's convictions about such phenomena as lying, the face, and war. Yet I am
willing to believe that one must be formed by John to read the stories'
central matters as I do. So that my readings be accessible to those not
formed by John, I have used several philosophical sources to clarify the
texts. Emmanuel Levinas's phenomenology of the face and his paradoxical understanding of the relationship between war and peace provide a
rich set of terms for reading "The Monster." The nexus of lying and
murder identified by "The Blue Hotel" can be helpfully read in relation to
Immanuel Kant's strictures on lying, which themselves stand in at least
oblique relationship to John.

To get the events of John 12 firmly in mind, as well as the Lazarus story
in John 11, a brief review may be useful. Chapter 11 opens with the

announcement that Lazarus is sick at Bethany. Jesus has recently escaped stoning for blasphemy in Jerusalem and gone "beyond Jordan into the place where John at first baptized" (10:40).[3] When he hears that Lazarus lies ill, Jesus says, "This sickness is not unto death, but for the glory of God, that the Son of God might be glorified thereby" (11:4). When he says further to the disciples, "Let us go into Judaea again," they understand what this means in terms of danger and death: "Master, the Jews of late sought to stone thee; and goest thou thither again?" (11:7–8). Jesus persists, but when they arrive at Bethany, Lazarus has been dead four days already. Running out to meet the group, Martha reproaches Jesus, "Lord, if thou hadst been here, my brother had not died" (11:21). When Jesus assures her that Lazarus "shall rise again," Martha responds that she knows he will rise at the last day, in the general resurrection. But Jesus now gives changed meaning to the resurrection hope: "I am the resurrection, and the life: he that believeth in me, though he were dead, yet shall he live: And whosoever liveth and believeth in me shall never die." Then he asks Martha directly, "Believest thou this?" and she responds that she believes him to be the Christ "which should come into the world" (11:23–27).

Next, Mary comes to Jesus, accompanied by a group of Jews who have been comforting her at her house. She also, in her grief, reproves Jesus, and when he sees both her and the Jews weeping, he too mysteriously weeps. When, at the tomb, he says, "Take ye away the stone," Martha hesitates, reminding Jesus that Lazarus has been dead four days and is already stinking. Jesus' response stresses again the glory of God: "Said I not unto thee, that, if thou wouldest believe, thou shouldest see the glory of God?" (11:39–40). Jesus commands Lazarus to "come forth," and "he that was dead came forth, bound hand and foot with graveclothes: and his face was bound about with a napkin." Jesus then says, "Loose him, and let him go," suggesting that the glory of God is manifested in the human being set free from bondage to death (11:43–44). Much of the rest of the chapter concerns the chief priests' decision that it is better for Jesus to die than for the nation to perish. Caiaphas argues "that it is expedient for us, that one man should die for the people" (11:50). The chief priests fear that the "Romans shall come and take away both our place and nation" (11:48). Fear of having their place usurped leads specifically to the betrayal of Jesus.

Chapter 12 begins with Jesus again in Bethany, sitting at table with Lazarus and Mary while Martha serves. When Mary anoints Jesus' feet with the costly spikenard, Judas rebukes her extravagance, asking why the oil had not been sold and the money given to the poor. Jesus' response initiates the motif of his moving toward death that dominates the chapter: "Let her alone: against the day of my burying hath she kept this" (12:7). Many people, at this time, come to Bethany to see not only Jesus but also Lazarus, "whom he had raised from the dead." Because many of the Jews are coming, through the miracle of Lazarus's raising, to "believe on Jesus," the chief priests resolve "that they might put Lazarus also to death" (12:9–11). Next, the chapter records the events commemorated now on Palm Sunday. Sitting on the ass's colt, associated by Zecchariah with Israel's king, Jesus turns toward death in Jerusalem. The crowd remains ever present: many have been there at the raising of Lazarus, many have come to the feast in Bethany, still others arrive who have heard the stories of the miracle. Taking their branches of palms, the crowd seem to acknowledge Jesus' Messiahship, crying, "Hosanna: Blessed *is* the King of Israel that cometh in the name of the Lord" (12:13). Indeed, the crowd's movement frightens the Pharisees further. Their policy seems to be failing, as "the world is gone after him" (12:19).

The themes of glory, light, and judgment dominate the second half of the chapter as Jesus faces death. Glory is first mentioned by John in reference to the disciples' failure to understand the significance of the crowd's cries of "Hosanna" or Jesus' riding the ass's colt: "These things understood not his disciples at the first: but when Jesus was glorified, then remembered they that these things were written of him, and *that* they had done these things unto him" (12:16). Later, Jesus uses the language of glory as he speaks of his death to the disciples and "certain Greeks" who have come to worship at the feast: "The hour is come, that the Son of man should be glorified." In the same speech, Jesus asks rhetorically, "Now is my soul troubled; and what shall I say? Father, save me from this hour: but for this cause came I unto this hour. Father, glorify thy name." And at that moment, a voice comes "from heaven, *saying*, I have both glorified *it*, and will glorify *it* again" (12:23–28). The crowd hears this, some saying it thunders, others, that an angel has spoken to Jesus, who responds that the voice has come "not because of me, but for your sakes." The Father's glory comes, then, not in saving Jesus from death but in His going to the cross. "Now," Jesus announces, is the beginning of the decisive eschatological moment: "Now is the judgment of this world: now shall the prince of this world be cast out. And I, if I be lifted up from the earth, will draw all *men* unto me" (12:30–32). The judgment of the world involves the Son's going to the cross to manifest the glory of the Father, which will draw all to it.

The remainder of the chapter identifies Jesus as "a light into the world," come in order that believers "should not abide in darkness" (12:46). He urges the crowd to "walk while ye have the light" and to "believe in the light, that ye may be the children of light" (12:35–36). Nevertheless, John makes clear that the crowd does not believe, citing what Isaiah has prophesied on his own glimpse of God's glory: "He hath blinded their eyes, and hardened their heart; that they should not see with *their* eyes, nor understand with *their* heart, and be converted, and I should heal them" (12:40). Some "among the chief rulers" do seem to believe, but, "lov[ing] the praise of men more than the praise of God" (12:42–43), they do not confess because they do not want to be removed from the synagogue. The chapter closes with Jesus' insisting that he comes not to judge the world but to save; the "word" that he speaks will judge, a word he has been commanded to speak by his Father: "life everlasting" (12:50).

The raising of Lazarus unsettles the borders between life and death. At table in John 12, he sits as one who has been dead now eating again with those who live. His presence destroys the distinctions between life and death on which the power of the authorities rests. Death has its terrors, but these have been brought under at least some control by the ruling powers. Lazarus's raising and continued presence call all those powers into question. Indeed, the geopolitical analysis of Caiaphas seems correct: any demonstration that God's glory lies in the human being set free from bondage to death will surely bring the most terrible counterreaction from the world's greatest armed power, imperial Rome.

Like Lazarus, Crane's Henry Johnson unsettles the boundaries between life and death and Whilomville's agreed-upon manner of containing death's terror and power. Whilomville is quite happy with Henry Johnson dead: his "raising" and return are what horrify. In death, he provides a number of people the opportunity for vicarious or reflected dignity. As the cots of Jimmie, Dr. Trescott, and Henry are carried from the scene of the fire, the narrator comments, "The men who bore the cots were well known to the crowd"—as present throughout this story as it is in John 11 and 12—"but in this solemn parade during the ringing of the bells and the shouting, and with the red glare upon the sky, they seemed utterly foreign, and Whilomville paid them a deep respect." Through closeness to the solemn mysteries of heroism and death, "each man in this stretcher party had gained a reflected majesty." The crowd seems to participate in the heightened importance of the moment, making "subtle obeisance to this august dignity derived from three prospective graves" (28–29).

Whilomville's reaction to Henry's "death" suggests Crane's insight into magical thinking as a way to counter death's terror. Townspeople judge "themselves stupid and ungenerous" (30) for being insufficiently helpful to Henry, thereby turning their attention away from what they do not want to face, their lack of control over death, to focus on themselves, their real or perceived failings. At the same time, Henry's name "became suddenly the title of a saint to the little boys"; to quote it in a quarrel was to, at once, overthrow one's "antagonist, whether it applied to the subject or whether it did not" (30). The sacred name contains power for the agon, that competitive gaming Crane understood so well, especially in its most intense and sublime form: war.

Crane knew the need of human beings to participate in powers greater than themselves. The fire scene in "The Monster" illustrates this need as the fire companies, and their respective advocates, engage in a competitive display analogous to war. When the sacred violence breaks out, the crowd feels lifted out of the routine of Whilomville and into a larger life: "The flames, towering high, cast a wild red light on their faces." "Perspiring citizens" fling "themselves into the fray," and boys dance "in impish joy at the displays of prowess." The fire threatens all with what Rene Girard calls a crisis of difference, and parties respond by supporting "the worth" of their favored fire companies "with no small violence."[4] Each part of Whilomville has its own allegiance to a particular fire company, and the town's placidity covers a war that simmers just below the surface of dailiness: "Feuds, which the boys forgot and remembered according to chance or the importance of some recent event, existed all through the town." Conflict develops over which company "owned [the] distinction" of getting the first water on the fire. Judgment settles on two rivals, and the "blood adherents of other companies were obliged to choose between the two on this occasion, and the talk waxed warm" (26–28).

The sacred ability of the fire to compel the crowd's fascination is enhanced by the apparent deaths of Jimmie and Henry and the savage burning of Trescott. "A great rumor went among the crowds," the narrator says, with distinctly biblical accent, followed by the falling of a "reverent silence." The great thing, with its power to compel, was in their midst: "The crowd did not even feel the police pushing at them. They raised their eyes, shining now with awe, toward the high flames." "The man who had information was at his best," describing "the whole affair" in "low tones," and, as the reader is privileged to know, getting all the details wrong. Seeking distinction through proximity to the sacred, "the man who had information" plays his part in the drama of the crowd's vicarious participation in the powers. In his last images of the fire before turning to focus on the procession of stretchers, Crane reemphasizes the warlike quality of the combat: "The crowd concentrated its gaze still more closely upon these flags of fire which waved joyfully against the black sky. The bells of the town were clashing unceasingly" (28).

Having seen the way Crane's fire scenes emphasize the competitive human striving to demonstrate worth, we are now in a position to speculate about the significance of Martha's last name: Good-one, Good-win— one who is determined to win by being the one who is good. Crane identifies this woman, so devoted to penitential labor to demonstrate her goodness, with war. Although "her fullest experience of violence" was to see "a hound clubbed," this "woman of peace, who had seen only peace, argued constantly for a creed of illimitable ferocity." "An invincible being like Napoleon," Martha "overrode all opponents with a sniff. This sniff was an active force. It was to her antagonists like a bang over the head, and none was known to recover from this expression of exalted contempt" (50). Martha's is a moral sniff, one that says she knows more than others about the far-flung matters to which she gives attention, one that looks down from the pinnacle of goodness she has built for herself through her labors. Critics have had difficulty knowing how to assess Martha, for Crane clearly suggests her refusal to join in the communal hysteria about Henry and anger at Trescott. This refusal, however, may derive from no particularly admirable motive in Martha. It may reflect only contempt for others and desire to distinguish herself absolutely from them—the desire that drives her labor to prove herself the one who is good, the winner. That desire is the engine of her "illimitable ferocity."

We have seen how Crane associates war with the human need to participate vicariously in powers larger than oneself and with the need to be distinguished, either by identification with a collectivity that proves its worth by defeating rivals or by turning one's life, as in Martha Goodwin's case, into a sacrificial labor of righteousness. Crane seems remarkably aware of these frantic attempts at transcendence of human limitations while, at the same time, stressing their utter futility. If we ask what would lead Crane to see, with such clarity, the futility of attempts at transcendence, we may find a possible answer in the New Testament chapter Crane gestures toward so broadly: John Twelve. Jesus predicts his own being "lifted up from the earth," a prediction fulfilled in his crucifixion and then in God's action of raising him from the dead. But this is, to any human notion, a curious kind of lifting up, not the transcendence sought by those who identify with the glory of one worldly power or another—from the Whilomville fire companies to the vast blue and gray demonstrations of nations at war. Rather, this "lifting up" involves turning toward death in Jerusalem, going directly at it and into it, and then being betrayed, tried, scourged, humiliated, and crucified. Yet Jesus predicts, too, that his being lifted up in this way will eventually draw "all men" to him, that all men will ultimately recognize His hugely paradoxical experience to be the very form of the Father's glory and the judgment of the world. The glorification of the Father's name through Jesus' going to the cross relativizes—one is tempted to say, trivializes—all human efforts at glory. How is one to regard all the various desperate ways in which human beings seek to glorify themselves—all of what Ernest Becker calls their "immortality heroics"[5]—if one takes seriously the idea that God has glorified his name and judged the world in Jesus' cross?

One might regard such heroics with the thoroughgoing irony characteristic of Crane, one continually aware both of the constancy of human efforts at glorification and their futility, or perhaps more accurately, irrelevance. A touching or pathetic irrelevance, perhaps, because the need to distinguish oneself in one's own glory seems so human. But pathetic or irrelevant nonetheless, and for the very reasons established in the raising of Lazarus and John 12. God has shown in the raising of Lazarus that his glory consists of the human being freed from the power of death. He wants to free, is glorified in freeing, human beings from the very power under which they remain in all their own frantic attempts to glorify themselves. All they need do is to participate in the glory of God— infinitely greater than any they themselves can demonstrate—through the following of Jesus.

Why, then, must Lazarus be put to death along with Jesus, as is contemplated in John: 12? Because he confounds the distinction between life and death; because he is the presence of that which was dead and is now alive again, not by virtue of any human power but by God's power alone. His being there constitutes evidence of God's relativizing all human power and attempts at distinction or glory. Henry Johnson's return from "death" similarly unsettles Whilomville, and if we read it from a point of view formed by John 11 and 12, we can see that unsettling to be one involving the very boundary between life and death.

Whilomville canonizes the dead Henry, but it knows not what to do with him once he returns. The question is taken up by Judge Hagenthorpe and Dr. Trescott as soon as it becomes clear that Henry may not die. When he visits Trescott as the latter attends Henry, the Judge seems to have "something further to say," which he is "kept from [saying] by the scrutiny of the unwinking eye" of Henry. Later, when the eye is no longer on him, the judge speaks up: "No one wants to advance such ideas, but somehow I think that that poor fellow ought to die" (31). The phrase "ought to die" seems ambiguous. Does it mean that Henry ought to be allowed to die for his own good in a kind of passive euthanasia? Or is it a recommendation to Trescott of a more active euthanasia? Or does it mean that somehow Henry is obligated to die, that it would be expedient—as is said of Jesus just after the raising of Lazarus—for one man to die for the people? Much of the rest of the story seems consistent with this last reading of the Judge's comment, for "the monster's" presence is profoundly dislocating to Whilomville. Surely its citizens would assent to its being expedient for Henry to die for them. The Judge argues further that it will be "a questionable charity" to preserve "this negro's life," for "he will hereafter be a monster, a perfect monster, and probably with an affected brain." The Judge assures Trescott that "no man" could observe him and not recognize that saving Henry Johnson has been "a matter of conscience" with him, but he fears the doctor is guilty of "one of the blunders of virtue" (31). Crane uses this last line to prepare the ironies of Whilomville's treatment of Dr. Trescott as "the monster" remains among them: everyone may regard Trescott's saving Henry to be a "matter of conscience," but they blame him anyway for the disturbing presence among them. Indeed, as the dead Henry has been canonized for heroism and the returned monster possesses a kind of untouchable sacredness, the people must look elsewhere for a scapegoat, for one responsible for loosing the terror among them. Thus the second half of Crane's story links the tale of Henry's growing monstrosity in Whilomville's eyes with the town's increasing desertion and even hatred of Trescott.

To the Judge's suggestion that preserving Henry's life is a blunder of virtue, Dr. Trescott responds effectively, *"Ich kann nicht anders"*—he cannot do otherwise: "'And what am I to do?' said Trescott, his eyes suddenly lighting like an outburst from smouldering peat. 'What am I to do? He gave himself for—for Jimmie. What am I to do for him?'" (32). Michael Warner has pointed to this section in his discussion of the way Crane "problematizes" ordinary notions of value, agency, and morality. Warner suggests that Trescott complains here not of a lack of "free will" but "that the right thing to do in his case had no connection to benevolence, moral courage, or anything that would make it the right thing to do." Warner sees in "Trescott's saving of Henry" an exact "parallel to Henry's saving of Jimmie in that in each case the act fails of its purpose, and in each case the value of moral courage feels appropriate even though no basis for that value is readily discernible."⁶ Warner is adamant that Trescott's problem of what to do is "neither one of interpretation nor one of action"; rather, it points to Crane's problematizing the notion of "agency" itself and the relation to "value" that Warner assumes to be essential to morality: "The crucial point is that a distinction has been made within the concept of choice; freedom obtains, but pure intent does not. This is part of what I have been calling the problematic of agency. One can still point to moral agents and their acts, but Crane has put in question the kind of relation between those agents and their acts that we must assume in order to understand our machinery of valuation" (85–86).

On Warner's model, moral agency depends on the ability of a "pure intent" to enact "value"; anything less problematizes agency and, with it, any notion of moral action. But it is hardly surprising that Crane problematizes agency conceived as such, for where has such a "pure intent," freed from all the contingencies of history, ever existed? The dilemma Crane constructs points to the value of something like Stanley Hauerwas's description of agency, wherein "to be an agent means I am able to locate my action within an ongoing history and within a community of language users." On this view, "I am not an agent because I can 'cause' certain things to happen, but because certain things that happen, whether through the result of my decision or not, can be made mine through my power of attention and intention. The 'causation' proper to agents and their actions is not rendered by cause and effect, but by the agent's power of description. My act is not something I cause, as though it were external to me, but it is mine because I am able to 'fit' it into my ongoing story."⁷ Hauerwas's model helps us see Trescott's problem as one of interpretation: he cannot really know what he is doing vis-à-vis Henry because he does not know what Henry will be on the other side of his "death." What Henry will "be" is itself a matter of interpretation between the Judge and Trescott. The Judge insists, "He will be your creation, you understand. He is purely your creation. Nature has very evidently given him up. He is dead. You are restoring him to life. You are making him, and he will be a monster, and with no mind." "He will be what you like, judge," Trescott cries out in return (32).

Henry will be, for others, what they interpret him to be. They will attempt to place him in some way or another within the stories they understand, as Crane emphasizes in Chapter 14, with its recounting of the barber shop conversation in which various townsmen try to imagine themselves into both Dr. Trescott's dilemma and Henry's condition of being without a face. Crane does "problematize" Trescott's situation, but he does so in a way that specifically involves interpretation and is much more radical than Warner allows. Warner is comfortable in saying that Trescott's saving Henry fails. But on what grounds does he do so? How does he make this judgment without interpretation, without reading Henry's experience within an ongoing narrative? It seems more reasonable to suggest, following Hauerwas, that moral action always takes place within a pattern of interpretation, within some understanding of what is going on. Trescott's problem lies in projecting how the faceless man he is saving will be interpreted by the community, for clearly Henry will present an interpretive problem to those others in whose hands his life will largely rest. I think it no accident that Crane uses the Judge to pose the difficulty of knowing what to do with Henry. The Judge is used to operating by assimilating cases to the law, by bringing antecedent criteria to bear on particulars. But what law covers the case of a faceless man? Under what criterion does one gather him? The closing note of Chapter 11 points directly to Crane's foregrounding of the interpretive problem: "After another silence, the judge said, 'It is hard for a man to know what to do'" (33). It is hard to know what to do because it is hard even to describe what is going on.

Stephen Crane was extraordinarily sensitive to the face. His work is filled with emphatic images of faces and of characters' facing one another. "The Upturned Face" provides a case in point: two officers and two privates work under fire to bury a third officer, whose face, "chalk-blue" and "star[ing] at the sky," dominates the story. After the privates have dug a shallow grave, the officers decide it would be appropriate for them to lift their comrade into it: "Both were particular that their fingers should not feel the corpse. They tugged away; the corpse lifted, heaved, toppled, flopped into the grave, and the two officers, straightening, looked again at each other—they were always looking at each other. They sighed with relief."[8] Crane insists here, as in "The Monster," on the uncanny presence of death and the men's desire to maintain clear distinction between the living and the dead. The remarkable first sentence of the quotation suggests that feeling is somehow only for the living, that it's inappropriate to feel a corpse. The corpse, on the other hand, seems bent on confusing the distinction between living and dead; it seems still able to act—lifting, heaving, toppling, and flopping as if on its own. Even more confusing is the continuing presence of the dead officer's face. As one of the privates begins filling the grave, "he lifted his first shovel load of earth and for a moment of inexplicable hesitation it was held poised above this corpse which from its chalk-blue face looked keenly out from the grave. Then the soldier emptied his shovel on—on the feet" (299). One of the officers, Timothy Lean, seems visibly relieved, as he had "felt that perhaps the private might empty the shovel on—on the face" (300). The remainder of the story is given, then, to the filling of the grave. One of the privates is wounded, and the officers must themselves take over the work of covering their comrade. "Soon there was nothing to be seen but the chalk-blue face," and Lean, who is filling the grave, cries out to the other officer, who is his senior, "Good God . . . Why didn't you turn him somehow when you put him in? This—." The face, staring chalk-blue at the sky over it, continues to bear a particular unsubstitutable identity; it continues to suggest an otherness that cannot simply be assimilated to the whole machinery of war. The adjutant, Lean's senior officer, "understood" Lean's stuttering, inconclusive, "This—." " 'Go on, man' [the adjutant] cried, beseechingly, almost in a shout." Here the beseeching cry is also an order, one that allows Lean and the adjutant to return to their roles and to be reassimilated into the totality of the army and the state it represents. They cry to be relieved of the pressure of acting as unique identities being appealed to by that transcendent face. The order gives Lean what he needs: "Lean swung back the shovel; it went forward in a pendulum curve. When the earth landed it made a sound—plop" (300).

Crane's feeling for the face seems much like that of phenomenologist Emmanuel Levinas, for whom the face makes ethics possible because it "resists possession, resists my powers. In its epiphany, in expression, the sensible, still graspable, turns into total resistance to the grasp. This mutation can occur only by the opening of a new dimension."[9] That new dimension is ethics, for which the "facing position" is fundamental. "The ethical relationship," for Levinas, is "not a species of consciousness whose ray emanates from the I; it puts the I in question. This putting in question emanates from the other" (*TI* 195)—specifically, from the face of the Other, whose alterity I am never able to reduce to a theme of my own. The face's resistance to the grasp "is not produced as an insurmountable resistance, like the hardness of the rock against which the effort of the hand comes to naught, like the remoteness of a star in the immensity of space." Rather, the face defies not simply my feeble powers but "my ability for power": "The face, still a thing among things, breaks through the form that nevertheless delimits it. This means concretely: the face speaks to me and thereby invites me to a relation incommensurate with a power exercised, be it enjoyment or knowledge" (*TI* 197–198). As Merold Westphal has put it, for Levinas, "it is face to face with the Other that I encounter the claim that puts my project of being the center of the world in question." The immediacy of the ethical relationship depends on my encountering "the infinity of another person incarnate in a face"; "violence," with which Levinas is continually concerned, "consists in seeing the Other not as a face but merely as a force."[10] In describing the ethical relationship, Levinas uses a metaphor that applies with striking accuracy to the men of Crane's "The Upturned Face": the hostage. I find myself a hostage "responsible for what [others] do or suffer."[11] This being a hostage is "like kinship, it is a bond prior to every chosen bond."[12] Is it not that "bond prior to every chosen bond" that requires the men of "The Upturned Face" to stay amid the bullets and bury their dead comrade? Moreover, it is the face, for Crane just as for Levinas, that holds the men hostage, claiming them against their will, insisting that they are responsible. Finally, the covering of the face is the precondition for the men's return to violence.

"The Monster" abounds in motifs of the face and facing. The most important of these is, of course, the facelessness of Henry Johnson after his return to life following the Trescott fire and his presumed death. But the emphasis on the face begins as early as the first chapter, Crane's parable of fallenness, in which "little Jim," playing train engine, knocks over a peony as his father mows in another corner of the yard: "He looked at his father and at the broken flower. Finally he went to the peony and tried to stand it on its pins, resuscitated, but the spine of it was hurt, and it would only hang limply from his hand. Jim could do no reparation. He looked again toward his father" (9). The paragraph points already to larger motifs in the story. Jim could not "resuscitate" the flower; he could not bring it back to life. He has not intended to sin, he has been innocently playing as any child might. But in the very process of living and acting, he has brought about consequences to another part of creation that cannot be undone. He would try to make reparation, but he cannot do so. In this condition of fallenness, where actions cannot be undone, Jim cannot face his father. The boy tries several times to show his father what he has done; Trescott has difficulty discerning the source of Jim's trouble and displays no anger, only courtesy and respect. Crane suggests, in short, that Jim has no reason to fear his father, who, when he finally discovers what is bothering the son, asks simply, "Well, Jimmie . . . I guess you had better not play train any more to-day. Do you think you had better?" Despite the father's mildness here, however, Jim does not face him: "During the delivery of the judgment the child had not faced his father, and afterward he went away, shuffling his feet" (10). It seems to me it would be wrong to read this scene out, psychoanalytically, in Oedipal terms, for there is no anger or vindictiveness in the father here. What Crane presents is considerably more sophisticated theology. Without intending to do so, we act in ways that inevitably have consequences for other parts of creation that cannot be undone—for which we cannot make reparation.[13] Our desire to make reparation, combined with an awareness of being unable to do so, leads to our inability to face the Father.

Crane's stress on the face continues in the opening line of Chapter 2: "It was apparent from Jimmie's manner that he felt some kind of desire to efface himself." Henry knows how to provide Jimmie solace during these times of effacement; he and Jimmie are "in complete but unexpressed understanding" on "all points of conduct as related to the doctor, who was the moon" (11). As an image for the doctor, the moon, emphasized repeatedly by Crane, seems curious. We might expect the doctor—as Jim's father, the ruler of the garden, Henry's employer—to be described as the sun, the sovereign source of light (an image Crane does employ in the story, but which he reserves for Martha Goodwin as she is looked on by those who defer to her when in her presence but laugh at her "afterward, under another sun" [50]). The moon has a face, but its light is reflected; it is not a source from which light goes out to disclose things against a horizon. Even in the opening scene, light does not seem to go out from Jim's father, as if he possessed penetrating insight, the ability to disclose, to drag or bring into the light Jim's crime. Jim must point several times to the peony, saying "There," before his father, only "after some trouble," finds what his son means. In short—and I stress the matter because it is important to the story's senses of light and glory I develop later—Jim's father is a reflector of light, an illumined moon, rather than a sovereign director of light who compels things into the open. The moon, however, can be "eclipsed," its face temporarily hidden, and it is during these times that Jimmie goes to the stable to "solace himself with Henry's crimes" (11).

Henry's own "face showed like a reflector as he bowed and bowed" to Miss Bella Farragut, who praises him to her mother with a rhetorical question, "Oh, ma, isn't he divine?" (16). Later, Mrs. Trescott "screamed" directly into "Henry's face," "Jimmie! Save Jimmie!" (21), triggering his immediate response of running into the burning house. When he falls unconscious in the laboratory, it is Henry's face that is exposed and vulnerable to the stream of sizzling, corrosive chemicals, described by Crane as a "ruby-red snakelike thing": "It coiled and hesitated, and then began to swim a languorous way down the mahogany slant. At the angle it waved its sizzling molten head to and fro over the closed eyes of the man beneath it. Then, in a moment, with a mystic impulse, it moved again, and the red snake flowed directly down into Johnson's upturned face" (24). The effect of light on another "upturned face" is mentioned by Crane just before the call of "Fire" goes throughout the crowd gathered to hear the band: "When the light fell upon the upturned face of a girl, it caused it to glow with a wonderful pallor. A policeman came suddenly from the darkness and chased a gang of obstreperous little boys" (17). The light here seems to disclose the little boys and brings with it force that would drag their defiances, their tiny contemplated crimes, into the open.

In addition to the face, several other motifs of Levinas's phenomenology are remarkably similar to those of "The Monster": home, vision, light, war, and hospitality. "Begin[ning] with the concrete relationship between an I and a world," Levinas argues that the I's maintaining itself as the same—the I's continuing ability to identify itself as I—is intimately bound up with a mode of being "against the world" produced by dwelling and the home. The I "finds in the world a site [*lieu*] and a home [*maison*]" where it dwells, a word that signifies "the very mode of *maintaining oneself* [*se tenir*], . . . as the body that, on the earth exterior to it, holds *itself* up [*se tient*] and *can*" (TI 37). Intimately related to this mode of maintaining oneself in dwelling is the identification of knowing with vision: "Vision moves into grasp. Vision opens a perspective, upon a horizon, and describes a traversable distance, invites the hand to movement and to contact, and ensures them." Vision is fundamental to a mode of existence that schematizes the world and experience in terms of the project: "The forms of objects call for the hand and the grasp," through which "the object is in the end comprehended, touched, taken, born and *referred* to other objects, clothed with a signification, *by reference to* other objects." "Empty space is the condition" for this mode of grasping objects and clothing them with signification by relating them to other objects. The emptying of space, the driving out of darkness, is the work of light. "Vision is not a transcendence," argues Levinas; transcendence involves the "face to face," where the Other can appear as if in itself and not simply as a thing to be grasped, an object to be brought within a schema of the I maintaining itself as the same. Vision "ascribes a signification by the *relation* it makes possible. It opens nothing that, beyond the same, would be absolutely other, that is, in itself. Light conditions the relations between data; it makes possible the signification of objects that border one another. It does not enable one to approach them face to face" (*TI* 191). The face of the Other opens in us the metaphysical desire for the infinite, for the possibility of an absolutely exterior being—possibilities forgotten by "vision in the light" because it continually causes us to apprehend beings on a horizon or in relation to one another. Still, light does have "another sense" as "origin of itself—as the source of light, in which its being and its appearing coincide, as fire and as sun." "Here," Levinas says, "is the figure of every relation with the absolute" (*TI* 191). The figure, however, is "only a figure." The "light as sun is an object," and the "sensible light qua visual datum does not differ from other data, and itself remains relative to an elemental and obscure ground." Making possible the "consciousness of radical exteriority" would require "a relation with what in another sense comes absolutely from itself": "A light is needed to see the light" (*TI* 192).

Levinas asks, in *Totality and Infinity*, whether "lucidity, the mind's openness upon the true," does not "consist in catching sight of the permanent possibility of war" (*TI* 21). Yet, for Levinas, "only beings capable of war can rise to peace." War and peace share a crucial presupposition: they both "presuppose beings structured otherwise than as parts of a totality" (*TI* 222). They are both opposed to a thinking, ontological and statist, that seeks to integrate all beings into a totality. That thinking resolves "*conflicts* between the same and the other . . . by theory whereby the other is reduced to the same—or, concretely, by the community of the State, where beneath anonymous power, though it be intelligible, the I rediscovers war in the tyrannic oppression it undergoes from the totality" (*TI* 47). I take Levinas to mean here that the I "rediscovers war" as it loses its face to the anonymous oppression of reason and the state. Existents drive, in war, to be themselves, not to be defined by their relation to other terms within a whole: "In war beings refuse to belong to a totality, refuse community, refuse law; no frontier stops one being by another, nor defines them. They affirm themselves as transcending the totality, each identifying itself not by its place in the whole, but by its *self.*" We might say, then, that the thought of peace must first go through the thought of war. "The exclusion of violence by beings susceptible of being integrated into a totality"—state, new world order, peace process—"is not equivalent to peace." Such exclusion merely masks the violence done to individual existents as they are brought into the totality. "Totality absorbs the multiplicity of beings," on which war insists and "which peace implies" (*TI* 222). Peace depends on eschatology, not philosophy, an eschatology in which "particular beings" would not "yield their truth in a Whole in which their exteriority vanishes" (*TI* 26). Crucial, then, to "a subjectivity born from the eschatological vision" is hospitality, "welcoming the Other." In hospitality "the idea of infinity," aroused by the revelation of exteriority in the face of the Other, is "consummated" (*TI* 27).

Chapter 6 of "The Monster" opens with an image of the Trescott house on the horizon, fading into darkness as the light of day dies: "The outlines of the house of Doctor Trescott had faded quietly into the evening, hiding a shape such as we call Queen Anne against the pall of the blackened sky" (20). The fire has already begun, although Crane has not yet made it clear that the Trescott house is the one burning. Crane never offers any causal explanation of the fire: it seems autochthonous, an "origin of itself," in Levinas's terms, "its being and its appearing coinciding." This seemingly unsourced light destroys the Trescotts' house, their home, the site that marks their place in the world, their project of being at the center of the world. Previously, the Trescotts lived comfortably enough in what Crane calls elsewhere the "truth of daylight" (45), where the infinite is excluded, but now Henry Johnson returns from death as a continual reminder of the infinite. His faceless face continually destroys attempts to represent it adequately, opening the possibility of existence in "radical exteriority." Despite Henry's being faceless rather than faced, Crane's strategy seems consistent with Levinas's sense of the face as "present in its refusal to be contained" (*TI* 94). It may be that Crane must make Henry, as an African American, faceless in order to make him faced.

As Crane's opening chapters emphasize, Henry has become extremely adept at offering others a social presentation that fits what they need. We might say he ceases to act as an Other to them; he is never able to destroy or overflow the idea of him in others because he is always anticipating that idea and presenting himself in its terms (making himself *adequate* to it). When Jimmie becomes the "victim of an eclipse," "Henry, with the elasticity of his race, could usually provide a sin to place himself on a footing with the disgraced one." If he does not follow this strategy of reducing himself to sameness with Jimmie, he takes on the authority of Dr. Trescott, still presenting himself not as an Other to Jimmie but as a representation of what Jimmie expects. Such a strategy again evinces "the elasticity of his race": "On the other hand, Henry would sometimes choose to absolutely repudiate this idea, and when Jimmie appeared in his shame would bully him most virtuously, preaching with assurance the precepts of the doctor's creed, and pointing out to Jimmie all his abominations" (11). Perhaps Crane suggests, then, that only after having his face burned away can Henry's face appear as the Other that continually overflows and destroys Whilomville's idea of him. Henry's life has arguably been a kind of systematic self-effacement. To end that self-effacement and allow Henry's face to appear as Other to the people of Whilomville, Crane eradicates it.

Levinas begins *Otherwise Than Being* with two epigraphs from Pascal: the first, "Men say, 'this is my place in the sun,' which marks 'the beginning and the image of the usurpation of the entire earth' "; and the second, "We have used concupiscence as far as was in our power to promote the general good; but it is no more than a sham and a false image of love; for at bottom it is nothing but hate."[14] The passages link the insistence on one's place in the sun with usurpation of the earth and with hatred—for Levinas, even murderous hatred. All of these ideas figure prominently in Chapter 20 of "The Monster," the last chapter in which Henry appears. Crane begins the chapter with Jimmie's difficulty in placing the "monster" after he has returned to living behind the stable at the Trescotts. After returning from temporary banishment to Connecticut, Jimmie is "at first much afraid" of the monster, because "he could not identify it in any way." "Gradually" fascination replaces his fear, and he "sidled into closer and closer relations with it" (52). This sidling into relations seems to be mostly a matter of Jimmie's mental processes, for Crane's presentation of "the monster" increasingly stresses his alterity, his existence without context—or in a context that resists acts of placing, identifying, or relating (however sidling). Even the gap between the chapter's first two paragraphs suggests the now autochthonous existence of the monster; paragraph 1 closes its account of Jimmie's mentation with his now imagined "closer relations." Then Crane moves abruptly: "One time the monster was seated on a box behind the stable basking in the rays of the afternoon sun. A heavy crepe veil was swathed about its head" (52).

Jimmie and his companions now engage in a game of taunting and daring one another to run toward Henry and touch the monster—the game, again, of distinction. Dared by an older boy who "habitually oppressed him to a small degree," Jimmie "went to the monster and laid his hand delicately on its shoulder": "'Hello, Henry,' he said, in a voice that trembled a trifle. The monster was crooning a weird line of negro melody that was scarcely more than a thread of sound, and it paid no heed to the boy" (53). Here the monster seems as removed from the surrounding context, as most nearly present in alterity, as we can perhaps imagine. Touching the Other suggests the need to reestablish relations with him, to bring him back from his context-defying crooning under the sun, to a place in relation to the group. Bringing the Other, the being of faceless face, to hand means glory for oneself and power over others. After Jimmie has done it, the boys turn their taunts to the larger boy, who declares his willingness to match Jimmie's feat but delays repeatedly, eliciting the ever more cynical "baiting" of the boys. Finally, he "cast an eye at the monster," shot "a glare of hatred at his squalling tormentors"—now described by Crane as a "mob"—and "with a formidable countenance . . . turned toward the impassive figure on the box." When this boy touches it, the "crowd of boys reverenced him at once, and began to throng into his camp, and look at him, and be his admirers." To all of this surrounding turmoil—the alternate taunting and reverence of the crowd, the screeching of Mrs. Hannigan "as if she was being murdered" when she discovers her Eddie is with the boys—the "monster" remains oblivious, exterior: "The monster on the box had turned its black crepe countenance toward the sky, and was waving its arms in time to a religious chant. 'Look at him now,' cried a little boy. They turned, and were transfixed by the solemnity and mystery of the indefinable gestures. The wail of the melody was mournful and slow. They drew back. It seemed to spellbind them with the power of a funeral. They were so absorbed that they did not hear the doctor's buggy drive up to the stable" (54–56). Critics of Stephen Crane have often differed over whether he should be regarded as a "religious writer."[15] Approaching this last description of "the monster" with Levinas's definition of religion in mind can perhaps help to clarify the matter.

Of the relationship between metaphysics and religion, Levinas writes in *Totality and Infinity*:

In metaphysics a being separated from the Infinite nonetheless relates to it, with a relation that does not nullify the infinite interval of the separation—which thus differs from every interval. In metaphysics a being is in a relation with what it cannot absorb, with what it cannot, in the etymological sense of the term, comprehend . . . For the relation between the being here below and the transcendent being that results in no community of concept or totality—a relation without relation—we reserve the term religion . . .

Religion, where relationship subsists between the same and the other despite the impossibility of the Whole—the idea of Infinity—is the ultimate structure. (*TI* 80)

In Crane's scene, relationship continues between "the monster" and the boys, yet they are unable to bring his "indefinable gestures" under any concept, any Whole that would include both him and them. They cannot comprehend or "absorb" him; indeed, Crane speaks of his unfathomable motions and sounds "absorb[ing]" the boys, so much so that they do not hear Trescott's approach. Crane has arrived at a kind of ultimate structure: a veiled faceless face gesturing and singing toward the sky in such a way as to transfix an audience that is utterly unable to make sense, in its own terms, of what it sees and hears. We might say, indeed, that insisting on "the impossibility of the Whole" has been part of Crane's major motif throughout, even in the story's form, with its various resistances to precise allegorization. Henry's return from "death" undoes death's privilege as the defining moment of life. He has, in his "last" acts, apparently defined himself as a hero and martyr, and yet he has returned from beyond his own end to rupture that identity—and the way others would narrate his history as a coherent whole.

Dr. Trescott's arrival breaks the spellbinding quality of the monster's performance on the box. When he asks the boys to go home, Crane comments: "They proceeded to the street much in the manner of frustrated and revealed assassins. The crime of trespass on another boy's place was still a crime when they had only accepted the other boy's cordial invitation, and they were used to being sent out of all manner of gardens upon the sudden appearance of a father or a mother. Jimmie had wretchedly watched the departure of his companions. It involved the loss of his position as a lad who controlled the privileges of his father's grounds, but then he knew that in the beginning he had no right to ask so many boys to be his guests" (56). Here Crane comes very close to the spirit of Levinas's reading of Pascal's *pensee* on the usurpation of the earth.

The whole scene has turned on the boys' touching—bringing to hand—
the Other, what fundamentally eludes their grasp, and achieving pride
of place, glory, by doing so: by making it familiar, making it comprehensible (as even the designation "monster" seeks to make the faceless
face comprehensible within one's own scheme of understanding rather
than the revelation of an Other who always undoes one's conceptual
schemes but is to be received hospitably nonetheless). This bringing to
hand, for Levinas, itself partakes of the logic of murder, "revealing" as
Crane puts it, the boys to be "frustrated . . . assassins." Moreover, Crane,
like Levinas, associates this revelation of one's murderousness with the
"crime of trespass on another boy's place," with, to use Pascal's language,
the marking out of places in the sun. Crane's passage provides an "image,"
as Pascal says, of "the usurpation of the entire earth."

The language of Crane's description of Dr. Trescott's approach and the
boys' departure is antithetical to the language of John in so many specific
ways that it reads almost like a parody of the Father-Son relationship as revealed in John. In Crane's passage, the "grounds" belong to Jimmie's father,
and Jimmie receives power and position as the one who "controls" the
"privilege" of access to his father's grounds. The boys are guilty of the
"crime of trespass" on the father's grounds even though they have "only accepted" Jimmie's "cordial invitation." In other words, the grounds have
really not passed over from the father to the son; they remain the father's
and Jimmie knows "in the beginning he had no right to ask so many boys to
be his guests." One should note here the ironic echo of the opening of
John—"in the beginning"—but the more important point is the way
Crane's depiction of the father-son relationship contrasts with the many
passages in John stressing the Father and Son's relationship of mutual self-
giving. In John, "All that the Father has is given to the Son" (16:15) and the
Son never seeks his own glory but always the glory of the Father who sent
Him. This is to say that the decisive mark of the Trinity is love, freely given
by the Father to the Son and given back, in a relationship of dynamic self-
communication, by the Son. As Arthur McGill puts it, the "relationship of
total and mutual self-giving" between the Father and the Son defines "the
essential mark of God's divinity." Identity for the Father and the Son is not a
matter of what they "possess and hold onto within themselves"; rather,
they have their identity "in terms of giving this reality to the other."[16]

Crane's Chapter 20 ends with a brilliant parody of the kind of glory
that is consistent with the patriarchal arrangements of power at Dr. Trescott's, a parody the interpreter formed by John is prepared to see be-

cause it derives from Crane's own Johannine understanding of the loving Logos. Where the father keeps his reality to himself, the son, like Jimmie, will seek distinction by giving out privileged access to the father's reality, and everyone must defend himself against trespass and usurpation of his place. Once the boys are back "on the sidewalk," however, they "speedily forgot their shame as trespassers" and the "large boy" who had so timidly gone up to the monster "launche[s] forth in a description of his success in the late trial of courage" (56). Meanwhile, the "little boy who had made the furtive expedition cried out confidently from the rear, 'Yes, and I went almost up to him, didn't I, Willie?'"—only to be "crushed" by a "few words" from the large boy (56–57). The human desire for distinction persists, the desire of the last to be first, either by virtue of their own claims or recognition by the "large" ones who are first: "The pace of the other boys was so manly that the tiny thing had to trot, and he remained at the rear, getting entangled in their legs in his attempts to reach the front rank and become of some importance, dodging this way and that way, and always piping out his little claim to glory" (57). The large crush the tiny while each pipes out his claim to glory. Crane's understanding of the drive for distinction underscores Levinas's insight that "peace" achieved through simply integrating beings into a totality necessarily imposes violence on existents driven to identify themselves by themselves—and not in relation to the whole. Crane, so insightful into war, stops short of a positive vision of peace, but his irony does point to the way peace can be made through a love that removes the need of each existent to mark out his place in the sun, to be defended against all others, or to establish his glory in a kind of ceaseless agon.

"War is kind," Crane writes in the title poem of his second volume of poetry, imploring the maiden whose lover has been killed not to weep. "War is kind," Crane repeats, because it provides men what they want, a completely self-contained reality, an agon ruled over by its own god, who is the projection of men:

> Hoarse, booming drums of the regiment,
> Little souls who thirst for fight,
> These men were born to drill and die.
> The unexplained glory flies above them,
> Great is the Battle-God, great, and his Kingdom—
> A field where a thousand corpses lie. (ll. 6–11)

Crane also implores the babe not to weep, the babe whose "father tum-
bled in the yellow trenches, / Raged at his breast, gulped and died" (ll.
13–14). War was kind to him, too, apparently, as Crane remarks with
bitter irony, because it provided the agon necessary for the ordering of
life according to "virtue" and "excellence":

> These men were born to drill and die.
> Point for them the virtue of slaughter,
> Make plain to them the excellence of killing
> And a field where a thousand corpses lie. (ll. 19–22)[17]

Crane's insight here seems similar to John Milbank's argument, made by
way of questioning MacIntyre, that ancient virtue necessarily and con-
ceptually depends on war for its testing and definition.[18]

Crane never makes his alternative to war entirely clear, but he does
perhaps suggest a way to peace in a poem from late in *The Black Riders*,
which he both liked better than his most famous portrayal of war, *The Red
Badge of Courage*, and regarded as "the more ambitious effort." In *Black
Riders*, Crane writes, "I aim to give my ideas of life as a whole, so far as I
know it, and the latter [*Red Badge*] is a mere episode,—an amplification."[19]
The poem begins with a challenging address to a god similar to the "God
of Battles" in "War Is Kind":

> Blustering god,
> Stamping across the sky,
> With loud swagger,
> I fear you not.
> No, though from your highest heaven
> You plunge your spear at my heart,
> I fear you not.
> No, not if the blow
> Is as the lightning blasting a tree,
> I fear you not, puffing braggart. (ll. 1–10)

In the second stanza, Crane again boldly declares that if this warrior god
can see into his heart, he will see that Crane fears him not and that "it is
right" not to fear (l. 14). In a line reminiscent of Henry Fleming's famous
"philippic,"[20] Crane addresses the sublime god of battles: "So threaten

not, thou, with thy bloody spears, / Else thy sublime ears shall hear curses" (ll. 15–16).

The third stanza of the poem brings a decided turn, as Crane confesses that there is a god whom he fears:

> Withal, there is one whom I fear;
> I fear to see grief upon that face.
> Perchance, friend, he is not your god;
> If so, spit upon him.
> By it you will do no profanity.
> But I—
> Ah, sooner would I die
> Than see tears in those eyes of my soul. (ll. 17–24)

The very formation of a soul, Crane seems to say—in Levinasian fashion—depends on the face to face, the movement coming from the Other who becomes the very "eyes of my soul." Here the face of the Other, a face highly suggestive of the spat-upon Jesus of the Passion, becomes the alternative to the sublime god of battles.[21]

The face of Henry Johnson appears no more in "The Monster" after the scene of his chanting and gesturing in Chapter 20. Crane has created for himself an immense narrative problem. Having presented Henry as nearly as possible in radical exteriority, how does he then narrate the remainder of his history? Perhaps this is why Crane makes such obvious gestures, as we have seen, toward John 11 and 12 in the chapters following Henry's last scene. Those chapters of John provide contexts within which we, as readers, might receive Henry hospitably without denying his otherness or effacing him through allegorical reading. The ending of Crane's story focuses specifically on a rejection of hospitality. As Whilomville increasingly demands that someone pay for the presence among them of one who confuses the boundary between life and death, Dr. Trescott plays the role of scapegoat. John Twelve and his group of twelve offer to take Henry off Trescott's hands, only to be met with the doctor's refusal: "It can't be done." But if Trescott "can't be done" with Henry, then Whilomville can seek to "be done" with the Trescotts: their neighbors, the Hannigans, move away; the doctor's patient list shrinks; the Winter family refuses to allow him to treat their daughter; all of the townswomen, except for Mrs. Twelve, boycott Grace's tea party. The one figure who, at least verbally, defies the opinion of "the whole town," thrown up to her by her sister Carrie, is Martha Goodwin, who supports Trescott and ridicules others for fearing Henry.

Martha is as bellicose as ever. When her sister tells her of Jake Winter's supposedly throwing Trescott out of his house, Martha exclaims, "If I had been Doctor Trescott . . . I'd have knocked that miserable Jake Winter's head off" (60). Martha also knows a lie when she hears one. When Carrie reports Jake Winter's saying that his daughter "Sadie had never been well since that night Henry Johnson frightened her at Theresa Page's party, and he held [Dr. Trescott] responsible," Martha "wheel[s] from the sink," advancing on the women who bear this lie and holding an "iron spoon . . . as if she was going to attack them" (59–60). Knowing that Sadie has been going to school every day, Martha is enraged by the lies she sees others willing to believe in the process of developing the justification to punish someone for what afflicts them all. Reading Martha in a Johannine way, we might say that she understands the link between the will to kill, to be done with the other, and the lie, unmasked by Jesus in John 8:44: "Ye are of your father the devil, and the lusts of your father ye will do. He was a murderer from the beginning, and abode not in the truth, because there is no truth in him. When he speaketh a lie, he speaketh of his own: for he is a liar, and the father of it." But Martha seems unable to get through the knowledge of war to the eschatology of peace, an inability that perhaps her name explains. She is still Martha Goodwin, the one who seeks to distinguish herself through work and be the one to win through being good—possibly even to be the one to "at-one" for the sin of surviving her lover, of being here in his place.

Trescott's response to John Twelve, "It can't be done," indicates not only his conviction that Henry ought not to be killed, but also his sense that his relationship to Henry cannot end. He cannot make up Henry's loss to him, he cannot be "even" with Henry, he cannot escape from the unaccountable gratitude he owes. Perhaps, in a Levinasian sense, Trescott's line should be read to suggest that once Henry has moved into a relationship with the Infinite that cannot be encompassed by our conceptualization—by any light that would go out from us to disclose it or lay it bare—"it can't be done," it cannot be finished, for him. To press this insight in a Johannine direction, we might say that "it can't be done" for Trescott or Henry, or for any of us, because we are in the process of being drawn into a relationship of love with and by the spat-upon face of the Other, Jesus, whose going to the cross in John 12 is the judgment of the world. No matter how much we long to bring things to an end on our terms, no matter how much we long to "be done" with the brother or the Other, ultimately we cannot do so, for Jesus has already, in part, brought the world to an end. "It can't be done" because the work has been done by Jesus. "It is finished" (19:30) by his cross and resurrection, which establish the Trinitarian love as the Light in which we have stood from the beginning, a light that does not disclose others in order for them to come to hand as implements for our projects. Rather, this Light, the very Logos manifested in Jesus, creates a community whose identifying quality is love. Indeed, as the first epistle of John puts it, it is through love that we, like Lazarus, know "we have passed from death unto life," for "He that loveth not his brother abideth in death" (3:14). That love is modeled on the Trinitarian love, which includes an affirmation of the goodness of the other within its movement from the beginning. In such a community, existents could continue in exteriority—defined in themselves—while simultaneously participating in patterns of free giving and freely offered return. The face to face would not be lost in the violence by which the "other is reduced to the same" through the anonymous power of theory or the state. Such a community would be peace and be characterized by hospitality.

Stephen Crane, of course, does not offer a fully realized vision of such a community or such peace. In many ways, however, he does point to an eschatological understanding of peace: by ironizing the ceaseless human efforts at glory through the agon; by confusing the boundaries of life and death through Henry's return; by situating Trescott in such a way that he must respond to Henry's *having already laid down his life* for Jimmie; by depicting Henry as a radically exterior being in a relation to the Infinite that is beyond our comprehension; by having Trescott refuse to allow Whilomville to "be done" with Henry, to end his story on its terms and enable it to retreat to the comfortable order it knew before he had passed from death to life; by specifically foregrounding hospitality throughout, especially in the final scene; and, most important of all, by framing his tale in relation to the events of John 11 and 12. If there are persistent Johannine patterns in Crane's work, I believe it is because Crane sensed that John revealed the finishing of a kind of love that made it possible for people to meet face-to-face in love freely given and freely returned—rather than in the killing clash of rivals. Perhaps, to adapt some of Crane's prevalent metaphors, preventing the face to face from becoming the leveling gaze of antagonists requires the simultaneous upturning of faces toward the One whose lifting up draws all to it, the One whose tears can become the very eyes of the soul.

Evidence from Crane's biography suggests a close relationship between "The Monster" and "The Blue Hotel," written within a few months of one another during 1897 and early 1898. Crane stressed their complementary quality in a letter to agent Paul Revere Reynolds: "It would be absurd to conjoin 'Death and the Child' with 'The Monster.' They don't fit. It would be rotten. Now, 'The Blue Hotel' goes in neatly with 'The Monster.' "[22] Given its relationship to "The Monster," we should not be surprised to find, as some critics have, Johannine motifs in "The Blue Hotel." My concern is not to work out allegorical correspondences, however, but to suggest how the whole of Crane's text invites reading in a Johannine way.[23] Crane's text specifically considers the relationship between lying and murder, as well as the link between lying and Satan's original lie, "Ye shall not surely die." The story's strong Johannine subtext is the passage I quoted earlier in relation to Martha Goodwin's hatred of the lie, John 8:44: "Ye are of *your* father the devil, and the lusts of your father ye will do. He was a murderer from the beginning, and abode not in the truth, because there is no truth in him." The text reads Crane's story very precisely, especially from the vantage point of its notoriously problematic second ending. Johnnie and the other men have arguably been murderers "from the beginning"; their murdering has first taken the form of abiding in the lies of the Blue Hotel. Moreover, Johnnie, and also the Swede, enact the "lusts" of the father, Scully, whose lies are versions of the original Satanic one. The story turns on a near reversal of the Johannine sense of love in which the Father offers everything that He is over to the Son and the Son makes a free response. "What things soever he [the Father] doeth, these also doeth the Son likewise," John writes. "For the Father loveth the Son and sheweth him all things that himself doeth" (5:19–20). In "The Blue Hotel," father and son continually work at cross-purposes; Johnnie never shows his father what he is doing, and Scully never shows his son what he is doing. They work together only on one occasion: in the fight against the Swede, in willing, we might say, the death of the other.

Hospitality is also a central matter in "The Blue Hotel." A hotel is a place of hospitality, and Pat Scully is fond of affirming, "A guest under my roof has sacred privileges."[24] The Blue Hotel seems less interested, however, in welcoming the other than in asserting itself against the world. To use Levinas's terms, the hotel seems bent on identifying itself "not by its place in the whole, but by its *self*": "The Palace Hotel at Fort Romper was painted a light blue, a shade that is on the legs of a kind of heron, causing the bird to declare its position against any background. The Palace Hotel, then, was always screaming and howling in a way that made the dazzling winter landscape of Nebraska seem only a gray swampish hush" (142). Crane's odd first paragraph suggests that the passengers who rode the rails through Romper "were overcome at the sight"; this "cult that knows the brown-reds and the subdivisions of the dark greens of the East expressed shame, pity, horror, in a laugh" on seeing the hotel. To the citizens of Romper, "Pat Scully had performed a feat. With this opulence and splendor, these creeds, classes, egotisms, that streamed through Romper on the rails day after day, they had no color in common" (142). In Levinasian terms, it seems significant that Crane's is a story of the frontier: his Westerners seem not to want to be defined by their relation to the East; they celebrate the bizarrely decorated hotel devoted to defining itself, insofar as possible, not in relation to the colors of the East but in itself.

The drive to define himself, by himself, rather than as part of the whole, perhaps accounts for Johnnie's cheating as well. Crane identifies only Johnnie by name among the players; the others are known by types: the cowboy, the Easterner, the Swede. The game represents a contract or law-governed activity in which all agree to submit to the same rules and chances. Johnnie's habitual cheating suggests the need to dominate and distinguish himself even in a game played just for fun—as does his partner, the cowboy's, board whacking. The contract is not strong enough to contain the drive for distinction compelling Johnnie to cheat and the cowboy to thunder "down his aces and kings" with such force that "the countenances of the Easterner and the Swede were miserable" (145).[25]

The Swede, the outsider, identifies Johnnie's cheating or lying with murder: "I suppose there have been a good many men killed in this room" (145–146). At first, one is tempted to dismiss this as paranoia or the result of an overactive imagination formed by dime novels. But Crane will not allow such an easy explanation. The fight reveals the will to kill in the cowboy, Scully, and the Easterner. The cowboy screams repeatedly to Johnnie, "Kill him, kill him," and Scully eggs his son on at every turn. The Easterner seems to want to stop the fight, until Johnnie miraculously lands a great blow and sends "the over-balanced Swede sprawling." Then the Easterner, too, consents to the will to kill: "The cowboy, Scully, and the Easterner burst into a cheer that was like a chorus of triumphant soldiery" (160–161).

The first indication that the Swede's reaction to Johnnie's lying represents more than simple paranoia comes as early as the story's section 3. As Scully comes to the Swede upstairs, the hotel owner's "wrinkled visage showed grimly in the light of the small lamp he carried . . . He resembled a murderer" (149). Scully and the men of the hotel do not, of course, directly murder the Swede, but he is murdered nonetheless, and his killing prompts the Easterner to propose his theory of joint responsibility in the story's so-called second ending: "We are all in it! This poor gambler isn't even a noun. He is kind of an adverb. Every sin is the result of a collaboration. We, five of us, have collaborated in the murder of the Swede" (170).

One hears a familiar phrase from John in the cowboy's comment that the saloon bartender, if he "had been any good," could "have gone in and cracked that there Dutchman on the head with a bottle in the beginnin' of it and stopped all this here murderin'" (169). The cowboy unintentionally points to precisely the problem posed by the Easterner's theory: When was "the beginning" of all this murdering, in this case, the Swede's? Or, to put the question slightly differently, to what extent is the systematic lying of the men of the Blue Hotel responsible for the Swede's murder?

One argument might say not at all. Such a reading would point to the gap in the story between events at the Blue Hotel and those in the saloon, a gap signified by the Swede's progress through the storm. On the other hand, the failure of hospitality at the hotel leads to the Swede's leaving and his murder. Moreover, the irrationality of the Blue Hotel contributes to the irrationality the Swede brings to the saloon. The Swede dies because he mistakes the "real" gambler of the saloon for the "false" gambler, Johnnie, over whom he has triumphed in the fight. He dies because he brings to the saloon an inflated "conceit" based on his experience at the hotel, whose fundamental lie he has imbibed and come to believe: "Ye shall not surely die."

At this point, it might be helpful to explore the connection between lying and violence. Charles Fried, influenced by both Augustine's and Kant's treatments of lying, presents the connection quite explicitly. To lie, Fried writes, is to "set up a relation which is essentially exploitative. It violates the principle of respect, for I must affirm that the mind of another person is available to me in a way in which I cannot agree my mind would be available to him . . . in lying to you, I affirm such an unfairly unilateral principle in respect to an interest and capacity which is crucial, as crucial as physical integrity: your freedom and your rationality. When I do intentional physical harm, I say that your body, your person, is available for my purposes. When I lie, I lay claim to your mind."[26] For Kant, lying also involves doing violence to oneself. Kant declares lying "the greatest violation of man's duty to himself merely as a moral being (to humanity in his own person)." Lying is a radical evil because it destroys rationality, undoes the purpose of language, and makes it impossible for persons to be regarded as rational ends in themselves. Through a lie, a person makes himself or herself "contemptible," "violates the dignity of humanity" in his or her own person, and forfeits his or her self-worth. Lying seems akin to self-murder, or suicide, because "by a lie a man throws away, and, as it were, annihilates his dignity as a man."[27]

An 1896 letter of Crane's to John Northern Hilliard suggests that he shared Kant's strong sense that lying involved not only a breach of duty to others but the most serious violation of one's duty to oneself. Crane's letter combines a devotion to personal honesty with a sense of the way humility and true moral self-esteem can be gained by the paradoxical process of attempting to live up to an ideal that one can never perfectly realize: "To keep close to my honesty is my supreme ambition. There is a sublime egotism in talking of honesty. I, however, do not say that I am honest. I merely say that I am as nearly honest as a weak mental machinery will allow. This aim in life struck me as being the only thing worth while. A man is sure to fail at it, but there is something in the failure."[28] For Crane, as for Kant, to lie is to forfeit one's self-worth, a forfeiture quite evident in the habitual liar, Johnnie Scully, with his desperate, even murderous need to demonstrate a goodness in which he does not believe.

Kant alludes to John 8:44 in a note following his treatment of lying in *The Doctrine of Virtue*: "It is noteworthy that the Bible dates the first crime, through which evil entered the world, not from *fratricide* (Cain's) but from the first *lie* (for even nature still rises up against fratricide), and calls the author of all evil a liar from the beginning and the father of lies."[29] Kant's argument suggests the connection between believing the first lie, "Ye shall not surely die," and that throwing away of personality he sees in lying. The connection rests, for Kant, on his sense that the moral agent acts not simply in himself or for himself but always also as a representative of humanity in his own person. In refusing to lie, the moral agent acts not only in some local context but also as a member of the realm of ends.

He acts in such a way as to uphold the ability of all people to make the contracts on which the free development of personality depends. The moral agent acts both in his own moment and as a participant in the "end": it is as if he has been to the end and seen there a realm marked by "a systematic union of rational beings" standing "under the law that each of them should treat himself and all others never merely as means, but in every case at the same time as an end in himself."[30]

The "end" Kant looks toward is a realm of rational, autonomous, moral agents, not the Kingdom of God. But we may see something like a Johannine movement in his thinking from the end. For John takes us to the end, to a decisive eschatological moment in which the crucified Jesus is revealed to be the very form of God's love. John presents Jesus loving "unto the end" and making that love possible for us. "Moved by God's act," writes Hans Urs von Balthasar, "the believer cannot but act in response; with that in mind, his action is therefore essentially eschatological or, since the word is charged with implications, let us say 'parousial'— the believer acts under the rubric of the second coming of Christ, the (timeless) and, from a Christian standpoint necessary, final act of all his acts in time, when he comes in the Glory of his revealed love which judges and rectifies all things."[31] The Christian acts, then, toward the neighbor not only in his or her local context and immediate moment but in a way that "is oriented toward the absolute future which is both in and beyond history" (92). God, according to von Balthasar, "thinks and acts progressively in this sense"—loving us, "not as we are, on account of our own merit, but as we *will be* as a result of his gift" (not unlike the way teachers ought to love students, one might add). "The fundamental law of Christian ethics," then, is "to join in doing what has already been done in its fullness, and to realize and fulfill what has been realized and fulfilled" (95). The form of God's glory has been manifested in Jesus' cross. The very form of loving to the end has been established: "Greater love has no man than this, that he lay down his life for his friends" (John 15:13). Jesus has made it possible for us to know love and to love because he first loved us. Our task is to "join in" fulfilling what has already, in one sense, been "finished." We do so from the faith that we "live in God through the power of Christ's death," to which we have been joined in baptism (93).

The Kantian, then, might endorse the Easterner's argument for joint responsibility in the Swede's death. Participation in the lies of the Blue Hotel does violence to the Swede, precipitating his own violent reaction. Johnnie's habitual cheating, and the efforts of the others to cover it, undermine rationality, beginning the process of sending the Swede spinning irrationally toward his doom at the saloon. The Johannine interpreter could agree with the Kantian on these points, but would, I believe, have something additional to say about the rootedness of lying in the original lie itself—something understood by Crane. The illusion of one's goodness is so important to Crane's characters that it must be maintained at any cost. "The conceit of man," which Crane calls "the very engine of life" (165), depends on the capacity for nearly unlimited self-deception. Crane understood as well as Reinhold Niebuhr that "Man loves himself inordinately" and that he often practices deceptions "in order to justify" a devotion to himself that the facts of his "determinate existence" do not warrant. His attempts to deceive "are constantly directed at other wills," but the "primary purpose is to deceive, not others, but the self."[32] The primary illusion is that he will not die—because he loves himself. John's Gospel unmasks this primary lie, which is so important to the self that human beings will kill to protect it. Giving it up requires seeing the consequences of such self-love nailed to the cross in Jesus. There the form of God's absolute love captures us, enabling us to love as part of the movement of His love and freeing us from the need to deceive others to justify our inordinate concern for ourselves.

The Johannine interpreter will detect the original lie in several places in Crane's story. One such place is the scene upstairs between the Swede and Scully, which Crane frames by remarking that Scully "resembled a murderer." The hotel owner asks the Swede whether he has truly feared for his life. When the Swede answers that he has, Scully responds, "Why, man, we're goin' to have a line of ilictric street-cars in this town next spring" and then goes on to mention other civic improvements: a railroad, four churches, a "smashin' big brick schoolhouse," even a factory (149–150). The underlying logic is easy to follow here: Scully says, in effect, that no one will kill the Swede, for the town is becoming civilized, its residents free from the will to kill. The rest of the story proves Scully wrong, but he is so committed to the fiction of himself as the benevolent keeper of a hospitable hotel that he cannot possibly understand his own motives. Scully lies to the Swede because he lies to himself.

Scully's deceptions are rooted in his own deep denial of death. Picking up the lamp that has earlier illumined his murderous visage, Scully urges the Swede to look at a picture: "Scully flashed the light high on the wall of his own chamber. There was revealed a ridiculous photograph of a little girl. She was leaning against a balustrade of gorgeous decoration, and the formidable bang to her hair was prominent. The figure was as graceful as an upright sled-stake, and withal, it was of the hue of lead. 'There,' said Scully, tenderly, 'That's the picter of my little girl that died. Her name was Carrie. She had the purtiest hair you ever saw! I was that fond of her, she—'" (150). The rhetorical context here is important: Scully illumines the picture of his daughter to prove his own benevolence. Through the gesture he declares again to the Swede, I can be trusted. You will not die. I am the kind of man who remembers his pretty little girl that died. You can count on me. In pointing to her picture, he points to his own goodness and indulges the tender mournfulness frequently evident in him. With its self-regarding indulgence, Scully's "tender" depiction of his dead daughter moves easily into his comments on the picture of his "oldest boy," Michael, whose success is also made to reflect Scully's goodness: "He's a lawyer in Lincoln, an' doin' well. I gave that boy a grand eddycation, and I'm glad for it now. He's a fine boy. Look at 'im now. Ain't he bold as blazes, him there in Lincoln, an honoured an' respicted gintleman" (151). Scully's self-indulgence leads naturally into his next producing the whiskey bottle he carefully hides from Johnnie and "the old woman" and sharing a drink with the Swede. Twice Scully urges the Swede to "Drink!" from the forbidden bottle (151), again performing his role as the benevolent host and confirming the men's new intimacy. He is also doing what Crane's drinkers—from the men of "George's Mother" to Pete and Jimmie and even the Johnsons of *Maggie*— invariably do: asking another to confirm him in his narcissism.

By insisting the Swede drink, Scully drives the process of bringing his son and the Swede into confrontation. Crane later emphasizes Scully's actively pushing the Swede toward the aggressive behavior that precipitates the fight. While the Swede "fizze[s] like a fire-wheel" at supper, Crane adds that "in all his madness he was encouraged by old Scully" (154). When the Swede proposes another game of High-Five, a game Scully knows to be potentially explosive, the hotel-keeper seems curiously passive, doing no more than "gently deprecat[ing] the plan at first" and then "subsid[ing]" when the Swede "turned a wolfish glare upon him." Then Scully withdraws, announcing that he must leave the hotel. Crane closely binds this withdrawal to the confrontation between the two younger men: "Scully said that he would presently have to go meet the 6.58 train, and so the Swede turned menacingly upon Johnnie. For a moment their glances crossed like blades, and then Johnnie smiled and said, 'Yes, I'll play'" (155).

Both Johnnie and the Swede act out the "lusts of the father," Scully, in the fight. For Johnnie, the fight represents a desperate bid to affirm his self-worth, here staked on defending a lie about his own honesty: "Well, he says I cheated! He says I cheated! I won't allow no man to say I cheated! If he says I cheated, he's a —— ——!" (157). Johnnie's lack of self-worth results from his never having achieved adequate separation from his father. The two play a perverse game of mirroring one another, sometimes in deceit, sometimes in sarcastic diminution of one another, sometimes in a sentimentalizing love. Johnnie fights both for himself and for his father. Scully seems paradoxically most able to own his son after Johnnie has been severely beaten by the Swede. Scully comes to "his son's side," crying "Johnnie! Johnnie, me boy?" in a "voice [that] had a quality of melancholy tenderness." This tenderness, however, does not lead him to save Johnnie from further harm. Instead, he asks, "Are you any good yet, Johnnie?" What follows is the son's pathetic confession, "No—I ain't—any good—any—more," accompanied by his breaking into tears occasioned not only by his "bodily ill" but also by "shame." But as if this confession of inadequacy before the father is intolerable to him, Johnnie immediately takes refuge in a lie, saying not that the Swede has been too good a fighter for him, but only, "He was too—too—too heavy for me." Johnnie pitifully seeks confirmation his ashamed father cannot offer and receives only one more lie to perpetuate his self-deception, " 'Yes, yes, Johnnie,' answered the cowboy, consolingly; 'he's hurt a good deal' " (160–162).

The Swede's part in acting out Scully's lusts involves confronting Johnnie with the accusation that he is cheating. The Swede's turning "menacingly" on Johnnie just before the last game recalls Scully's gesture of wheeling to face his son, repeated no fewer than five times in the earlier scene in which he seeks to find out what has gone on during the first game among the men. Having imbibed Scully's bad will with the whiskey, the Swede enacts the father's part. Johnnie's cheating has been his way of asserting his will and thus of subverting his father's benevolent tyranny over the hotel. The Swede serves Scully's desire to bring this subversion out into the open but without his having to accuse Johnnie directly—for that would compromise his own beliefs in the hotel's hospitality and in his own goodness. Because Scully and Johnnie are overinvested in one another, Scully cannot accuse Johnnie directly, for to do so would be to accuse himself. But if Scully can manipulate the Swede into confronting and fighting Johnnie, then he stands to gain no matter what the result. If

Johnnie defeats the Swede, even kills him in the fight—as the men truly will him to do—then Johnnie and his father together will be vindicated, their honesty and moral worth upheld, the hospitality and the benevolence of its keeper reaffirmed. In that case, the dead Swede could be dismissed as merely a pathological case who got what was coming to him. If the Swede should defeat Johnnie, on the other hand, Scully will at least have proven to himself his son's lack of worth. He will then have won the struggle for control that is the real issue in Johnnie's cheating, and he can mourn for himself over his son's inadequacy.

The original lie is also in force at the saloon, where the gambler thrives by encouraging other men in their self-deceptions. The gambler supplies the respectable men of Romper a way to indulge their murderous will while yet maintaining the illusion of their own relative superiority. He is "so delicate in manner" and "judicious in his choice of victims" that "in the strictly masculine part of the town's life he had come to be explicitly trusted and admired." What he allows the town's "important men" is an opportunity to "prey" vicariously on his victims without compromising the sense of moral superiority on which their self-worth depends. As a matter of policy, "he invariably distinguished between himself and a respectable Romper man so quickly and frankly that his manner actually appeared to be a continual broadcast compliment" (166–167).

Crane seems as aware as Kant that "men love to compare themselves with others" to support the vain illusion of "self-favor." The gambler provides Romper's "important men" the deceptions they need to continue in what Kant calls "an unwarranted state of self-approbation." As a liar in a system of deception, he seems the appropriate agent of the Swede's death: "There was a great tumult, and then was seen a long blade in the hand of the gambler. It shot forward, and a human body, this citadel of virtue, wisdom, power, was pierced as easily as if it had been a melon" (168–169). The violence of the lie leads to the violence of murder: the assumption that the Swede's mind has been available to others in a way that he could not, for himself, will has led to the similar penetration and disposal of his body.

The Johannine interpreter will thus see the logic of the Easterner's claim that all the men of the Blue Hotel have been involved in the Swede's death. To support this claim, let me give a brief reprise of how the events of the story might appear to such an interpreter. An outsider, an other, comes to what seems a house of hospitality but is actually the scene of a barely submerged and potentially "murderous" conflict between a father who does not show his son what he is doing and a son who secretly subverts the purposes of a father whom he cannot face. The son's drive for distinction causes him to engage in systematic lying, directed now at this outsider. He is joined in his lies by another, who loves domination, and a third, who fears the consequences of breaking the shared deception. The outsider, however, challenges the deception, identifying it (in a seemingly paranoid but ultimately right fashion) with the will to murder. The father now begins subconsciously to orchestrate a conflict between the son and the outsider. When the fight erupts, it becomes clear that the conflict of father and son can be forgotten insofar as it can be directed outward at an enemy. In this case, the outsider wins the fight, receives from his victory the illusion of invulnerability, and then dies later at the hand of one whose modus vivendi turns on his extraordinarily subtle understanding of power. He makes the space for his life between the powerful and their would-be victims, enacting the "wolfish" desires of the powerful while always deferring in such a way as to leave intact the powers' illusion of invulnerability.

I believe there is ample evidence of Crane's familiarity with the Gospel of John to suggest that his reading of John explains his ability to see with such clarity what happens when the father does not show the son what he is doing and the son cannot face the father. Whatever the truth of this assertion as a literary-critical claim about Crane, the Johannine interpreter will read "The Blue Hotel" as decisive evidence of the need for all human father-and-son relations to be disciplined by the model of love between Father and Son as depicted in John. By connecting destruction of the other, lying, and submerged conflict between father and son, Crane's story points ironically to the connection between hospitality to the other, truth telling, and the Trinitarian love in which the Father gives everything to the Son and the Son is utterly free to offer it in return.

"The Blue Hotel" points further to the need for a form of life that would accommodate both the individual's drive for distinction and hospitality to the other. Johnnie's cheating, his will to dominate even a game played just for fun, suggests that pure contractualism cannot contain the drive for distinction. Kant attempts to bring all into a universal contract founded on Reason in which each will would freely renounce the desire to use others as means to its own end. Truth telling is critical for him both because contractual relations depend on it and because moral agency involves the strictest scrutiny of one's own motives: the ability to distinguish truthfully between one's inclinations and the demands of the moral law. Lying is primarily a violation of duty to oneself because, without utter sincerity, one cannot develop as a moral agent or realize "the essential ends of humanity in one's own person."[33] But to put it as Levinas might, the person who becomes a participant in the universal contract founded on Reason has already simply "rediscover[ed] war" in submitting to "anonymous power" (*TI*, 47). And Crane would surely agree. For if there were ever an approximation to the Kantian realm of ends, it would seem to be the situation Crane invents: a game played just for fun. In such a game, each player would seem to have the strongest possible reasons to renounce his or her own inclinations in order to participate indefinitely in an activity of benefit to all, one in which no player would ever be diminished by the success of any other. Yet Johnnie cheats, lies about his cheating, and finds others willing to accede to the deceptions of the Blue Hotel. Even where the game structure seems to make need or interest irrelevant, Johnnie and the others cannot agree to regard one another as a systematic interplay of rational ends all subject to the same law. Particularity of interest simply cannot be bracketed so easily.

"The Blue Hotel" seems to leave us, then, with an impression of the permanence of war. The game suggests not only the inevitability of conflict between the individual and the general, but also—as it is a game played in pairs—the way cooperation itself leads to conflict between groups. The conflict of father and son seems forgettable only in mutual hatred of the other, and even the son who resents the father will go into battle to prove himself worthy of the father's regard—perhaps to prove himself worthy of his history.[34] If Crane suggests an alternative to the permanence of war, he does so through the notorious second ending: especially through the Easterner's insistence that all the men have cooperated in the death of the Swede by countenancing Johnnie's lies and through the cowboy's unintentional problematizing of the "beginnin'" of "all this here murderin.'" When was the "beginnin'" of "all this here murderin'"? Crane's story asks. And if events could be otherwise, if history could be other than a history of murder, would it be on the rediscovery or retrieval of a different beginning?

The Johannine interpreter will see the ironies of Crane's story pointing to a different beginning, one rooted in the Trinitarian love wherein the Father shows the Son all that He is doing and the Son offers love back freely in return. With this emphasis on the Father's existing in His giving himself to the Son, the doctrine of the Trinity means that "there is, from all eternity, otherness *in the life of God*."[35] A community formed by the Spirit that proceeds from this Father and Son will thus be characterized by hospitality, and hospitality requires truth telling, as Augustine recognized in his treatise *Against Lying*. Commenting on "the Apostle's words," "Put away lying and speak truth each one with his neighbor, because we are members of one another" (Ephesians 4:25), Augustine argued that these words should not be understood "to permit telling a lie to those who are not yet members with us of the body of Christ." In explaining the text, Augustine maintains: "The words were spoken thus because each one of us ought so to count a man as we wish him to be, even if he has not yet become what we wish. Even so has the Lord shown the alien Samaritan as the neighbor of him to whom he showed mercy. Thus, he with whom it is our business to see that he not remain a stranger must be regarded as a neighbor and not as a stranger."[36] If the men of the Blue Hotel had regarded the Swede "not as a stranger" but as one in the process of becoming a neighbor, events in that story might well have been otherwise. Obviously, they did not see it as their business to regard him as a neighbor.

The Gospel of John, and specifically John 12, does not give Christians the option of regarding the stranger as less than a neighbor. For as Jesus announces, if the Son of Man "be lifted up from the earth," He "will draw all *men* unto him." All people are in the process of being drawn to the Son of Man, which means that the Christian acts, as von Balthasar puts it, under the rubric of the parousia. The Christian "join[s] in doing what has already been done in its fulness" (95). As regards truth telling, this means that we are to tell the truth in all cases, for the very integrity of faith is bound up with our truth telling. As Augustine remarks in *Lying*, "Faith has received its Latin form from the fact that what is said is done. Hence, it is evident that a person who is lying does not show faith."[37] Moreover, justifying lying to promote one good or another, even the highest one of teaching the faith, leads to "mak[ing] every brother appear suspect to every other brother," with the result "that faith is accorded to no one." To tell the truth in all circumstances is to expose oneself to the risk of martyrdom; indeed, as Augustine comments about the Priscillianists, who justified lying to protect their faith, to follow such a course "altogether removes the possibility of holy martyrdom."[38] The encounter with the other includes the possibility of martyrdom, but this is something we are to take upon ourselves, in truth, rather than to visit upon the other through lying, as in "The Blue Hotel." As Crane implied in one of his curious poems from *The Black Riders*, it is better to find an assassin than a victim: "A man feared that he might find an assassin; / Another that he might find a victim. / One was more wise than the other."[39] Crane knew the will to be done with the other and the difficulty of speaking the truth, as is evident from another of his cryptic poems, one quite appropriate to conclude with here, as it focuses specifically on lying and is highly amenable to Johannine interpretation:

> Yes, I have a thousand tongues,
> And nine and ninety-nine lie.
> Though I strive to use the one,
> It will make no melody at my will,
> But is dead in my mouth.[40]

Crane cannot, of his own will, speak the truth; the word is dead in his mouth. The living word must come from without, from the Other, to be received in the mouth. Perhaps in that Word lies the alternative to the permanence of war, for that Word wills, from all eternity, the goodness of the other within the movement of His love.

afterword

POSTLIBERAL CHRISTIAN SCHOLARSHIP:

AN ENGAGEMENT WITH RORTY

AND STOUT

In 1995, I proposed, at my state university, to teach a course in literature and ethics that would bring literary texts into conversation with Aristotelian, Kantian, and Christian approaches to ethics. Among my texts was Stanley Hauerwas's *The Peaceable Kingdom,* which I chose because its emphasis on the community formed by Scripture seems to me to have clear implications for a Christian literary criticism. Because I recognized that the current version of church-state separation on campuses means, to many people, that no religious convictions must ever be granted more than antiquarian interest, I was explicit in my course description. I specifically welcomed all students but made it clear that the section of the course devoted to Christian ethics would take Christian convictions with seriousness and consider whether they made a difference for ways of doing literary criticism and ethics.

Several weeks later, my chairman received a strong complaint about my course from the Philosophy Department. The writer informed my chairman that ethics involved the study of impersonal principles in a disinterested manner and argued that my course might be appropriate in Sunday school but not in the university. Soon after, a colleague from Religion also challenged my course, and I found myself in a minor skirmish of the so-called culture wars.

I cite the incident for its suggestion of the curious condition of the university caught between Enlightenment and postliberal or postmodern assumptions. To argue that teaching in the humanities is disinterested is to deny perspectivalism and postmodern assumptions about language. There simply is no God's-eye view from which to teach disinterestedly. "The data," to paraphrase Alasdair MacIntyre, do not "present themselves and speak for themselves."[1] Much postmodern teaching acknowledges this frankly and conceives teaching as advocacy: feminists advocate feminism; Marxists advocate Marxism; ecocritics advocate green politics. Yet it is difficult for university departments to acknowledge the inevitably ideological quality of their courses and their instructors' methodologies. The governing fiction, perhaps necessary to retain funding, especially at state institutions, is that the courses to be taught, the order of topics to be considered, and the methodologies to be employed are matters of consensus based on common rationality. Scholars' concentration on limited problems within their disciplines and communal hiring and promotion practices generally produce enough ideological overlap within departments to obscure the most significant differences in methodological approaches and pedagogical goals. Conflict can generally be contained for the sake of funding, although in recent years, episodes in the culture wars have come more frequently to public attention as people outside academia increasingly recognize that curricula are political statements, justifiable, at best, pragmatically.

Against this postmodern background, it is possible to conceive what George Marsden has called "the outrageous idea of Christian scholarship." Marsden traces the exclusion of faith-informed perspectives from the university to "the disestablishment of Protestantism as the semiofficial religion in America."[2] Ironically, Protestantism's cultural dominance in the university, persisting through most of the nineteenth century, made it relatively easy to disestablish, as culture Protestants had little need to think out the intellectual consequences of their theological convictions. Once questioned, they had little with which to respond. Marsden argues that universities have now simply replaced one orthodoxy, Protestant Christianity, with another—call it established nonbelief, secular humanism, or unchallengeable naturalism. Believing that we have "overcorrected" in the direction of exclusive secularism in the university, Marsden calls for "a better balance among both religious and nonreligious voices" (24). Achieving this balance will depend first on scholars' articulating the consequences of their faith convictions for their scholarship. Marsden's book is an excellent place to begin familiarizing oneself with the ongoing Christian scholarship in many disciplines.

What postliberal Christian scholarship might look like is much too large a question to take up here. I hope to have made some contribution to that scholarship in this book, and in a moment I want to briefly show the intellectual consequences of faith convictions in one last engagement with two prominent postmoderns, Richard Rorty and Jeffrey Stout. First, however, let me make clear what I am *not* advocating in speaking of Christian scholarship.

With Marsden, I believe that there is no possibility of the reestablishment of Christianity in American universities. Moreover, even if there were, I would vehemently oppose any such return to Constantinianism. I dissent even from Stephen Carter's Tocquevillean argument that "the religions" (his term) should be encouraged by the state, through a form of affirmative action, precisely for their taking "positions that differ from approved state policy." "Taking an independent path," Carter asserts, is "part of what religions are *for*."[3] I agree with Carter that a healthy democratic polity depends on subsidiary institutions that prevent the state from absorbing and dominating every area of life. But even this is not what Christianity "is *for*." Christianity is for proclaiming God's revelation in Jesus Christ. The Church's justification does not lie in anything it can provide either society or state, not even resistance or virtuous citizens; its justification lies only in God's raising Jesus Christ from the dead for the forgiveness of sins.

Ironically, I find myself sympathetic to the colleagues who tried to block my course in 1995. They no doubt feared that I intended to advocate Christianity. This I would have been most careful not to do, out of a respect for the students grounded in Christian faith. Just as the first three commandments prohibit using God for any purpose, however laudable, so the last six prohibit using the neighbor.[4] Christians have had, unfortunately, a sorry record of not loving or respecting their neighbors. Liberals like Rorty and Stout rarely miss an opportunity to point out that liberal states developed as a way to confine the violence of the wars of religion. Christians must always remember the shameful history of their alliance with the powers, their record of hatred, imperialism, and violence in the spread of the faith and the "blessings" of Western civilization. We should be thankful for all those secularists who have made a return to Christian triumphalism impossible and unthinkable. If mainstream Christianity in the United States and Western Europe is in the process of disestablishment and death, Christians should look on this as a necessary dispossession, the self-emptying required of a servant people. If, as Simone Weil put it, "religion, degraded to the rank of a private matter, reduces itself to the choice of a place in which to spend an hour or two every Sunday morning," then we should look on this, as she did, as "how the *anathema sit* have to be paid for."[5]

The systematic disengagement from all alliances with force should, in my view, lead us to see the rightness of there being no knock-down, coercive, once-for-all arguments for Christian claims. "Perfect clearness would be of use to the intellect," Pascal observes, but it "would harm the will." "God prefers rather to incline the will than the intellect," both "to humble pride" and to convert the whole human being to charity. Pascal insists we cannot know God without the heart's being converted to love. Even "the truth" alone would not be enough: "We make an idol of truth itself; for truth apart from charity is not God, but His image and idol, which we must neither love nor worship."[6] Thus we should rejoice in God's hiddenness, His decision not to compel all rational minds, for it reveals to us that the world does not exist "to instruct man of God." Rather, in Pascal's view, it exists "for Jesus Christ," for the infinite love of the Cross that changes the will and the heart (182).

Perhaps the best place to begin engaging Rorty and Stout is with Rorty's understanding of faith's relation to the public sphere. As a pragmatist and postmodern bourgeois liberal, Rorty has typically consigned religion to the private sphere. He follows Jefferson, who "thought it enough to privatize religion, to view it as irrelevant to social order but relevant to, and possibly essential for, individual perfection."[7] Rorty argues that there are two sides, the "absolutist" and the "pragmatic," to the "Jeffersonian compromise concerning the relation of spiritual perfection to public policy." The absolutist side says "that every human being, without the benefit of special revelation, has all the beliefs necessary for civic virtue," and that he does so because he possesses a "conscience," which is understood to be "the specifically human essence of each human being." The pragmatic side "says that when the individual finds in her conscience beliefs that are relevant to public policy but incapable of defense on the basis of beliefs common to her fellow citizens, she must sacrifice her conscience on the altar of public expediency" (PD 175).

The "tension" between the absolutist and pragmatic sides of the compromise can be "eliminated by a philosophical theory that identifies justifiability to humanity at large with truth." The Enlightenment "idea of 'reason' embodies such a theory: the theory that there is a relation between the ahistorical essence of the human soul and moral truth, a relation which ensures that free and open discussion will produce 'one right answer' to moral as well as to scientific questions" (PD 175–176). In other words, if a position or an argument were true, it could be demonstrated in terms that reason, possessed by everyone, would recognize. In effect, then, no one really ever had to sacrifice "true" convictions of conscience if they could not be publicly demonstrated, for the inability to demonstrate them publicly meant that they could not pass the test of reason and were untrue or irrational.

In our century, Rorty writes, this "rationalist justification of the Enlightenment compromise has been discredited," with the consequent polarization of liberal theory. We can "stay on the absolutist side," in which case we will "talk about inalienable 'human rights' and about 'one right answer' to moral and political dilemmas without trying to back up such talk with a theory of human nature." Or we can "swing to the pragmatist side," abandon most rights talk, and accept that every account of rationality is tradition-bound. If one adopts the pragmatist approach, as Rorty does, the most important question becomes distinguishing the "sort of individual conscience we respect from that we condemn as 'fanatical.'" That sort of conscience "can only be something relatively local and ethnocentric— the tradition of a particular community, the consensus of a particular culture. According to this view, what counts as rational or as fanatical is relative to the group to which we think it necessary to justify ourselves— to the body of shared belief that determines the reference of the word 'we'" (PD 176–177).

Rorty makes no attempt to justify the traditions of his group philosophically. Rather, he simply offers a pragmatic comparison between his own tradition and others: "we" should be Western liberal social democrats not because we "think there are such things as intrinsic human dignity" or "intrinsic human rights" but because the Western democracies have done a better job of protecting dignity than states embodying other traditions.[8] (He does not confront the possibility that the Western democracies may have done a "better job" of protecting dignity because they thought it "real.") Rorty divides Kantians from Hegelians. The first believe in "such things as intrinsic human dignity"; the second, with whom Rorty identifies, "say that 'humanity' is a biological rather than a moral notion, that there is no human dignity that is not derivative from the dignity of some specific community, and no appeal beyond the relative merits of various actual or proposed communities to impartial criteria which will help us weigh those merits" (PBL 583). Persons have "only the comparative dignity" of the groups with which they identify, and the dignity of any particular community derives only from "contrast-effects—

comparisons with other, worse communities." "Persons have dignity not as an interior luminescence," but insofar as "they share in such contrast-effects" (PBL 586–587).

Rorty quite directly confronts a major objection to his position through an arresting story:

> The . . . objection is that on my view a child found wandering in the woods, the remnant of a slaughtered nation whose temples have been razed and whose books have been burned, has no share in human dignity. This is indeed a consequence, but it does not follow that she may be treated like an animal. For it is part of the tradition of *our* community that the human stranger from whom all dignity has been stripped is to be taken in, to be reclothed with dignity. This Jewish and Christian element in our tradition is gratefully invoked by free-loading atheists like myself, who would like to let differences like that between the Kantian and the Hegelian remain "merely philosophical." The existence of human rights, in the sense in which it is at issue in this meta-ethical debate, has as much or as little relevance to our treatment of such a child as the question of the existence of God. I think both have equally little relevance. (PBL 588–589)

This story offers a good entry point for a Christian critique of Rorty. My first reservation involves the metaphor he uses for the conferring of dignity on the human stranger. Can one give another dignity as one gives him or her clothes? Is the dignity of another person purely a matter of "our" giving? Doesn't dignity, like its related term "respect," point to something another has, or is owed, purely as an other—quite independently of any ability of mine to confer it? If we come to think of dignity as something that is ours to confer, like clothes to be put on the stranger, then we will soon lose the ability to think the idea of dignity, or respect—at least as these have been carried by the Jewish and Christian traditions Rorty invokes. Surely there is a curious tension, too, between Rorty's invoking those traditions and his closing remark that "the existence of God" is without relevance to "our" treatment of the child. Was the existence of God irrelevant to Jews and Christians as they evolved the traditions of respect Rorty invokes? Is not the ground of respect in those traditions the affirmation that God is the God of all people? Have not Christians been told that the encounter with the stranger may well be an encounter with God?

Rorty's story falsely eliminates conflict. The child is helpless; we are the powerful and gracious rescuers. It costs us nothing to attribute respect to her. A better test of "our" community is whether we would attribute respect, as Christianity insists, to one opposed to our interests and powerful enough to be a meaningful enemy. Interestingly, Rorty says nothing about the identity of the child's enemies; all we know is that they are not "us" (though presumably they represent some other group that considers itself superior to the child's culture through "contrast-effects"). Christians who are aware of their own sinfulness will see themselves in all three of the story's roles: not only as rescuer but also as child and victimizer. In doing so, they will grasp simultaneously the interdependence of the two great commandments: to love God and the neighbor. Relying on contrast-effects to establish our goodness might be sufficient as long as we are confident of always being the liberators in the stories we tell ourselves. But will reliance on contrast-effects alone, without recognition of some form of perfection, allow us to recognize ourselves when we become the oppressors? It seems no accident, for example, that Thoreau—to invoke one central to Rorty's cherished tradition—combined insistence "that there be some absolute goodness somewhere" with awareness of his country's culpability in slavery and in aggression against Mexico. His reasoning for the imperative need to resist his own government contrasts eerily with Rorty's story of the child: "When a sixth of the population of a nation which has undertaken to be the refuge of liberty are slaves, and a whole country is unjustly overrun and conquered by a foreign army, and subjected to military law, I think that it is not too soon for honest men to rebel and revolutionize. What makes this duty the more urgent is the fact, that the country so overrun is not our own, but ours is the invading army."[9]

My point is that Rorty's stress on comparative cultural evaluations and contrast-effects remains vulnerable to Kant's argument that human beings will select the comparisons they need to shore up their self-deceits. A similar criticism applies to his selection of the artistic narratives he now relies on to justify the "institutions and practices" of a particular group. The arts "develop and modify a group's self-image" by "apotheosizing its heroes, diabolizing its enemies, mounting dialogues among its members, and refocusing its attention" (PBL 587). This seems descriptively accurate as an account of group behavior, but I think we should resist Rorty's apparent normative claim. His account leaves the narrative constructors dangerously unaccountable. As such, they seem likely to construct self-justifying narratives. If narrative constructors have concluded that postmodern bourgeois liberalism of the American type represents the apex of human civilization, then they will seek out ancestors pointing to themselves, read them in a way that serves their own ends, and perhaps even exclude others who possess good historical reasons to think themselves part of the group in question.

Rorty frequently mentions Emerson and Whitman among his "strong poets" who have prepared the way for bourgeois liberalism. Harold Bloom, from whom the "strong poet" language derives, similarly declares Emerson "merely the mind of America."[10] Emerson and Whitman also play a large part in Jeffrey Stout's defense—against Hauerwas—of his version of a substantive, rather than merely procedural, liberalism. I admire both Emerson and Whitman, but they can be read as problematic ancestors even for the pluralism Rorty and Stout espouse. Perhaps the only declaration more imperialistic than Bloom's on Emerson is Emerson's own assertion that "to believe what is true for you in your private heart is true for all men."[11]

Emerson thought the strong poet should be praised for "dar[ing] to write his autobiography in colossal cipher, or into universality." He argued that no "genius" had yet appeared in America who, "with tyrannous eye . . . knew the value of our incomparable materials."[12] This last phrase must have been among those that brought the simmering Whitman to a boil; his greatest poem begins with the blithely tyrannous assertion that what is true of him is true for all: "I celebrate myself, and sing myself, / And what I assume you shall assume."[13] This seems harmless enough, but sometimes the implications of Whitman's vision are more obviously disturbing: "I know that what answers for me an American must answer for any individual or nation that serves for a part of my materials."[14] Is this the antecedent of democratic diversity or of a global capitalism that seeks to transform the world into "materials" for what answers the needs of Americans? Stout sees "normatively charged openness to difference" in *Leaves of Grass.*[15] Whitman's book might also be read as the prototype of a national mass culture, where every feature of particular identity is lost in incorporation into the whole. At its center, after all, is a consecration of the war of American unification. Perhaps it should be read, then, as if by Weil, as a necessary document in the state's claiming all sacrifice for itself, as the American version of the process by which modern states have destroyed every particular kind of rootedness in order to focus love idolatrously on the state—a process required to produce masses of force large enough for the conflicts of the late nineteenth and twentieth centuries.[16]

If MacIntyre and Hauerwas see greater confusion in our moral languages than Stout, perhaps this reflects their writing from within an institution, the Church, that is more inclusive than those within which Stout writes. Rorty's "post-modern bourgeois liberalism," although certainly intended to be inclusive, links political philosophy specifically to a particular class and level of income. I applaud Rorty's defense of the bourgeoisie, his quite accurately criticizing intellectuals for contempt of the middle class. But to idealize the relative peace of the bourgeois democracies may block the asking of important critical questions. To what degree does that peace depend on unlimited economic growth? What are the social and personal costs of growing an economy fast enough so that consumerist envy of the neighbor remains manageable? Does the economic power requisite to maintaining bourgeois peace in the Western democracies depend on disproportionate consumption of the world's resources and arguably exploitive relations with the developing countries? Wendell Berry has argued that economics has been "elevated" in America "to the position of ultimate justifier and explainer of all the affairs of our daily life."[17] If this is so, is it the price of maintaining a liberal society where virtue is irrelevant to social order? Does unlimited economic growth require the conversion of every piece of human "material" into worker, consumer, and taxpayer? If so, what are the consequences for love, for children, for families, for the poor, for those unable—for whatever reason—to contribute to national economic life?

Stout laments the "idolizing" of "external goods" in American society today (291). But he does not ask whether his version of American liberalism has not always depended on encouraging individuals to focus on external goods as a way of containing conflict. As Crèvecoeur observed well over two hundred years ago, what kept the Catholic, the German Lutheran, the seceder, and the Low Dutchman from quarreling in America was the focus of each on his own prosperity. The Low Dutchman may "implicitly believ[e] the rules laid down by the synod of Dort," but what marks him as an American is that "his house and farm [are] the neatest in all the country; and you will judge by his wagon and fat horses that he thinks more of the affairs of this world than of those of the next."[18] According to Crèvecoeur, to be an American has always meant to be focused on external goods.

Stout charges MacIntyre and Hauerwas—unfairly, in my view—with wanting to impose premature closure on moral discourse. But there is more than one way to limit discourse: excluding voices from one's bricolage or narrative accomplishes such limitation. Consider Rorty's point that our institution-justifying narratives involve "apotheosizing heroes" and "diabolizing enemies." Elsewhere, Rorty argues that one can avoid becoming a "wet liberal" whose sense of selfhood dissolves only by maintaining a "capacity to feel contempt." "Nazis and the fundamentalists" (offered up without moral differentiation) are among those people to whom bourgeois liberals react with "indignation and contempt."[19] Rorty's judgment seems to suggest that religious fundamentalists are unworthy of inclusion in moral conversation or attempts at understanding. They function only as enemy or scapegoat by which to define our sense of who "we are" by knowing what "we" are not.

The Christian scholar will resist diabolizing anyone, precisely from the conviction that we all participate in crucifying the One who is our infinitely qualitative superior. We scapegoated the One who is impossible to blame; thus, the scapegoat mechanism becomes visible to us and allows us to resist it. We cannot live from contempt for anyone. We will understand religious fundamentalism in order to converse with it. We might ask, for example, whether American fundamentalism does not represent resistance to a mainstream culture perceived to be driven by idolatrous focus on external goods. Perhaps the insistence on scriptural inerrancy should be seen as the means to maintain a minority culture against the overwhelming political, economic, and educational power of the American establishment. Perhaps the turn to fundamentalism represents the result of mainstream Christianity's failure to develop and widely disseminate a rich theology capable of entering into productive dialogue with modern science. Before condemning the religious right's tendency to identify America as a Christian nation, we should do extensive surveys of the percentage of military veterans in conservative congregations. I suspect it will be higher than that in more liberal congregations or among the secular public, especially its more affluent sectors. If this is the case, we may have learned that the tendency to conflate religion and nation correlates closely with the amount of blood people have been asked to spill for their country. A similar question might be inspired by Stout's interesting discussion of how opposition to homosexuality correlates with sharply defined and stereotypical divisions between masculine and feminine roles (154). It would be useful to ask whether groups that maintain sharp divisions between sexual roles have relatively high levels of military service. If men are likely to be called away to defend a homeland or die for a country, women will likely be allotted the continuous caregiving required by children over a long period of time. If there is greater homophobia in conservative churches than in the general population, perhaps this reflects higher rates of military service rather than peculiar moral benightedness. We might reduce homophobia not by chartering homosexuals to kill in military service but by seeking ways to create peace and thus to free all segments of our society from the need to maintain rigidly divided gender roles.

Rorty relies heavily on the distinction between persuasion and force in defending his version of ethnocentrism against the charge that abandoning the search for a "true self" for man will leave pragmatic liberals to depend on terror in the manner of the Nazis: "There is an important difference between saying 'we admit that we cannot justify our beliefs or our actions to all human beings as they are at present, but we hope to create a community of free human beings who will freely share many of our beliefs and hopes,' and saying, with the Nazis, 'we have no concern for legitimizing ourselves in the eyes of others.' There is a difference between the Nazi who says 'we are good because we are the particular group we are' and the reformist liberal who says, 'we are good because, by persuasion rather than force, we shall eventually convince everybody else that we are.'"[20] It seems legitimate to ask, however, whether a sharp, or even workable, distinction between force and persuasion can survive the abandonment of Enlightenment reason in a world of very unequal powers. The distinction seems grounded in the Enlightenment idea that reason could be persuaded by good reasons quite apart from the identity of the reason giver. If description or narration were a matter of reading off an antecedent reality, then it might be plausible to argue that one inquirer could be freely persuaded by another. But if moral sentences are understood to be always perspectival, and to refer only to other sentences, how are we ever to sort out what has been accepted through persuasion rather than force—even among Stout's stock of moral platitudes? Moreover, Rorty's persuasion-force distinction seems either naïve or mystifying given the unrelenting attempts of corporate powers, private and public, to fashion publics for their products and policies.

Thus far I have been distinguishing the implications, as I see them, of Christian convictions from positions held by Rorty and Stout. The Christian scholar ought not, however, to rest in making distinctions. Christianity must never divide only for the sake of division; when it divides, it must do so from the desire for real reconciliation for all. It also believes in the possibility of real reconciliation for all, not because it has seen peace in the world but because it sees Jesus, who seems to divide in many ways but also proclaims that if the Son of Man is lifted up, he will draw all people to him.[21] As Kierkegaard argued, one must not rest in earthly distinctions, or even think it enough to struggle against earthly distinctions, in an earthly way. For to do so is inevitably to set one distinction aside and put another in its place—and thus to "really wor[k] for distinction." The Christian will rather go straight to the mark, "merely express[ing] what to him was a Christian need—to love his neighbour," to "will to exist equally for every human being without exception."[22]

In the spirit of reconciliation appropriate to the postliberal Christian scholar, I will try a mediation in the conversation among Hauerwas, MacIntyre, Stout, and Rorty. Stout fears that Hauerwas and MacIntyre "may well be contributing to the erosion of habits and virtues essential to democracy." He mentions, for example, Hauerwas's persuading "Christians that democratic collaboration in the struggle for justice is a 'bad idea' for the church" (343). Here Stout misses Hauerwas's claim that justice is itself a problematic term. For Christians to uncritically align themselves with justice, apart from some relatively thick notion of the good, may simply aid in underwriting the promise of unlimited fulfillment for all that presses the Western democracies toward imperialism.[23] A further consideration of Hauerwas's argument could lead Stout to see that here and elsewhere he is concerned that Christians, to borrow a phrase from Rorty, regain "semantic authority" over themselves. If Hauerwas is more willing than Stout to explore how far down postmodern differences go, it may be that he trusts, as a Christian, that these can ultimately be reconciled. As one told by Jesus to take differences immediately to his brother, Hauerwas may know that denial of differences where they truly exist leads only to anger, resentment, and the destruction of community. There is much to be said, I believe, for Arthur W. Frank's analysis of postmodernity in terms of postcolonialism, which he defines "in its most generalized form [as] the demand to speak rather than being spoken for and to represent oneself rather than being represented, or, in the worst cases, rather than being effaced entirely."[24] We have all, to some extent, been colonized by modernity. Democracy presumes too much if it regards itself to be "after Babel." Capitalism presumes too much if it believes everyone's silence can ultimately be bought. People will tell their own stories because they die. Under the Holy Spirit, all can speak so as to be understood in the native tongue of the listener. No state, however, not even the most democratic, is the upper room. Democracies need to face this.

Stout fears MacIntyre's stress on the confusion of our moral languages and his call for a new St. Benedict at the end of *After Virtue*. "Many readers," Stout notes, "have taken him to be advising withdrawal from democratic engagement into a circle of virtuous, like-minded souls at the margins of society" (342). Stout might be heartened to know that MacIntyre has been similarly criticized from a Christian point of view by John Milbank, who argues that returning to paradigms of virtue derived ultimately from the Greek city-states means returning to a politics of war. Milbank seems concerned, to cite the title of his chapter on MacIntyre, about "the difference of virtue and the difference it makes."[25] But MacIntyre might reasonably respond that until we know what differences virtue makes, Christians are likely to be absorbed into the building of the tower—where, absent different languages, differences cannot even be recognized or articulated. We might say that Christians need to pursue the differences virtue makes in order to find a more real reconciliation further on in the conversation. Part of MacIntyre's effort might be seen as a means to establish an orderly peace based on justice in polities rather than a heightening of conflict. He has insisted that an account of the good life for human beings, a rational ordering of goods, must precede deliberation about justice in polities. Attempting to do justice without a prior account of the good for human beings simply leads to the barely disguised war of all against all that we now accept as liberal politics.

Stout might find an ally in MacIntyre on some matters if he were to turn from *After Virtue* to MacIntyre's essay on *Veritatis Splendor*, although doing so may cause Stout to revise some of his assumptions. Stout defends an ethics of bricolage throughout *Ethics after Babel*, but he also insists that he is not a relativist. He believes in moral truth, offering repeatedly a paradigmatic instance: "slavery is evil." Defined as "the coercive practice of buying, selling, and exercising complete power over other human beings against their will," slavery "is evil, [and] it makes perfect sense to say that it has always been evil—whenever and wherever it can be found in the historical record" (22). He makes this claim despite rejecting the force of any "culture transcendent thing-in-itself, like the Moral Law or a Realm of Values." These can be of little help, either as criteria or explanations, "to us human beings who are not culture-transcendent, whose every knowing is culturally embedded" (24).

"Part of what justifies" our "believing slavery to be evil," Stout argues, "is a failure, over the long haul of moral reasoning, to make clear what could conceivably justify treating people assigned to the role of slave in ways that we do not tolerate for other people." Among the beliefs that once underwrote slavery is "that no society could survive without slavery," a belief that has "not survived critical scrutiny." What it means to say that "proponents of slavery" in the American South were unjustified in holding slaves is simply that "their reasons and arguments just weren't good enough, in the presence of reasons and arguments on the other side." We may, however, "imagine a time, or discover one through historical inquiry, when belief in slavery was justified, relative to available reasons and evidence" (29).

Stout closes his discussion of moral diversity with the insistence that we "keep in view another possibility, only implicit until now." Wanting to guard against turning "comparative inquiry into an exercise in self-congratulation," he points out that "we might, after all our dialogue with the dead or the foreign, decide to change *our* minds on the moral issue in question." Through examining "another group's ideological distortions," we may discover distortions of our own; we may discover additional reasons for the past group's beliefs, "reasons that persuade us that their judgments, and not ours, are true"; we may "come to admire them as a people and wish to be like them" (32).

My question for Stout, then, is whether any change in epistemic context could ever change our belief that slavery is evil. Are there any further discoveries—ideological distortions of our own, additional reasons for past judgments, new admiration for slaveholding gentility—that could change the truth that slavery is evil? If it could be demonstrated that our culture's survival did depend on slavery, would that change the truth? Or would we rather die than affirm that slavery is anything other than evil? Would we not say, as Thoreau did about slavery and aggression in 1848, that "this people must cease to hold slaves, and to make war on Mexico, though it cost them their existence as a people" (CD 390)? I believe Stout would affirm, with Thoreau, that in some cases we "must do justice, cost what it may" (CD 390). If he would do so, then it seems inconsistent to assert that "philosophy cannot explain the nature of truth or what it is for a moral proposition to be true" (24). When we say that slavery is evil, we are saying at least three important things: first, that there is no further evidence of any kind that would change this conviction; second, that we would die rather than change this conviction, for it is impossible to compromise on this matter and still be ourselves; and third, that on this matter, there is no distinction between what holds for our community and any other. In this case, "we" includes all the human beings who have ever lived, and thus the idea of "contrast-effects" is irrelevant.

To affirm the truth "slavery is evil" is to say there can be no further negotiation on this issue, for it is rooted in what we are—our nature. It means further that this truth now becomes part of the moral inheritance with which we examine present and future circumstances, to see, for example, how other economic and social arrangements might resemble slavery. It seems inadequate to claim, with Stout, that "to hold our beliefs is precisely to accept them as true" (24), for we need a stronger separation between belief and truth to distinguish what can be revised from that which is unrevisable: slavery is evil.

If Stout affirms the unrevisability of "slavery is evil," then his implicit sense of truth seems much like that informing MacIntyre's Thomist account of natural law in his discussion of *Veritatis Splendor.* Stout's insistence that slavery is and always has been evil seems very like John Paul II's insistence that "the *negative precepts* of the natural law" oblige *"semper et pro semper,* without exception, because the choice of this kind of behavior is in no way compatible with the goodness of the will of the acting person, with his vocation to life with God and to communion with his neighbor."[26] Stout might want to eschew talk about a vocation to God or to the good, but it is not clear that he can do so and hold slavery to be unrevisably evil. As MacIntyre explains, "The conception of a final good for human beings is that of a good that cannot be weighed against any other, a good whose loss could not be compensated for by any other."[27] To say that slavery is evil is to say that there is no good arising from slavery that could ever outweigh the loss of freedom and dignity it represents. Indeed, it is to reject the notion that weighing of goods can be intelligible in regard to slavery. Nothing can compensate the slave for loss of freedom and dignity; nothing can compensate the slaveholder for the distortion of his rationality caused by existing in a system of domination so at odds with "the permanent structural elements" of human beings. The slaveholder is "inadequately rational," on MacIntyre's view, because he fails to see that his true good cannot be achieved apart from obedience to "negative exceptionless precepts" like Stout's or the Pope's "slavery is evil" semper et pro semper.[28]

Stout and MacIntyre could begin conversation on the matter of how a truth like "slavery is evil" can hold semper et pro semper and yet be discovered, or made, in time. MacIntyre might ask Stout to examine his stock of moral platitudes to ascertain whether they are "exceptionless prohibitions" whose force is necessary to our discovering our rational natures. He might ask Stout further whether Aquinas seems a master bricoleur precisely because he is committed to discovering natural law. On the other hand, MacIntyre might show Stout how the background conditions enabling the historical judgment that "slavery is evil" derive from obedience to previously accepted consequences of natural law thinking. A place to begin might be with the experience of the body. Stout says that slavery's advocates could no longer make their case "in the presence of reasons and arguments on the other side" (29). This, in my view, goes too far toward separating reasons from persons. I suspect that what brought an end to slavery was not the failure of "reasons and arguments" in favor of it but rather the daily pain, suffering, humiliation, and death of the slaves. Slaves brought the end of slavery by suffering it. Weil spoke of labor as a daily death, a consent each day to be used up, to be reduced to the status of a thing.[29] Arguments for slavery could not be made "in the presence of" the suffering bodies of slaves forced to undergo this daily dying only to have the results of their labor appropriated by others. Perhaps slavery ended when no amount of argumentation could disguise what it *really* involved, apprehensible to those who had become sufficiently rational to see it.

Rorty believes that the past two centuries should be understood "not as a period of deepening understanding of the nature of rationality or of morality" but "as one in which there occurred an astonishingly rapid progress of sentiments."[30] He approves of the emergent "human rights culture" while rejecting human rights foundationalism. He argues that "the nineteenth and twentieth centuries saw, among Europeans and Americans, an extraordinary increase in wealth, literacy, and leisure," an increase that "made possible an unprecedented acceleration in the rate of moral progress" (TP 175), which he tends to equate with ending slavery, extending the franchise, promoting women's rights, and encouraging tolerance. Without diminishing the importance of any of these accomplishments, I think it has to be said that the record of the rich Eurocentric countries over the past two centuries is more ambiguous than Rorty suggests. Nearly all of the countries in that group built their wealth, at least in part, on imperialism. From the end of the eighteenth century to the middle of the twentieth, they engaged in a series of ever more violent and murderous wars, moved, in part, by the need to control resources essential to national wealth building and to creating the kind of mass needed for survival in a world where killing has become as technologically efficient as it has. Rorty takes heart from our learning, in the past two centuries, "that human beings are far more malleable than Plato or Kant had dreamed" (*TP* 175). That malleability seems to some of us, however, mainly evident in the hitherto unimaginable crimes of the twentieth century. Surely, one lesson of the past century is that human beings can be made capable of doing just about anything to one another.

Rorty believes that the most serious problem facing us now is to persuade people everywhere to regard membership in our biological species as equivalent to membership in the moral community. He argues that the breaking down of rigid group identities can best be advanced by "security and sympathy." Security means for him "conditions of life sufficiently risk-free as to make one's difference from others inessential to one's self-respect, one's sense of worth" (*TP* 180). Kierkegaard argues that Christianity goes straight to the heart of the task Rorty identifies here. Jesus commands, "You *shall* love thy neighbor." "Never has any greater security been found" than in this "You shall," for "When one *shall*, it is for ever decided; and when you will understand that you *shall* love, your love is for ever secure" (*WL* 48–49). Moreover, one is always secure in having a neighbor to love; death cannot take him or her from you, "for if it takes one, life immediately gives you another" (*WL* 76). That Jesus is the One who commands to love makes an infinite difference: our self-respect rests secure in our being worthy to be commanded to love by the One whose surpassing righteousness makes an infinite qualitative difference.

For Rorty, sympathy is rooted in material security; as people's lives become less risky, they are able to respond more sympathetically to others unlike themselves: "The tougher times are, the more you have to be afraid of, the more dangerous your situation, the less you can afford the time or effort to think about what things might be like for people with whom you do not immediately identify" (*TP* 180). If this were true, one would expect to find fewer historical examples of the more materially secure countries attacking the less secure. Surely one of the things that makes weaker peoples less secure is the presence, often as neighbors, of stronger, more secure and aggressive ones. The case is still out, it seems to me, even for Rorty's identifying security and sympathy on the personal level. After all, how much security is enough? Are not the striving for security and the risk taking needed for sympathy fundamentally at odds? Is it reasonable to believe that acquisitive Western consumers will, at some point, decide they have enough and begin giving to the poor? Is it possible that a too great exclusion from the ordinary risks of humanity will make people less, rather than more, sympathetic to others? Against Rorty's analysis we should set Jesus' story of the rich man whose ground "brought forth [so] plentifully" that his current barns could not hold all the fruits. What does he resolve to do? Build bigger barns (Luke 12:16–21).

Christians can certainly agree with Rorty that an important task of the moral educator is to answer the question "Why [should I] care about a stranger, a person who is no kin to me, a person whose habits I find disgusting?" (TP 185). The straightforward answer is because Jesus commands us to love. Hospitality to the stranger is a theme with deep Christian roots. MacIntyre might answer the question by saying that we will never realize our true good if we fail to follow the radical interpretations Jesus gave to the negative prohibitions of the Decalogue. Clearly, it involves radical trust to follow Jesus: there may well be no immediately perceptible benefit to those who take the risk of caring for the stranger. As our true good will be revealed only in God's own time, it requires trust, or faith, engendered by seeing Jesus, to go on. Rorty emphasizes the centrality of trust, rather than obligation, to the moral life. Christians can certainly agree on the importance of trust, but they may find counterintuitive Rorty's opposition of trust and obligation. Surely the entering into and fulfilling of obligations among people builds trust. Likewise, trust leads to the connectedness and mutuality within which obligations arise while also empowering people to fulfill those obligations. Christians and Rorty might well enter into discussion about how to create the trust and risk taking required for people to move beyond the extended kinship group to universal fellowship. Christians can affirm, with Rorty, that it is unfortunate that many philosophers "are still trying to hold on to the Platonic insistence that the principal duty of human beings is to *know*" (TP 184). The principal duty of Christians is to love God with all one's heart and soul and mind and to love one's neighbor as oneself. Trusting fulfillment of this duty will lead to our recognizing that we love ourselves rightly when we love ourselves as we love our neighbors. But again, Christians will resist Rorty's tendency to split apart qualities that should be held together. Love moves us to know, and knowledge guided by love will seek to know more in order to serve love. Being loved and forgiven by God allows us the freedom to examine all our own commitments to see where we are mired in self-justifications that constrain our feelings, disable our trust, distort our knowledge, and dry up our loves.

What I have attempted here is the kind of intervention between rival standpoints called for by MacIntyre's "university of constrained disagreement." In that university, the notion of rationality within particular traditions, each in conversation with one another, would supplant the idea of a tradition-free rationality as the governing concept of the humanities and social sciences. Those engaged in "teaching and enquiry" would be required both "to advance enquiry from within [their] particular point of view" and "to enter into controversy with other rival standpoints"—both to disprove "what is mistaken" in the rival and to "test and retest" their own theses.[31] Such a conception faces obvious practical and intellectual problems. It seems unlikely that any of today's multiversities, either private or public, would be willing to risk possibly highly visible conflicts in disciplines considered so marginal to the overall enterprise. Nor are they likely to be patient enough to support the extended, painstaking work required for scholars to recapture the rival traditions. Moreover, it would take the utmost goodwill on all sides to prevent scholars from subverting the efforts of those with competing standpoints. Negotiating among the standpoints, as I have tried to do, would be both critical and difficult, for it means taking the standpoint of another with entire seriousness, proceeding with a minimum of desire for self-justification, and being willing to assent to rival positions when they are more persuasively argued. Perhaps the Christian, freed by the love command to rise above earthly distinctions, can play a particularly useful role in negotiating among standpoints. In fact, the "university of constrained disagreement" may have to be Christian, for it seems a profound venture of radical trust to finance and encourage the work of those seemingly opposed to one's own views. There is no reason to fear the "university of constrained disagreement," however, for those who believe that *"to ask about the good . . . ultimately means to turn towards God"* (VS 19).

The Christian university must be "teleologically ordered to peace," as Hauerwas and Charles Pinches have said of Christian accounts of the virtues.[32] If it is to be a "university of constrained disagreement," it should be so under what James Denney has called the further "constraint of an infinite love."[33] Christians within such a university would seek to regain "semantic authority" over themselves, but always with the intent of serving the world God creates and loves. While exploring the difference made by the virtues, we must remember that these are not our accomplishments but gifts from the God of all people whose goodness first moves our search for virtue. Christians within the "university of constrained disagreement" should say, with Rorty, "We admit that we cannot justify our beliefs or our actions to all human beings as they are at present, but we hope to create a community of free human beings who will freely share many of our beliefs and hopes." Our difference from Rorty's liberalism involves the location of the good our communities honor. Rorty's reformist liberal says, "We are good because by persuasion rather than force, we shall eventually convince everybody else that we are" (CWE 214). Christians must say, on the other hand, We are not good because of anything we are in ourselves but only insofar as we are related to the One who has persuaded us that he is good and who, we hope, will persuade you too—but only in his own way, by offering you his free and abundant and eternal life.

notes

Introduction

1 Alasdair MacIntyre, "Does Applied Ethics Rest on a Mistake?" *The Monist* 67 (1984): 499.

2 Liberalism "tempts us to believe that freedom and rationality are independent of narrative—i.e., we are free to the extent that we have no story." Stanley Hauerwas, *A Community of Character: Toward a Constructive Christian Social Ethic* (Notre Dame, IN: University of Notre Dame Press, 1981), 12.

3 George Grant, *English-Speaking Justice* (Notre Dame, IN: University of Notre Dame Press, 1985), 4.

4 George Grant, "The Triumph of the Will," in *The George Grant Reader*, ed. William Christian and Sheila Grant (Toronto: University of Toronto Press, 1998), 143.

5 Grant, *English-Speaking Justice*, 9–10. For Heidegger on these matters, see "The Question Concerning Technology" and "The End of Philosophy and the Task of Thinking," in *Martin Heidegger: Basic Writings*, ed. David Farrell Krell (New York: Harper and Row, 1977), 287–317, 373–392.

6 Charles Paine, "Relativism, Radical Pedagogy, and the Ideology of Paralysis," *College English* (1989): 563.

7 For Heidegger's analysis of *Bestand* (standing reserve), see "The Question Concerning Technology," 298.

8 Henry David Thoreau, *Walden*, in *Walden and Civil Disobedience* (New York: Penguin, 1983), 118.

9 For an excellent condensation of these articles, see Andrew Delbanco, "The Decline and Fall of Literature," *The New York Review of Books*, November 4, 1999, 32–38.

10 MacIntyre suggests a model for the "university of constrained disagreement" in *Three Rival Versions of Moral Enquiry: Encyclopaedia, Genealogy, and Tradition* (Notre Dame, IN: University of Notre Dame Press, 1990), 216–236. For Milbank's reservations about MacIntyrean virtue, see *Theology and Social Theory: Beyond Secular Reason* (Oxford: Blackwell, 1990), 332.

11 Stanley Fish, *There's No Such Thing as Free Speech and It's a Good Thing, Too* (New York: Oxford University Press, 1994), 41.

12 Stanley Hauerwas, *The Peaceable Kingdom: A Primer in Christian Ethics* (Notre Dame, IN: University of Notre Dame Press, 1983), 1.

13 Ibid., 29.

14 H. R. Niebuhr, *The Responsible Self: An Essay in Christian Moral Philosophy* (New York: Harper and Row, 1963), 56, 60.

15 Stanley Hauerwas, *In Good Company: The Church as Polis* (Notre Dame, IN: University of Notre Dame Press, 1995), 179–181.

16 For a suggestive account of repentance in Christian reading of texts, see David Lyle Jeffrey, *People of the Book: Christian Identity and Literary Culture* (Grand Rapids, MI: Eerdmans, 1996), 87, 204, 353–373, 378.

17 Edward Said, "Restoring Intellectual Coherence," *MLA Newsletter* 31, no. 1 (spring 1999): 3.

18 Martha Nussbaum, *Love's Knowledge: Essays on Philosophy and Literature* (New York: Oxford University Press, 1990), 23–24.

19 "Aridity" is Grant's word; see *English-Speaking Justice*, 11–12.

20 Delbanco, "The Decline and Fall of Literature," 34.

21 For a Christian response to "ideological" criticism, see Daniel E. Ritchie, *Reconstructing Literature in an Ideological Age: A Biblical Poetics and Literary Studies from Milton to Burke* (Grand Rapids, MI: Eerdmans, 1996), especially 1–20.

22 The quotations from Emerson are, in order, from *The Journals and Miscellaneous Notebooks of Ralph Waldo Emerson*, ed. Alfred R. Ferguson (Cambridge, MA: Harvard University Press, 1964), 4:278; "Self-Reliance," in *Selected Writings*, ed. Brooks Atkinson (New York: Modern Library, 1940), 145; "Circles," in *Selected Writings*, 285. My paraphrase of Emerson on history and biography derives from "History," in *Selected Writings*, 127.

23 See Gerald Graff, "Teach the Conflicts," in *The Politics of Liberal Education*, ed. Daryl J. Gless and Barbara Herrnstein Smith (Durham, NC: Duke University Press, 1992), 57–73.

24 1 John 3:14.

1 Literary Criticism and Christian Ethics in Service to One Another

1 See Alasdair MacIntyre, *After Virtue: A Study in Moral Theory* (Notre Dame, IN: University of Notre Dame Press, 1984); *Whose Justice? Which Rationality?* (Notre Dame, IN: University of Notre Dame Press, 1988); and *Three Rival Versions of Moral Enquiry: Encyclopaedia, Genealogy, and Tradition* (Notre Dame, IN: University of Notre Dame Press, 1990).

2 Stanley Fish, *There's No Such Thing as Free Speech and It's a Good Thing, Too* (New York: Oxford University Press, 1994), 41. Cited hereafter in the text.

3 Bernard Williams, *Morality: An Introduction to Ethics* (New York: Harper and Row, 1972), 29–39.

4 Mark Schwehn, *Exiles from Eden: Religion and the Academic Vocation in America* (New York: Oxford University Press, 1993), 15–16. Cited hereafter in the text.

5 Jeffrey Stout, *Ethics after Babel: The Languages of Morals and Their Discontents* (Boston: Beacon Press, 1988), 182.

6 Richard Rorty, "The Priority of Democracy to Philosophy," in *Essays on Heidegger and Others* [*Philosophical Papers*, Vol. 2] (Cambridge, England: Cambridge University Press, 1991), 189.

7 Alasdair MacIntyre, "How Can We Learn What *Veritatis Splendor* Has to Teach?" *The Thomist* 58 (1994): 187.

8 Josef Pieper, *The Four Cardinal Virtues* (Notre Dame, IN: University of Notre Dame Press, 1966), 189.

9 Annette Kolodny, "Dancing through the Minefield: Some Observations on the Theory, Practice, and Politics of a Feminist Literary Criticism," in *Falling into Theory: Conflicting Views on Reading Literature*, ed. David H. Richter (Boston: Bedford Books, 1994), 280. Cited hereafter in the text.

10 St. Augustine, *Confessions*, trans. R. S. Pine-Coffin (Baltimore: Penguin, 1964), 78.

11 For a defense of appropriate resentment and moral hatred, see the chapters by Jeffrie Murphy in Jeffrie G. Murphy and Jean Hampton, *Forgiveness and Mercy* (Cambridge, England: Cambridge University Press, 1988), especially 14–34, 88–110.

12 Rorty, "The Priority of Democracy to Philosophy," 194. The phrase "terminal wistfulness" seems to have been used first by Jeffrey Stout in "Virtue among the Ruins: An Essay on MacIntyre," *Neue Zeitschrift fur Systematische Theologie und Religionsphilosophie* 26 (1984): 256–273. It reappears in the title of Chapter 10 of *Ethics after Babel*, "Liberal Apologetics and Terminal Wistfulness," a chapter based, in part, on the earlier essay.

13 MacIntyre, *After Virtue: A Study in Moral Theory*, 263.

14 Wayne Booth, *The Company We Keep: An Ethics of Fiction* (Berkeley: University of California Press, 1988), 172. Cited hereafter in the text.

15 Aristotle, *The Ethics of Aristotle: The Nicomachean Ethics*, trans. J. A. K. Thomson, rev. Hugh Tredennick (New York: Penguin, 1976), 128–129. Cited hereafter in the text as *NE*.

16 J. Hillis Miller, *The Ethics of Reading* (New York: Columbia University Press, 1987), 1. Cited hereafter in the text.

17 Immanuel Kant, *Foundations of the Metaphysics of Morals and What Is Enlightenment?* 2d ed., trans. Lewis White Beck (New York: Macmillan, 1990), 17.

18 Two points need to be made about Miller's reading of Kant's example of the lying promise. First, Kant's point is about the subjective maxim adopted in guiding the will, not about whether one will, or can, fulfill the requirements of a promise at some future date. Quite apart from future contingencies that may affect my ability to keep a promise, it does seem logically incoherent for me to adopt the making of lying promises *as my maxim* when the institution of promising depends on promises' being believed. Second, it may be helpful to consider Kant's and Miller's views on lying and promising in relation to violence. Chapter 6 gives attention to Charles Fried's Kantian view that lying involves violence in that to lie is to claim access to the mind of another in a way that the other could not will for himself or herself. Kant's refusal of the lying promise, then, is a way of binding oneself not to do violence to the other. Miller, however, seems to want to insist on retaining the ability to lie, to keep one's secret or secret language, to resist binding himself with the promise, to resist that giving

over of himself to another that a promise involves. He seems to write from the position of one to whom violence has been done rather than one capable of doing violence. Insisting on the unreadability of the text or person is a way of resisting the culture of surveillance, policing, and totalizing explanation that Miller fears. All this seems very important in Miller, and I am in deep sympathy with it. I simply wish the protection of freedom Miller desires could be achieved without our assuming the universality of lying. Perhaps what is needed is a community devoted to keeping promises from a sense that promises can be assuredly kept—because God has kept his promises. Such a community would not lie because their keeping faith with one another would be seen as part of God's keeping faith with them. Members of such a community would be truthful with strangers because strangers would be seen in the light of the reconciliation already accomplished by God in the cross and resurrection—though, of course, not yet realized. Finally, no one would need ever fear the violence of totalizing explanation because his or her secret as singular, unsubstitutable individuality would be rooted in relationship to the Wholly Other. For more on these matters, see Chapter 6. For Fried on lying as violence, see *Right and Wrong* (Cambridge, MA: Harvard University Press, 1978), 54–78.

19 Martha Nussbaum, *Love's Knowledge: Essays on Philosophy and Literature* (New York: Oxford University Press, 1990), 23. Cited hereafter in the text as *LK*.

20 James's first two remarks cited here are from "The Art of Fiction," reprinted in *The Portable Henry James*, ed. Morton Dauwen Zabel, rev. Lyall H. P. Powers (New York: Viking, 1968), 399, 411. For James's remark to Wells, see Zabel's introduction to the same volume, p. 5.

21 Martha Nussbaum, *The Fragility of Goodness: Luck and Ethics in Greek Tragedy and Philosophy* (New York: Cambridge University Press, 1986), 1. Cited hereafter in the text as *FG*.

22 Stanley Hauerwas, with Richard Bondi and David B. Burrell, *Truthfulness and Tragedy: Further Investigations in Christian Ethics* (Notre Dame, IN: University of Notre Dame Press, 1985), 19–20. Cited hereafter in the text as *TT*.

23 Stanley Hauerwas, *The Peaceable Kingdom: A Primer in Christian Ethics* (Notre Dame, IN: University of Notre Dame Press, 1983), 18. Cited hereafter in the text as *PK*.

24 Stanley Hauerwas, *A Community of Character: Toward a Constructive Christian Social Ethic* (Notre Dame, IN: University of Notre Dame Press, 1981), 9. Cited hereafter in the text as *CC*.

25 H. Richard Niebuhr, *The Responsible Self: An Essay in Christian Moral Philosophy* (New York: Harper and Row, 1963), 56, 60.

26 George Lindbeck, *The Nature of Doctrine: Religion and Theology in a Postliberal Age* (Philadelphia: Westminster, 1984), 118. For Hauerwas's comments on Lindbeck, see *Against the Nations: War and Survival in a Liberal Society* (Minneapolis: Winston Press, 1985), 1–9.

27 Stanley Hauerwas, *Suffering Presence: Theological Reflections on Medicine, the Men-*

tally Handicapped, and the Church (Notre Dame, IN: University of Notre Dame Press, 1986), 182, 211. Cited hereafter in the text as *SP.*

28 See Stanley Hauerwas, "The Difference of Virtue and the Difference It Makes: Courage Exemplified," *Modern Theology* 9 (1993): 249–264.

29 Michael Warner, "Value, Agency, and Stephen Crane's 'The Monster,'" *Nineteenth-Century Fiction* 40 (1985): 85–86.

30 "If cacophony had not forbidden, *Emma* could and I think would have been entitled *Influence and Interference.* Or it might have been called more generically *Solicitude.* Jane Austen's question here was: What makes it sometimes legitimate or even obligatory for one person deliberately to try to modify the course of another person's life, while sometimes such attempts are wrong? Where is the line between Meddling and Helping?" (280). Gilbert Ryle, "Jane Austen and the Moralists," in *Collected Papers* (New York: Barnes and Noble, 1971), 1:276–291.

31 See Bernard Williams, *Moral Luck: Philosophical Papers, 1973–1980* (Cambridge, England: Cambridge University Press, 1981), especially 20–39. Nussbaum has written about "moral luck" in both *The Fragility of Goodness* and *Love's Knowledge.*

32 Jane Austen, *Emma* (London: Penguin, 1985), 37. Cited hereafter in the text.

33 Stanley Hauerwas, *Dispatches from the Front: Theological Engagements with the Secular* (Durham, NC: Duke University Press, 1994), 58.

34 MacIntyre, *After Virtue,* 242–243.

35 See Hauerwas, "Constancy and Forgiveness: The Novel as a School for Virtue," Chapter 1 of *Dispatches from the Front,* 31–57.

36 See Nussbaum's chapter "Perceptive Equilibrium: Literary Theory and Ethical Theory," in *Love's Knowledge,* 168–194.

37 George Marsden, *The Outrageous Idea of Christian Scholarship* (New York: Oxford University Press, 1997).

38 Hauerwas, *Dispatches from the Front,* 56.

39 Nathaniel Hawthorne, *The English Notebooks,* ed. Randall Stewart (New York: Russell and Russell, 1962), 433.

40 On this point, see John Howard Yoder, "How H. Richard Niebuhr Reasoned: A Critique of *Christ and Culture,*" in Glen H. Stassen, D. M. Yeager, and John Howard Yoder, *Authentic Transformation: A New Vision of Christ and Culture* (Nashville, TN: Abingdon Press, 1996), especially 68–71. Yoder responds to Niebuhr's famous five-part typology of options within the Christian tradition for the resolution of the "problem" of Christ and culture (see H. Richard Niebuhr, *Christ and Culture* [New York: Harper and Row, 1951]). Yoder offers a searching critique of Niebuhr, one whose most important point is that Niebuhr's way of setting the problem is itself not sufficiently guided by New Testament affirmations of the Incarnation, Christ's Lordship, and the inseparability of "the man Jesus of Nazareth" from "the Christ who is Lord" (68). Niebuhr sets up, on the one hand, an autonomous,

monolithic culture and then poses against it a Christ understood primarily as a "moralist" who "points away from" culture "towards something else incomparably more important" (59). Given this way of posing the issue, it's not clear on what grounds one could effect a resolution of the "problem," and Yoder finds even Niebuhr's preferred transformationist option "not so much wrong as empty" (68). To confess the man Jesus of Nazareth as Christ the Lord means that one cannot see Him as "'pointing us away from' full and genuine human and historical existence." Because "the humanity of Jesus was a cultural reality," Jesus' disciples "are also within culture, not by accident or compromise, or out of weakness or inconsistency or in spite of themselves, but *by virtue* of their being his disciples" (68).

The need of the Christian interpreter of culture, then, "is precisely *not* to get the kind of total formal answer around which" Niebuhr's "treatment is oriented." Rather, the Christian's interpretation from within culture will move by discernment, accepting some aspects of culture "within clear limits," categorically rejecting others, giving new motivation to still others (69). The "assignment" is to "represent within society, through and in spite of withdrawal from certain of its activities, as well as through and in spite of involvement with others, a real judgment upon the rebelliousness of culture and a real possibility of reconciliation for all" (70–71).

41 Simone Weil, "Reflections on the Right Use of School Studies with a View to the Love of God," in *The Simone Weil Reader*, ed. George A. Panichas (Mt. Kisco, NY: Moyer Bell, 1977), 44. Cited hereafter in the text.

42 MacIntyre, *Three Rival Versions of Moral Enquiry*, 233.

43 John Milbank, *Theology and Social Theory: Beyond Secular Reason* (Oxford: Blackwell, 1990), 332, 363. Cited hereafter in the text.

44 Hauerwas and Charles Pinches have commented on Milbank's critique of MacIntyrean virtue in *Christians among the Virtues: Theological Conversations with Ancient and Modern Ethics* (Notre Dame, IN: University of Notre Dame Press, 1997), 61–69. Largely agreeing with Milbank, they introduce a helpful distinction between Christians' "using" "Greek accounts of the virtues" and "building upon them." These terms "name two quite different things. To use requires that one apply a thing within a framework significantly other than the one in which it originally appeared, which is precisely what Christianity requires insofar as it refounds human life on the life, death, and resurrection of Jesus Christ, God made flesh" (68). For more on these matters, see the afterword.

2 Toward a Christian Ethics of Reading, or, Why We Cannot Be Done with Bartleby

1 J. Hillis Miller, *Versions of Pygmalion* (Cambridge, MA: Harvard University Press, 1990), 18. Cited hereafter in the text. For a similar analysis of the way I inevitably sacrifice obligations in the exercise of preference, see

Jacques Derrida, *The Gift of Death*, trans. David Wills (Chicago: University of Chicago Press, 1995), 69.

2 John Rawls, *A Theory of Justice* (Cambridge, MA: Harvard University Press, 1971), 12.

3 St. Augustine, *Enchiridion: Faith Hope and Charity*, trans. Louis A. Arand (New York: Newman Press, 1947), 52.

4 For Derrida, there is an inescapable aporia in responsibility, which "demands on the one hand an accounting, a general answering-for-oneself with respect to the general and before the generality, hence the idea of substitution, and, on the other hand, uniqueness, absolute singularity, hence nonsubstitution, nonrepetition, silence, and secrecy" (*The Gift of Death*, 61). I very strongly share two of his concerns about the discourse of responsibility. First, if philosophy or ethics gives priority to the manifest "over the hidden or the secret," to "universal generality" over the individual, then there would seem to be "no absolutely legitimate secret" (63). Second, in the general cultural talk about ethics and responsibility of "the moralizing moralists and good consciences," it is too often forgotten that "the simple concepts of alterity and of singularity constitute the concept of duty as much as that of responsibility." In short, the "preaching" about ethics too often ignores the duties I have "in my singularity to the absolute singularity of the other" (67–68).

5 Greg Jones, "Alasdair MacIntyre on Narrative, Community, and the Moral Life," *Modern Theology* 4 (1987): 67.

6 Martin Luther, "The Freedom of a Christian," in *Luther's Works*, ed. Harold J. Grimm (Philadelphia: Muhlenberg Press, 1957), 31:371.

7 Derrida, *The Gift of Death*, 75.

8 Stanley Hauerwas, *The Peaceable Kingdom: A Primer in Christian Ethics* (Notre Dame, IN: University of Notre Dame Press, 1983), 93. Cited hereafter in the text as *PK*.

9 See Charlotte Walker Mendez, "Scriveners Forlorn: Dickens's Nemo and Melville's Bartleby," *Dickens Studies Newsletter* 11 (1980): 33–38; David Jaffe, *"Bartleby the Scrivener" and Bleak House* (Hamden, CT: Archon Books, 1979); Brian Foley, "Dickens Revised: 'Bartleby' and *Bleak House*," *Essays in Literature* 12 (1985): 241–250.

10 Dan McCall, *The Silence of Bartleby* (Ithaca, NY: Cornell University Press, 1989), 99–102.

11 H. Richard Niebuhr, *The Responsible Self: An Essay in Christian Moral Philosophy* (New York: Harper and Row, 1963), 56–60.

12 See William B. Dillingham, *Melville's Short Fiction, 1853–1856* (Athens: University of Georgia Press, 1977), 45; Robert Weisbuch, *Atlantic Double-Cross: American Literature and British Influence in the Age of Emerson* (Chicago: University of Chicago Press, 1986), 44, 45–47; Hershel Parker, "The 'Sequel' in 'Bartleby,'" in *Bartleby the Inscrutable: A Collection of Commentary on Herman Melville's Tale "Bartleby the Scrivener,"* ed. M. Thomas Inge (Hamden, CT: Archon Books, 1979), 163–164.

13 John Howard Yoder, *The Politics of Jesus* (Grand Rapids, MI: Eerdmans, 1972), 122.

14 See ibid., especially 110–113. Characterizing the way Protestant ethics has tended to cast the choice between *"the political and the sectarian,"* Yoder writes.

> In the tradition of Ernst Troeltsch, Western theological ethics assumes that the choice of options is fixed in logic and for all times and places by the way the Constantinian heritage dealt with the question. Either one accepts, without serious qualification, the responsibility of politics, i.e. of governing, with whatever means that takes, or one chooses a withdrawn position of either personal-monastic-vocational or sectarian character, which is "apolitical." If you choose to share fully in the duties and the guilt of government, you are exercising responsibility and are politically relevant; if you choose not to, it is because you think politics is either unimportant or impure, and are more concerned for other matters, such as your own salvation. In so doing you would have Jesus on your side, but having Jesus on your side is not enough, for there are issues to which Jesus does not speak . . . We must therefore supplement and in effect correct what we learn from him, by adding information on the nature and the goodness of the specifically "political" which we gain from other sources.

"This disjunction," Yoder argues bluntly, is illegitimate "if Jesus is confessed as Messiah" (110–111). Yoder has more recently extended his critique of H. R. Niebuhr's classic *Christ and Culture* (New York: Harper and Row, 1951), to which my own language about the "options" for relating Christ to culture is inevitably indebted. Yoder argues that Niebuhr's typology of five basic options is excessively rigid and that it especially puts "people called 'radical' in a box in which they do not recognize themselves" (46); that Niebuhr's definition of culture is "monolithic" and too often simply synonymous with government; that Niebuhr actually advocates a unitarianism of the Father despite his Trinitarian claims; and that Niebuhr's unstated but apparent preference for the fifth option of his book—Christ transforming culture—remains vague and underestimates the power of evil. Yoder advocates an understanding of Christian community that draws especially on New Testament language about the "powers," which are both "good creatures of God" and "fallen, evil, oppressive." On this view, "everything we call 'culture' is both in some way created and creative and positive, and in other ways rebellious and oppressive," though obviously not in some "fifty/fifty" mix (85). The task of the Christian community is to "exercise discernment" into the operation of the powers or culture while remaining faithful to Christ's Lordship. See "How H. Richard Niebuhr Reasoned: A Critique of *Christ and Culture,*" in Glen H. Stassen, D. M. Yeager, and John Howard Yoder, *Authentic Transformation: A New Vision of Christ and Culture* (Nashville, TN: Abingdon Press, 1996), 31–89.

15 Lydia Maria Child, *Letters from New York* (New York: C. S. Francis and Co.,

1844). Cited hereafter in the text. Mrs. Child's book may have provided Melville details of the spectacular Colt-Adams murder and the dramatic suicide of Colt in the Tombs just before his scheduled hanging. For more on the Colt-Adams murder, see n. 20 below. Child's treatment of Wall Street is very suggestive of Melville's, and her exposure of the substitutionary logic of capital punishment may well have stimulated Melville's story of one who refuses to be other than his singular self. That Melville understood the sacrificial dimension of capital punishment is indicated by *Billy Budd*. For an interesting reading of Child's and Melville's sense of urban space in New York, see Wyn Kelley, *Melville's City: Literary and Urban Form in Nineteenth-Century New York* (Cambridge, England: Cambridge University Press, 1996), 55–59.

16   Herman Melville, *The Piazza Tales and Other Prose Pieces, 1839–1860,* ed. Harrison Hayford et al., in *The Writings of Herman Melville* (Evanston, IL: Northwestern University Press and the Newberry Library, 1987), 9:24. Cited hereafter in the text.

17   See James F. Childress, "'Answering That of God in Every Man': An Interpretation of George Fox's Ethics," *Quaker Religious Thought* 15, no. 3 (1974): 2–41.

18   Dale Aukerman, *Darkening Valley: A Biblical Perspective on Nuclear War* (New York: Seabury Press, 1981), 44.

19   See Frederick Busch, "Thoreau and Melville as Cellmates," *Modern Fiction Studies* 23 (1977): 239–242; Robert E. Morsberger, "'I Prefer Not To': Melville and the Theme of Withdrawal," *University College Quarterly* 10 (1965): 24–29.

20   On September 17, 1841, Samuel Adams, the proprietor of a New York printing shop, went to the office of John C. Colt, who owed Adams money for a printing job. Adams disappeared; his body was discovered on the 26th on board the ship *Kalamazoo*, where it had been stuffed into a crate and consigned to New Orleans. Colt later admitted that he had killed Adams with a hatchet and boxed the body, but he claimed to have committed the crime in self-defense. A sensational trial followed, a jury condemned Colt to hang, and several appeals proved unsuccessful. On November 18, 1842, a crowd gathered in the prison yard to witness Colt's hanging, scheduled for 4 o'clock. At a few minutes to 4, a delegation went to Colt's cell to conduct him to the gallows, but found him dead, stabbed through the heart, the wound self-inflicted. At about the same time, a fire broke out in the cupola of the Tombs, which some thought had been set to divert attention from a possible escape attempt by Colt. Melville was in the Galapagos at the time of the murder, in Tahiti at the time of the trial. Thus the source of his knowledge of the crime has been a subject of some discussion. One possibility is the volume by Lydia Maria Child, *Letters from New York,* mentioned above. Child treats the case at length in the book, using it to expose what she sees as the falsely sacrificial purpose of capital punishment. For further details about the crime and its relation to "Bar-

tleby," see T. H. Giddings, "Melville, the Colt-Adams Murder, and 'Bartleby,'" *Studies in American Fiction* 2 (1974): 123–132. For Child's treatment, see *Letters from New York*, 220–231. For McCall's comments on the case and "Bartleby," see *The Silence of Bartleby*, 26–27.

21 McCall, *The Silence of Bartleby*, 26–27.

22 Paul Ramsey, *Nine Modern Moralists* (Englewood Cliffs, NJ: Prentice-Hall, 1962), 224.

23 William Werpehowski and Stephen D. Crocco, introduction to *The Essential Paul Ramsey: A Collection*, ed. William Werpehowski and Stephen D. Crocco (New Haven: Yale University Press, 1994), xv.

24 Paul Ramsey, *Christian Ethics and the Sit-In* (New York: Association Press, 1961), 125.

25 Hans Frei, *The Identity of Jesus Christ: The Hermeneutical Bases of Dogmatic Theology* (Philadelphia: Fortress Press, 1975), 65. For Frei's reading of several modern literary figures, often considered "Christ figures," including Billy Budd, see 63–84.

26 David Yeago, "Literature in the Drama of Nature and Grace: Hans Urs von Balthasar's Paradigm for a Theology of Culture," *Renascence* 48 (1996): 97.

27 Hans Urs von Balthasar, *A Theology of History* (New York: Sheed and Ward, 1963), 16–17.

28 H. Bruce Franklin, *The Wake of the Gods: Melville's Mythology* (Stanford: Stanford University Press, 1963), 128. Cited hereafter in the text.

29 David Yeago, Unpublished theology typescript (Columbia, SC: Lutheran Theological Southern Seminary, 1993), pt. 2, 322. I wish to thank Professor Yeago for permission to cite this and other quotations from his typescript.

30 Ibid., pt. 2, 168.

31 Charles Dickens, *Bleak House*, ed. Duane DeVries (New York: Crowell, 1971), 137. McCall reviews the scholarship on Dickens and Melville; see *The Silence of Bartleby*, 10–13. Jaffe has pressed the connection between Bartleby and Nemo especially; see *"Bartleby the Scrivener" and Bleak House*, 10. Also relevant is Pearl Chesler Solomon, *Dickens and Melville in Their Time* (New York: Columbia University Press, 1975).

32 St. Thomas Aquinas, *Summa Theologiae*, 2a–2ae, xlvii., 3, *ad* 2 in *Saint Thomas Aquinas: Philosophical Texts*, trans. Thomas Gilby (New York: Oxford University Press, 1960), 333.

33 Josef Pieper, *The Four Cardinal Virtues* (Notre Dame, IN: University of Notre Dame Press, 1966), 3. Cited hereafter in the text.

34 St. Thomas Aquinas, *Quaestiones disputatae de veritate*, 27, 5 *ad* 5, quoted in ibid., 36.

35 Paul Wadell, *The Primacy of Love: An Introduction to the Ethics of Thomas Aquinas* (New York: Paulist Press, 1992), 131–132. Cited hereafter in the text.

36 St. Thomas Aquinas, *Summa Theologiae*, 2a–2ae. 23, 8, trans. R. J. Batten O.P. (London: Blackfriars, 1964), 34:33.

37 For extensive comparison of "Bartleby" and *A Christmas Carol,* see Solomon, *Dickens and Melville in Their Time,* 8–42, 78–84.

38 Charles Dickens, *A Christmas Carol* (New York: Stewart, Tabori and Chang, 1990), 7. Cited hereafter in the text.

39 On the matter of perfection as a perennial "reaching forward" rather than as stasis, see Bishop Kallistos Ware, *The Orthodox Way* (Crestwood, NY: St. Vladimir's Seminary Press, 1990), 185.

40 Immanuel Kant, *Foundations of the Metaphysics of Morals and What Is Enlightenment?* 2d ed., trans. Lewis White Beck (New York: Macmillan, 1990), 46. Cited hereafter in the text.

41 The quote from Aquinas is from *Summa Theologiae,* 2a–2ae, xlvii, 9 *ad* 2, trans. Thomas Gilby, O.P., vol. 36 (London: Blackfriars, 1974), 30.

42 Alasdair MacIntyre, *After Virtue: A Study in Moral Theory* (Notre Dame, IN: University of Notre Dame Press, 1984), 46. Cited hereafter in the text.

43 For suggestions of Bartleby's anorexia, see Edwin Haviland Miller, *Melville* (New York: Persea Books, 1975), 263; Robert N. Mollinger, "Bartleby the Anorexic," *Psychoanalysis and Literature* (New York: Nelson-Hall, 1981), 85–96.

44 Paolo Freire, "The 'Banking' Concept of Education," in *Ways of Reading: An Anthology for Writers,* 3d ed., ed. David Bartholomae and Anthony Petrosky (Boston: Bedford Books, 1993), 206–219.

3 The "Best Blessing of Existence": "Conscious Worth" in *Emma*

1 Lionel Trilling, *The Opposing Self: Nine Essays in Criticism* (New York: Viking, 1955), 207. Cited hereafter in the text.

2 Alasdair MacIntyre, *After Virtue: A Study in Moral Theory,* 2d ed. (Notre Dame, IN: University of Notre Dame Press, 1984), 190. Cited hereafter in the text as *AV.*

3 Alistair Duckworth, *The Improvement of the Estate: A Study of Jane Austen's Novels* (Baltimore: Johns Hopkins University Press, 1971), 160.

4 Alison Sulloway, *Jane Austen and the Province of Womanhood* (Philadelphia: University of Pennsylvania Press, 1989), 39.

5 Judith Wilt, *Ghosts of the Gothic: Austen, Eliot, and Lawrence* (Princeton, NJ: Princeton University Press, 1980), 147, 154. Cited hereafter in the text.

6 Edmund Wilson, "A Long Talk about Jane Austen," in *Jane Austen: A Collection of Critical Essays,* ed. Ian Watt (Englewood Cliffs, NJ: Prentice-Hall, 1963), 39; Marvin Mudrick, *Jane Austen: Irony as Defense and Discovery* (Princeton, NJ: Princeton University Press, 1952), 206.

7 Wayne Booth, *The Company We Keep: An Ethics of Fiction* (Berkeley: University of California Press, 1988), 435. Cited hereafter in the text as *CK.*

8 Wayne Booth, *The Rhetoric of Fiction,* 2d ed. (Chicago: University of Chicago Press, 1983), 259.

9 Alasdair MacIntyre, *Three Rival Versions of Moral Enquiry: Encyclopaedia, Genealogy, and Tradition* (Notre Dame, IN: University of Notre Dame Press, 1990), 79. Cited hereafter in the text as *TRV.*

10 Stanley Hauerwas and Charles Pinches, *Christians among the Virtues: Theological Conversations with Ancient and Modern Ethics* (Notre Dame, IN: University of Notre Dame Press, 1997), ix.

11 Martha Nussbaum, *Love's Knowledge* (New York: Oxford University Press, 1990), 23.

12 For Ryle, see "Jane Austen and the Moralists," in *Collected Papers* (New York: Barnes and Noble, 1971), 1:276–291. Lewis's "A Note on Jane Austen" is available in *Jane Austen: A Collection of Critical Essays*, ed. Ian Watt (Englewood Cliffs, NJ: Prentice-Hall, 1963), 25–34. Also relevant is Gene Koppel, *The Religious Dimension of Jane Austen's Novels* (Ann Arbor: UMI Research Press, 1988).

13 Bernard Williams, *Morality: An Introduction to Ethics* (New York: Harper and Row, 1972), 29.

14 Nussbaum has been concerned with the matter of "moral luck" in both *The Fragility of Goodness: Luck and Ethics in Greek Tragedy and Philosophy* (Cambridge, England: Cambridge University Press, 1986), and *Love's Knowledge.* Her work draws on Bernard Williams's paper on moral luck in *Moral Luck: Philosophical Papers, 1973–1980* (Cambridge, England: Cambridge University Press, 1981), 20–39.

15 My text of *Emma* is the Penguin edition, which "follows that of the first edition except for the dividing of the novel into three volumes" (31). Jane Austen, *Emma*, ed. Ronald Blythe (London: Penguin, 1985), 37. Cited hereafter in the text.

16 Ryle, "Jane Austen and the Moralists," 1:280.

17 Duckworth notes also "Jane Austen's careful choice of a religious vocabulary in the closing chapters: we hear, for example, of Emma's 'contrition' and 'penitence'" (*The Improvement of the Estate,* 177).

18 To Francis Austen, 26 July 1809, in *Jane Austen's Letters*, ed. Deirdre Le Faye (Oxford: Oxford University Press, 1995), 178. Cited hereafter in the text.

19 Nussbaum, *The Fragility of Goodness,* 338. Cited hereafter in the text as *FG.*

20 Mrs. Norris's use of the word "mite" suggests that she likens herself to the widow of the Gospel story when she proposes to Sir Thomas that they take one of Fanny's children into their care: "I entirely agree with you in the main as to the propriety of doing every thing one could by way of providing for a child one had in a manner taken into one's own hands; and I am sure I should be the last person in the world to withhold my mite upon such an occasion" (4). What Mrs. Norris does from first to last, in regard to Fanny, is to withhold her mite, while continually calling attention to her own goodness. Her real love is for money, as Austen remarks twice in the early chapters. See *Mansfield Park*, ed. James Kinsley (Oxford: Oxford University Press, 1990), 6, 22.

21 For a reading of Mrs. Norris as one whose "irritating officiousness" derives

from "a woman's imaginative energy misdirected by her dependence and social uselessness," see Mary Poovey, *The Proper Lady and the Woman Writer: Ideology as Style in the Works of Mary Wollstonecraft, Mary Shelley, and Jane Austen* (Chicago: University of Chicago Press, 1984), 216. Where Poovey and I agree is in her analysis of how Mrs. Norris seeks, even in arranging Fanny's adoption, to "reinforc[e] what meager power she has": "the activity of moral instructor reinforces Mrs. Norris's tenuous sense of her own superiority—especially when the lessons she prescribes all project onto her little niece the worthlessness, inferiority, and indebtedness she is so anxious to deny in herself" (216). I agree that the need of the pharisaic personality frequently is to use the claim to moral superiority as justification for power over another, a need that often springs from a sense of unworthiness and inferiority. The Gospel at once humbles the moral drive and exalts the sinner, conferring an otherwise inconceivable worth through God's choosing to die for him or her.

22 John Halperin sees decisive change in Austen's religious views between the letters of January 24, 1809, and November 18–20, 1814, change he attributes to her growing "more conservative" with age; see *The Life of Jane Austen* (Baltimore: Johns Hopkins University Press, 1984), 263. Mary Poovey cites the two letters' remarks about Evangelicalism as "one example of Austen's apparent self-contradiction." See *The Proper Lady and the Woman Writer*, 265, n. 2. For a valuable discussion of Jane Austen and the Evangelicals, see Irene Collins, *Jane Austen and the Clergy* (London: Hambledon Press, 1994), 179–195.

23 Fanny Knight responded to Austen's letter of November 18–20, 1814, with its suggestion that "we perhaps ought all to be Evangelicals." Fanny apparently took issue with the suggestion, for Austen wrote in her next letter to her niece: "I cannot suppose we differ in our ideas of the Christian Religion. You have given an excellent description of it. We only affix a different meaning to the Word *Evangelical.*" Jane Austen to Fanny Knight, 30 November 1814, in *Letters*, 287.

24 Ellen Moers reads these comments as suggesting that Austen regards Mrs. Weston's rearing of Emma as a "botched" job; she will "teach her own daughter no better, whatever Emma thinks, for having practiced on a surrogate." I differ from Moers in taking seriously both Mrs. Weston's and Knightley's points of view on the good as well as the contribution of *both* to Emma's development. See *Literary Women* (Garden City, NY: Doubleday, 1976), 216.

25 Nussbaum works out her views throughout *The Fragility of Goodness*, but see especially 1–21, 318–371, and 384–387. What I have called the "moral luck conundrum" depends on the Kantian separation of value into moral and nonmoral realms. In its large outlines, Nussbaum's argument is something like the following: Plato and Kant attempt to isolate the good from harm, from influence by all sorts of factors external to the agent (i.e., luck); yet the living of a good life, a life of excellences and eudaimonia, can

clearly be affected by factors external to the agent, a matter that Greek tragedy repeatedly emphasizes; therefore, we must recognize that the good, the moral life or worth, is susceptible to luck. But it seems to me that Nussbaum is never really successful in her critique of Kant. Her key move is the first one, defining the "ethical" question as "How should one live?" as part of her Aristotelian inquiry. Clearly, luck can affect the capacity for human flourishing, but to grant that is not finally to say anything about the particular realm Kant called the moral (i.e., that concerning the maxims that direct one's willing). Nussbaum, at times, seems insufficiently clear about the tradition within which her own interpretations are offered, and thus, as Hauerwas has said about her work, "what we get is the claim that by reading Aristotle we can recapture the essential human insights about the finiteness and fragility of our lives that are simply there"—to be read off, as if in the manner of "objective scholarship." See Hauerwas, "Can Aristotle Be a Liberal? Nussbaum on Luck," *Soundings* 72 (1989): 687. Important to remember is Nussbaum's purpose as it concerns the way Kantian assumptions might form agents. With Bernard Williams, she shares the sense that Kant's demarcating a realm of moral value *and* insisting that moral value "is of overwhelmingly greater importance than everything else" (*FG* 4) can lead to a hard invulnerability in agents. As Williams puts it, insisting "that *what I most fundamentally am*" is "beyond luck" can lead to making "admiration or liking or even enjoyment of the happy manifestations of luck" seem to be "treachery to moral worth" (*Moral Luck*, 38). However much I agree with this, I wish to insist just as vehemently that "excellence" and "worth" are not equivalent, as Nussbaum often implies or assumes.

26 Trilling, *The Opposing Self*, 207–208.

4 Honor, Faithfulness, and Community in Anthony Trollope's *The Warden* and *He Knew He Was Right*

1 Stanley Hauerwas, *Dispatches from the Front: Theological Engagements with the Secular* (Durham, NC: Duke University Press, 1994), 58. Cited hereafter in the text as *DF.*

2 See Stanley Hauerwas, "A Story-Formed Community: Reflections on *Watership Down*," in *A Community of Character: Toward a Constructive Christian Social Ethic* (Notre Dame, IN: University of Notre Dame Press, 1981), 9–35. Cited hereafter in the text as *CC.*

3 Stanley Hauerwas, *Naming the Silences: God, Medicine, and the Problem of Suffering* (Grand Rapids, MI: Eerdmans, 1990), 1–38; Peter DeVries, *The Blood of the Lamb* (Boston: Little, Brown, 1969).

4 Karl Barth, *The Doctrine of Creation*, pt. 4, vol. 3 of *Church Dogmatics*, ed. G. W. Bromiley and T. F. Torrance (Edinburgh: T. and T. Clark, 1961), 649. Cited hereafter in the text as *DC.*

5 Peter Berger, "On the Obsolescence of the Concept of Honor," in *Revisions:*

Changing Perspectives in Moral Philosophy, ed. Stanley Hauerwas and Alasdair MacIntyre (Notre Dame, IN: University of Notre Dame Press, 1983), 172–181.

6 Alasdair MacIntyre, *After Virtue: A Study in Moral Theory*, 2d ed. (Notre Dame, IN: University of Notre Dame Press, 1984), 242.

7 Shirley Letwin, *The Gentleman in Trollope: Individuality and Moral Conduct* (Cambridge, MA: Harvard University Press, 1982), 65. Cited hereafter in the text.

8 Stanley Hauerwas, *The Peaceable Kingdom: A Primer in Christian Ethics* (Notre Dame, IN: University of Notre Dame Press, 1983), 89. Cited hereafter in the text as *PK*.

9 Anthony Trollope, *The Warden*, ed. Robin Gilmour (London: Penguin, 1986), 2, 3. Cited hereafter in the text.

10 J. Hillis Miller, *The Ethics of Reading* (New York: Columbia University Press, 1987), 97.

11 Søren Kierkegaard, *Works of Love*, ed. and trans. Howard V. Hong and Edna H. Hong (Princeton, NJ: Princeton University Press, 1995), 307. The passage immediately preceding the one quoted is perhaps just as suggestive in reference to Mr. Harding's abiding in love: "Can anyone determine how long the silence must last before it can be said that now there is no more conversation; and if that can be determined, one can still know whether it is so in the particular case only in the sense of the past, since the time must indeed be past. But the one who loves, who abides, continually emancipates himself from his knowledge of the past. He knows no past; he is only waiting for the future" (307).

12 Anthony Trollope, *Anthony Trollope: An Illustrated Autobiography* (Wolfeboro, NH: Alan Sutton, 1989), 109. Earlier in the passage from which the quote derives Trollope articulates an even more positively conceived moral purpose: "There are many who would laugh at the idea of a novelist teaching either virtue or nobility—those, for instance, who regard the reading of novels as a sin, and those also who think it to be simply an idle pastime. They look upon the tellers of stories as among the tribe of those who pander to the wicked pleasures of a wicked world. I have regarded my art from so different a point of view that I have ever thought of myself as a preacher of sermons, and my pulpit as one which I could make both salutary and agreeable to my audience" (109). Trollope presents himself here in terms nearly antithetical to Miller's interpretation of him: Miller assumes the novelist played a well-respected and stabilizing role in reflecting society's values to itself but that Trollope subverted these expectations by undermining moral expectations and authority. Trollope makes it plain that the novel was the last place many of his contemporaries would be likely to look for confirmation of their moral notions, but that he has taken the novel's moral possibilities seriously.

13 Elizabeth Epperly, *Patterns of Repetition in Trollope* (Washington, DC: Catholic University of America Press, 1989), 82.

14 Anthony Trollope, *He Knew He Was Right* (London: Oxford University Press, 1963), 1. Cited hereafter in the text.

15 John Milton, *Complete Poems and Major Prose*, ed. Merritt Y. Hughes (Indianapolis: Odyssey Press, 1957), 469. Cited hereafter in the text.

16 Søren Kierkegaard, *The Sickness unto Death: A Christian Psychological Exposition for Upbuilding and Awakening*, ed. and trans. Howard V. Hong and Edna H. Hong (Princeton, NJ: Princeton University Press, 1980), 30. Cited hereafter in the text.

17 Ernest Becker, *The Denial of Death* (New York: Free Press, 1973), 76.

18 Explaining himself to Maria Gostrey at the end of *The Ambassadors*, Strether claims finally to understand what would make his whole complex experience in Paris somehow "right": "That, you see, is my only logic. Not, out of the whole affair, to have got anything for myself." Henry James, *The Ambassadors* (New York: Charles Scribner's Sons, 1909), 2:326.

19 L. Gregory Jones, *Embodying Forgiveness: A Theological Analysis* (Grand Rapids, MI: Eerdmans, 1995), 6.

20 Karl Barth, *The Doctrine of Reconciliation*, pt. 1, trans. G. W. Bromiley, vol. 4 of *Church Dogmatics*, ed. G. W. Bromiley and T. F. Torrance (Edinburgh: T. and T. Clark, 1936–1977), 448. Cited hereafter in the text as *DR*.

21 Nigel Biggar, *The Hastening That Waits: Karl Barth's Ethics* (Oxford: Clarendon Press, 1993), 7–8. Cited hereafter in the text.

5 The "Very Temple of Authorised Love": Henry James and
The Portrait of a Lady

1 Henry James, *Notes of a Son and Brother* (New York: Charles Scribner's Sons, 1914), 171. Cited hereafter in the text.

2 Henry James Sr., *The Literary Remains of the Late Henry James*, ed. William James (Boston: James R. Osgood, 1885), 12–13.

3 In Henry James Sr., *Christianity the Logic of Creation* (New York: D. Appleton, 1857), 169. Cited hereafter in the text as *CLC*.

4 Hans Urs von Balthasar, *A Theology of History* (New York: Sheed and Ward, 1963), 16–17.

5 David Yeago, "Literature in the Drama of Nature and Grace: Hans Urs von Balthasar's Paradigm for a Theology of Culture," *Renascence* 48 (1996): 97.

6 Henry James Sr., *Society the Redeemed Form of Man* (Boston: Houghton, Osgood and Company, 1879), 445–446. Cited hereafter in the text as *SRF*.

7 In James Sr., *The Literary Remains of the Late Henry James*, 17.

8 See Harold Bloom, *The American Religion: The Emergence of the Post-Christian Nation* (New York: Simon and Schuster, 1992); cited hereafter in the text. Bloom has referred to the elder James as "an American Gnostic speculator" in his introduction to *Henry James's The Portrait of a Lady*, ed. Harold Bloom (New York: Chelsea House, 1987), 2.

9   From *Moralism and Christianity* (1850), in *Henry James, Senior: A Selection of His Writings*, ed. Giles Gunn (Chicago: American Library Association, 1974), 126. Cited hereafter in the text as *MC*.

10 Giles Gunn, introduction to *Henry James, Senior: A Selection of His Writings*, 5; the citation from Daniel Aaron is from *Men of Good Hope* (New York: Galaxy Books, 1961), 133.

11 Yeago, "Literature in the Drama of Nature and Grace: Hans Urs von Balthasar's Paradigm for a Theology of Culture," 98.

12 The example of the elder James can help us to see how much is at stake in Stanley Hauerwas's reminders that the "most fundamental way to talk of God" is through "story" and that "claims such as 'God is creator' are simply shorthand ways of reminding us that we believe we are participants in a much more elaborate story, of which God is the author." Part of Hauerwas's purpose seems to be to warn against a theologizing about Nature or Creation that treats these as independent categories and not as second-order language whose purpose is to help us better understand the meaning of the scriptural narratives themselves. See *The Peaceable Kingdom: A Primer in Christian Ethics* (Notre Dame, IN: University of Notre Dame Press, 1983), 25–26.

13 David Baily Harned, *Creed and Personal Identity: The Meaning of the Apostles' Creed* (Philadelphia: Fortress, 1981), 38.

14 David Yeago, Unpublished theology typescript (Columbia, SC: Lutheran Theological Southern Seminary, 1993), pt. 2, 168, 175.

15 Josef Pieper, *About Love*, trans. Richard Winston and Clara Winston (Chicago: Franciscan Herald Press, 1974), 26.

16 Henry James, *The Portrait of a Lady* (New York: Charles Scribner's Sons, 1908), 2:235. Cited hereafter in the text.

17 The remark is in James's "Preface to the New York Edition," in *The Portrait of a Lady*, 1:xxi.

18 Richard Poirier finds the "consummate irony" of James's novel in "the degree to which Osmond is a mock version of the transcendentalist"—of the Emersonian stamp. See *The Comic Sense of Henry James: A Study of the Early Novels* (London: Chatto and Windus, 1960), 219. Harold Bloom echoes this judgment in his introduction to *Henry James's The Portrait of a Lady*, 8–9. Alfred Habegger argues that Osmond "represents the dark side of . . . his author's male parent," the authoritarianism of James Sr. with which the son is in psychic struggle throughout *Portrait*. Habegger contends that James betrays his cousin Minny Temple through Isabel's return to Osmond, a conclusion that signifies James's capitulation to his father's repressive notions of marriage. See *Henry James and the "Woman Business"* (Cambridge, England: Cambridge University Press, 1989), 178–181.

19 Henry James, *The Complete Notebooks of Henry James*, ed. Leon Edel and Lyall H. Powers (New York: Oxford University Press, 1987), 15.

20 Immanuel Kant, "Jealousy and Its Offspring—Envy and Grudge," in *Lectures on Ethics*, trans. Louis Infield (New York: Harper and Row, 1963), 217. Cited hereafter in the text as *JEG*.

21 Immanuel Kant, *The Metaphysics of Morals*, trans. Mary Gregor (Cambridge, England: Cambridge University Press, 1993), 252. Cited hereafter in the text as *MM*.

22 Ernest Becker, *The Denial of Death* (New York: Free Press, 1973), 152.

23 For a fascinating treatment of curiosity, see Ross Posnock, *The Trial of Curiosity: Henry James, William James, and the Challenge of Modernity* (New York: Oxford University Press, 1991). Following the argument of Hans Blumenberg that the "turbulent history" of curiosity "has played a central role in defining 'the legitimacy of the modern age,'" Posnock situates Henry James as one interested in the rehabilitation of curiosity, over against what Posnock deems an Augustinian "prohibition" on the one hand and, on the other, an Enlightenment tendency to devalue curiosity as a "worldly sin" against the imperatives of applied science. For the relevant sections of Blumenberg, see *The Legitimacy of the Modern Age*, trans. Robert Wallace (Cambridge, MA: MIT Press, 1983), 312, 385, 388.

24 Gilbert Meilaender, *The Theory and Practice of Virtue* (Notre Dame, IN: University of Notre Dame Press, 1984), 138. Meilaender cites the Rex Warner translation of the *Confessions* (New York: New American Library, 1963). Meilaender is, in my view, unnecessarily defensive about the supposed antiscientific import of Augustine's treatment of curiosity. What Augustine understands by curiosity could never sustain the prolonged and disciplined inquiry of science or theology; wonder at creation, as he well knew, is needed.

25 St. Augustine, *Confessions*, trans. R. S. Pine-Coffin (Baltimore: Penguin, 1961), 239. Cited hereafter in the text.

26 H. Richard Niebuhr, *The Responsible Self: An Essay in Christian Moral Philosophy* (New York: Harper and Row, 1963), 56, 60.

27 James Sr., *Lectures and Miscellanies* (1852), in *Henry James, Senior: A Selection of His Writings*, 135.

28 Henry James, *The Ambassadors* (New York: Charles Scribner's Sons, 1909), 2:326. It's doubtful that even Strether is in a position to take up his own logic, for, as Maria Gostrey reminds him, "But with your wonderful impressions you'll have got a great deal." Cited hereafter in the text.

29 Søren Kierkegaard, *Works of Love*, trans. Howard and Edna Hong (New York: Harper and Row, 1962), 34–35, 39.

30 In Walter Harding, *The Days of Henry Thoreau* (New York: Knopf, 1970), 457.

31 On availability, fidelity, and "being for" the other, see Gabriel Marcel, *Creative Fidelity*, trans. Robert Rosthal (New York: Farrar, Straus, Giroux, 1964), 38–57, 147–174; and *Homo Viator: Introduction to a Metaphysic of Hope*, trans. Emma Craufurd (1951; rpt. Gloucester, MA: Peter Smith, 1978), 125–134.

32 James, *The Complete Notebooks of Henry James*, 15.

33 A textual apparatus listing all of the "substantive" variants between the editions is conveniently available in *The Portrait of a Lady*, ed. Robert D.

Bamberg (New York: Norton, 1975), 493–575. For the 1881 reading cited here, see 508–509.

34 Martha Nussbaum, *Love's Knowledge* (New York: Oxford University Press, 1990), 173; cited hereafter in the text as *LK.* For James, see also 125–147, 148–167, 195–219. For the Aristotelian "starting point," see 23–29.

35 See William H. Gass, "The High Brutality of Good Intentions," in *Perspectives on James's The Portrait of a Lady: A Collection of Critical Essays*, ed. William T. Stafford (New York: New York University Press, 1967), 208; Tony Tanner, "The Fearful Self: Henry James's *The Portrait of a Lady*," in *The Merrill Studies in The Portrait of a Lady*, ed. Lyall H. Powers (Columbus, OH: Merrill, 1970), 107–108.

36 Alasdair MacIntyre, *After Virtue*, 2d ed. (Notre Dame, IN: University of Notre Dame Press, 1984), 46.

37 The point about substitutability reflects the way MacIntyre and Nussbaum depict Kantian rationality. Kant, however, seems to argue that absolute nonsubstitutability is integral to the definition of "objective ends (i.e., beings whose existence is an end in itself)." "Such an end," Kant writes, "is one in the place of which no other end, to which these beings should serve merely as means, can be put." *Foundations of the Metaphysics of Morals*, trans. Lewis White Beck (New York: Macmillan, 1990), 45.

38 Dorothea Krook, *The Ordeal of Consciousness in Henry James* (Cambridge, England: Cambridge University Press, 1967), 365–366. See Carren Kaston, *Imagination and Desire in the Novels of Henry James* (New Brunswick, NJ: Rutgers University Press, 1984), 54.

39 Virginia Fowler, *Henry James's American Girl: The Embroidery on the Canvas* (Madison: University of Wisconsin Press, 1984), 82. Cited hereafter in the text.

40 Priscilla Walton, *The Disruption of the Feminine in Henry James* (Toronto: University of Toronto Press, 1992), 53, 64.

41 Habegger, *Henry James and the "Woman Business,"* 165; Habegger is discussing Joseph Wiesenfarth's treatment of Isabel in "A Woman in *The Portrait of a Lady*," *Henry James Review* 7 (1986): 18–28.

42 Edwin Sill Fussell, *The Catholic Side of Henry James* (Cambridge, England: Cambridge University Press, 1993), 54.

43 After reading the first two numbers of *Portrait*, Grace Norton wrote James in December 1880 to ask about the relationship between Isabel and Minny Temple. James responded: "You are both right & wrong about Minnie Temple. I had her in mind & there is in the heroine a considerable infusion of my impression of her remarkable nature. But the thing is not a portrait. Poor Minny was essentially incomplete & I have attempted to make my young woman more rounded, more finished. In truth, every one, in life, is incomplete, & it is the mark of art that in reproducing them one feels the desire to fill them out, to justify them, as it were." Letter of December 28, 1880, quoted in Habegger, *Henry James and the "Woman Business,"* 160. Habegger thinks James "betrayed" Minny in his depiction of Isabel from the need

to appease his father, who had "vigorously instructed" him "not to believe in Minnie's or anyone else's free intrepidity" (88). Closer to my treatment is Philip Horne, who emphasizes the "absolute force" of the "warning" to Grace Norton "not to identify Isabel with Minny"; James requires "a more differentiating account of their relation" from his "interested reader." See *Henry James and Revision* (Oxford: Clarendon Press, 1990), 189.

44 Rowan Williams, "Balthasar and Rahner," in *The Analogy of Beauty: The Theology of Hans Urs von Balthasar,* ed. John Riches (Edinburgh: T. and T. Clark, 1986), 21–22.

45 Bloom, introduction to *Henry James's The Portrait of a Lady,* 12.

6 A Light That Has Been There from the Beginning: Stephen Crane and the Gospel of John

1 Stephen Crane, *The Works of Stephen Crane: Tales of Whilomville,* ed. Fredson Bowers (Charlottesville: University Press of Virginia, 1969), 7:49. Cited hereafter in the text.

2 Daniel Knapp, "Son of Thunder: Stephen Crane and the Fourth Evangelist," *Nineteenth-Century Fiction* 24 (1969): 253–291; Donald Gibson, *The Fiction of Stephen Crane* (Carbondale: Southern Illinois University Press, 1968), 137–139; Charles E. Modlin and John R. Byers Jr., "Stephen Crane's 'The Monster' as Christian Allegory," *Markham Review* (May 1973): 110–113. A list of religious readings of Crane must begin with R. W. Stallman's interpretation of *The Red Badge of Courage* and the notorious "wafer" image; see *Stephen Crane: A Biography* (New York: George Braziller, 1968), 168–180. Daniel Hoffman reads Crane's poems as a religious psychodrama, with Crane split between the rigorous Methodism of his mother's family, the Pecks, and the gentler theology of the Reverend Jonathan Crane; see *The Poetry of Stephen Crane* (New York: Columbia University Press, 1957), 43–99.

3 For biblical quotations, I have used the King James translation as that likely most familiar to Crane. When there is a quotation within a citation of a secondary source, I have maintained the translation used in the source.

4 My understanding of social crises of differentiation has been greatly influenced by Rene Girard, *The Scapegoat,* trans. Yvonne Freccero (Baltimore: Johns Hopkins University Press, 1986), especially the chapter "Stereotypes of Persecution," 12–23.

5 Ernest Becker, *The Denial of Death* (New York: Free Press, 1973), 148–158.

6 Michael Warner, "Value, Agency, and Stephen Crane's 'The Monster,'" *Nineteenth-Century Fiction* 40 (1985): 85. Cited hereafter in the text.

7 Stanley Hauerwas, *The Peaceable Kingdom: A Primer in Christian Ethics* (Notre Dame, IN: University of Notre Dame Press, 1983), 42.

8 Stephen Crane, "The Upturned Face," in *Tales of War,* ed. Fredson Bowers, in *The Works of Stephen Crane* (Charlottesville: University Press of Virginia,

1970), 6:298. Cited hereafter in the text. The uncanny encounter with the face of a dead soldier is also critical to Henry Fleming's experience in *The Red Badge of Courage*. During Henry's wanderings after running from battle, he comes upon a chapel-like place in the woods, where, "near the threshold," he becomes "horror-stricken at the sight of a thing. He was being looked at by a dead man who was seated with his back against a column-like tree." The strangeness of the encounter that follows turns especially on the seeming ability of the dead face to continue to look at Henry. See *Works*, ed. Fredson Bowers (Charlottesville: University Press of Virginia, 1975), 2:47.

9   Emmanuel Levinas, *Totality and Infinity: An Essay on Exteriority*, trans. Alphonso Lingis (Pittsburgh: Duquesne University Press, 1969), 197; cited hereafter in the text as *TI*. Jacques Derrida emphasizes the way the ethical relation in Levinas singularizes the self by putting it in question. Derrida contrasts Levinas with Kierkegaard, who identifies the ethical with the general and the religious sphere with singularity. See *The Gift of Death*, trans. David Wills (Chicago: University of Chicago Press, 1995), 78.

10   Merold Westphal, "Levinas and the Immediacy of the Face," *Faith and Philosophy* 10 (1993): 492.

11   Emmanuel Levinas, "Substitution," in *The Levinas Reader*, ed. Sean Hand (Oxford: Basil Blackwell, 1989), 101.

12   Emmanuel Levinas, "Language and Proximity," in *Collected Philosophical Papers*, trans. Alphonso Lingis (Dordrecht, Netherlands: Martinus Nijhoff, 1987), 123.

13   For Crane's sense of sin as separation from God, poem 33 from *The Black Riders and Other Lines* is instructive. After beginning "There was One I met upon the road / Who looked at me with kind eyes," the poem involves a dialogue between the speaker and this One. Each time the One asks the speaker to show his "wares," and each time the One answers, "It is a sin." "At last," the speaker "cried out: 'But I have none other,'" and the poem concludes: "He looked at me / With kinder eyes. / 'Poor soul,' He said." In *The Complete Poems of Stephen Crane*, ed. Joseph Katz (Ithaca, NY: Cornell University Press, 1972), 35.

14   Emmanuel Levinas, *Otherwise Than Being or Beyond Essence*, trans. Alphonso Lingis (The Hague: Martinus Nijhoff, 1981), vii.

15   In addition to the sources in n. 2, one should mention David Halliburton's discussion of the "apocalyptic" mode in Crane, especially the poetry, in *The Color of the Sky: A Study of Stephen Crane* (Cambridge, England: Cambridge University Press, 1989), 304–321, and an unpublished dissertation by Clarence Oliver Johnson that offers the most systematic attempt to trace the influence on Crane of works by his Methodist forebears, "A Methodist Clergyman—of the Old Ambling-Nag, Saddle-bag, Exhorting Kind": Stephen Crane and his Methodist Heritage (Oklahoma State University, 1983).

16   Arthur McGill, *Suffering: A Test of Theological Method* (Philadelphia: Geneva Press, 1968), 70.

17 Crane, *The Complete Poems*, 81.

18 John Milbank, *Theology and Social Theory: Beyond Secular Reason* (Oxford: Blackwell, 1990), 331–332. It is Crane's deep suspicion of "virtue" that makes me unwilling to accept the thesis of Keith Gandal in *The Virtues of the Vicious: Jacob Riis, Stephen Crane, and the Spectacle of the Slum* (New York: Oxford University Press, 1997). Heavily indebted to Foucault's *Discipline and Punish: The Birth of the Prison*, trans. Alan Sheridan (New York: Vintage, 1977), Gandal argues that Crane's *Maggie: A Girl of the Streets* should be read as a vindication of the virtues of urban toughs like Jimmie and Pete, who rebel against "Protestant, disciplinary society" (17). In my view, Gandal misreads Crane's ironic view of Jimmie and Pete's "virtues." No less than those who oppress them, they are, in the words of Crane's "War Is Kind," "Little souls who thirst for fight."

19 Crane to *DeMorest's Family Magazine* 32 (May 1896), in Stanley Wertheim and Paul Sorrentino, *The Crane Log: A Documentary Life of Stephen Crane 1871– 1900* (New York: G. K. Hall, 1994), 180–181.

20 Henry's "philippic," "Hell——," immediately precedes Crane's famous image of the wafer: "The red sun was pasted in the sky like a wafer" (*Works*, 2:58).

21 For the poem, see *The Complete Poems*, 57. Hoffman presses the poem toward a transcendentalist conclusion: "The eyes, we note, are not glaring down from the brows of heaven; they are 'of my soul'—in transcendental fashion Crane merges the Divine in himself with the Divinity. Those eyes would weep were he to violate the compassionate nature of the Divinity within him." Noteworthy in their absence from both Hoffman's citation of the poem and his interpretation are lines 18–21, those most suggestive of the face of Jesus (*The Poetry of Stephen Crane*, 66–67).

22 Wertheim and Sorrentino, *The Crane Log*, 289.

23 See Knapp, "Son of Thunder," 268–273. For an interpretation making specific use of Girard's understanding of the scapegoat mechanism, see William A. Johnsen, "Rene Girard and the Boundaries of Modern Literature," *Boundary* 2 9 (1981): 277–290.

24 Stephen Crane, *Works: Tales of Adventure*, ed. Fredson Bowers (Charlottesville: University Press of Virginia, 1970), 5:154. Cited hereafter in the text.

25 Crane perhaps follows Genesis in linking the falling of the countenance with eventual murder. When God "had not respect" for Cain's offering, "Cain was very wroth, and his countenance fell" (4:5).

26 Charles Fried, *Right and Wrong* (Cambridge, MA: Harvard University Press, 1978), 68.

27 Immanuel Kant, *The Metaphysics of Morals*, trans. Mary Gregor (Cambridge, England: Cambridge University Press, 1991), 225–226.

28 Stephen Crane to John Northern Hilliard [January 1896], in *The Correspondence of Stephen Crane*, ed. Stanley Wertheim and Paul Sorrentino (New York: Columbia University Press, 1988), 1:195–196.

29 Kant, *The Metaphysics of Morals*, 227.

30 Immanuel Kant, *Foundations of the Metaphysics of Morals*, 2d ed., trans. Lewis White Beck (New York: Macmillan, 1990), 50.

31 Hans Urs von Balthasar, *Love Alone: The Way of Revelation*, ed. Alexander Dru (London: Burns and Oates, 1968), 92. Cited hereafter in the text.

32 Reinhold Niebuhr, *The Nature and Destiny of Man* (New York: Charles Scribner's Sons, 1949), 1:203. I was directed to this passage in Niebuhr by the excellent treatment of self-deception by Stanley Hauerwas with David B. Burrell, "Self-Deception and Autobiography: Reflections on Speer's *Inside the Third Reich*," in Hauerwas with Richard Bondi and Burrell, *Truthfulness and Tragedy: Further Investigations in Christian Ethics* (Notre Dame, IN: University of Notre Dame Press, 1985), 82–98. Especially interesting is the essay's connection between integrity and self-deception. Paradoxically, it is the person of integrity's very drive for wholeness and consistency that can make him or her especially susceptible to self-deception. Crane, then, might have the powerful insight into self-deception in "The Blue Hotel" because of his very concern for integrity. For Hauerwas and Burrell, what we need to minimize self-deception (which cannot be wholly avoided) is a story that enables us to "recognize and acknowledge the evil we perpetrate and to confront ourselves without illusion and deceit" (98). Understanding himself primarily as an architect who cared little for politics, Albert Speer "began his engagement with life with a story inadequate to articulate the engagements he would be called upon to undertake" (94). Finally, for the authors, to "accept the Gospel is to receive training in accepting the limits on our claims to righteousness before we are forced to" (98).

33 As Mary Gregor explains, "sincerity with oneself" is, for Kant, "not so much a specific virtue as rather the 'formal condition' of all virtues." *Laws of Freedom* (Oxford: Basil Blackwell, 1963), 157.

34 See Hauerwas's point that "war reaffirms our history by offering us the opportunity to be worthy of our history by making similar sacrifices." *Against the Nations: War and Survival in a Liberal Society* (Minneapolis: Winston Press, 1985), 185.

35 David S. Yeago, Unpublished theology typescript (Columbia, SC: Lutheran Theological Southern Seminary, 1993), pt. 2, 175.

36 St. Augustine, *Against Lying*, trans. Harold B. Jaffee, in *Saint Augustine: Treatises on Various Subjects* in *The Fathers of the Church*, ed. Roy J. Deferrari, trans. Sister Mary Sarah Muldowney et al. (Washington, DC: Catholic University of America Press, 1965), 14:140–141.

37 St. Augustine, *Lying*, trans. Sister Mary Muldowney, in *Saint Augustine: Treatises on Various Subjects*, 14:106.

38 St. Augustine, *Against Lying*, 14:134, 14:128.

39 Crane, *The Complete Poems*, 60.

40 Ibid., 6.

Afterword

1 Alasdair MacIntyre, *Three Rival Versions of Moral Enquiry: Encyclopaedia, Genealogy, and Tradition* (Notre Dame, IN: University of Notre Dame Press, 1990), 16. Cited hereafter in the text as *TRV.*

2 George Marsden, *The Outrageous Idea of Christian Scholarship* (New York: Oxford University Press, 1997), 23. Cited hereafter in the text.

3 Stephen Carter, *The Culture of Disbelief: How American Law and Politics Trivialize Religious Devotion* (New York: Doubleday, 1993), 37.

4 Walter Brueggemann, public lecture, Second Presbyterian Church, Roanoke, VA, March 4, 2002.

5 Simone Weil, *The Need for Roots*, in *The Simone Weil Reader*, ed. George Panichas (Mt. Kisco, NY: Moyer Bell, 1977), 208.

6 Blaise Pascal, *Pensees*, trans. W. F. Trotter, in *Pensees and The Provincial Letters* (New York: Modern Library, 1941), 190–191. Cited hereafter in the text.

7 Richard Rorty, "The Priority of Democracy to Philosophy," in *Objectivity, Relativism, and Truth* [*Philosophical Papers*, vol. 1] (Cambridge, England: Cambridge University Press, 1991), 175. Cited hereafter in the text as PD.

8 Richard Rorty, "Postmodernist Bourgeois Liberalism," *Journal of Philosophy* 80 (1983): 583. Cited hereafter in the text as PBL.

9 Henry David Thoreau, "Civil Disobedience," in *Walden and Civil Disobedience* (New York: Penguin, 1983), 389–391. Cited hereafter in the text as CD.

10 Harold Bloom, introduction to *Henry James's The Portrait of a Lady* (New York: Chelsea House, 1987), 3.

11 Ralph Waldo Emerson, "Self-Reliance," in *Selected Writings*, ed. Brooks Atkinson (New York: Modern Library, 1940), 145.

12 Emerson, "The Poet," in *Selected Writings*, 338.

13 Walt Whitman, "Song of Myself," in *Leaves of Grass: Comprehensive Reader's Edition*, ed. Sculley Bradley et al. (New York: Norton, 1965), 28.

14 Whitman, "Preface 1855," in *Leaves of Grass*, 728.

15 Jeffrey Stout, *Ethics after Babel: The Languages of Morals and Their Discontents* (1988; rpt. Princeton, NJ: Princeton University Press, 2001), 348. All citations of Stout in this chapter are to this 2001 edition, cited hereafter in the text.

16 Weil, *The Simone Weil Reader*, 209–212.

17 Wendell Berry, *What Are People For?* (San Francisco: North Point Press, 1990), 129.

18 Hector St. John de Crèvecoeur, "What Is an American?" in *Letters from an American Farmer*, in *The Norton Anthology of American Literature: Shorter Edition*, ed. Nina Baym et al. (New York: Norton, 1986), 202.

19 Richard Rorty, "On Ethnocentrism: A Reply to Clifford Geertz," in *Objectivity, Relativism, and Truth*, 203. Cited hereafter in the text as OE.

20 Richard Rorty, "Cosmopolitanism without Emancipation: A Response to

Jean-Francois Lyotard," in *Objectivity, Relativism, and Truth*, 214. Cited hereafter in the text as CWE.

21 See John Howard Yoder, *The Politics of Jesus* (Grand Rapids, MI: Eerdmans, 1972), 94–114.

22 Søren Kierkegaard, *Works of Love*, trans. Howard V. Hong and Edna H. Hong (New York: Harper and Row, 1962), 83, 92. Cited hereafter in the text as *WL.*

23 Stanley Hauerwas, *After Christendom?* (Nashville, TN: Abingdon Press, 1991), 61–62.

24 Arthur W. Frank, *The Wounded Storyteller: Body, Illness, and Ethics* (Chicago: University of Chicago Press, 1995), 13.

25 John Milbank, *Theology and Social Theory: Beyond Secular Reason* (Oxford: Blackwell, 1990), 326–379.

26 John Paul II, *The Splendor of Truth: Veritatis Splendor* (Boston: St. Paul Books, 1993), 70. Cited hereafter in the text as *VS.*

27 Alasdair MacIntyre, "How Can We Learn What *Veritatis Splendor* Has to Teach?" *The Thomist* 58 (1994): 178–179.

28 Ibid., 177.

29 Simone Weil, *Gateway to God*, ed. David Raper (New York: Crossroad, 1982), 47.

30 Richard Rorty, *Truth and Progress* (Cambridge, England: Cambridge University Press, 1998), 185. Cited hereafter in the text as *TP.*

31 MacIntyre, *Three Rival Versions of Moral Enquiry*, 231.

32 Stanley Hauerwas and Charles Pinches, *Christians among the Virtues* (Notre Dame, IN: University of Notre Dame Press, 1997), 68.

33 James Denney, *The Death of Christ* (London: Tyndale, 1951), 84.

bibliography

Aaron, Daniel. *Men of Good Hope.* New York: Galaxy Books, 1961.

Aquinas, St. Thomas. *Summa Theologiae.* 2a–2ae. 23, 8. Vol. 34. Trans. R. J. Batten O.P. London: Blackfriars, 1964.

——. *Summa Theologiae.* 2a–2ae, xlvii, 9 *ad* 2. Vol. 36. Trans. R. J. Batten O.P. London: Blackfriars, 1964.

——. *Summa Theologiae,* 2a–2ae, xlvii, 3 *ad* 2. In *Saint Thomas Aquinas: Philosophical Texts,* trans. Thomas Gilby. New York: Oxford University Press, 1960.

Aristotle. *The Ethics of Aristotle: The Nicomachean Ethics.* Trans. J. A. K. Thomson. Rev. Hugh Tredennick. New York: Penguin, 1976.

Augustine, St. *Against Lying.* Trans. Harold Jaffee. In *Saint Augustine: Treatises on Various Subjects.* In *The Fathers of the Church,* ed. Roy J. Deferrari, trans. Sister Mary Sarah Muldowney et al. Vol. 14. Washington, DC: Catholic University of America Press, 1965.

——. *Confessions.* Trans. R. S. Pine-Coffin. Baltimore: Penguin, 1964.

——. *Confessions.* Trans. Rex Warner. New York: New American Library, 1963.

——. *Enchiridion: Faith Hope and Charity.* Trans. Louis A. Arand. New York: Newman Press, 1947.

——. *Lying.* Trans. Sister Mary Sarah Muldowney. In *The Fathers of the Church,* ed. Roy J. Deferrari, trans. Sister Mary Sarah Muldowney et al. Vol. 14. Washington, DC: Catholic University of America Press, 1965.

Aukerman, Dale. *Darkening Valley: A Biblical Perspective on Nuclear War.* New York: Seabury Press, 1981.

Austen, Jane. *Emma.* Ed. Ronald Blythe. London: Penguin, 1985.

——. *Jane Austen's Letters.* Ed. Deirdre Le Faye. Oxford: Oxford University Press, 1995.

——. *Mansfield Park.* Ed. James Kinsley. Oxford: Oxford University Press, 1990.

——. *A Theology of History.* New York: Sheed and Ward, 1963.

Balthasar, Hans Urs von. *Love Alone: The Way of Revelation.* Ed. Alexander Dru. London: Burns and Oates, 1968.

Barth, Karl. *The Doctrine of Creation.* Pt. 4, Vol. 3 of *Church Dogmatics,* ed. G. W. Bromiley and T. F. Torrance. Edinburgh: T. and T. Clark, 1961.

——. *The Doctrine of Reconciliation.* Pt. 1. Trans. G. W. Bromiley. In *Church Dogmatics,* ed. G. W. Bromiley and T. F. Torrance. Vol. 4. Edinburgh: T. and T. Clark, 1936–1977.

Becker, Ernest. *The Denial of Death.* New York: Free Press, 1973.

Berger, Peter. "On the Obsolescence of the Concept of Honor." In *Revisions:*

Changing Perspectives in Moral Philosophy, ed. Stanley Hauerwas and Alasdair Mac-Intyre. 172–181. Notre Dame, IN: University of Notre Dame Press, 1983.

Berry, Wendell. *What Are People For?* San Francisco: North Point Press, 1990.

Biggar, Nigel. *The Hastening That Waits: Karl Barth's Ethics.* Oxford: Clarendon Press, 1993.

Bloom, Harold. *The American Religion: The Emergence of the Post-Christian Nation.* New York: Simon and Schuster, 1992.

——. Introduction to Henry James's *The Portrait of a Lady.* Ed. Harold Bloom. New York: Chelsea House, 1987.

Blumenberg, Hans. *The Legitimacy of the Modern Age.* Trans. Robert Wallace. Cambridge, MA: MIT Press, 1983.

Booth, Wayne. *The Company We Keep: An Ethics of Fiction.* Berkeley: University of California Press, 1988.

——. *The Rhetoric of Fiction.* 2d ed. Chicago: University of Chicago Press, 1983.

Busch, Frederick. "Thoreau and Melville as Cellmates." *Modern Fiction Studies* 23 (1977): 239–242.

Carter, Stephen. *The Culture of Disbelief: How American Law and Politics Trivialize Religious Devotion.* New York: Doubleday, 1993.

Child, Lydia Maria. *Letters from New York.* New York: C. S. Francis and Co., 1844.

Childress, James F. "'Answering That of God in Every Man': An Introduction to George Fox's Ethics." *Quaker Religious Thought* 15, no. 3 (1974): 2–41.

Collins, Irene. *Jane Austen and the Clergy.* London: Hambledon Press, 1994.

Crane, Stephen. *The Complete Poems of Stephen Crane.* Ed. Joseph Katz. Ithaca, NY: Cornell University Press, 1972.

——. *The Correspondence of Stephen Crane.* Ed. Stanley Wertheim and Paul Sorrentino. 2 vols. New York: Columbia University Press, 1988.

——. *The Works of Stephen Crane: The Red Badge of Courage.* Ed. Fredson Bowers. Vol. 2. Charlottesville: University Press of Virginia, 1975.

——. *The Works of Stephen Crane: Tales of Adventure.* Ed. Fredson Bowers. Vol. 5. Charlottesville: University Press of Virginia, 1970.

——. *The Works of Stephen Crane: Tales of War.* Ed. Fredson Bowers. Vol. 6. Charlottesville: University Press of Virginia, 1970.

——. *The Works of Stephen Crane: Tales of Whilomville.* Ed. Fredson Bowers. Vol. 7. Charlottesville: University Press of Virginia, 1969.

Crèvecoeur, Hector St. Jean de. *Letters from an American Farmer.* In *The Norton Anthology of American Literature: Shorter Edition,* ed. Nina Baym et al. New York: Norton, 1986.

Delbanco, Andrew. "The Decline and Fall of Literature." *The New York Review of Books,* November 4, 1999, 32–38.

Denney, James. *The Death of Christ.* London: Tyndale, 1951.

Derrida, Jacques. *The Gift of Death.* Trans. David Wills. Chicago: University of Chicago Press, 1995.

DeVries, Peter. *The Blood of the Lamb.* Boston: Little, Brown, 1969.

Dickens, Charles. *Bleak House.* Ed. Duane DeVries. New York: Crowell, 1971.

———. *A Christmas Carol.* New York: Stewart, Tabori and Chang, 1990.

Dillingham, William B. *Melville's Short Fiction: 1853–1856.* Athens: University of Georgia Press, 1977.

Duckworth, Alistair M. *The Improvement of the Estate: A Study of Jane Austen's Novels.* Baltimore: Johns Hopkins University Press, 1971.

Edel, Leon. *Henry James: The Untried Years, 1843–1870.* Philadelphia: Lippincott, 1953.

Emerson, Ralph Waldo. *The Journals and Miscellaneous Notebooks of Ralph Waldo Emerson.* Ed. Alfred R. Ferguson. Vol. 4. Cambridge, MA: Harvard University Press, 1964.

———. *Selected Writings.* Ed. Brooks Atkinson. New York: Modern Library, 1940.

Epperly, Elizabeth. *Patterns of Repetition in Trollope.* Washington, DC: Catholic University of America Press, 1989.

Fish, Stanley. *There's No Such Thing as Free Speech and It's a Good Thing, Too.* New York: Oxford University Press, 1994.

Foley, Brian. "Dickens Revised: 'Bartleby' and *Bleak House.*" *Essays in Literature* 12 (1985): 241–250.

Foucault, Michel. *Discipline and Punish: The Birth of the Prison.* Trans. Alan Sheridan. New York: Vintage, 1977.

Fowler, Virginia. *Henry James's American Girl: The Embroidery on the Canvas.* Madison: University of Wisconsin Press, 1984.

Frank, Arthur W. *The Wounded Storyteller: Body, Illness, and Ethics.* Chicago: University of Chicago Press, 1995.

Franklin, H. Bruce. *The Wake of the Gods: Melville's Mythology.* Stanford: Stanford University Press, 1963.

Frei, Hans. *The Identity of Jesus Christ: The Hermeneutical Basis of Dogmatic Theology.* Philadelphia: Fortress, 1975.

Freire, Paolo. "The 'Banking' Concept of Education." In *Ways of Reading: An Anthology for Writers,* 3d ed., ed. David Bartholomae and Anthony Petrosky. 206–219. Boston: Bedford Books, 1993.

Fried, Charles. *Right and Wrong.* Cambridge, MA: Harvard University Press, 1978.

Fussell, Edwin Sill. *The Catholic Side of Henry James.* Cambridge, England: Cambridge University Press, 1993.

Gandal, Keith. *The Virtues of the Vicious: Jacob Riis, Stephen Crane, and the Spectacle of the Slum.* New York: Oxford University Press, 1997.

Gass, William H. "The High Brutality of Good Intentions." In *Perspectives on James's The Portrait of a Lady: A Collection of Critical Essays,* ed. William T. Stafford. 206–216. New York: New York University Press, 1967.

Gibson, Donald B. *The Fiction of Stephen Crane.* Carbondale: Southern Illinois University Press, 1968.

Giddings, T. H. "Melville, the Colt-Adams Murder, and 'Bartleby.'" *Studies in American Fiction* 2 (1974): 123–132.

Girard, Rene. *The Scapegoat.* Trans. Yvonne Freccero. Baltimore: Johns Hopkins University Press, 1986.

Graff, Gerald. "Teach the Conflicts." In *The Politics of Liberal Education,* ed. Daryl J. Gless and Barbara Herrnstein Smith. Durham, NC: Duke University Press, 1992.

Grant, George Parkin. *English-Speaking Justice.* Notre Dame, IN: University of Notre Dame Press, 1985.

———. *The George Grant Reader.* Ed. William Christian and Sheila Grant. Toronto: University of Toronto Press, 1998.

Gregor, Mary. *Laws of Freedom.* Oxford: Basil Blackwell, 1963.

Gunn, Giles. "An Introduction." In *Henry James, Senior: A Selection of His Writings.* Ed. Giles Gunn. 3–29. Chicago: American Library Association, 1974.

Habegger, Alfred. *Henry James and the "Woman Business."* Cambridge, England: Cambridge University Press, 1989.

Halliburton, David. *The Color of the Sky: A Study of Stephen Crane.* Cambridge, England: Cambridge University Press, 1989.

Halperin, John. *The Life of Jane Austen.* Baltimore: Johns Hopkins University Press, 1984.

Harding, Walter. *The Days of Henry Thoreau.* New York: Knopf, 1970.

Harned, David Baily. *Creed and Personal Identity: The Meaning of the Apostles' Creed.* Philadelphia: Fortress, 1981.

Hauerwas, Stanley. *After Christendom?* Nashville, TN: Abingdon Press, 1991.

———. *Against the Nations: War and Survival in a Liberal Society.* Minneapolis: Winston Press, 1985.

———. "Can Aristotle Be a Liberal? Nussbaum on Luck." *Soundings* 72 (1989): 675–691.

———. *A Community of Character: Toward a Constructive Christian Social Ethic.* Notre Dame, IN: University of Notre Dame Press, 1981.

———. "The Difference of Virtue and the Difference It Makes: Courage Exemplified." *Modern Theology* 9 (1993): 249–264.

———. *Dispatches from the Front: Theological Engagements with the Secular.* Durham, NC: Duke University Press, 1994.

———. *In Good Company: The Church as Polis.* Notre Dame, IN: University of Notre Dame Press, 1995.

———. *Naming the Silences: God, Medicine, and the Problem of Suffering.* Grand Rapids, MI: Eerdmans, 1990.

———. *The Peaceable Kingdom: A Primer in Christian Ethics.* Notre Dame, IN: University of Notre Dame Press, 1983.

———. *Suffering Presence: Theological Reflections on Medicine, the Mentally Handicapped, and the Church.* Notre Dame, IN: University of Notre Dame Press, 1986.

Hauerwas, Stanley, with Richard Bondi and David B. Burrell. *Truthfulness and Tragedy: Further Investigations in Christian Ethics.* Notre Dame, IN: University of Notre Dame Press, 1985.

Hauerwas, Stanley, and Charles Pinches. *Christians among the Virtues: Theological Conversations with Ancient and Modern Ethics.* Notre Dame, IN: University of Notre Dame Press, 1997.

Hawthorne, Nathaniel. *The English Notebooks*. Ed. Randall Stewart. New York: Russell and Russell, 1962.

Heidegger, Martin. *Basic Writings*. Ed. David Farrell Krell. New York: Harper and Row, 1977.

Hoffman, Daniel. *The Poetry of Stephen Crane*. New York: Columbia University Press, 1957.

Horne, Philip. *Henry James and Revision*. Oxford: Clarendon Press, 1990.

Jaffe, David. *"Bartleby the Scrivener" and Bleak House*. Hamden, CT: Archon Books, 1979.

James, Henry. *The Ambassadors*. 2 vols. New York: Charles Scribner's Sons, 1909.

——. *The Complete Notebooks of Henry James*. Ed. Leon Edel and Lyall H. Powers. New York: Oxford University Press, 1987.

——. *Letters*. Ed. Leon Edel. Vol. 2. Cambridge, MA: Harvard University Press, 1975.

——. *Notes of a Son and Brother*. New York: Charles Scribner's Sons, 1914.

——. *The Portable Henry James*. Ed. Morton Dauwen Zabel. Rev. Lyall H. P. Powers. New York: Viking, 1968.

——. *The Portrait of a Lady*. Ed. Robert D. Bamberg. New York: Norton, 1975.

——. *The Portrait of a Lady*. 2 vols. New York: Charles Scribner's Sons, 1908.

James, Henry, Sr. *Christianity the Logic of Creation*. New York: D. Appleton, 1857.

——. *Lectures and Miscellanies*. In *Henry James, Senior: A Selection of His Writings*. Ed. Giles Gunn. 92–104, 134–147, 173–182. Chicago: American Library Association, 1974.

——. *The Literary Remains of the Late Henry James*. Ed. William James. Boston: James R. Osgood, 1885.

——. *Moralism and Christianity*. In *Henry James, Senior: A Selection of His Writings*. Ed. Giles Gunn. 81–91, 123–133. Chicago: American Library Association, 1974.

——. *Society the Redeemed Form of Man*. Boston: Houghton, Osgood and Company, 1879.

Jeffrey, David Lyle. *People of the Book: Christian Identity and Literary Culture*. Grand Rapids, MI: Eerdmans, 1996.

John Paul II. *Splendor of Truth: Veritatis Splendor*. Boston: St. Paul Books, 1993.

Johnsen, William A. "Rene Girard and the Boundaries of Modern Literature." *Boundary 2* 9 (1981): 277–290.

Johnson, Clarence Oliver. *"A Methodist Clergyman—of the Old Ambling-Nag, Saddle-bag, Exhorting Kind": Stephen Crane and His Methodist Heritage*. Ph.D. diss., Oklahoma State University, 1983.

Jones, L. Gregory. "Alasdair MacIntyre on Narrative, Community, and the Moral Life." *Modern Theology* 4 (1987): 53–69.

——. *Embodying Forgiveness: A Theological Analysis*. Grand Rapids, MI: Eerdmans, 1995.

Kant, Immanuel. *Foundations of the Metaphysics of Morals and What Is Enlightenment?* 2d ed. Trans. Lewis White Beck. New York: Macmillan, 1990.

——. *Lectures on Ethics*. Trans. Louis Infield. New York: Harper and Row, 1963.

——. *The Metaphysics of Morals*. Trans. Mary Gregor. Cambridge, England: Cambridge University Press, 1991.

Kaston, Carren. *Imagination and Desire in the Novels of Henry James*. New Brunswick, NJ: Rutgers University Press, 1984.

Kelley, Wyn. *Melville's City: Literary and Urban Form in Nineteenth-Century New York*. Cambridge, England: Cambridge University Press, 1996.

Kierkegaard, Søren. *The Sickness unto Death: A Christian Psychological Exposition for Upbuilding and Awakening*. Ed. and trans. Howard V. Hong and Edna H. Hong. Princeton, NJ: Princeton University Press, 1980.

——. *Works of Love*. Trans. Howard V. Hong and Edna H. Hong. New York: Harper and Row, 1962.

——. *Works of Love*. Ed. and trans. Howard V. Hong and Edna H. Hong. Princeton, NJ: Princeton University Press, 1995.

Knapp, Daniel. "Son of Thunder: Stephen Crane and the Fourth Evangelist." *Nineteenth-Century Fiction* 24 (1969): 253–291.

Kolodny, Annette. "Dancing through the Minefield: Some Observations on the Theory, Practice, and Politics of a Feminist Literary Criticism." In *Falling into Theory: Conflicting Views on Reading Literature*, ed. David H. Richter. 278–285. Boston: Bedford Books, 1994.

Koppel, Gene. *The Religious Dimension of Jane Austen's Novels*. Ann Arbor, MI: UMI Research Press, 1988.

Krook, Dorothea. *The Ordeal of Consciousness in Henry James*. Cambridge, England: Cambridge University Press, 1967.

Letwin, Shirley Robin. *The Gentleman in Trollope: Individuality and Moral Conduct*. Cambridge, MA: Harvard University Press, 1982.

Levinas, Emmanuel. *Collected Philosophical Papers*. Trans. Alphonso Lingis. Dordrecht, Netherlands: Martinus Nijhoff, 1987.

——. *The Levinas Reader*. Ed. Sean Hand. Oxford: Basil Blackwell, 1989.

——. *Noms Propres*. Montpellier, France: Fata Morgana, 1976.

——. *Otherwise Than Being or Beyond Essence*. Trans. Alphonso Lingis. The Hague: Martinus Nijhoff, 1981.

——. *Totality and Infinity: An Essay on Exteriority*. Trans. Alphonso Lingis. Pittsburgh: Duquesne University Press, 1969.

Lewis, C. S. "A Note on Jane Austen." In *Jane Austen: A Collection of Critical Essays*, ed. Ian Watt. 25–34. Englewood Cliffs, NJ: Prentice-Hall, 1963.

Lindbeck, George. *The Nature of Doctrine: Religion and Theology in a Postliberal Age*. Philadelphia: Westminster, 1984.

Luther, Martin. "The Freedom of a Christian." In *Luther's Works*, ed. Harold J. Grimm. Vol. 31. Philadelphia: Muhlenberg Press, 1957.

MacIntyre, Alasdair. *After Virtue*. 2d ed. Notre Dame, IN: University of Notre Dame Press, 1984.

——. "Does Applied Ethics Rest on a Mistake?" *The Monist* 67 (1984): 498–513.

——. "How Can We Learn What *Veritatis Splendor* Has to Teach?" *The Thomist* 58 (1994): 171–195.

———. *Three Rival Versions of Moral Enquiry: Encyclopaedia, Genealogy, and Tradition.* Notre Dame, IN: University of Notre Dame Press, 1990.

———. *Whose Justice? Which Rationality?* Notre Dame, IN: University of Notre Dame Press, 1988.

Marcel, Gabriel. *Creative Fidelity.* Trans. Robert Rosthal. New York: Farrar, Straus, Giroux, 1964.

———. *Homo Viator: Introduction to a Metaphysic of Hope.* 1951. Trans. Emma Craufurd. Gloucester, MA: Peter Smith, 1978.

Marsden, George M. *The Outrageous Idea of Christian Scholarship.* New York: Oxford University Press, 1997.

McCall, Dan. *The Silence of Bartleby.* Ithaca, NY: Cornell University Press, 1989.

McGill, Arthur. *Suffering: A Test of Theological Method.* Philadelphia: Geneva Press, 1968.

Meilaender, Gilbert. *The Theory and Practice of Virtue.* Notre Dame, IN: University of Notre Dame Press, 1984.

Melville, Herman. *The Piazza Tales and Other Prose Pieces, 1839–1860.* Ed. Harrison Hayford et al. In *The Writings of Herman Melville.* Vol. 9. Evanston, IL: Northwestern University Press and Newberry Library, 1987.

———. *Pierre or The Ambiguities.* Ed. Harrison Hayford et al. In *The Writings of Herman Melville.* Vol. 7. Evanston, IL: Northwestern University Press and Newberry Library, 1971.

Mendez, Charlotte Walker. "Scriveners Forlorn: Dickens's Nemo and Melville's Bartleby." *Dickens Studies Newsletter* 11 (1980): 33–38.

Milbank, John. *Theology and Social Theory: Beyond Secular Reason.* Oxford: Blackwell, 1990.

Miller, Edwin Haviland. *Melville.* New York: Persea Books, 1975.

Miller, J. Hillis. *The Ethics of Reading.* New York: Columbia University Press, 1987.

———. *Versions of Pygmalion.* Cambridge, MA: Harvard University Press, 1990.

Milton, John. *Complete Poems and Major Prose.* Ed. Merritt Y. Hughes. Indianapolis: Odyssey Press, 1957.

Modlin, Charles E., and John R. Byers Jr. "Stephen Crane's 'The Monster' as Christian Allegory." *Markham Review* (May 1973): 110–113.

Moers, Ellen. *Literary Women.* Garden City, NY: Doubleday, 1976.

Mollinger, Robert N. "Bartleby the Anorexic." In *Psychoanalysis and Literature.* New York: Nelson-Hall, 1981.

Morsberger, Robert E. "'I Prefer Not To': Melville and the Theme of Withdrawal." *University College Quarterly* 10 (1965): 24–29.

Mudrick, Marvin. *Jane Austen: Irony as Defense and Discovery.* Princeton, NJ: Princeton University Press, 1952.

Murphy, Jeffrie G., and Jean Hampton. *Forgiveness and Mercy.* Cambridge, England: Cambridge University Press, 1988.

Niebuhr, H. Richard. *Christ and Culture.* New York: Harper and Row, 1951.

———. *The Responsible Self: An Essay in Christian Moral Philosophy.* New York: Harper and Row, 1963.

Niebuhr, Reinhold. *The Nature and Destiny of Man.* 2 vols. New York: Charles Scribner's Sons, 1949.

Nussbaum, Martha Craven. *The Fragility of Goodness: Luck and Ethics in Greek Tragedy and Philosophy.* Cambridge, England: Cambridge University Press, 1986.

——. *Love's Knowledge: Essays on Philosophy and Literature.* New York: Oxford University Press, 1990.

Paine, Charles. "Relativism, Radical Pedagogy, and the Ideology of Paralysis." *College English* (1989): 557–570.

Parker, Hershel. "The Sequel in 'Bartleby.'" In *Bartleby the Inscrutable: A Collection of Commentary on Herman Melville's Tale "Bartleby the Scrivener,"* ed. M. Thomas Inge. 159–165. Hamden, CT: Archon Books, 1979.

Pascal, Blaise. *Pensees.* Trans. A. J. Krailsheimer. Baltimore: Penguin, 1968.

——. *Pensees* in *Pensees and The Provincial Letters.* Trans. W. F. Trotter. New York: Modern Library, 1941.

Pieper, Josef. *About Love.* Trans. Richard Winston and Clara Winston. Chicago: Franciscan Herald Press, 1974.

——. *The Four Cardinal Virtues.* Notre Dame, IN: University of Notre Dame Press, 1966.

Pizer, Donald. "Stephen Crane: A Review of Scholarship and Criticism since 1969." *Studies in the Novel* 10 (1978): 120–145.

Poirier, Richard. *The Comic Sense of Henry James: A Study of the Early Novels.* London: Chatto and Windus, 1960.

Poovey, Mary. *The Proper Lady and the Woman Writer: Ideology as Style in the Works of Mary Wollstonecraft, Mary Shelley, and Jane Austen.* Chicago: University of Chicago Press, 1984.

Posnock, Ross. *The Trial of Curiosity: Henry James, William James, and the Challenge of Modernity.* New York: Oxford University Press, 1991.

Ramsey, Paul. *Basic Christian Ethics.* New York: Charles Scribner's Sons, 1950.

——. *Christian Ethics and the Sit-In.* New York: Association Press, 1961.

——. *The Essential Paul Ramsey: A Collection.* Ed. William Werpehowski and Stephen D. Crocco. New Haven: Yale University Press, 1994.

——. *Nine Modern Moralists.* Englewood Cliffs, NJ: Prentice-Hall, 1962.

Rawls, John. *A Theory of Justice.* Cambridge, MA: Harvard University Press, 1971.

Ritchie, Daniel E. *Reconstructing Literature in an Ideological Age: A Biblical Poetics and Literary Studies from Milton to Burke.* Grand Rapids, MI: Eerdmans, 1996.

Rorty, Richard. *Essays on Heidegger and Others* [*Philosophical Papers,* Vol. 2]. Cambridge, England: Cambridge University Press, 1991.

——. *Objectivity, Relativism, and Truth* [*Philosophical Papers,* Vol. 1]. Cambridge, England: Cambridge University Press, 1991.

——. "Postmodernist Bourgeois Liberalism." *Journal of Philosophy* 80 (1983): 583–589.

——. *Truth and Progress* [*Philosophical Papers,* Vol. 3]. Cambridge, England: Cambridge University Press, 1998.

Ryle, Gilbert. "Jane Austen and the Moralists." In *Collected Papers*. Vol. 1. 276–291. New York: Barnes and Noble, 1971.

Said, Edward. "Restoring Intellectual Coherence." *MLA Newsletter* 31, no. 1 (spring 1999): 3–4.

Schaefer, Michael W. *A Reader's Guide to the Short Stories of Stephen Crane*. New York: G.K. Hall, 1996.

Schwehn, Mark. *Exiles from Eden: Religion and the Academic Vocation in America*. New York: Oxford University Press, 1993.

Solomon, Pearl Chesler. *Dickens and Melville in Their Time*. New York: Columbia University Press, 1975.

Stallman, R. W. *Stephen Crane: A Biography*. New York: George Braziller, 1968.

Stout, Jeffrey. *Ethics after Babel: The Languages of Morals and Their Discontents*. Boston: Beacon Press, 1988. Reprint. Princeton, NJ: Princeton University Press, 2001.

———. "Virtue among the Ruins: An Essay on MacIntyre." *Neue Zeitschrift fur Systematische Theologie und Religionsphilosophie* 26 (1984): 256–273.

Sulloway, Alison G. *Jane Austen and the Province of Womanhood*. Philadelphia: University of Pennsylvania Press, 1989.

Tanner, Tony. "The Fearful Self: Henry James's *The Portrait of a Lady*." In *The Merrill Studies in The Portrait of a Lady*, ed. Lyall H. Powers. 106–122. Columbus, OH: Merrill, 1970.

Thoreau, Henry David. *Walden and Civil Disobedience*. New York: Penguin, 1983.

Trilling, Lionel. *The Opposing Self: Nine Essays in Criticism*. New York: Viking, 1955.

Trollope, Anthony. *Anthony Trollope: An Illustrated Autobiography*. Wolfeboro, NH: Alan Sutton, 1989.

———. *He Knew He Was Right*. London: Oxford University Press, 1963.

———. *The Warden*. Ed. Robin Gilmour. London: Penguin, 1986.

Wadell, Paul. *The Primacy of Love: An Introduction to the Ethics of Thomas Aquinas*. New York: Paulist Press, 1992.

Walton, Priscilla. *The Disruption of the Feminine in Henry James*. Toronto: University of Toronto Press, 1992.

Ware, Bishop Kallistos. *The Orthodox Way*. Crestwood, NY: St. Vladimir's Seminary Press, 1990.

Warner, Michael D. "Value, Agency, and Stephen Crane's 'The Monster.'" *Nineteenth-Century Literature* 40 (1985): 76–93.

Weil, Simone. *Gateway to God*. Ed. David Raper. New York: Crossroad, 1982.

———. *The Simone Weil Reader*. Ed. George A. Panichas. Mt. Kisco, NY: Moyer Bell, 1977.

Weisbuch, Robert. *Atlantic Double-Cross: American Literature and British Influence in the Age of Emerson*. Chicago: University of Chicago Press, 1986.

Wertheim, Stanley, and Paul Sorrentino. *The Crane Log: A Documentary Life of Stephen Crane 1871–1900*. New York: G.K. Hall, 1994.

Westphal, Merold. "Levinas and the Immediacy of the Face." *Faith and Philosophy* 10 (1993): 486–502.

Whitman, Walt. *Leaves of Grass: Comprehensive Reader's Edition.* Ed. Sculley Bradley et al. New York: Norton, 1965.

Wiesenfarth, Joseph. "A Woman in *The Portrait of a Lady.*" *Henry James Review* 7 (1986): 18–28.

Williams, Bernard. *Morality: An Introduction to Ethics.* New York: Harper and Row, 1972.

——. *Moral Luck: Philosophical Papers, 1973–1980.* Cambridge, England: Cambridge University Press, 1981.

Williams, Rowan. "Balthasar and Rahner." In *The Analogy of Beauty: The Theology of Hans Urs von Balthasar,* ed. John Riches. Edinburgh: T. and T. Clark, 1986.

Wilson, Edmund. "A Long Talk about Jane Austen." In *Jane Austen: A Collection of Critical Essays,* ed. Ian Watt. 35–40. Englewood Cliffs, NJ: Prentice-Hall, 1963.

Wilt, Judith. *Ghosts of the Gothic: Austen, Eliot and Lawrence.* Princeton, NJ: Princeton University Press, 1980.

Yeago, David. "Literature in the Drama of Nature and Grace: Hans Urs von Balthasar's Paradigm for a Theology of Culture." *Renascence* 48 (1996): 95–109.

——. Unpublished theology typescript. Columbia, SC: Lutheran Theological Southern Seminary, 1993.

Yoder, John Howard. "How H. Richard Niebuhr Reasoned: A Critique of *Christ and Culture.*" In Glen H. Stassen, D. M. Yeager, and John Howard Yoder, *Authentic Transformation: A New Vision of Christ and Culture,* 31–89. Nashville, TN: Abingdon Press, 1996.

——. *The Politics of Jesus.* Grand Rapids, MI: Eerdmans, 1972.

Index

Fritz Oehlschlaeger is Professor of English at Virginia Polytechnic Institute and State University. He is co-author, with Peter Graham, of *Articulating the Elephant Man: Joseph Merrick and His Interpreters* (Johns Hopkins, 1992); editor of *Old Southwest Humor from the St. Louis Reveille, 1844–1850* (Missouri, 1990); and co-editor, with George Hendrick, of *Toward the Making of Thoreau's Modern Reputation* (Illinois, 1979).

Library of Congress Cataloging-in-Publication Data

Oehlschlaeger, Fritz.
Love and good reasons : postliberal approaches to Christian
ethics and literature / Fritz Oehlschlaeger.
p. cm.
Includes bibliographical references and index.
ISBN 0-8223-3053-9 (cloth : alk. paper) — ISBN 0-8223-3064-4
(pbk. : alk. paper)
1. American fiction—History and criticism. 2. Christianity and
literature—United States. 3. Christianity and literature—Great
Britain. 4. English fiction—History and criticism. 5. Christian
ethics in literature. 6. Ethics in literature.
I. Title.
PS374.C48 O38 2003
813.009'382—dc21   2002011438